Library of
Davidson College

WEST INDIAN SLAVERY

SELECTED PAMPHLETS

NEGRO UNIVERSITIES PRESS
WESTPORT, CONNECTICUT

Originally published in 1816-1827, London

Reprinted in 1970 by Negro Universities Press
A Division of Greenwood Press, Inc.
Westport, Connecticut

Library of Congress Catalogue Card Number 75-100310

SBN 8371-2954-0

Printed in the United States of America

CONTENTS

No. 1 An examination of the principles of the Slave Registry Bill and of the means of emancipation.
G. W. Jordan 1816

No. 2 Considerations on the abolition of negro slavery and the means of practically effecting it.
J. F. Barham 1823

No. 3 An appeal to the religion, justice and humanity of the inhabitants of the British Empire, in behalf of the negro slaves in the West Indies.
William Wilberforce 1823

No. 4 A review of some of the arguments which are commonly advanced against parliamentary interference in behalf of the negro slaves 1823

No. 5 The report of the committee of the legislature of Dominica, appointed to enquire into and report on certain queries relative to the condition, treatment, rights and privileges of the negro population of that island 1823

No. 6 A report of a committee of the Council of Barbadoes, appointed to inquire into the actual condition of the slaves in this island 1824

No. 7 Negro emancipation and West Indian independence, the true interest of Great Britain.
John Taylor 1824

No. 8 The Rural Code of Haiti, in French and English.
.... 1827

No. 9 The West Indian Reporter, Nos. I and II ... 1827

AN   No. 1.

EXAMINATION

OF THE

𝔓rinciples

OF THE

SLAVE REGISTRY BILL,

AND OF THE

MEANS OF EMANCIPATION,

PROPOSED

BY THE AUTHORS OF THE BILL.

By G. W. JORDAN, Esq. F. R. S.
COLONIAL AGENT FOR BARBADOS.

LONDON:
PRINTED FOR T. CADELL AND W. DAVIES, STRAND.

1816.

AN EXAMINATION

OF THE

Principles

OF THE

SLAVE REGISTRY BILL,

&c. &c.

The time is at length arrived, when for the protection of the persons, for the security and preservation of the rights, liberties, and properties of the British Colonists of the West Indies, I shall appear ranged in opposition to those who profess themselves to be the advocates of freedom. I had hoped that this effort would have been spared to my life, and that my name would not go abroad to the world, or descend to posterity subjected even to the suspicion of entertaining opinions and feelings hostile to the great cause of the liberties of all mankind. That hostility for myself and for mine, I disavow, I disclaim. The Colony which I represent, during the progress of the proceedings for the Abolition of the Slave Trade, positively enjoined me to give no opposition to the measure. On the subject of the slavery of the West India Colonies, my own opinions are contained in the following public declarations and expostulations made for myself and other British Colonists, and opposed to one of those invasions of colonial rights so frequently meditated.

" We take this occasion to deprecate the odium
" which the agricultural system of these Colonies
" may have excited against us. We have suc-
" ceeded to the system and continuance of slavery.
" We are equally guiltless of the production with
" our brethren in Europe, who stand in an equal
" degree and distance of relation with us from the
" original authors, and we are equally zealous with
" them to do whatever is practicable, whatever is
" safe. We consider the system as oppressive to
" master as well as to slave, as tending to injure of
" both the moral characters, to plague persons, and
" to pejorate families. The proudest and most
" prosperous among us would wish time to go
" back, to replace our ancestors in Europe, and to
" give to chance the power of determining for us
" our conditions in Great Britain, where all are
" free, rather than to occupy the highest and most
" distinguished stations in these Colonies, where
" many are slaves."

This public act of the Colony, these spontaneous expressions of individual feeling and opinion may fairly be advanced in front, and insisted upon as proofs that nothing can have been done to counteract the Abolition of the Slave Trade, that nothing could remain undone to render the condition of the black slaves comfortable and consistent with the personal safety of the Colonists, and with the agricultural and colonial systems of the West Indies. But these avail not for us or for others. My public duty, therefore, commands, and my private affections urge me to stand up in defence of my countrymen and my brethren of the Colonies. I appear only as the advocate of British rights and of British subjects, and I come prepared to defend these against all aggression, from whatever quarter it may proceed, whatever it may presume or pretend.

I come not to defend slavery either in the abstract or the particular. I will not vindicate the black slavery of the West Indies in its origin or in its continuance. To any question which may respect the existence of the Slave Trade, an answer is already given. To any question which may respect the existing slavery of the Colonies, the answer is already given. In defence of our political freedom, our existence, our establishments, I come forward to exhibit to the united British Parliament, and to the world, by what invasion of rights, what hazard of persons, what danger to property, the emancipation of the negroes in the Colonies is now proposed to be accomplished—to state the sacrifices, private and public, it will require, however, and whenever effected, and to leave to them to judge of the measure, and to decide respecting the means.

We know, we feel the evils inseparable from a state of slavery, and under this feeling, when in addition to these, charges imputing all the crimes which are of man, and of every state of society, are accumulated upon us, we submit in silence, from whatever sources they may be derived, or by whatever motives they may be dictated. But silence and submission would be criminal, when the course of proceeding contemplated and avowed respects our dearest interests, would violate political rights, endanger personal safety, extinguish the agricultural system of the Colonies, with the commerce dependent thereon, and overwhelm in general ruin the expensive establishments and valuable plantations of the islands.

On the 13th of June, 1815, Mr. Wilberforce moved in the House of Commons for leave to bring in a Bill to prevent the clandestine importation of Slaves into the British Colonies. Previously thereto, copies of a pamphlet, entitled, " Reasons for esta-

"blishing a Registry of Slaves in the British Co-
"lonies, being a report of a Committee of the Afri-
"can Institution, published by order of that Society,"
were delivered to the several members of both
Houses of Parliament. In making his motion, Mr.
W. referred to and adopted this pamphlet as advocating the measure, and indicative of a course of
proceedings to be subsequently adopted by Parliament, and to lead to the general emancipation of
the black slaves in the West Indies. On the 5th
of the following July, the Bill was brought in, and
by order printed, as preparatory to the revival of
the measure, during the succeeding Session of Parliament.

To this Bill, as in itself destitute of all parliamentary grounds of fact or circumstance for its
support, as invasive by internal legislation of the
rights of the Colonial Assemblies, as not being sanctioned by the unquestioned right of the British Parliament to commercial regulation, as transgressing
limits which the British Parliament has prescribed
to itself in matters of revenue, as violating by excess
all the principles of penal law which it respects not,
and all the rights of property in others whom it
entirely disregards, these enumerated objections are
opposed.

Of these, the first and last apply to the Bill itself,
the others to the *extent* of British parliamentary
jurisdiction.

These objections are opposed to the Bill—to its existence—to its principle—to its enactments.—But when the measure is considered in its origin and objects, when contemplated in its causes and consequences, its means and ends, the primary purposes it is insidiously contrived to effect, the ultimate it is avowedly intended to accomplish, all the evils that attend and will follow its existence, course and progress, beginning in a violation of public, and a disregard of private rights, leading to destruction, depreciation, and abandonment of properties, to massacres and deportation of persons, and to be consummated by conflagration and destruction, and by the extinction of establishments, individual and national, of agricultural and commercial wealth, and of naval power, dependent upon these—all these evils rise up in horrible array, and in prospect not remote. Already have those movements been perceived, which threaten to lead the afflicted master to measures of necessary precaution and infliction, and would compel him, with his own hands to sacrifice a portion of his property in personal characters and existences, that he may preserve himself and the remainder.

To Emancipation, all these horrors are to be referred, to the Emancipation of the Black Slaves in the West Indies, now for the first time openly contemplated, and as that to which this whole course of irregular and violent proceeding is to lead, now for the first time publicly avowed, under the following circumstances, intended to justify the course of proceeding, even to its last terrible consummation.

To Emancipation, all these horrors have a thousand times been objected, as necessary consequences to be expected from the measure either contemplated or effected. As often have they been encountered by a direct, positive, absolute denial, that Emancipation was meditated or intended, a denial formally and publicly made by those very persons, who now come forward and avow the principles and practices developed in the following exposition of past events narrated in their own words.

" Accused by their opponents of meditating a ' general Emancipation, they denied the charge, but " it was denied only in the insidious meaning of the " imputation itself. They did not aim at an Emancipation to be effected by insurrection."

The fact therefore is admitted and established, that the charge of meditating a general Emancipation was made, and as positively and directly denied.

This denial, however, is now stated to have been made under a secret mental reservation, that it was not intended by means of insurrections, and all their trains of attendant horrors. These, as the means of Emancipation, it is stated, were insidiously imputed, not openly expressed in the charge of their opponents. They were therefore insidiously not declaredly included in the denial. Thus under a suggested mental reservation of their opponents, a mental reservation is admitted in themselves, by which they would now justify the breach of a solemn public pledge, given at another time, and under other circumstances. This is an original species of morality, which would justify fraud committed by the imputation or suggestion of fraud intended. The non-existence however, of what is imputed, is capable of being most exclusively established, and the violation of a solemn engagement, made and admitted to have been made in the face of the public, and of the world, is further aggravated by an attempt to defend, and to justify it, by affirming the thing which was not, the thing which could not be.

It never was, it never could have been insidiously imputed, nor publicly charged that murder and massacre, and conflagration, and destruction were the means by which Emancipation was to be effected. These evils, indeed, as apprehended *consequences*, were then openly as now deprecated, never as *means*, never as the course of proceeding by which emancipation was to be accomplished. That the agitation of the question, that the establishment of the measure would be followed by insurrections and massacres as effects to be produced, not as causes producing, was always openly charged. Never was it stated, or suggested, or imagined that Emancipation was aimed at or to be effected *by these horrors,* but that these horrors would be produced *by Emancipation* contemplated or established. The existence therefore of any concealed insidious meaning was impossible. The suggestion is of the present time, and raised upon the occasion. The statement that it existed, and was known and operated to induce an insidious covert counter-declaration, is entirely unsupported and disproved, and the accuracy of statements by which the breach of a solemn engagement would be justified, is equal to the morality.

This avowed mental reservation of a party under a supposed or suggested mental reservation of their opponents, a mental reservation impossible in itself, and now for the first time suggested to defend a breach of engagement, can never be justified. It belongs to political profligacy alone to employ all means to attain its ends, to fanatical depravity alone to justify the means by the end.

To qualify however the denial thus unadvisedly if not profligately made, and to exclude these conclusions which necessarily flow from, and are thus legitimately established against the declaration, as well as its authors, it is stated in continuance, not very consistently with what precedes, that they never denied that " they did look forward to a future ex-

"tinction of Slavery in the Colonies, by the same
" happy means which formerly put an end to it in
" England, by a revolution in opinions and manners,
" by encouragement of manumissions, by progres-
" sive melioration of the condition of the Slaves, till
" it should *slide* insensibly into general Freedom, in
" short to an Emancipation, of which the masters
" should be the willing authors."

How the covertly qualified denial of the charge of meditating general Emancipation, has been disposed of by its own internal evidence, already appears. Let this admission of an openly qualified denial be now referred to and compared with that and with their present conduct, and unqualified declarations.

Upon what evidence a Committee of the African Institution made such a report, it is unnecessary to inquire. The nature of the statement excludes the possibility of producing evidence to establish, the necessity of producing evidence to disprove it. No evidence can exist to support, none is required to impugn that which is in itself impossible. Although not required, evidence is not however wanting to negative the affirmation, " that all the Abolitionists " professed themselves to be as earnest as Mr. Wil- " berforce himself to abolish Colonial Slavery." Mr. Stephen, the brother-in-law of Mr. Wilberforce, in a letter dated so late as January 15, 1813, declares "the charge of meditating Emancipation, to be the "renewal of a stale and idle charge against Mr. Wil- "berforce as well as himself, both being equally "incapable of entertaining a purpose they have pub- "licly disclaimed." For this fact, taken from p. 93, of "Thoughts, &c. and an Examination of the "Registry Bill Report," I am indebted to its author, and I seize this occasion for myself, and for all, to thank him for this, and for all his intelligent and zealous exertions in the cause of the Colonies.

For the credit of the African Institution, the only question that can be raised, respects the existence of any report, or of any committee appointed by themselves, according to the usual form and style of creation of committees, to inquire into the matter and to report the same, and the minutes of their proceedings, and of the evidence taken before them, together with their observations thereupon.

If no such committee was appointed, no proceedings had, no minutes of evidence taken, no report made—the title-page of the pamphlet presents a statement of, and affirms things which are not, of a committee, of a report published by order of the Society; and the Society have only to deny these statements, to withdraw themselves from exposure to the preceding and following observations.

The pamphlet may indeed be the production of

an individual, and the Institution unquestionably may adopt it, and as such it may be published by the order, and, if such an application of their funds be warranted, at the expense of the Society. Unquestionably the Society, if they cannot truly, may not state it to be a report of a committee of their body. Such an unsupported statement, when the pernicious effects to be produced by it are considered, is even divested of that colour of innocence by which a celebrated moral philosopher, Paley, has accurately distinguished certain inaccurate statements.

The nature indeed of these statements, the internal evidence of the work itself, lead irresistibly to the inference that it is not what it professes to be. I will not indeed believe the work to be what it pretends, what its title-page so unblushingly announces it to be—the thing is impossible, and I relieve my mind from the painful consideration of referring it to so respectable a body, by treating it as a composition which has not been considered or approved of by the great and respectable part of the Society. Whatever may be wrong, I attribute to an inferior agency of persons, such as, from sordid motives, contrive to introduce themselves into ostensible situations in all public institutions and societies, that they may avail themselves of their means, and powers, and influence—and against such alone are these animadversions directed. As this agency may be inferred from general practices, so is its existence and operation unquestionably established and exhibited by the publication itself, and its attendant circumstances.

Many of the principal Members of the African Institution, I respect, reverence and personally regard. All I do not know. To all worthy of regard, reverence or respect, I appeal against the unfounded allegations and malignant inferences which have been uncontradictedly permitted to appear under their sanction, and so have been presented to the High Inquest of the Nation, compromising at once the credit, the honour and the intelligence of the Society.

To all worthy of regard, reverence or respect, I appeal against the cruel calumnies with which the British Colonists and Legislatures have been assailed —Calumnies against all truth and decency accumulated upon men in all things most just and honourable, of his Majesty most faithful and loyal subjects, of the United Kingdom the dutiful and affectionate children and brethren, in education and intelligence inferior to none on an average of extent of district and number of persons. Of my own Colony I would vouch for more, not as among Colonies, for this would be invidious, but as of countries in general. Many of the Colonies have been, that in particular was colonized by the best blood of England, flying from the invaders and usurpers of the church and throne. In the Colonies last of all the King's dominions, in Barbados, last of all the Colonies, from this honourable circumstance, and from priority of settlement, justly styled most ancient and most loyal, flew the royal flag when democracy and puritanism triumphed over the monarchy. In that Colony I have been one of a company of seventeen or eighteen gentlemen, all educated at Cambridge and Oxford. Nor is this said with the view of distinguishing any one among the Colonies; " I speak that which I do know" of one, and leave to be inferred for all. It is done for the purpose of upholding all against observations which would degrade all, and have even contrived to introduce themselves into office through persons in whom they are calumnies, and who, admitted to advise in colonial affairs, compromise those who commit themselves to their agency, by their blind prejudices and anxious endeavours to debase the characters of the inhabitants of the Colonies, whom they feel that they injure.

Of the several legislatures I will affirm that they are all fully competent to their various duties. In support of this proposition I refer myself to all who, by personal residence in the Colonies, and actual observation, are judges of the question under the view now to be exhibited and illustrated by comparisons by no means intended to degrade or disparage. I speak of times gone, and of persons who have passed away. Has not every Colonial legislature, as a legislature, been at all times and in all respects, from ability, talent and information, as fully fitted for its functions as the King's epresentative, chosen and delegated by his Majesty to the office of Governor? There can be nothing odious in a comparison which would sink none but raises all, and which, by referring to objects placed naturally, as it were, side by side, and thus exposed to direct observation, renders the judgment respecting that one which alone is submitted for question, obvious and intuitive. There have been at all times in both Colonial houses of legislation, the council and assembly of each Colony, the first appointed for life by his Majesty, the other elected by the people, many individuals who need not shrink from a general comparison of personal merits, either with a respected chief, or with individuals among the first of both Houses of Parliament in the United Kingdom. That there have been persons delegated by popular election, whom popular election alone would delegate, is true of the Colonial Assemblies as of the Imperial Parliament. The Imperial Parliament also has had her ——————, but I forbear to name them, nor will I be driven by ruffian outrage to practise outrage, or even for self-justification and defence, expose the bosom to be torn open, and the natural infirmities to be displayed of a mother whom I love and honour.

On the Evidence produced to support the Bill.

The objections to the measure proposed, divide themselves, as before stated, into two classes, one of which respects the Bill itself, and the other the extent of British parliamentary jurisdiction.

The fairest mode of estimating all those of the first class, is by considering them as regularly submitted against the Bill, to a Parliament having the unquestioned right of entertaining it, to a Colonial Legislature, to that of Barbados, for instance.

In the first place, it is destitute of all parliamentary grounds of support. It is proposed as a remedy for an evil that does not exist, that could not exist without being known, which is known not to exist. In Barbados, a single African could not be imported and concealed. In a community where a complete communication of whatever occurs is immediately diffused and eagerly circulated, where every thing and every person is known to every body, in a country of small extent, closely inhabited, neither by woods or mountains affording a single place of concealment, a solitary African could neither pass in open air, nor lurk in secret shade, without being observed. In some of these circumstances of condition, the other Windward Islands may differ, in dimensions of considerable extent, Jamaica alone varies; but in all, illicit importation is equally capable of being, and is as distinctly and positively denied as it can be, or is denied by Barbados, and for all it is completely disproved by the returns made from all to Government, and printed by order of the House of Commons, in July, 1815. This non-existence of an illicit import, renders enactments to prevent it unnecessary and futile. Under this impossibility of existence, without being known, and discovered, and, when discovered, subjecting the party to the pains and penalties of the Abolition Laws, to a charge of, and to the punishments of felony, to call upon a legislature to enact new laws under such circumstances, is to abuse and to misapply and to waste its powers, and the proposal would deserve to be repelled, not merely by a silent—by an indignant rejection.

In Barbados it might in the next place be observed, that there are annual returns of Slaves, made upon oath, and under adequate penalties, which would infallibly discover any irregular increase of numbers by clandestine import, if otherwise concealable. The registration in the public offices, of all deeds, conveying Slaves, is also by law required to give effect thereto, within a short given time. In most of our islands, the report itself which advocates the Registry Bill admits, "that annual returns of Slaves are required for the purposes of internal revenue, and in most, or all the islands, the enrolment of deeds is required within a limited time, to pass the estate granted;" and it is added, that "the Registry proposed, would do little more than provide a clearer specification of property, as if the whole cumbersome machinery of the Bill, of officers to be appointed, and offices established in each of the Colonies, and in Great Britain, of returns to be made, of duties to be performed, of fees to be paid, fines inflicted, penalties incurred, and forfeitures suffered of estates in lands to any extent, for the omission of a single name, were little more than a clearer specification of property.

The Bill therefore is not only destitute of all parliamentary grounds of support in itself, but is also rendered unnecessary by regulations which exist within that and most of the other Colonies, regulations similar to these which are proposed, and enforced by no violations of principles and rights.

Under these circumstances, under the existence of no necessity to justify, and during the existence of regulations that would meet any such necessity, should it occur, can it be expected that any intelligent or independent Legislature would consent to impose upon the community it represents, such a load of personal duties, offensive in their origin, chargeable in themselves, and vexatious as unnecessary, or subject their constituents to fees, fines, penalties and forfeitures violating in principle, and in excess, all penal laws and institutions, and all the rights of property? Is it to be supposed, that any free British Colonial Assembly will ever be induced, by the adoption of the Trinidad order in council, to assimilate its own condition to that of a conquered Foreign Colony, to that subsisting state of conquest, which they all deplore, not only in itself, (and as it affords an excuse for practices and ordinances, at which the spirit of a Briton revolts,) but as, by its example and its continuance, tending to affect, to weaken, and to impair their own undoubted rights and franchises ? Such might be the deserved fate of the Bill, if offered to the Colonial House of Assembly in Barbados for enactment. Let Barbados, however, speak for herself. She has spoken by her two Houses of Legislature in resolutions, two of which, the second and fifth, are here exhibited, to disprove the charge of illicit import, and the unjust and unfounded imputation that the Colonial Assemblies will do nothing. They do honour to the Colony.

2d. *Resolved*, That the allegation contained in the said Bill, namely, that there is an illicit importation of Slaves into the West Indies, as far as respects this island, is totally void of foundation ,this House feeling the most thorough conviction, that the only Africans imported here, since the abolition of the Slave Trade, have been either brought in as prize to his Majesty's navy, or for the purpose of recruiting his army.

5th. *Resolved*, That although there is an Act, at present in force in this island, which requires, under a heavy penalty, the annual return upon oath of the Slaves of each Proprietor; yet, to evince the cordial desire which this House feels to co-operate in any measure deemed necessary for carrying into effect the Acts of the Imperial Parliament, for Abolishing the Slave Trade, it declares that it is most willing to adopt, by an Act of the Legislature of this island, such parts of the Registry Bill as are compatible with the legitimate rights and local circumstances of the inhabitants of this island, and which may be more adequate to ascertain the Slave *population*.

That the British Parliament will, as would a Colonial Parliament, in defect of all parliamentary grounds for its support, reject the measure, independently of all other considerations, may fairly be expected from its good sense and wisdom. But as it may be necessary to establish that before a British Parliament, by duly exhibited evidence, which, to a Colonial Parliament, would be, and is known by direct observation, by self conviction, by intuition, by information, which each to other, as composing the same inquest, every member might, and is bound to impart, and as the establishment of the facts necessary to justify a proceeding, is of right demandable from the actors and promoters of the measure, neither law nor reason requiring the proof of a negative proposition—An examination of the evidence produced by the Report, which advocates the measure, becomes necessary, and is undertaken to save, as much as possible, a discussion, necessarily involving those further higher considerations, which form the second class of observations, opposed to the Bill.

The evidence to be produced before the British Parliament, should unquestionably be the highest, which the nature of the case admits, and establishing facts sufficient by their number, magnitude and importance, to warrant an exercise, even of its ordinary and unquestioned right of jurisdiction.

An apology is made for the non-production, which admits, and would account for the non-existence of such evidence, and which endeavours to supply the defects of that other confessedly inferior evidence, which is produced. The proof is opened by stating, not that there is abundant *evidence* to establish, but " abundant *reason* to conclude," that there has been an illicit import of African Negroes, into *some,* if *not* all of our islands : that this is to be inferred from the case of Saint Croix, (Danish, and now in Danish possession,) in which island, the collector of the customs, supposing " that there was abundant reason to conclude," that illicit import existed, advertised rewards for discovery, which produced neither information nor evidence to convict : That this is to be inferred in the absence of evidence, which, although possessed, is not exhibited, because it has been obtained in a manner, that does not admit of its production, " by communications from persons, who dare not appear as witnesses: and that this is to be inferred in the absence of that highest evidence, which might be demanded, because, from the want of informers, and of competent witnesses, that highest evidence *exists not*.

A document is in the next place referred to, dated July 25th, 1814, purporting to be " a Return " of all ships and vessels, condemned under any of " the Acts for the Abolition of the Slave Trade," which took place on the 1st of May, 1807. In seven years to 1814, the vessels from Africa, condemned in the West Indies, amounted to eight, not one of which appeared bound to a British port, or " could well be suspected to be so," as the Report admits, though it adds, without any alleged grounds for the charge, that " it cannot reasonably be doubted, that many of the Slaves were destined circuitously for the British Colonies." Of sixteen cases of smaller vessels, the Report observes, that the numbers of Slaves found on board, were so small, that they do not average four to each vessel, and this, it is argued, establishes a smuggling trade among the islands. All consideration of time is however carefully abstained from. These condemnations of sixteen sloops and schooners, were of seven years, barely two to a year, and of sixty-four Slaves, barely nine to a year, for all the West Indies; and judging, from the names of ships or masters, thirteen, at least, of the vessels were foreign. Any objection to the smallness of these numbers, in themselves, or as of a long period of years, is encountered by stating, in obviously unfounded and contradictory terms, that the mischievous tendency of this illicit trade depends not upon its extent, upon *its actual degree,* "the known practicability of *clandestine* import in one island would be enough for the effectual and *open* supply of all the rest."

In the absence confessed of that highest evidence which is required, and in defect of other sufficient evidence to prove, the Report infers the existence of an actual or *potential* contraband Slave Trade, (potential resource, p. 51 of Report,) from suggestions and presumptions, for the most part neither legitimately established, nor logically deduced, many contradicted by facts, many convertible against the points they would prove, all irrelevant and inadmissible as evidence. As evidence, therefore, they are here rejected. As calumnies, they call for, and shall receive future consideration and confutation.

Those to whom the charge of Colonial interests is committed, submit, as documentary evidence, the papers relating to the West Indies, printed by order of the House of Commons, in July 1815, to prove, that there has been no illicit import, calling for further legislation, within the limits either of the Imperial or Colonial parliamentary jurisdictions, and are prepared to confirm the same, by further evidence and the testimony of witnesses, establishing a negative in the only way in which it can be maintained, by the entire exclusion of the affirmative proposition.

Here then the evidence might be closed on both sides, and summed up, to consist, on one side, of apologies for evidence, of defective evidence, of unfounded and inadmissible allegations and presumptions; on the other side, of evidence, as complete and sufficient as the case is capable of receiving, and entirely subversive of that to which it is opposed. To the decision which should follow such an exhibition of evidence, the parliamentary case is submitted.

———

There is therefore no illicit import of slaves into the Colonies. By the Abolition Laws, " to " carry on from British ports, from Africa *in British* " *ships,* or to prosecute the Slave Trade at sea, or " *in any* FOREIGN *part of the world,* on account " of, or by British subjects," [so the Report qualifiedly states for its own purposes, but the Act itself says,] " to carry, or aid and assist in carrying as " Slaves, any persons from Africa, or from *any other*

"*country or place,* immediately, or by tranship-
"ment at sea, directly or indirectly, on account of,
"or by British subjects," to import into any Island
or Colony, to ship or embark on board *any* vessel
or boat, any Slave or Slaves, to hire or employ for
these purposes *any* vessel, to fit out, command, enter
on board of, or navigate *any* vessel so employed,
constitutes all persons, British subjects, so offending,
felons, and " has been made as difficult, as danger-
" ous as Parliament could possibly make it. The
" penalty of death can only be superadded."

In the face of these laws, and of the preceding evidence establishing their practical efficacy, it is contended, that an illicit import is to be presumed, present or future, immediate or prospective, actual or potential, because there has been no amelioration of the condition of Slaves, and no protection has been secured to them—they may be sold for debts, and have not been attached to the soil—they are the subjects of a poll-tax laid for all without distinction on the master, and of pecuniary compensations in make-good leases—that manumissions are obstructed, and religious instruction prohibited—because in opposing the abolition measure, illicit import, it was argued, could not be prevented, that, therefore, it has existed to *the full extent* of the demand!—and because a legal presumption of slavery from colour, excludes from all legal redress in the

Colonies, and in Jamaica subjects a free man of colour to be sold into slavery with his manumission in his hand. No one of these statements, if all be admitted, proves any breach of the Abolition Laws, the conclusions to be deduced from many, are directly hostile to the views of the authors, and they are advanced rather to excite clamour and prejudice, than to justify any parliamentary proceeding.

The charge, for instance, that manumissions are obstructed, might be admitted, and it might be answered and contended, could we descend so low as to imitate the weak course of argumentation pursued in the "Report of Reasons," that the Abolition Acts having effectually cut off all the sources of external supply, it is adviseable to limit, by all possible means, the diminution of the existing number of slaves, and that, therefore, manumissions are discouraged, as tending to lessen those numbers.

Make-good leases in the West Indies, are for terms of years longer or shorter, and for the security of the lessor, an appraisement is made upon oath, of the value of the property, exclusive of the lands, at the commencement and at the termination of the lease, and the difference in value is paid or received by the lessor or lessee. It is contended, that the lessor reserves pecuniary payment, because he looks forward to supply deficiencies of slaves by purchase.

What, and if he has to pay the difference? If the number of slaves had been to be made up by the lessee, it might have been said with equal justice, that *he* stipulated for a return of numbers, in contemplation of illicit import, enabling him to do it at less cost than the first valuation.

Because it was objected argumentatively to the Abolition Acts, that they could not prevent the illicit import of slaves into the islands, that, *therefore,* an illicit import, and *to the extent of the demand,* has existed, thus endeavouring to establish by inference founded on inference, what is unsupported by any, and contradicted by all evidence, and expecting Parliament to believe, to admit, and to act upon the statement as duly established, is a serious trifling, that deserves reprobation.

I wish I could give the same character and answer to the statement that a poll-tax continues to be laid upon the master, the direct consequence of which, to the slaves he possesses, is destruction of life and of increase, and the inferred, an immediate or potential resource in illicit import.

" This tax attaches on them from the birth to the
" grave, without any allowance for infancy, infir-
" mity, or age. If a mother be relieved from labour
" on account of pregnancy, or her duties as a nurse,

" the master is yet rated for her and for her infants
" too. If feeble life is kindly cherished after the
" hope of productive labour has ceased, the poll-
" tax still continues, and operates *in effect* as a dis-
" couragement to humanity and justice."

It can only operate *in effect* by destruction of life. In Barbados, the only poll-tax that exists, is applicable to the purposes of the government, and amounts to 1s. 10½d. currency, or about 18 pence sterling *per annum*. This is the amount of the payment, and of the supposed inducement to sacrifice human life in its commencement, or in its decline. But this is not all. There are numerous pecuniary charges established *per capita*, on all slaves. The apothecary's daily care is remunerated by an annual allowance for each. The occasional attendance of a physician, in many plantations, is secured by similar payments. These " attach on infancy as well " as age." The allowance of food, clothing, and of general supplies, never to be diminished on account of age or infirmity, together with these, cannot, in the whole, be estimated at less than from £10 to £12 currency *per annum ;* and the infant, from its birth, receives a daily allowance delivered to its mother, as a support and encouragement to her. In some of the Colonies, the poll-tax may be higher than in Barbados. In all, the general charges must be nearly equal. If life can be sacrificed to avoid payment of the poll-tax, how can existence be preserved against this load of annual charges and murderous inducements?

This is not all. The Registry Bill, in addition to these, would lay on a set of consolidated annual charges *per capita*, "without any allowance for in-" fancy, infirmity, or age," that altogether would amount to more than triple the Barbados poll-tax; and these already existing in Trinidad, are further increased by a direct poll-tax, under a recent *Order in Council*, to nine times the amount.

Such is the humane consistency of these advocates for Emancipation. Blinded by sordid motives, they act, as if in others as in themselves, the power existed not of distinguishing truth or falsehood under the garb of hypocrisy and fanaticism, and have thus advanced these weak and impotent arguments, merely to introduce the soft flow, the canting and inconsistent jargon of release from maternal duties leading to infantine destruction, and feeble life cherished to be destroyed.

What shall I say of the statement—what shall I say of the inference—what shall I say of the motives—would not the harshest terms be deservedly applied to all? How much would it be regretted if such men could be admitted to advise, or have power to influence a government!

Thus far are these statements, with all their inferences, disposed of.

The examination is necessary of a statement formally made that there exists a legal presumption that a man of colour is a slave, which in all the Colonies excludes him from all the means of legal redress, and that in Jamaica particularly there exist laws " consistently with which a freeman may be sold " into slavery with his deed of manumission in " his hand."

Unfortunately these statements prove too much and against the points they are invented to establish. If colour excludes a negro from all legal redress, how is the evidence of freedom under the Registration Bill to avail him, if in Jamaica a negro may now be sold with his registered Jamaica manumission in his hand, how is the New Registration Evidence to protect him? I speak of these statements as invented upon the occasion, because they have no other source of existence in the nature of things. It would well have become the Report in making such charges thus extensively dilated upon, to have referred to any law of a Colony, and to that particular law of Jamaica which, and which alone could, and being referred to would at once have substantiated them. How impossible is it to find that which by its non-existence would mock all search! No laws are made in the Colonies for coloured persons, without the added specification of free or slave; " negro, mulatto, or other slaves" is the constant description of such persons expressed in all laws. No law, therefore, or legal disqualification can exist but as applied to slaves—to existing slaves. The very law of Jamaica, under which a vagabond or runaway slave, as a measure of police, is sold, according to the statement of the Report itself, can only be applied to a *slave*, and the price is reserved for the master of the slave until he shall appear to claim it, and slaves alone therefore are contemplated. If every vagrant slave taken up by the police, by giving no account of himself or his master, and claiming to be free, could without further inquiry obtain his discharge, a most necessary and useful law would at once be rendered a dead letter. This further inquiry is made by the usual advertisements, stating the detention of the individual, and the publication of the case is for his benefit as well as for the ends of justice. No freeman of colour could exist in the Colony under the execution of a law that would sell him as a slave with his manumission in his hand.

In the Colonies where the proportion of slaves to freemen of colour is so considerable, the moral probability that every man of colour is a slave is great. In Barbados, taking, according to the last returns, the numbers respectively as 70,000 and 3,000, the moral probability or moral presumption that any coloured individual is a slave, is as twenty-three nearly to one; in Jamaica it is considerably greater.

No other moral or legal presumption whatsoever concerning colour as evidence of slavery exists or can possibly exist in the Colonies, and the statement is absolutely unfounded. Stated and considered as true, it is employed to introduce the most odious comparisons and reflections on the legislatures, laws, courts of justice and inhabitants of the British Colonies, continued through thirteen pages of the Report, from 56 to 69. Let these pages be carefully perused, and afterwards the following.

If a man of colour in the West Indies should make application to any magistrate or lawyer for legal redress, the moral probability before stated would perhaps lead to an inquiry respecting the free condition of the man. In the smaller Colonies where every person almost is known, even this would not probably occur. Known to be the slave of a neighbour, if such an application could possibly occur, he would be treated as a slave. Known to be a freeman of the country, his case would be attended to most carefully, if within the pale of criminal jurisdiction, by the magistrate; by the practising lawyer, if within his province of employment.

Let it be inquired of any lawyer who has practised in the Colonies, if upon the application of a coloured man, for his professional assistance in a civil or a criminal case, he would have answered " looking at his condition recorded in his face," My good fellow! your case is remediless, your skin is black. The inquiry has been made, I have made it. Mute astonishment at the question, as not being what the words imply, has always been followed by a negation couched in terms of disgraceful reprobation and peremptory denial.

The Seventh Report of the African Society, in 1813, only two years before, states the case of a black man named John George Whiston. Having been manumitted by his mistress, who was only a tenant for life, he was after her death, in 1812, claimed as a slave, and as such being arrested, was, by writ of *habeas corpus,* subsequently released. The question of freedom was tried in the Island of Saint Vincent, and the verdict of a jury, established the Slavery. The generous advocate who defended the Negro, prevailed on the Court to reserve the point of law, pledging himself to pay one hundred pounds sterling, in *satisfaction* of the claim, provided no reversal of the judgment should be effected within a twelvemonth, by further proceedings.

This case affords an example worthy of imitation, where, by regular course of proceeding, and a due conservation of the rights of others, a man who had enjoyed freedom during a long course of years, was saved from again descending into that slavery, from which he had formerly been raised. The benevolence of Mr. Keane, and of the directors who advanced the money necessary on the occasion, deserves all praise.

Here then is an instance of a black man, notwithstanding the colour of his skin, coming into a Colonial Court upon an *habeas corpus*, and having the question of slave or free, publicly tried and determined. The decision was indeed unfavourable to the individual, he was in fact a slave, and must have been so known to be. Yet, both a black and a slave, he is not as either, excluded from a regular trial of his title to freedom.

This case could not be, was not unknown to any committee framing the Report of Reasons, and is glanced at by the following observation, in itself contradictory of all its other statements: "If free-"dom be asserted for them by *habeas corpus*, at the "instance of some bold and generous patron, their "colour is a presumption of slavery, which he could "not repel," *unless*, by competent witnesses, to prove the necessary facts.

Yet, with this case existing, and establishing these points, the Report has ventured to state, that remedies for detention in slavery, of free Blacks, and the right of even alleging the wrong in a civil action, are barred by objecting that the man is a slave: that upon a question of slave or free, the Colonial

Courts have excluded from all redress, by one short rejoinder, " the man's skin is black :" That " the *Assemblies* have absolved the master from any other trouble in proving title to an alleged *slave* beyond the production of the party whose *condition* is recorded in his face :" and all this upon a legal presumption of slavery from the skin, which neither assemblies, nor courts, nor advocates, ever entertained.

In the West Indies, as in England, the law truly knows no distinctions of persons, parties to suits, but what may be put in issue between them. If the declinatory plea of slavery be pleaded, like the plea of alien enemy in the present, or of Villeinage in ancient time, or any other similar plea, it may be put in issue and abate the suit, or upon a judgment of *respondeat ouster* the suit will be continued. Upon the master also, or upon him who pleads, the burthen of proving his own plea lies, although the Report states that " the *Assemblies* have cast the " burthen of proof on the weaker and helpless " party, upon the alleged slave himself." A practice of this sort would be against all legal principle, and I call for the production of any act of any assembly that ever existed to this effect.

A wilful and pitiful misrepresentation and misstatement both of law and of facts is made and maintained in this case, by confounding the meaning and use of the terms negro and slave, and substituting each for the other to support a verbal argument that has no foundation whatsoever, except in the convertibility, not immediately to be perceived, of one word for another, whilst each is in common parlance applied at different times to mean the same or different things. By calling a *negro* a *slave*, and a *slave* a *negro*, and naming this, or that, when the other is intended, a verbal and sophistical course of argumentation is prolonged through 20 pages, to the opprobrium and disgrace of that respectable body, who have most unadvisedly thus committed themselves to others for fair, and legitimate, and honourable argumentation. When it is stated, that in a civil action, the objection that " *the man is a slave*" cannot be removed, the equivocation is on the word *slave.* If the objection really be that " the man is a slave," it may be removed if unfounded, and if true, that it may avail, it must be established by the objector: If that " the man is a negro," his condition indeed cannot be changed, but the objection would not avail nor be received. The Report states *slave,* but wishes *negro* to be understood.—If " a *slave* is disabled from applying to the law in any case," this does not disable a free *negro.*—To the question of slave or free should [not the Colonial courts, as is stated,] but the party in the cause " shortly rejoin," " his skin is black," how would this meet the question? This course of pleading is novel in Westminster Hall, and I venture to affirm that would not be offered to or received by any Colonial court existing. When the master produces the alleged slave, what is that " condition which is recorded in his face?" *slave* or *negro*? If *slave* it ought to avail against him. If negro it avails nothing. Then which is it? It can only be *negro*, his skin is black. Only as *slave* can it avail to maintain the argument of the Report. Against the inexcusable ignorance or wilful misrepresentation displayed by these observations and statements, we appeal to the British public and to the Institution itself, calling upon them " to do us somehow noble justice," and to discharge from their confidence and consideration the authors of these calumnies, and upon Parliament to reject a measure derived from these sources, and supported by these proofs of its necessity.

Of the remaining presumptive propositions, amelioration of condition, protection of persons, religious instruction, sale for debts, attachment to the soil, all consideration is for the present waved. It is due to public opinion and expectation that they should be treated with some consideration, and they shall in due time receive the fullest, particularly as connected with the subject of Emancipation, when the general condition of slaves in the Colonies shall come to be considered in itself, and apart from that measure of registration to which it affords no ground of support. To these, therefore, as proofs of any breach of the Abolition Acts, we apply the exception that excludes them, as not establishing any thing in point if admitted. All further consideration of the question of manumission is also, for the present, and might altogether be declined from the powerful inference it affords against any actual or expected supply of slaves by illicit import. We disclaim the inference as founded on a principle which exists not. But a consideration of the state and condition of the free coloured people, by no means correctly represented or understood, is necessary in itself and in its relations to that mode of Emancipation suggested in the Report, and will also as a part of the subject of Emancipation be duly considered.

It is, however, even here denied that there has been no amelioration of condition—that there is no protection for slaves. The amelioration laws of several of the Colonies, of Jamaica for instance, notwithstanding the indecent and unfounded suggestions of the Report respecting them, are appealed to. The protection of these laws against masters, and the never failing protection of slaves by their masters against strangers, contradict both the preceding statements. They are contradicted by the observation of all in the West Indies, now that the abolition of that cruel trade has removed from among the coloured population the appearance of many unfortunate subjects of slavery in a foreign country, and a native peasantry is now exhibited with fewer objects of squalid commiseration than any other country affords. That slaves continue liable to be sold for debts, and are not attached to the soil, are points involving so many considerations which respect not only the public and the master, but the slave himself,—the beneficial policy, respect being had only to the slave, is so equivocal that the best of men would pause, and doubt, and delay before he decided, and so perhaps would not decide at all. No prohibition has been opposed to Religious Instruction in any Colony, except what the prudent care of the magistracy has exercised to preserve the peace and morals of the country against characters of a description incapable of affording any religious, moral, or beneficial instruction whatsoever.

As matters of general political consideration, many of these topics will hereafter be discussed more at large. I spare to encumber with further observations that which is adduced, and is to be taken only as evidence to prove the point in issue; breach or not of the Abolition Laws. To that which is, and may be received as evidence, the question is committed.

On the Extent of Parliamentary Jurisdiction.

After all, the question is not of Abolition. Abolition is only the pretext. It is indeed on all sides known, it is felt, it is admitted that there has been no violation of the Abolition Laws; none that requires the enactment of any new or more coercive laws. The question is not whether a registry of slaves shall be established in the Colonies or not. In almost all, annual returns of numbers which would discover illicit increase, are already regularly made; in all, recorded Registrations of persons and numbers, are publicly made, and may always be consulted. Abolition and Registration are only pretences.

The object is by that which calls itself a Registry Bill, and affects to be only a registration of slaves, although accompanied with clauses that would constitute it rather a Bill of pains, penalties and forfeitures, to induce Parliament to violate the exclusive rights of internal legislation of the Colonial assemblies in a case of no great apparent interest, that the promoters of the measure may be enabled afterwards, through Parliament, as has been done by Orders in Council for the recently conquered Colonies, to proceed to legislate for all the Colonies of Great Britain.

There are indeed most high and important considerations which arise from a view of the state in which these Colonies remain, considerations which respect the general rights of British Colonists, the duty of the executive, and the responsibility of its advisers. The general right of British Colonists to British laws and a British form of Government, becomes weakened by the precedent and example of a Colony retained after final cession by a treaty of peace, in its ancient state of subjection to a despotism which the British Constitution rejects, and British feeling would abhor. So impressed was I with the consequences to all of this proceeding, that I considered it my duty, although neither directly nor indirectly connected with that Colony, to remonstrate, as a British Colonist, against this conduct in the case of Trinidad, at a very early period after the final cession of that Colony. The answer I received from the then Secretary of State, the late Earl of Buckinghamshire, was worthy of a British minister. " We are as anxious as yourself " to give a British Constitution to Trinidad, and " will certainly do so as soon as it can prudentially " be effected. Such, however, is the present state of " that Colony, that to a General Representative " Assembly, if established, there would be mem-" bers returned, whom you," addressing himself to me, " would regret to see holding places in any " Colonial Assembly."

Two years ago, upon a suggestion that a registration of slaves in all the Colonies, similar to that which had been established in Trinidad, would tend to enforce the Abolition of the Slave Trade, a measure alike favoured by myself and my constituents, I obtained a copy of the Trinidad Order in Council, which I transmitted to the Colony, and recommended, under the Annual Poll-Tax Returns, a more particular specification of names and descriptions of persons, as all that was necessary or proper to be done, and this more from respect to what I considered to be the wish of Government, than from any conviction of its use or necessity. What I felt as a man, as a Colonist, and an Englishman, when I perused that Order in Council, and contemplated the powers exercised, and, the form in which it had been imposed on that unfortunate Colony, I cannot describe, but I can never forget,—I seemed to cease, at the moment, to be a freeman of a free country. The horror I felt I failed not to express to my constituents, and from this circumstance probably, as well as from the total absence of any necessity for legislative interference, nothing was then done.

I cannot but observe upon the caution with which this ordinance for Trinidad is mentioned in the Registry Report; once only is it mentioned as a new law; the legislators are not hinted at, and when formally referred to, it is designated as an " *instrument* before alluded to," being the Order in Council of the Prince Regent for registering slaves in Trinidad.

In 1812 this ordinance was imposed upon Trinidad. It was not, as is now proposed for that and for all the British Colonies, a British Statute made by a British Parliament, undertaking to legislate for a British Colony. It was not an Act passed by an Assembly of the Colony, for no such legislative body exists within it. It was imposed upon the

Colony contrary to the general wishes of the inhabitants, in the form of an Order in Council, by right of conquest I presume, for I know of no other right that can be pretended.

Is it not by force of that innate principle in human nature, by which power once possessed is always fondly retained, that these men have been enabled to persuade his Majesty's Government to hold and to exercise against what might perhaps be considered as a sound discretion, the power of making ordinances for British Colonies and British persons? Have they not availed themselves of the power thus retained, to send out their registry ordinance to Trinidad and the other ceded Colonies of St. Lucie and the Isle of France? Is not the Registry Bill unquestionably an insidious attempt on the part of the same persons, but by other means, and with equal disregard of the sacred rights of Britons, to introduce into all the Colonies a similar law, by the agency of Parliament, in the hope that having thus once surmounted all the muniments of Colonial rights, they may proceed to those further violations contemplated and avowed of jurisdiction and of property? As such we meet the attempt with the following vindication of Colonial rights.

The British Parliament has, in time past, claimed the right of legislating for the British Colonies in all cases whatsoever. This right has always been denied by every Colony possessing a duly constituted legislature.

This question involves two others; the original right of the British Parliament to British legislation, and the extent of that right as referrible to Colonial legislation.

Unquestionably the British Parliament owes its existence and its powers to those original rights, and rights of representation which are vested in, and inseparable from, persons and freeholds. Conformably to these principles, and in execution of the royal duties, a separate summons, by letter or writ, is sent to each Peer of Parliament, and a writ to the sheriffs and bailiffs, commanding Returns of Representatives by freeholders or others.

These principles which impart the powers, define also the limits of British Parliamentary Jurisdiction, and prescribe the course of proceeding to be pursued, upon the accession of persons or of districts to those already represented. This claim of the British Parliament can only be founded on a right connate with itself, of extending the powers it possesses to other communities and countries besides those from and for which it has been elected. Such a claim is, however, against principle, and is not warranted by those rights of representation, to which alone Parliament, under a due exercise of the royal prerogative, owes its creation and existence *, and which are derived from, and limited to particular persons and places.

Against this claim the antient law-authorities declare themselves. " A Tax by the Parliament of " England shall not bind Ireland, because they are " not summoned to Parliament. Ireland hath a " Parliament of its own, and maketh and altereth " laws, and our Statutes do not bind them, because " they do not send knights to our Parliament." Year Book—1 Henry VII.

---

* Parliament owes its existence to the Crown, in virtue of the prerogative, creating and convening it. The Crown created peers and tenants *in capite*. As inferior courts baron were constituted by the inferior tenants of each, so those constituted the royal court baron, or common council of the realm. In one house, barons and tenants continued personally to sit, until of the tenants a representation by election was made, and a delegation established of knights from counties, of burgesses from tenant-boroughs, of citizens from corporations corporate tenants elected according to charter. Finally, a division was effected into two houses, one of barons in their own rights, and one of representatives, this latter house carrying with it and reserving to itself the right of originating all taxes. Subsequently to William I. A. D. 1066, these establishments began. Between 1250 and 1300, the representation of tenants was established. In 1327, the division of houses was effected. In 1422, the qualification of 40s. freeholders was enacted. Thus the frame and constitution of the British parliament was completed, and a government formed which combines all rights of king, peers, people, legislating for themselves directly, or by representation, and embraces practically through boroughs all interests as well as persons.

Parliament has indeed in practice waved this claim of self extension, and returned to a recognition of those principles to which it owes its existence, and which not to know argues itself unknown.

Extension of parliamentary power can only be effected by extension of parliamentary representation. In cases of added population, in all cases of extended dominion, the British principle and practice has always been to proceed by extended representation united and inclusive, or separate and exclusive. Cases of the former kind are of Wales and of Ireland finally, though at first, as a kind of Colony, to be ranked among the latter: cases of the latter kind, of representation separate and exclusive, are of the Colonies.

Ireland was originally conquered and "planted by the English, as a kind of colony," vi. Blackstone, vol. 1. p. 100. For a long time it was held in a state of subjection, such as never has been practised towards any British Colony. When, upon a due consideration of the state and circumstances of that conquest, and from propriety, expediency, and necessity, English laws, and a parliament had by the King been duly constituted therein, the powers and the duties of that Parliament, were, by indirection subsequently reduced to a nullity, by their submitting to entertain no Bill, of which the heads had not previously been transmitted to England, and approved of by the British Government, and their subjection was further enforced, by an appeal from the

Courts in Ireland, to the Courts of Westminster. Thus a subordinate judicature was superadded to that which was not subordinate, but a mockery of legislation.

Jamaica was conquered in 1655. In 1661, the King's representative was duly empowered by his Majesty, to erect British courts of judicature, and, with the advice of a council, *to be elected by the inhabitants*, to pass laws suitable to the exigencies of the Colony. Subsequently a commission issued to the governor, directing him to call an assembly, to be indifferently chosen by the people at large, to pass laws for their own internal regulation and government. This practice of making ordinances, by a governor and council, during the unsettled or unceded state of a Colony, and upon final settlement or cession, as soon as circumstances permit, of establishing a general Assembly, composed of the King by representation, and of two legislative houses, a council, and a representative assembly, is regular and right. An attempt was made in Jamaica, to subject their legislation to the restraints, and confine it practically within the limits of Poyning's Law, but this was properly and effectually resisted.

During the latter part of the reign of James the First, Barbados was occupied under a grant by letters patent to the Earl of Marlborough, afterwards waved in favour of the Earl of Carlisle, to whom the proprietaryship of the Island was granted, by letters patent, under the great seal, giving to the said Earl of Carlisle, for the government of the said Province, with the consent of the free inhabitants thereof, thereunto to be called, power to make laws, as convenient and agreeable as may be to the laws of England, and ordaining that the said province be of the King's allegiance, and that all persons born therein, be subjects of the Crown of Great Britain, as free as those born in England, and shall freely, quietly and peaceably, have and possess, all the liberties, franchises and privileges, of natural born subjects and liege persons. The Barbados settlers carried with them all British laws, and in the course of a very few years, from the first settlement, after passing through the necessary administration of a governor and council, the British Constitution also was fully imparted to the Colony, by the establishment of a general assembly, composed of the governor, council, and representatives of the people, being freeholders, freely elected by and from the freeholders of every parish in the Island, and lawfully empowered by commission from the Earl of Carlisle, thereto empowered by letters patent from the King.

In February 1762, the French island of Grenada surrendered upon capitulation to the British arms, and was finally ceded by the treaty of peace in February 1763. October the 7th, 1763, his Majesty, by proclamation, states, that " for the speedy set-
" tling various governments, of which Grenada is
" one, and from his paternal care for the security
" of the *liberties* and *properties* of the inhabitants,
" he had given express power and direction to the

"Governor thereof, that as soon as the state "and circumstances of the Colony will admit, "he shall, with the advice and consent of his "Majesty's Council, summon and call Gene- "ral Assemblies, and, together with his Majesty's "Council, and the Representatives of the people, "freely elected by the freeholders and inhabitants "thereof, in General Assembly, make laws and "statutes to bind the people thereof, as near "as may be agreeable to the laws of England." In April 1764, a Governor was by commission appointed, with full powers, and before the end of 1765, a General Assembly was actually formed and convened in the Colony.

Conformably to the charter of King John, that the King would summon Peers himself, and the Commons by Sheriffs and Bailiffs,—conformably to these precedents, and to the same principles, the rights of persons and of freeholds, to which the British Parliament owes its existence and powers, and in execution of the same royal duties, are Colonial Parliaments formed and convened. Every member of the Upper Houses of Legislature in the Colonies, is called to sit therein by letter or commission, signed by the King's own hand, whilst the Lower Houses of Representatives are formed by writs issued on the occasion to the proper officers, commanding a return of members duly elected to serve therein. The King, by representation, exercises the royal right of approving or rejecting all bills—money bills originate only in the Houses of Representatives—each House possesses and exercises all the legislative privileges and powers of each House of Parliament in England—and the general resemblance of the Colonial to the Imperial Parliament, is complete in their modes of creation, existence, constitution, and powers.

These principles and these precedents deny to the British Parliament that right and power of self-extension, by which it would exclude Colonial Parliaments, and occupy their districts of jurisdiction, in violation of the rights of persons and of freeholds.

There are indeed instances in which the assistance of the British Parliament has been invoked, and joined with the powers of the prerogative under particular circumstances, as in the case of Canada, to give by successive enactments, conformably to the practice of the Crown acting by and for itself—first, by 14 Geo. III. c. 83. a Governor and Legislative Council to make *ordinances*—and subsesequently, by 31 Geo. III. c. 31. a duly constituted Legislature composed of the King by representation, a Council appointed by the King, and a body of Representatives freely elected by the freeholders and inhabitants of the Colony to make *laws*. But the exercise of this power, or even the possession of the power attributed to the British Parliament by Blackstone, of new modelling and reforming the whole of a colonial constitution, gives no right of internal legislation either to the King or to the Parliament, when, and after the constitution is settled. That it remains not in the King, the Grenada case has decided, and the principle of that case, and all reason, would equally take it out of the British Parliament, after the formation of a government fully capable of making laws in all cases, subject to the royal negative.

That to the King properly and exclusively, according to his own discretion, and as circumstances shall admit of its exercise, belongs this power of imparting the British constitution and constitutional forms of government to the British Colonies, is unquestionably established. The King, in the due exercise of his prerogative, gives existence to the British Parliament by convening it. The King creates Peers. The King created boroughs in England, until the union with Scotland prevented any new creation that would change the relative numbers of the representatives of the two kingdoms. The King has always possessed and exercised the power of intermediate regulation of all conquests. Lord Mansfield, in Campbell *v.* Hall, states distinctly, " that " in the case of Ireland, no man ever said the " Crown did not do it, that the Crown could not

" do it:"—" That which is called the Statute of
" Wales, is certainly no more than regulations made
" by the King in Council for the government of
" Wales :"—" Berwick, after the conquest of it,
" was governed by charters from the Crown, with-
" out the interposition of Parliament, till the reign
" of James I.; that the King has this right was
" never denied in Westminster Hall, was never ques-
" tioned in Parliament." The King, therefore, has
in himself the undoubted right " of subordinate" regulation, that is, of regulation " *subordinate* to his
" own authority in Parliament," when he pleases to
submit it, " but without any power to make changes
" contrary to fundamental principles," to the British Constitution and Laws, " in all cases of con-
" quest," and I will add, of Colonies conquered or
to be settled.

As soon as settled, or ceded and settled, and circumstances permit, the duties of the prerogative
require the establishment in every Colony of the British Constitution and forms of Legislation, and of
British Laws, if they did not previously exist, to be
modified to the existing state of each Colony by its
own Legislature, subject to the royal negative.
Nothing else can regularly be done. A Governor
alone—a Governor and Council are intermediate
states—a Governor, Council, and Assembly of Representatives, perfect states of Government. When
too long a time has passed without establishing this

last form of government, and change of circumstances may require it, the King joins Parliament to himself, or himself to Parliament, for duly effecting the same purposes.

This power of forming and imparting a British Constitution and Laws once exercised by the King, is no longer in him, and this is established and admitted in Campbell *v.* Hall—exercised by Parliament invoked by the King, and in aid of the King, and by his assent, for without his invocation it would not, and without his assent it could not act, it is equally out of the King, and, by all reason and analogy, out of the Parliament. The King's power to act without Parliament is unquestionable. Parliament cannot act without the King. It is this occasional agency of Parliament, and the not distinguishing between a perfect and this imperfect constitution, this intermediate state of regulation which Parliament assists to new model and reform, that has led Mr. J. Blackstone, in a general work, and upon an occasion in which accuracy of information or observation has not been possessed or exercised, to state, that " the Legislation of the Colonies is sub- " ject to the revision and controul of the King in " Council," instead of the simple royal negative which may be exercised, and to attribute to Parliament the general power of " new modelling and " reforming Colonial constitutions." This new modelling and reforming can only be of the intermediate state of regulation which is in the King. To the Act, Parliament would not and could not proceed, but in aid of, and invited by, the King, and this once performed, as it ends the intermediate power of regulation in the King, so it ends that power which exists only as invoked and as auxiliary thereto. The Act that imparts a British Constitution and Laws, establishes powers fully adequate to, and entitled to perform all the works of Legislation, either for Laws, Constitution, or form of Government, subject to the King's negative. With the original auxiliary aid of Parliament, therefore, that of new modelling and reforming also is gone. No power can it possess of new modelling and reforming the British Constitution, and no other can King or Parliament have given, or have undertaken to give to British subjects.

The power therefore of self extension for the purposes of internal Colonial Legislation, is not in the British Parliament by original right, or by the occasional exercise of its powers in forming constitutions for particular Colonies, and it is excluded therefrom absolutely and of right, by the establishment of these Constitutions, and the existence of olonial Parliaments duly constituted like itself, and possessed of equal powers within their several districts and jurisdictions.

There is therefore in the British Parliament no

original right of internal Colonial Legislation. If any such could ever have been supposed to exist, it is divested by Acts of the British Parliament itself.

To British considerations, Acts of Parliament possess powers before which all legal opinions and judicial decisions disappear. If they differ, they are controuled thereby—if they agree, they are merged therein. I pass over those acts of commercial regulation, which are not to be considered as acts of internal Colonial Legislation, and those occasional acts of direct violation of the exclusive Colonial right, which can never impart right resisted or not, and come to direct positive enactments which controul all these.

By the 6th of Geo. I. c. 5. it is declared, that the King's Majesty, with the consent of the Lords and Commons of Great Britain in Parliament, hath power to make laws to bind the people of Ireland.

By the 6th of Geo. III. c. 12. it is declared, that the King's Majesty, with the Lords and Commons of Great Britain in Parliament, have power to make laws to bind the people of the British Colonies in all cases.

By the 18 Geo. III. c. 12. it is declared and enacted, that the King and Parliament of Great Britain will not lay any tax, duty or assessment whatever payable in any Colony, except duties necessary for the regulation of Commerce, the nett proceeds of which shall be paid to the use of the Colony, in which they shall be levied, to be at the disposal of the general assembly thereof.

By the 23 Geo. III. c. 28. it is declared and enacted, that the right claimed by the people of Ireland to be bound only by laws enacted by his Majesty and the Parliament of that kingdom in all cases whatever, is thereby established and ascertained for ever, and shall at no time thereafter be questioned or questionable.

Here then are four British Statutes, the two first of which assert a power in the British Parliament, to make laws to bind Ireland and other British conquests and dependencies in all cases. The third concedes to the British Colonies, the right of taxation claimed under the general right of Legislation asserted. The fourth concedes to the people of Ireland, the right claimed by them of being legislated for only by their own Parliament, declaring it to be a right, established and ascertained for ever, and thus establishing and ascertaining it for ever, for all the dependencies and Colonies of Great Britain, similarly circumstanced.

The Act the 6th Geo. III. c. 12. advanced a

claim to the general right of legislation, to support a claim to the particular right of taxation. In a subsequent case the particular claim is as formally withdrawn as the general claim was made, and with the particular claim or object, the whole measure was, and the general claim was fairly considered as abandoned. If only then partially, although actually, it now stands virtually and generally repealed by the then existing General Right subsequently declared for Ireland within five years after, by the 23 Geo. III. and by its enactments operating as an actual repeal for all.

The Colonial Assemblies claim exclusive internal Legislation by right original and indefeasible : as incident to their distinct creation and separate existence : as established by the modes and purposes of their creation, by principle and analogy, by propriety, expediency and necessity : by right not impaired by exercise of the admitted right of Commercial Regulation in the British Parliament, nor by petty violations of their general right of Legislation, because not always nor captiously resisted : by right confirmed against all claim, all invasion, all judicial opinions and legal enactments, by enactments operating in principle and in effect, to relinquish, redress, reverse, and repeal all these.

The original and indefeasible rights, under which the Colonial Assemblies are entitled to exclusive internal legislation, are those original unquestionable rights of representative legislation and representative election vested in and inseparable from persons and freeholds, and so declared to be by Lord Chief Justice Holt, confirming the ancient principle before referred to in the Year-book, 1 Henry VII. If this right be admitted, and it cannot be questioned, it is in its nature exclusive, as well as inclusive—it establishes beyond all question the rights of the inhabitants and freeholders of the Colonies to elect representatives, and of those representatives as part of a Colonial General Assembly or Parliament, to legislate for them their constituents, and it establishes also those rights of the Colonists and of the Colonial Legislatures within their own districts, to the exclusion of all claims not representative of their persons and freeholds.

I can only weaken by attempting to dilate upon this right. But I cannot refrain from confirming and illustrating it by reference to the following Resolutions recently passed in the Honourable the Houses of Assembly of Jamaica and Barbados, declaratory of these rights as founded in the indefeasible rights of persons—resolutions to be adopted by every Colony of the Empire—and upon these I take my stand.

Jamaica Resolutions.

"*Resolved*, 1. That the free British subjects who conquered and settled in Jamaica, or have since removed to and established themselves in this island, are bound by the like allegiance as every other subject of the realm, and carried with them, have enjoyed, and ought of right to enjoy, all liberties and immunities of free and natural born subjects, to all intents and purposes, as if they had been born and remained within the realm, modified and adapted to their peculiar situation as Colonists : and particularly have enjoyed, and ought of right to enjoy, so long as their Knights and Burgesses are not called to sit in Parliament, a distinct and entire civil government, of the like powers, pre-eminence, and jurisdictions, within the said island, as are established in the British government, in respect of the British subjects within the realm, which government, according to the constitution of Jamaica, is composed of his Majesty the King of Great Britain and Ireland, the Council appointed by his Majesty, and the representatives of the people, freely elected and met in general assembly.

2d.—*Resolved*, That the most important of the rights, privileges, immunities, and franchises, which are inherent in British subjects as their birth-right, and have by them been brought to this island, is to consent to those laws by which they are to be governed by the exercise of the right to send their Representatives to the said General Assembly, who, with his Majesty, and the Council, can and of right ought to do, all such acts and matters of legislation, respecting the internal government of the island, as the Imperial Parliament can do within the United Kingdom of Great Britain and Ireland.

3d.—*Resolved*, That it is the peculiar privilege of the free British subjects settled in Jamaica, by their Representatives met in General Assembly, to give and grant all aids and subsidies to his Majesty ; and to impose all rates, duties, taxes, fees, fines or penalties whatever ; and that laying and levying any taxes, fees, fines or penalties, other than such duties of customs as are mere regulations of trade, on the inhabitants, by any other authority than the Legislature of this island, composed as aforesaid, is altogether unconstitutional, and a violation of their dearest rights.

4.—*Resolved*, That the inhabitants of this island have not had the liberty and privilege of electing and sending any Knights and Burgesses or others, to represent them in the High Court of Parliament, and explain the condition of their country, and ought not to be bounden by laws, or touched and grieved by subsidies, fees or penalties enacted, granted and imposed, without their assent, other than such external regulations, in respect of commerce, as are necessary for the common weal of the Empire.

8th.—*Resolved*, That we have seen with surprise and concern the draught of a Bill said to have been printed by order of the Commons House of Parliament, entitled " A Bill for effectually preventing the unlawful importation of Slaves, and the holding free persons in slavery, in the British Colonies," which assumes a right of legislation within the island, upon a subject of mere municipal regulation and internal police, exercises a power over the estates and property of the inhabitants, imposes the most grievous penalties and forfeitures, to be inflicted at the will of a single officer, without trial by jury, and levies fees and gratuities to the use of the said officer and others, on the inhabitants, not given or consented to by their Representatives in General Assembly; by which enactments, penalties, forfeitures and assessments, not only the constitutional right of internal legislation is infringed, but the pledge in respect of taxation, given to the Colonies by the Statute of 18 Geo. III. c. 12. is violated.

Barbados Resolutions.

1st.—*Resolved*, That this House, having received from its Agent in London, the copy of a Slave Registry Bill, lately introduced into the House of Commons, conceives itself most urgently called upon to protest against the infringement which this Bill attempts on the rights of our Colonial Legislature.

3d.—*Resolved*, That although the ostensible object of the Bill is to obtain a Registry of Slaves, it obviously proposes to attain that by imposing a tax upon every Slave Proprietor within the Colony, in manifest violation of that sound and just principle of the British Constitution, that " representation and taxation are inseparable."

4th.—*Resolved*, That the *sole* right of imposing taxes on the inhabitants of this Island, or of passing laws for internal regulation, is now, and hath been for a length of time past, vested in the House of Assembly with consent of the Council, and of the King or his Representative here for the time being:—a right which can never be safely or advantageously exercised by those who are utter strangers to these Colonies, and must necessarily want that local information which is so essential to the important work of legislation.

Not only by original right, but by actual existence the Colonial Legislatures are exclusive. This, as of natural bodies, excludes all others from the places they fill. Their existence and the exercise of the powers by which they occupy their particular districts, naturally and necessarily, politically and practically exclude the existence and exercise by all persons of similar powers within their jurisdictions.

If to avoid the political solecism of *Imperium in imperio*, and the existence of two concurrent legislatures of equal and absolute powers within the same limits of jurisdiction, one must necessarily exclude the other, that must certainly prevail which duly established, legally existing, possessing the right and exercising the power, excludes all others by and from all these, and even from the Right of Claim. The Colonial Parliament is admitted to be duly constituted and legally subsisting. Possessing and exercising its powers *de jure & de facto*, they are as necessarily exclusive, as they are rightfully established, and the *imperium in imperio* is rather to be applied against that Parliament which claims to possess, and to exclude against rightful and actual possession.

By positive institution as well as by the purposes of institution, the Colonial Legislatures exclude all others from their districts. When the King, by virtue of his Royal prerogative, and in execution of his Royal duties, as soon as the state and circumstances of any settled or conquered Colony, to be determined by his Majesty in the exercise of a sound discretion, aided by responsible advisers, will admit, and for the security of the liberties and properties thereof, constitutes and convenes a Colonial Parliament or General Assembly, composed of his representative, a council duly appointed by himself, and representatives freely elected by the inhabitants and freeholders thereof, such Parliament or General Assembly possesses all the rights, privileges and powers of a Parliament, and of internal Legislation, to the exclusion of all other Parliaments or Legislative Bodies constituted and convened by the same royal powers for any other separate part or district, or united parts or districts of the realm.

Of the Parliaments of Great Britain, of Ireland before the Union, of Jamaica, Barbados, Grenada, each created and convoked by the same power for its particular district, none can possess the right of legislating for or within the jurisdictions of the others.

The declared purposes of constituting Parliaments, are for securing the liberties and properties of persons. These purposes can only be accomplished by exclusive internal legislation,—by internal legislation obviously, by exclusive necessarily. Legislation must be exclusive as well as internal, or it is nothing. It must exclude, or it will be excluded. Internal exclusive legislation can alone secure liberties and properties—there is neither liberty nor property to him who holds them at the arbitrament of another over whom he has no controul, with whom he is connected by no privity, no relation political or legal, to whom he has delegated no power.

It has been shewn that the express purpose for which Colonial Parliaments have been constituted, is the security of the liberties and properties of the Colonists, and that exclusive internal legislation is necessarily consequent as indispensable to that great purpose. If now it can be shewn that in any case of properties or liberties the power of legislation claimed has been effectually resisted and denied to, and by the British Parliament itself abandoned, that is established by positive law, which was before inferred from principle, and any one case or precedent of a settled or conquered colony or district, is extendible by analogy to all.

The case of property is fully settled and secured by a formal abandonment by the British Parliament, of the right of taxation, by the 18 Geo. III. c. 12. before referred to, and which might be, as before observed, and was considered as a failure and abandonment of the general claim advanced to support it.

The other purpose for which Colonial Parliaments were constituted, the security of the liberties of the Colonists, is also effectually secured by enactments

[65]

of the British Parliament itself, conceding the right of exclusive internal legislation to the claims of one of the dependencies of the British Crown by the 23 Geo. III. c. 38. abandoning the whole British parliamentary claim to the *declared and ascertained* right of the people of Ireland, and declaring that his Majesty and its own Parliament alone have a right to make laws for them. Principle and analogy extend these exclusive powers and privileges to Jamaica, and Barbados, and Grenada, and to all.

By abandonment of a part of the general claim to the Colonies, the right to the whole was weakened, and indeed extinguished under the circumstances of advancement and abandonment. By abandonment of the whole claim against one as contrary to general declared existing right, the right to the whole is abandoned as against all similar territorial dependencies of the empire, and the claim of the Colonies to exclusive legislation is established and confirmed in part, and in the whole, by positive enactments, by principle, and analogy.

By propriety, expediency and necessity, they possess exclusive legislation against the impropriety, impracticability and impossibility of its being generally, or effectually, or duly exercised by the British Parliament sitting at the distance of between 4000 and 5000 miles, without any local knowledge, without any practical knowledge whatsoever—and they hold it

not impaired by any apparent incroachments which the admitted right of commercial regulation in the British Parliament justifies, or by any petty, but more direct violations of the general right, violations which can never give or take away rights. They hold it confirmed by the Acts, and by the sweeping clause effects of the Acts before referred to, removing every judicial or legislative declaration, decision, or enactment opposed to them.

To this claim of the Colonies, the Report opposes the argument of *Imperium in imperio*, which has already been disposed of, and the following objections: " that the lawgiver is the sovereign," a proposition which if admitted would render the Parliament of the United Kingdom the sovereign of the United Kingdom, and is therefore disproved by the argument *ex absurdo :* that it would constitute a virtual independence of the Colonies, as if the admission would expel his Majesty from his sovereignty, and abrogate that right of negative, and those other powers of controul which indissolubly bind and unite the Colonies to the Crown of the United Kingdom: that it would place the sugar islands in the same relation " *to us* as Hanover, with this unjust and degrading difference, that we should be bound to protect, though not allowed to govern."—If by *us* be meant the people of England, we answer; that we are British subjects, the children and the brethren of the people of the United Kingdom, which the people of Hanover are not:—if by *us* be meant the sovereign and king of the United Kingdom, we refer the Report for an answer to the lowest of the legal profession, who will inform him that Hanover belongs to the person of the King, the Colonies to the Crown of the United Kingdom:—if the term *us*, as applied to the obligation to protect, be intended of men who write Reports for Institutions, we deprecate the protection—equally ignorant of general law and Colonial policy must he be, who confounds Hanover with the British Colonies, or it might be with Hampshire—the general defence and preservation of the empire with the protection of the Colonies: That parliament has acted erroneously in confining itself most commonly to commercial regulation, and leaving internal regulation to the Colonial Assemblies: that for commercial regulation, Parliament has exercised legislation, as well within as without the Colonies, and that other laws, not of commercial and maritime regulation, have been made invasive of Colonial rights, and therefore destructive of them: that the admitted right of enacting commercial regulation, is only a branch of, and establishes the general right of legislation in the British Parliament, and that the acquiescence in violations of the Colonial rights, by the enforcement of these, and the erection of official establishments on shore in the Colonies, is a concession by the Colonies of the whole rights claimed :

To these objections, and to the demand that the Colonial Right should be surrendered, or commercial and maritime regulation distinguished from general legislation, and these territorial invasions from others not of similar origin, it is answered; that we have never contended with Great Britain for the empire of the ocean, that we have never contended for any right beyond our respective limits, and that within these limits we confine all assertion or defence of rights.

Other violations indeed there have been of Colonial Rights, violations which neither give nor take away rights, but the establishments incident to commercial regulation when duly limited, neither are, nor are to be considered as violations.

The right of the British Parliament to enact commercial regulations limited in their operation to the ocean, in and over which Great Britain possesses all the rights of empire, not to be questioned certainly by her own subjects, and extended to the shores of all the Colonies, on which necessarily are erected the establishments required for their maintenance and enforcement, has never been denied. But can it be inferred or supposed that we have abandoned and forfeited all the rights of men and of Britons, because we have not complained of encroachments upon our territory, necessarily exceeding those of the ocean, and have not required and insisted, that custom-houses should be erected only below high water-mark? No Colonial right is affected or impaired, by exercise of the admitted right of the British Parliament to commercial regulation extrinsic to Colonial limits, nor by the formation of establishments, fiscal and judicial on the physical lines which bound the jurisdictions of the different Legislatures, and are necessarily drawn upon the Colonial territory.

The British Parliament has itself declared and enacted, that whenever any imposed duties, necessary for commercial regulation, shall be payable in any Colony, the same shall be at the disposal of the Colonial Legislature, and has thus recognized, and in so much admitted and established their exclusive legislative rights, even against itself, as well as the arguments of the Report:

That if local legislation may be admitted as necessary in these cases, the Registry Bill also may be enacted as a necessary regulation to effectuate abolition, and being thus justified by, and as auxiliary to commercial and maritime regulations, may be received among them, and considered as one of them: thus the Registry Bill becomes a law of trade: thus the Acts for registering deeds in Yorkshire and

Middlesex, are laws of trade: Thus all the Acts in the Colonies, for registering deeds are laws of trade, although the objects of all are, as is the principal object of the Registry Bill, to furnish evidence to Courts of Common Law, in matters of title, and of title to freedom, distinct from questions of maritime jurisdiction, and commercial regulation.

Physical lines do not, like mathematical lines, bound two surfaces without being parts of either. On the line of shore therefore, which bounds the sea although part of the land, and of necessity, are the establishments placed, which a maritime jurisdiction requires. But, to extend in argument the breadth of this physical line, to the occupation of all the soil, and of all its rights—because a legislation, commencing for, and on, and operating over the surface of the ocean, reaches its limits—by extending to the shore which bounds it. To contend that legislation may begin within the land, operate over the whole territory, establish itself in the heart of the soil, and extend itself to the utmost limits of its surface, under pretence of being, and by calling itself maritime regulation, is only to be equalled by offering this sophistry to the British Parliament, and calling it reasons, or by any name, that may suppose the power of ratiocination in the person or persons addressing, or the possession of intelligence by the persons addressed.

That the Act, the 6 Geo. III. c. 12, has settled the question: That by the 18 Geo. III. c. 12, Parliament only partially receded from this general assertion of legislative authority, in the case of taxation, for the sake of conciliation, which not even the renunciation of the general claim would have produced—as if this failure of effect might enure to defeat the law itself.

This failure of effect cannot indeed be exhibited to abrogate the law itself. It is however carefully coupled with observations on the limited nature of the concession, in order to resist the inference, that whatever of pretension, or of right was advanced to support the claim, was of course abandoned with the claim. The strength of the inference is thus demonstrated by the preparations made to oppose it. The practical inference and general expectation was, that the claim of legislation was abandoned with the claim of taxation.

I cannot but admire the dexterity with which the question of taxation, as applied to the Registry Bill, is artfully evaded. The Act, the 18 Geo. III. c. 12, by which the claim to taxation was abandoned, is introduced, merely to " remove an objection, resting upon a mistake," respecting its operation as a renunciation of the general claim of legislation, and is stated to have been passed, "partially to *qualify* this assertion of legislative authority." The Act therefore, "enacts *or promises*," (were such words ever exhibited in, or applied to the enacting clause of any British Statute?) that Parliament will not impose any tax, duty or assessment whatever, payable in any Colony. The question of its extent of operation in repealing the Act of the 6 Geo. III. c. 12, will not here be revived. The Act unquestionably abandons the right of taxation. The Registry Bill imposes a tax payable in the Colonies. Does this "objection rest upon a mistake respecting its operation?"—Why is this not shown?—Why is the question carefully avoided?—It cannot, however, with all this subtilty, be evaded.

By the 18 Geo. III. c. 12, it is enacted, that the King and Parliament of Great Britain will never impose *any* duty, tax, or assessment whatever, payable in any of his Majesty's Colonies in America or the West Indies, except duties for the regulation of commerce, the nett produce of which shall be at the disposal of the respective General Assemblies. August 7th, 1815, a poll-tax of two dollars on each slave, amounting on 30,000 persons to 60,000 dollars, was imposed in his Majesty's name, by Order in Council, on the British subjects of Trinidad, held in a state of conquest, without any General Assembly.—I offer this fact to the consideration of Parliament, and to British feelings.

The Bill indeed imposes a tax payable in the Colonies, a tax operating as, and being indeed a Poll-Tax, and of an excessive amount. We have already stated it to triple, at least, the amount of the existing Poll-Tax in Barbados, which is 1*s*. 6*d*. sterling for each person. This for 70,000 persons, would amount annually to 10,750*l*. sterling, at 40 per cent. upwards of 14,000*l*. currency, per annum.

The only defence that has been offered of the Bill, against this objection, is a suggested distinction between a tax imposed for the purposes of the Colony itself, and one raised for the benefit of another country. Against this distinction, I rely on the words of the preamble, which speaks of the justice of raising taxes under the authority of the general assembly of the Colony, and of the Act, declaring that Parliament will not " impose any tax, duty, or assessment whatever, payable in any Colony."

Will it be said, that it is not a tax because imposed in the form of fees,—because applied to pay officers for services performed,—because collected by the officer who is to receive,—because the collection and application are cotemporaneous,—because the ways and means, and the expenditure, meet at the same moment, in the same person and place? The general and principal objects of taxation, are the payments of officers, persons in office from the highest to the lowest, from the first lord of the treasury to the clerk. Will a tax upon land, or upon malt, cease to be a tax by its mode of application, or is the tax diminished, because a part is applied to the expenses of collecting, and paid to, or retained by the officers collecting? Parliament cannot impose any tax, duty or assessment,—the Registry Bill imposes what is equally a tax, a duty, and an assessment of a given sum on and for every Slave returned and registered, combined with other charges which swell this distinct charge, to an enormous tax *per capita*, to an oppressive and additional Poll-Tax.

The 23 Geo. III. c. 28, establishes for all the dominions of the Crown of Great Britain, the existence of a general paramount indefeasible right, and directly repealing the 6 Geo. I. c. 5, for Ireland, which was in the nature of a Colony, and by direct consequence, the 6 Geo. III. c. 12, for the Colonies has thus abrogated this last law also, and extinguished the general claim to legislation, advanced in it:

That the King has no authority to make laws for Colonies, in which *representative assemblies exist*, and therefore Parliament must do the work itself, or leave it to the Colonial assemblies. That neither Parliament nor the King has the right, has been shewn, nor will the suggested alternative give the right to Parliament, "although the work, if left to the Colonial Assemblies, certainly will not be done," *as it is proposed to be done.* It is not necessarily in the Parliament, although not legally in the King. Not being in the King, but legally and actually in the Colonial Assemblies, it is not either legally or necessarily in the British Parliament.

Any question respecting the supremacy or sovereignty of the British parliament can only be answered by referring to or repeating the preceding statements. Supreme or sovereign executive—supreme or sovereign legislative are terms of abstract and metaphysical jurisprudence, never to be confounded with British law. By not adverting to this distinction and division of powers, received indeed by himself, Blackstone states generally, that sovereignty and legislature are convertible terms, not qualifying the term sovereignty, and thus excluding the executive—and the Report, rushing on beyond him to its own objects, from powers to persons, making the lawgiver the sovereign, arrives at that absurd extreme case which in every system of reasoning establishes the absurdity of the intermediate, and would establish the Parliament of the United Kingdom, the sovereign of the United Kingdom, whilst the maker of the Berlin decree is contemplated, and foreign despotism confounded with British legislation. As a British lawyer, I know only King and Parliament, and I know their powers.

Those of parliament are, as hereinbefore stated, exhibited, and established from history, by principle, and by precedent. To the metaphysical jurist I leave to satisfy himself, by finding out among these any powers he may choose to include under those or any of his terms. For information I refer the British lawyer to former statements. The dependence, connection, uniformity of institutions in the Colonies, are preserved by the controul and exercise of the prerogative of the Crown. Their commercial regulations and external relations are settled and arranged, those by the parliament, these by the King, the sole sovereign of all.

I know nothing of that *absolute despotic* power which *must* be vested somewhere, and therefore is in parliament. The *necessary* existence of such a power in terms I do not see—I do not see that it is in parliament—I see in parliament certain general superintending powers, *not despotic*—these may be defined, and stated, and enumerated, and this is all I know. I admit the whole enumeration of parliamentary powers, detailed in Blackstone, vol. i. p. 160; and from the whole paragraph I would only strike out the words, stating parliament to be " the " *place* where *absolute despotic* power resides," as neither necessary to the sense nor agreeable to British law. How exists this absolute power against the *fundamental* and *essential* conditions of the union with Scotland and with Ireland? How against antient paramount rights to which parliament itself owes its existence and powers?—Against those rights, declared by and existing independently of its own acts *ascertaining* not creating them? I admit not the right, and therefore I contemplate not the existence of a power in parliament, the exercise of which would dissolve the whole frame of the constitution, and therein its own rightful existence.

If parliament, indeed, possesses the power of taking away original declared rights, by repealing the Acts, declaratory of these, taking the 18 Geo. III. c. 12, for an example, should we be more safe under its own words, "*declares and enacts,*" or those supplied for it by the Report, "*enacts or promises,*"—and of which is the immorality greater, the violation of a right or of a promise? Such a violation of all principle, even the Report itself has not yet arrived at.

Thus is the claim of the British Parliament to internal Colonial legislation disposed of,—thus is the right of the Colonial Assemblies to exclusive internal legislation within their separate jurisdictions, established in itself, and confirmed against all objections.

In the Newtonian philosophy, we query the truths we would consider as established. In imitation of that great master, I will give to the principal propositions, which embrace the disputed points of Imperial and Colonial parliamentary jurisdiction, the form of queries. It is more respectful, and it may be more grateful, that they should rather remain as questions, referred even to that honorable body itself, which every British subject respects and regards, and which he the more regards, the better he understands the nature of its existence, and the exercise of its powers, as dependent upon British principles, and British practices, unmixed with all others.

Does not the British Parliament owe its existence and its powers to those original rights, and rights of representation, which are vested in, and inseparable from persons and freeholds?

Is not the British Parliament restricted and limited in legislation by this right of representation, to the persons and places whom it thus represents?

Can the British Parliament extend itself and its powers, or can they be extended to other persons and places, but by extended representation?

Conformably to these principles, has not the practice been, to extend parliamentary legislation and powers, by extended representation and union, and where this has been unadvisable, or inconvenient, has not separate legislation been established?

Is not the security of liberty and property, the great object and purpose of these legislative establishments, whether united or separate?

What security for, what liberty or property has he, who holds them at the arbitrament and disposal of others, over whom he has no controul? and does not this necessarily constitute each, exclusive of the others?

Is not the separate legislation, thus duly established, necessarily exclusive of that legislation to which it has not been united, by all the principles which have established both, of creation, of representation, of necessity forbidding or delaying union? Of many separate Legislatures thus duly established, and dependent each for its existence and powers, upon the distinct representations of different persons and places, communities, and countries, can any one, or more, possess the right of interfering with any one, or more of the others, of controuling their powers, or of exercising its own, or any powers within their districts and jurisdictions?

Are not all legal opinions, depending as they do, for their acceptance, only upon their reasonableness and conformity to right; are not all judicial decisions admitted to be obligatory, because considered to be declaratory of existing law; are not all legislative enactments, invasive of these rights, unjustifiable in themselves, and for ever subject to be rejected, reversed and repealed?

Is not an Act or Statute of the British Parliament, of sufficient authority and power, to controul, reverse and repeal, by its enactments, all legal opinions, judicial decisions, and preceding British Statutes, repugnant to its own subsequent enactments, and is it not in itself, by principle and analogy, extendible, and to be extended to all cases and circumstances, similar to those for which it has once provided and settled, by its declarations and enactments?

Are not all British subjects who conquer or settle a Colony bound by the same allegiance as all other British subjects, and do they not carry with them and enjoy all their liberties and rights to be modified and adapted to their situations as Colonists, and particularly, so long as their Knights are not called to sit in Parliament, to a distinct Civil Government, by a General Assembly, composed of his Majesty by representation, a council appointed by his Majesty, and the representatives of the people freely elected, which General Assembly alone, of right, can, or ought to do all such acts and matters of legislation for the internal government of the Colony as the Imperial Parliament can do for that of the United Kingdom of Great Britain and Ireland?

By the cases and precedents of Jamaica, Barbados, Grenada, and by the words of his Majesty's royal proclamation declaring the same in the case of Grenada, is it not settled and established as the constitutional law and practice, that every settled and conquered and ceded Colony, as soon as its condition and circumstances will admit thereof, is entitled to British laws, to the British Constitution, and to the British form of government by a Legislative Body, composed of the Governor, or King's Representative, a Council duly appointed by the King, and an Assembly freely elected by the freeholders and inhabitants of the Colony, and that it is among the duties of the Crown, judging of condition and circumstances, in the exercise of a sound discretion, aided by responsible advisers and in its paternal care for the security of the liberties and properties of the Colonists to constitute this form of government within the Colony?

In the principles of creation and existence of the separate Legislatures of Great Britain, Ireland, Jamaica, Barbados, Grenada, each constituted declaredly for the same general purpose of securing liberties and properties, and each duly and separately convened conformably to their several rights, and by the same Sovereign, acting by himself or by delegation, by virtue of his royal prerogative, and in execution of his royal duties, is there any thing to give to either of these Legislatures the right of legislating for any other, of interfering with any other, of excluding any other from its proper legislation, and which might not, if by any, by every one be claimed?

Where from omission on the part of the Crown to form a duly constituted Representative Legislature, where from lapse of time, varying circumstances, or the expediency of making changes not clearly within the limits of the royal prerogative, it has been judged necessary by the King himself not to act but with the assistance and concurrence of Parliament, in forming and establishing such a Legislature or Legislatures, can the right thus exercised by the King and the two British Houses of Parliament, jointly, but which, if it remains, is in the King alone, or the right claimed for all jointly, being a question partly between the King and the British Parliament, and partly between the Imperial and the Colonial Parliament, of forming, forming anew, and new modelling the whole of the Constitutions of the Colonies, give to the Imperial the right of internal Colonial legislation? The formation of a Legislature, and the exercise of legislation are for ever distinct and not to be confounded. The King forms in the first instance a Colonial Legislature. That gives him no right of legislation, but in fact, excludes him and all others from all further and future right of formation and legislation. If the Parliament, of which the King is a part, forms a Colonial Legislature, is not the Parliament for ever excluded, as in that Colony, from the power of formation and legislation, having created a Representative Body competent to both works?

If to avoid the political solecism of *imperium in imperio*, and the co-existence of two Legislatures of equal powers within the same limits of jurisdiction, one must necessarily exclude the other, which shall exclude, or be excluded, that which *de facto* and *de jure* possesses and exercises the powers of internal legislation, and by possessing and exercising excludes all others, or that which claims to possess, and to exercise, and to exclude?

The admitted right of commercial regulation extends the right of Imperial Parliamentary jurisdiction to the shores of every Colony as its limits. Can the erection of custom-houses and of Vice-Admiralty Courts, necessary to commercial regulation, upon the lines not mathematical but physical, which bound the rights of internal Colonial legislation and external imperial commercial regulation, and which are necessarily drawn upon the Colonial territory not within high-water mark, be considered as invasions on one side and acquiescences on the other, of sufficient force to abrogate the Colonial right of exclusive internal legislation?

Can any invasion of right in itself impart right? Can any invasions of rights, however numerous, because not continually or captiously resisted, destroy, or establish rights in others, and do they not rather maintain between the parties, under a sense of hostile aggression, a perpetual right of vindication and recaption?

Was not the attempt of the British Parliament to raise a revenue in the Colonies by taxation an invasion of their right of property, one of those great rights, or branches of right, for the security of which, Representative Assemblies were formed? Was it not so admitted to be, and as such, afterwards, and for ever abandoned by the British Parliament itself, by the Act of Parliament, the 18th of George III. c. 12, repealing insomuch the preceding Act of the 6th George III. c. 12, claiming a right in the British Parliament to make laws to bind the Colonies in all cases whatsoever? Was not this which even gave to the Colonial Assemblies the right of applying any duties eventually raised within their jurisdiction by exercise of the admitted right of commercial regulation, and as necessary thereto, an admission of the right of exclusion, and of exclusive internal legislation of the Colonial Assemblies in all matters of property? and was not this abandonment of the claim to taxation, an abandonment of the claim to legislation advanced to support it?

Ireland was conquered and planted by the British Crown—so was Jamaica. Ireland and Jamaica had each its separate Parliament. The Parliament of Ireland was persuaded to pass Poynings's law, which reduced its legislative powers to a shadow. An attempt was made to prevail upon Jamaica to adopt Poynings's law, but it was resisted and failed. The Act of 6 Geo. I. c. 5, for Ireland, and the 6 Geo. III. c. 12, for Jamaica, as a Colony, asserted a power in the British Parliament to make laws to bind both in all cases whatsoever. The Act the 23 Geo. III. c. 28, declares and enacts, that the King of Great Britain with the Parliament of Ireland alone have power to make laws to bind Ireland in all cases. Can any but his Majesty, with the Legislature of Jamaica, have power in any case to make laws to bind Jamaica? Is not every preceding enactment repugnant hereto repealed by the enacting part? Does not every succeeding enactment stand controuled by the declared paramount principle which it would violate?

Is not the 23d Geo. III. c. 28, a declaratory Act, and does it not, as such, establish an old, not create a new right, a general existing right, existing and applicable to whatever exists, and applicable to, and including Jamaica, and every other Colony of Great

Britain, possessing a duly constituted Representative Legislature?

Does not this law not only declaring, but enacting, controul, reverse, and repeal all opinions, decisions and laws contrary thereto, and together with 18th Geo. III. c. 12, establish for all the Colonies perfect security of liberties and properties, by settling in his Majesty alone, together with the general Assembly of each Colony, the right of making laws to bind each Colony in all cases whatsoever? And can these *declared and ascertained* rights for Ireland and for the Colonies be destroyed or extinguished by the repeal of those laws, or by any enactments whatsoever, without the violation of all right, of all faith, of all honour?

Is not the exclusive legislation thus established in the Colonial Assemblies by principle and analogy as a right, justified and maintained as a measure of propriety, expediency, and moral necessity? The representative right entitles to union, or to separate, and if to separate, to exclusive legislation. If separate legislation rather than union is indicated for the Colonies by state and condition, by distance, various climate, differing agriculture, mixed population, and if union would seem to be forbidden, which would constitute a general Parliament, only partially fitted to legislate for Colonial affairs in proportion to the accession and number of Colonial

Representatives, does not this which forbids union, deny legislation to a Parliament totally unqualified in practice and in principle to legislate for the Colonies in the absence of all Colonial representation? Thus all right, all propriety, all expediency, moral and natural necessity, render it unsafe and unwise, and impossible for the British Parliament to legislate for these distant dependencies.

Contending for these established and unquestionable rights, and using all the legal and constitutional means of resistance they possess, can the Colonies be legislated for without being conquered? If Parliament will proceed thus to legislate for us we are conquered—We submit to be conquered, and Orders in Council may then go out to the Colonies with, or as now, without the formality of parliamentary acquiescence. Then it is that those who now assert will deprecate in the British Parliament a power which can never constitutionally nor conveniently be exercised, and will see to whom they will have delivered over the British Colonists: To office, which sees only with the eyes of others, and in Colonial affairs has never in the Colonies or in Great Britain used the best—to the inferior agents of institutions and joint stock companies—to the men who write reports for the African Institution—and to July jobbers of Acts of Parliament.

On the proposed Means of Emancipation.

The population of the British Colonies consists of three classes of persons.

1. White persons:

2. Free persons of various intermediate colours between those of negroes and of white persons, inclusive of the former and exclusive of the latter: and

3. Slaves, consisting almost entirely of negroes, with a few individuals of mixed origin.

Of these last we shall first speak.

In proceeding to speak of the institutions of slavery, if I should speak of benefits incidentally arising from the condition, let it not be supposed that my intention is to defend or to recommend it.—From my heart I abhor and detest all slavery, as pernicious and not to be endured. I hesitate not to declare that the system ought to be abolished, whenever this may be effected by means less pernicious in their principles and consequences than the system itself: and in secret, as I proceed, I breathe the humble and sincere prayer that this defence of ourselves, and assertion of our own rights, may not be, or be converted to the injury of others, more particularly, of these, our unfortunate slaves and fellow-creatures—and that what is best for all may be dispensed to all.

What the condition of slavery really and practically is, may best be estimated and known by comparison with servitude, that state of freemen to which it is most nearly assimilated.

The grand distinctions which exist between slavery and service respect both the masters and the labourers. In service, the compensation follows the labour, and dissatisfaction on either side terminates the contract.

In the indissoluble contract of slavery, the means of supporting life in health, strength, and comfort, the considerations for which service labours, being of necessity, duly secured, and regularly received, to withhold the labour thus purchased and paid for, constitutes a crime incapable of compensation in the circumstances under which it originates, and requiring to be prevented by punishment, which may restrain the commission. That which in service as a breach of contract may be repaired or provided against by exclusion from employment, is thus in slavery exalted into an offence of an higher, of a criminal nature, and can only be remedied by coercion. Thus to slavery the infliction of corporal punishment is inseparably incident, and the necessity of constant supervision, in order to diminish its necessity and frequency—a supervision general as well as constant, notwithstanding the varieties of character incident to all societies, and, which even in slavery, distinguish the good and the industrious from the profligate and the indolent. That the power thus possessed will never be abused by wantonness or excess is not to be expected from human nature. It is this abuse which is the sting of slavery as it respects the slave, the necessity, coupled with the use, however proper, is the sting of slavery as it respects the master, to whose regrets and injury indeed the abuse also is superadded. From neither the use as a system, nor the abuse can he deliver himself; the good slave may suffer incidentally from the abuse of power—the master, even when the power is duly used, against the bad.

Without thus commanding the labour, that power which is to move all, it is impossible to commence, conduct or continue the system dependent upon it, and it is weak to suppose, that in such a state of society, such a mixed population, in such countries and such climates, that to classes of persons can be applied that power of enforcement, that necessity which applied to free individuals in other societies produces, but not always unfailingly and unsparingly, the exertions of power, and the labours that are repaid simply by what is adequate to the sustentation of life, whilst in those other societies, individual capitalists by possessing the natural means, or artificial instruments, lands, houses, machineries, establishments, stock, acquire great profits, duly operating by their reaction and accumulation for the benefit of all.

If it be inquired what are the rights of persons subjected to the condition of slavery, and how may the persons be secured in them, the first part of the question may be answered by referring, comparing and assimilating the condition of the slave, whilst the slavery endures, as nearly as may be to that servitude which endures for ever among freemen, and in and under which nine-tenths of mankind for ever labour—by securing to him those unalienable and indefeasible rights to which labour entitles all her children, and compensating him for the loss of those rights which disappear before the power of enforcement, unavoidably substituted for that necessity which is the main-spring of free powers, by provision secured for him in infancy, infirmity and age, such as improvident freedom seldom lays up in store for itself, but which is due before Heaven and before man from every society to the labour, whether free or enforced, by which it ultimately subsists.

Nor is this declaration of rights made as of rights denied. They are understood, admitted, acted upon—only in particular cases, blazoned indeed as

of all, are they disregarded or violated, as are all human institutions.—Systematically and generally respected, they are only violated by the individually bad, who are of every age, of every station, and of every society.

When a distressed or wicked master respects not these rights or abuses this power, behold one of those cases inseparably incident to slavery, which constitute its principal ills, and make it what it is, which make the state of the slave to depend upon the temper and condition of the master. These cases are not indeed frequent; they are, in fact, exceptions to the general state and condition, which they by no means represent. They receive that notoriety which distinguishes them, from a malignant spirit which passing from all that is good and amiable, more rejoiceth over one such instance of depravity, than over thousands of just persons who perform their duties conscientiously. When by a good master a full provision is made for, and received by a slave, of food, raiment, and domestic comforts, under a due conservation of domestic rights; and to the possession and enjoyment of these is added a sense of security and an assurance in the provision made for him in health, sickness, and old age, by his master, as his *savings-bank*, as his *benefit or friendly society box*, without any of the cares and self-denials, and perplexing forethought of ordinary and common life, it cannot be denied that the supply of the slave, not the condition, as some think, is better than that of the freeman. I cannot indeed admit, as other good and feeling men contend, that a state of slavery can under any circumstances be preferred to, or compared with, a state of freedom. In this particular my own opinion is founded upon high and exalted considerations of liberty—that of others upon what they may consider as a better formed estimate of benefits and evils, and of all things incident to human life, such as it is, and is of the great body of the human race. That the state of slavery in the West-Indies is generally what interested advocates report, or prejudiced hearers believe, I deny.

Such are the rights of slavery, to which in general all rights have been denied. The wrongs of slavery are of two classes—those of the master and those of others.

Against the wrongs of others, against all other wrongs, the master is to the slave the sure defence and certain means of redress.

In the Colonies, the remedies for injuries done to slaves are by right of action in the master. It is for the benefit of the slave, that it should be so, rather than that he should be abandoned or compelled to seek redress for himself. Under the protection of his master who considers every wrong done to his slave, not only as an injury done, but as a personal violation offered to himself, the vindication of which interest, honour, and I hope I may be allowed to add feeling, urge him to demand, the slave is more secure than the whole class of free persons, black, coloured, or poor whites, who are left to their own remedies.

Possessed of these indefeasible rights, and thus practically and effectually secured against one whole class of wrongs, how is the slave to be protected against those which are of the master and his agents, against the abuse of powers which that title confers, and in the enjoyment of those compensatory rights which his condition claims?

Every thing has been done for these purposes that can be done. To the obligations of moral duty the sanctions of legal enforcement have been added.

In several of the Colonies, the murder of a slave had formerly been punished by fine on the master, or by fine on a stranger, superadded to the compensation due to the master. In all, for several years past, by the repeal of former laws, the punishment of death is inflicted on the murderer. Yet this additional security for life, operating both by terror and by infliction, is not admitted into the negative catalogue which charges that nothing has been done to meliorate the condition of the slaves in the Colonies.

When for these purposes principally, when in compliance with the wishes of good men, and to silence the clamorous expostulations of agitators, Jamaica undertook to revise and consolidate her Slave Laws, and by enactments of positive law to assign limits to the formerly undefined exercise of discretionary powers and punishment, and to regulate and secure to the labourer those compensatory supplies of food, clothing, and other comforts to which he is entitled;—when having done every thing that by law could be effected by enactments in their nature alike monitory and prohibitory;—when the difficulties arising to the execution of these laws, which result from the state and condition of slavery, and which they and all Colonists knew and felt, and which alone have delayed in many the adoption of similar measures, though not required by any defects in their own existing domestic regulations; when these difficulties came to be observed in the execution of these laws, these same agitators, who called for them, now object to the Colonists the enactment of these very laws, which they now call mock laws, and speak of as being laughed at and forgotten. These statements are however unfounded. These laws would not be unavailing and useless were they only rules of conduct, prescribed and recommended by none but their innate authority to the consideration and observance of all. They would teach to the unfeeling and the penurious the limits, inclusive and exclusive, of his powers and his duties. But when they assume the force of legal enactments, and when the performance of duties to which justice as well as interest prompts, is required under legal sanctions, they must and they do avail, and they are effectual to a considerable, if not to the whole extent contemplated.

By this exposition, therefore, the statement, that nothing has been done, nothing of any effect, is disproved. All has been done to protect the slave against the wrongs, arising from his very condition as a slave. Unfortunately no laws in the Colonies or in the world can protect against the irregular sallies of violence and injustice, and all the bad passions of men.—Against the wrongs of others, his very condition, as before shewn, is his best and complete defence. —The incompetency of his testimony in particular cases, (for the rejection thereof in all cases is an incorrect statement,) is founded upon those principles which in every legal system establish an incompetency of witnesses, dependent upon station and condition. The incompetency of one witness in no system operates to exclude all other testimony and evidence, and these have never been wanting to vindicate the master's rights and the injuries done to his slave.

———————

There exists in every Colony a class of free persons more or less numerous, intermediate in colour and condition between the whites and the negro slaves. To manumissions from various motives, and to natural increase, they owe their origin and numbers. Scarcely separated in the beginning from slaves, they continue in their habits and lives, and manners, scarcely distinguished from them. However considerable the political rights obtained—however exalted their political state, they are not in their social state much advanced in the consideration of the whites, nor in their own, above the better classes of slaves. They are so retained by their own sense of its propriety, and from the political prudence and necessity of preserving unimpaired those distinctions of colour and of class upon the observance and continuance of which primarily depend the peace and safety of all. Raised ever so high above the slaves, they may not, from moral and social considerations, from political and prudential reasons, be mixed and confounded with the whites.—The feelings of the whites, their own, the feelings of the slaves forbid it, the interests of all forbid it. From them, as in England from persons of different condition, as from the domestic servant or respected tradesman, the observance of certain forms indicative of distinction, respect, and civility, is expected, and never fails.

But their legal and political rights are the same with those of the domestic and tradesman, except in one or two points in one or two of the Colonies. What are they in Barbados? His testimony is subjected to the same limits of competency with that of the slaves, from among whom he was taken. He cannot elect or be elected a member of assembly or vestry. He cannot serve as a juror on the trial of real actions. These are all. Of only one of these restrictions has he any reason to complain, of the narrow limits to which his competency, as a witness, is restrained. Of the other two, one is for his benefit, the exemption from service as a juror; of both the propriety is obvious. Of the population of Great Britain do nine-tenths possess the elective franchise, and are they not excluded by positive law in defect of qualification?

Of a slave, the testimony, narrowed by the established legal limits of testimony, is further narrowed by his condition, in questions between free white persons. If one of the parties be his master, of course he cannot be admitted. And how in any doubtful case is the testimony to be accepted of one over whom any person has the power of a master, although that person be not as a legal party legally interested?

In all questions therefore between white parties, the production of a slave, as a witness, is never contemplated, is by law forbidden, and can it be said, without reason? In all questions however among slaves, or confined to slaves, and here generally, a slave's interests are at issue, the contest of master in slave, or slave in master, against similar parties, is reduced to an equality of motives and interests, that admit slaves as witnesses on all sides.

Against free persons of colour also the testimony of a slave is by law expressly received.

The competency therefore of a slave has necessarily been reduced to narrower limits, and confined to cases arising between the coloured population alone. By and to this standard the competency of all coloured persons also was reduced, as persons not more worthy of general credit than slaves, from whom they were not easily distinguishable. Unfortunately this limitation in cases of freemen of colour in which the King is the party, confines the proof to other evidence, and testimony not of the party aggrieved, if a freeman of colour. This may occasionally be a grievance. But as general justice never excludes from its consideration evidence of which it may avail itself, and to which the disqualifications of slavery do not apply, a better consideration which respects general as well as individual interests, is proceeding to remove this single invidious exception, which exists, I believe, in only one other Colony.

With the single exception, therefore, in one or two of the Colonies of the elective franchise, which Great Britain denies to more than one half of her freemen, and a tenth never use, and with a beneficial exemption from a particular public service, the legal condition of the coloured freemen may be stated to be in all respects the same as of the white Colonists. In most of the Colonies it differs not at all. The only differences which exist, and are mistaken for legal disabilities, are in the moral and social distinctions of persons, such as manners and habits establish, and which in all societies differ with conditions.

These statements are made for the purpose of informing the British public, and others, who not accurately distinguishing between the moral and legal condition of the freemen of colour, have erroneously inferred a diminution of legal rights, from a difference in social distinctions.

They are made to shew at once how desperate are all expectations of succeeding in the *projet* of the West India agitators, who, by extending and increasing this class, and by proceeding through them in imitation of WHITE villeinage, according to their *sliding* system, would establish a general emancipation of the slaves.

They are made as applicable to, and bearing upon the case of Trinidad, connected as it is with the Registry Bill, and to the measures adopted by these men, the advocates of freedom, to deceive his Majesty's ministers, and to keep that unfortunate Colony and its population of free persons of all colours and descriptions under subjection to Spanish despotism and the right of conquest regulations, imposed as Orders in Council.

Such was the state of the free coloured people in the British Colonies, possessed, with very few exceptions, of all the rights of Britons, and not more affected, being already free, than the whites themselves, by the laws intended to prevent addition to their numbers, when the Colony of Trinidad was finally ceded to the British Crown, and became a British Colony.

Since that time the population of the Colony has experienced, as was to be expected, considerable changes, and the number of free British born subjects has increased to several thousands, so as now fully to equal and exceed that of all the other combined Spanish and French inhabitants. Since that time several applications have been made by the inhabitants of the Colony, and their friends in Great Britain for a British constitution and laws. Mr. Wyndham, when in office, proposed, and was proceeding to accomplish, this desirable work, as a thing of course. The conduct and the declarations written and oral of Lord Buckinghamshire, were favourable to the measure as soon as circumstances would permit.

In 1810, the freeholders of Trinidad petitioned for a change of political system. All that it was necessary or proper for his Majesty's government to do, to give to Trinidad a British constitution and laws, was, by proclamations and letters patent similar to those of Grenada, to establish the same. These would have included all free persons without distinction in its provisions. To all it would in the first instance have imparted the same equal rights and privileges, and if at any future time any attempts had been made by the constituted Legislature derogatory to these rights, they could only have been effected by the Royal assent, and this might have been petitioned against by the persons or interests affected. All that the free coloured people had to do was to wait in patience the result of this application. Every friend of these persons would so have advised them. Agitators however in the Colony, equally the enemies of the whites and coloured freemen, anxious only to defeat an application, which, if successful, would put an end to all their schemes for annoying the British Colonists, disturbing the Colony, and making experiments upon its varied population, prevailed upon a considerable number of these ill-advised persons to adopt a sort of counter-petition, most injurious to their own best rights and interests, under an agency of persons from their own body, into which some of the worst characters of the Colony contrived to introduce themselves. They came forward asking in terms for " *something*" without specifying what, without knowing, when questioned, what they should ask; and finally, by specifications, which, as before stated, might have induced them to refrain from asking any thing. In the mean time the conduct and developement of character of some of their leading men, produced a feeling by which all their true friends were grieved. Unfortunate men! you came forward to resist an application, which, under the due superintending care of the British government, would have given you, and the whites without distinction, all the rights and privileges of British subjects, and by the same superintending care, you would have been protected and preserved in them. This would have been the conservation and consummation of more than all those enumerated rights of capitulation which were claimed by, or for you, even after final cession, beyond which capitulation extends not; and you would have had them by the better claim and title of British subjects. Your own application has been considered among the principal reasons for refusing to all a British constitution and laws, which now, or hereafter, can only be regularly established, as it then might have been, by imparting equal rights undistinguishably to all, by a due course of Royal proceeding, similar to that practised in the case of Grenada, or if now rendered necessary by lapse of time and change of circumstances, of Parliamentary proceeding, pursuing a similar course.

Such is the state and condition, such are the rights of coloured free persons in all, except the conquered Colonies.

The only question that can remain, and this has been raised by others, respects the increase of their numbers as a measure of wisdom, policy and safety.—

Undoubtedly " for the encouragement of good conduct among those who are slaves," justice and policy would advise " to make enfranchisement the prize of great individual merit." The rule is admitted, and the strict application of the rule, which circumstances hereafter narrated might perhaps justify, would confine it to the individual, a measure more harsh than any of these which are complained of.

The first objection that offered itself to the eye of political prudence in the Colonies, was the creation of an inferior class of persons, who, necessarily mixing with, might vitiate the black population by their habits of indolence, and by the vices that flow therefrom—of receivers and retailers of what was received.

The second objection that occurred, was; that the existence of such a class, if honestly employed, occupied the places and employments of artificers and handicraft workmen, to the exclusion and injury of the inferior classes of white men, who would thus be left destitute of the means of supporting life.

None of these coloured freemen ever became agriculturists or labourers, a circumstance worthy of observation.

With these radical objections to the extension of this class, we solaced ourselves under their unrestrained increase by these same considerations which are now presented to us by others. And it could be wished that this were the last occasion in which the unfortunate Colonist is reasoned for by others, who, strangers to every thing that belongs to himself or condition, would deny to him the possession, whilst by their gratuitous recommendation, they suggest the absence of all reasoning powers within himself, for himself, or the things which are his.

We looked upon this intermediate population as tending to establish the security of the whites, as men, who, in every question or conflict that might arise from the slave population, would unquestionably be on the part of the whites. This expectation has been disappointed. The experiment has been made and has failed. Danger has been found to exist in a free coloured population, danger commensurate to its extent, and, therefore, it is that in many of the Colonies, "laws to restrain manumissions have originated within a very few years." These acts are spoken of by the report in terms which are justified by no evidence.

The case and the laws of Grenada are referred to as constituting a cruel mockery, "enhancing the pain of the oppression." The Legislature of Grenada in 1797 required a deposit of £100 on manumissions, and granted an annuity of £10 for life to the person manumitted. In 1806 they retained the deposit without making any annual allowance. This conduct of the Legislature is accounted for by the Chief Justice, who has published the laws of Grenada, stating that the provision had been abused, and improper advantages taken of it. The report states the law, but omits the justificatory exposition of the Chief Justice which accompanies. The establishment of manumission-deposits and annuities dependent thereon is of antient practice on good principles in all the Colonies, and their subsequent increase of amount is to be attributed to, and may be defended in all, by the following history of events which occurred in Grenada.

In the beginning of March, 1795, a rebellion broke out among the free coloured people of Grenada. They seized in the first moments of the insurrection 45 principal proprietors and inhabitants, and carried them off prisoners to their camp, where, for several weeks they endured all the indignities, privations, and miseries to which such a condition exposed them, personally knowing, and being personally known to, their rebellious captors. Removed at length to Mount Quaqua, the highest station of Fedon, the Mulatto rebel general's camp, and confined all within a wooden tenement, on the night of the 7th of April one of these unfortunate gentlemen awakened the rest by informing them that he had heard one of the centinels tell another that an order had been issued for putting all the prisoners to death. Another gentleman stated that he had heard the words, and that they did not bear any such import. When the next morning the guard entered to turn them out severally for slaughter, the former gentleman could not refrain from exulting even in the moment of death, in the correctness of his information, exclaiming—Gentlemen, you find I was accurate. A line of coloured rebels was drawn up at a short distance from the wooden house, and fronted towards it. A party entered and turned out these unfortunate individuals singly to the death which each received, as he was made to turn off in walking to the right, from one of the Mulattos in line stepping forward, putting his musket close to his back, and discharging the ball through his body. Among the prisoners were a surgeon, Mr. Hay, and the Rev. Mr. M'Mahon, the rector of St. Patrick's parish, the residence of Fedon. Mr. Hay was preserved by order, because his assistance was necessary to the rebels. One of the rebels sent in undertook to save the life of the clergyman, and leading him out attempted to pass him through the line. One of those in line stepped back, and with the butt-end of his firelock struck at the priest in order to drive him back. The attention of Fedon, who sat down at a small distance, viewing and superintending the massacre, was attracted by these circumstances, and the observation of Mr. Hay, who separated and saved from among the rest was seated by him, and he called out, waving with his hand, Spare that man. Thus saved, the rector was supported, for his half-covered feet were wounded and torn by preceding marches, and led to, and seated, for he could not stand, where Fedon was sitting, and thence he beheld the slaughter of his remaining fellow-prisoners. The Lieutenant-Governor the Honourable Ninian Home fell. Archibald Campbell, the illustrious patriot of Grenada, a name for ever dear to every British Colonist, as the bold assertor of their rights, came forth, and opening his bosom to the rebels, called upon them to give fire, received it, and fell. Of other individuals, as the ball passed through the body, the hand was applied to the wound at which it passed out through the breast, and the unhappy individual raising, and looking at his bloody hand, sunk and expired. Thus many perished. Many, as the shot was received, sprang up convulsed, and fell dead. To the heads of those who did not immediately expire, muskets were applied, and effectually discharged. The shrieks and outcries were terrible of a British lad who would not come out, and was murdered within the lodge. Three persons only survived this bloody scene. The names of the 42 sufferers are recorded on a public monument erected to their memory in the Colony.

I leave to this narration the justification of Grenada. Other Colonies did not shut their eyes to what was passing in Grenada. They saw the failure of the only principle upon which the gradual increase of the intermediate class had been acquiesced in. They did not however resort to actual prohibitions, nor to the harsh measure of confining the reward of personal merit to the person—they opposed difficulties to enfranchisement, from whose operations they expected effects that would diminish and restrain their numbers within the limits of peaceful safety. The increase of manumission-deposits is thus accounted for. If under the exasperation of the moment, at a time and under circumstances not favourable to correct calculation, some may have exceeded, the excess is also to be referred to the same causes. The other causes stated by the Colonial Legislatures justify the demand and retention of an adequate deposit, not extending in effect beyond the objects of purview.

These men were in possession of all the rights of Britons. They possessed them by the establishment of a British Constitution and Laws. Of none could they after the settlement of the Government have been deprived, except by laws to which the King and assented. Yet this availed not. The same also would have been the case with the free coloured inhabitants of Trinidad. Any charter of settlement, any capitulation upon surrender derogatory of these British rights is in itself void. Settlements are of Britons. Capitulations of temporary existence, and applicable only to the intermediate time which precedes final cession.—Settled or conquered, every Colony is entitled under the conditions and limitations expressed in the Grenada proclamations to a British Constitution and Laws.

This insurrection and massacre, it has been considered, was only a French rebellion, and to be attributed to French principles. This, though not exactly so, may yet be admitted. But when the Commissioners of the National Convention at Guadaloupe sought for instruments in Grenada to effect their purposes, to whom did observation lead them? There were in the Colony Frenchmen, French freemen of colour, French negroes. The whites were neglected, though they joined afterwards. The Commissioners preferred, they selected and seduced the coloured freemen, possessing all the rights of Britons, as their fittest and most convenient instruments, in consequence of, and from a consideration of their intermediate condition and station in society, from their connections with, and the influence their example might have upon the slaves, and that it might appear and be considered only as a contest with the whites for freedom, that so the whole coloured population might be identified, as seeking the recovery of rights, emancipation from tyranny and oppression.

In the same spirit, and with the same views, the agitators of Trinidad practised upon the free coloured population of the Colony, and prevailed upon a few of not the most respectable, to resist a measure which could not but have terminated for their advantage, as has been already shewn, in the due and regular establishment of the British Constitution and Laws, to a full participation of which they would have at once been admitted without any distinction of persons or colours, and in which they would have been secured against all violation, which, if even meditated, could never have been effected but by the Royal assent, which might, whenever necessary, have been deprecated. Intending to annoy the whites, and to deprive them of all power to interfere with or interrupt their projects or plans respecting the slaves, they judged the middle population to be fit instruments for their purposes, practised and tampered with them accordingly, and whilst they would covertly sink, confound, and identify them with the slaves, persuaded them to resist, instead of joining with all free persons in a measure intended to exalt and improve the conditions of all freemen, and this, that the agitators themselves might keep possession of the Colony and its government, and make experiments dangerous and injurious to the peace, happiness, and safety of all.

In the same spirit, and with the same views, is not the African Institution now practising with the coloured population,—with the people of colour in all the Colonies, privately agitating and intriguing with them, whilst their inferior agents, in their periodical publications, have recommended that they should " be sent for," and maintained at the general expense, as mercenaries and auxiliaries in that war, which they are for ever waging against the British Colonists? By these it has been proposed " to raise a " fund for bringing over to England a few witnesses of " the class of persons of colour, from each Colony, to " give testimony of Colonial practices." In an Address from the African Institution to the public, dated January 22, 1816, it is stated, "that the si- " tuation of the slaves AND *coloured population* in " our West India islands has been a subject of con- " stant and increasing solicitude with the Institution, " and a determination is expressed to persevere until " public feeling shall overcome those deep-rooted " prejudices and mistaken views, which are opposed " to the happiness and rights of *the enslaved Afri-* " *cans and people of colour* in these Colonies." Can I understand the words of the preceding sentence, printed in Italics, in any other than their commonly received acceptation, by which the terms coloured population and people of colour, are applied to free persons in the Colonies, not whites? Coloured population is clearly contradistinguished from slaves in the first place—in the second, enslaved, may be referred both to people of colour and Africans, although enslaved people of colour is a term never used. Is the object thus insidiously concealed, that it may be avowed or disclaimed as may be convenient? I must understand the words, in their usual sense and application. The people of colour in nearly all, with trifling exceptions in a few Colonies, possess all the rights of Britons. All that remains for the Institution to do, is to introduce them to the boards and beds of the white Colonists.

Is there a man of any class, colour, or description in the Colonies, who does not start, with horror, at such a suggestion. Yet is it the only inference that can remain to be made, when the happiness and rights of men who possess all the rights of Britons, are to be advanced. To no legal disabilities are they subjected. By moral distinctions alone are they separated. These boundaries are all that remain to be removed or overleaped.

Is there an inhabitant of Great Britain, who would not start at a determination expressed by any association of persons, "to persevere until the general "feeling of the British public should gradually over- "come those deep-rooted prejudices and mistaken "views so long opposed to the happiness and rights "of the inferior orders of society" in Great Britain, by which they have been and are excluded from the tables and beds of the higher classes, of *the privileged order* (so they call the white Colonists) in Great Britain. Of this violation, the evils in a succeeding generation of all white persons, might disappear; but what shall we say of submitting the daughters of Great Britain, or of the Colonies, to the embraces of persons, towards whom there is in fact, and confessedly an instinctive feeling, not merely "a prejudice or a mistaken view," which the strongest and most brutal of passions is not always able to overcome, and which (in the last extremity) would abate even the joy of a mother, that a man child is born into the world.

If upon the equivocal terms used, it should be denied, that this is contemplated by the Report or Address of the Society, yet such is the state to which by the projected mode of emancipation, the report of their committee, if such it be, proposes to bring the population of the Colonies, and such is to be the *Euthanasia* of Colonial slavery.

I cannot refrain, upon the present occasion, from

expostulating with the noble Earl, who communicated to the Colony, through the Governor, the rejection by government of the application from Trinidad for a British constitution and laws. In the official letter, it is stated in terms applicable alike to Colonists and Colonial Assemblies, that, " they have " been educated, or *suppose themselves to be edu-* " *cated*, in the knowledge of them," the British constitution and laws. Never, in so few words, were men and legislatures at once so disqualified, and more than disqualified.

The Colonies, in considerably more than their just proportion as compared with other parts of the British dominions, abound with men completely educated in all the knowledge of past and of present times, in whatever literature, philosophy, general or particular policy can teach, in all the knowledge of the British and Colonial constitutions and laws. What will be the feeling of every Colonist who reads this letter?

The dispatch is official: the words may be of office. I ascribe them to the suggestions of those who seize every occasion to degrade the West India character, and have particularly busied themselves in the affairs of Trinidad. To the same men I ascribe the false impressions made on government, leading them to conclude, that to grant to British subjects the British constitution and laws established in the other British Colonies, would lead to the direct, or to any invasion or abridgment of the political and legal rights of the free coloured population of Trinidad, or to any regulations respecting the same, except what the British government might approve, and his Majesty must assent to. They have thus doubly committed government on points of Colonial personal estimation and general policy and law. These persons, or persons of this same character, are now misleading the good and honourable members of the African Institution, by misrepresenting and confounding the moral and social with the legal and political condition of the free people of colour in the West Indies. To watch over the abolition of the Slave Trade is a great and noble object.—When this no longer affords employment—when the civilization of Africa, which calls for, and will exhaust all their means, ceases to proceed—when the source of the Congo shall be ascertained, for the benefit of geography, although no commerce may thrive, as none can now land upon its inhospitable banks, possessed by nations fierce and barbarous, who use, who require no articles of innocent import.—Let not the Society, in imitation of the slave dealers, to whom they have succeeded, voyaging from Africa to the West Indies with equally base and cruel freights, purchased, and collected, and to be employed in their West India labours, under the same violations of persons and of rights which existed in the slave trade, seek to amuse public expectation, and support their own existence, by speculations in an equally base and sordid traffic carried on for the benefit and on account, but not risk, of their inferior agents.

Am I not justified in imputing sordid motives when I see men enriched in themselves and in their relatives—when I see professions and trades exercised, and more prosperously and safely than in ordinary circumstances, under the influences, and with the means of others exerted and employed upon various occasions? Can these renewed agitations be referred to any other principle but that of covering and protecting the title to what has been acquired, and of leading to other and further acquisitions?

These two classes thus described, together with the first class of white inhabitants British subjects, forming the principal class of masters of slaves, constitute nearly the whole mixed population of the Colonies.—Of the slaves of this population, thus composed and conditioned, an emancipation is now for the first time distinctly proposed.

Of this as a question of magnitude and of danger

unparalleled—of vital importance to all in the Colonies and in Great Britain—to the contemplation—to the consideration—to the agitation of this question, we are compelled, by a necessity which we deprecate, under a responsibility at which we tremble for ourselves and for all. For ourselves, therefore, and for all, and for itself, we invoke the justice of the nation for all consequences upon the heads of those who have moved it.

The question is to be considered as it respects national interests—individual interests, even of those for whom it is proposed—and the means proposed for effecting it.

To all national interests, emancipation, however, and whenever effected, gives the death-blow. The naval power which depends upon the commerce, the commerce which depends upon the agriculture, will all fall with the agriculture. Never can the agriculture of the Colonies, and the emancipation of the labourers co-exist.—Never can the agriculture be maintained under any state that shall deny to it that controul over persons, and the possession of powers, which it now retains, and by which, during every day of labour in the year, it is enabled to command and to apply them. Even now the agriculture in detail is only and exactly commensurate to the extent of these powers and of this controul, and the assured possession of them during the whole succession of days, months, and years. The labours of West India cultivation continue through the whole period of crops which require more than a year to begin and be completed. On every one of the six days of every week, in every month, in the whole year, the whole of the population of every plantation or village, for such it truly is, has allotted labours to perform, adapted to the powers of the various classes into which the persons are distributed. These works, as times or seasons require, are for the first classes, the most laborious of preparing, planting, or reaping the crop which should repay the capitalist, or provisions to sustain the population; and for the other classes, works of inferior labour, or auxiliary to those of the first classes.

Notwithstanding these arrangements for the year, the urgency of particular occasions frequently renders it necessary to procure auxiliary labour, that whilst one essential work is in progress, another equally indispensable may, in due season, be accomplished. All these require such a constant and continued command and controul of active powers, that without them they would languish, and must fail. I appeal to all, who know the West Indies, for a confirmation of these things; and I appeal to posterity upon the result of and against the experiment, if the experiment shall ever be tried.

Under absolute emancipation this controul can never exist—under any qualified or supposed emancipation which shall maintain this controul, all the evils complained of, and magnified in the existing slavery, will remain. They will always remain whilst a power of man over man remains, which wicked persons and passions will not fail as now to abuse. Neither the apprenticeships of England or of Sierra Leone afford any hope, that West India apprenticeships would produce better treatment or afford more protection than is now enjoyed. That under any thing short of absolute emancipation, abuses will continue—that under absolute emancipation neither the agriculture, the commerce, or the naval power will continue, I state, not intending to infer or decide that this or that is to be preferred, nor will I maintain that because these may be lost, that shall be abandoned. To those to whom the fates of empires are committed I leave the decision. Towards them, towards my country, I have performed my duty by this exposition.—It yet remains to be performed towards individuals. Attachment to the soil, the state of villeinage, proposed for imitation and adoption, would yield, whilst it continued, no additional protection against evils similar to the present, to be derived from lords and bailiffs.

Emancipation must of necessity be immediate and direct, or future and to be produced by the insensible operation of time and circumstances effecting the change.

That it can be immediate and direct is impossible. This is inconsistent with all the individual as well as national interests implicated, and is even by the agitators themselves of the Colonies admitted so to be.

In the first place, the train of compensations it would naturally draw along with it, for property taken, or destroyed, or rendered of no value, exceeds all the ability of the United Kingdom to discharge, even were the Colonies called upon to contribute their full share of the expense. Great Britain never takes, for public uses or objects, individual property, without a full and duly estimated compensation. Compensation the Colonists are unquestionably entitled to demand, and beyond all doubt they are equally entitled to demand from parliament, and do now demand protection and safety for property, and respect for rights, by declarations that shall guarantee them against all future attacks to be made thereon, under cover of parliamentary proceeding.

To the unfortunate slaves themselves no proceeding could be more fatal or disastrous. The wretched white population might be withdrawn by a *middle voyage* of miseries and deaths to other countries, the black population would proceed through massacres and destruction to establish another Africa in the American islands, and convert the settlements of British power and wealth into provision grounds of Arum and Convolvulus-Batatas roots.

If emancipation then must be of future time, why is it not abandoned to future time? Eight years have passed since the first Abolition Act was enacted. In eight years an individual scarcely emerges from infancy. In the ages of nations and societies eight years are as nothing. The Villeinage of England fully established at the time of the Conquest, continued until the 15th James I. in which year the last legal case of Villeinage occurred, (omitting all consideration of the 12 Car. II. which extinguished the real tenure) during a period of 550 years, and was at last effected, as the Report states, by a revolution in opinions and manners, by particular manumissions, and by melioration of condition. Without questioning these causes or their operation, I hesitate not to affirm that more has been done within these eight years, in these respects, for the Colonial slaves, than any 50 years in England ever effected for its villeins. How far these, any continuance of these, any progressive improvement or extension of these measures may, during any period, by the operation of these, and of time alone, extinguish the slavery, will hereafter appear from the reasons which shall be assigned.

I proceed now to examine the particular modes or means proposed of effecting emancipation. Two examples from history are exhibited, Roman slavery and English villeinage, the one for illustration, the other for imitation. The supplies of captives once cut off, they both, it is stated, gradually declined, and were extinguished by time and other causes. The precise time during which Roman slavery gradually disappeared, cannot be so accurately estimated as for English villeinage. The causes to which the extinction of each is ascribed, I am not inclined to admit. Of the extinction of Roman slavery, having no talent for invention, I forbear to speak. For the extinction of English villeinage, manumissions may have done a little, but so far was melioration of condition from effecting the change, that the total neglect of the lord for his villeins, during periods of acquiescence in their independent condition, either extinguished all memory of his title or established a legal limitation of right by time, which prevailed in the Courts against his title. If the principle of this acquiescence be sought for, it will be found in the nature of the services which were either predial and occasional, and might therefore be omitted, or personal, and not always required and claimed. But above all, the grand and most important distinction that appertained to English villeinage, was the natural condition of the person. The English villein was a WHITE MAN. Those words exclude at once all comparison of persons or adaptation or adoption of systems. The English villein by not being naturally distinguished among freemen frequently became a freeman, and becoming a freeman was no longer distinguishable in society as having been a villein.

In the Colonies a coloured man when manumitted becomes not one of, constitutes not a part of the population of whites whose privileges he has obtained. He is a free man but he does not become a white man. For ever he remains distinguished by nature and separated by manners, and by social institutions which may not be considered as other than wise and provident.

Villeinage in England was of various sorts, pure and absolute, privileged and limited.—Villeins were *in gross* and personal, or *regardant* and atttached to lands. The state of the Colonial slaves is as nearly as can be that of villeins in gross. This is by all authors described as the least oppressive in its nature. This was primarily extinguished in fact, whilst the real tenure remained until the 12th of Car. II. Yet from this state of independent villeinage, it is proposed to reduce negro slaves to the attached state, through which, it is considered that they may more comfortably be conducted, to final emancipation, and to restore at this day in the Colonies what has been abrogated in Great Britain by positive law. To this measure these objections are opposed.

Indissoluble attachment to the soil, which is contended for, is adverse and opposed to that plan which proposes now to arrive at emancipation by particular manumissions. The two parts of the plan are at variance with each other. In cases of villeinage or of attachment to the soil, emancipation to be effectual by particular manumissions must be accompanied in cases of attached villeinage by the power of detaching from the soil; and yet the present cry is, Attach to the soil,—attach and you may not detach. If the object be emancipation and detachment from the soil by manumissions, why begin by attachment? Attachment, therefore, inseparable from the soil, is inconsistent with the proposed plan of emancipation.

But neither will emancipation, nor detachment from the soil by manumissions, however general, produce that state of society which naturally followed in the cases of English villeinage or Roman slavery. There the only question was slave or free, slave or villein; the slave or the villein manumitted took at once his station in a society of which he became immediately an integrant undistinguishable part.

The union of a West India population is by mechanical intermixture, not natural combination. There are repulsions between the various parts, which will for ever keep them from forming any other kind of association than the present, except by the extinction of the whites, and the subsequent depression of white mixtures in society, until they shall be neglected as unworthy of consideration in the dark-coloured medium through which they will be found, if existing, indissolubly to float.

Even if the agriculture should survive this state of things, the natural, all connexion between the Colonies and parent state will be dissolved, and it will be discovered in Great Britain, as it is now felt in the Colonies, that all respect, all regard for British or white connexion or dependence begins in the Colonies in the first place, and subsequently extends itself to Europe, and that to weaken or destroy that, is to break asunder the connecting line of union which passes through all.

The question of attachment to the soil, as every other question arising among persons, such as are these, so combined in political society, is to be considered and disposed of under a double reference, which should respect the rights of others over, and in those persons, as well as the rights of the persons themselves who are to be so attached, how far the interests of those are compromised, what of benefit or injury will accrue to these.

The measure would be unquestionably a gross violation of the rights of property, not only as it respects immediate proprietors, but as it would affect the claims of creditors of every description. It could never indeed have been contemplated, nor would it have been even for a moment endured, except in such a species of property.

There are even in slavery certain paramount indefeasible rights, securing to the slave all things necessary to support and solace life, food, raiment, lodging, family rights, such as service, labour, a due exertion of bodily power can every where obtain, and without which labour and life itself may not be preserved and continued in existence or succession. Against these rights I admit none other under the slavery to prevail. The question then is, how far these rights of property to be controuled are opposed to those rights of persons, and if opposed, whether the present state of unattached, or that proposed of slavery indissolubly attached to a particular soil, and place, and situation, trenches most on these rights so as to forbid or recommend the change.

In the Colonies, the plan of attaching slaves to the soil has generally been advocated by men in distressed circumstances, as combined with certain preliminary legal processes for enforcing payment of debts to which delays would be incident, and expenses and a command of capital would be required through sales, receivers, or trustees, such as no general creditor would submit to, or might possess. The pretences have been sometimes of a public nature for preventing the dilapidation and destruction of plantations, and sometimes of a private, for securing the slaves against the inconveniences of removals; but the motives have been obviously of particular convenience and of the persons proposing. The arguments derived from such sources will be duly appreciated, and perhaps the removal from an establishment thus conditioned may not be dreaded by the slaves themselves.

There are indeed benefits obtained as well as injuries suffered by the dissociation from an establishment where every thing is settled and arranged. On the other hand, there are benefits also obtained by the change. There are benefits obtained, or injuries secured against by the attachment. There are benefits lost and injuries suffered by the attachment. Upon a due consideration of these, it is extremely difficult to decide, and hazardous to advise a change.

Perhaps the proper objection is to the system itself, as a system overwhelming every thing, and changing every thing, and which, when established, may operate to purposes never contemplated, with a power of action and motion not to be controuled or restrained when put in operation. If to the master remain, and who can take away without consent, without compensation, the power of disposing of, the power of detaching—these powers, those interests, which are of the master, and belong to his creditor if he has any, cannot be taken away from either, and why should a power be denied to the laws of doing that for justice'-sake which the master may do for his own sake? For the sake of humanity the exercise of this power may be regulated without injury to master or slave, and these regulations through the master will be extended to others, and the extent and due conservation of the master's rights will be the principles to guide in, and to be extended to all cases.

The evils complained of, which arise from the sale for debt, and dissociation or removal of persons, may be remedied in themselves by partial regulations specially applied and submitted to the test of experience. That savours more of revolutionary practice which begins by destroying in order to renew. This is more consonant to British principles proceeding by regulations which shall controul the evils without producing greater or other.

And after all, what do the men in Great Britain and in the Colonies who recommend the system, know of the attached villeinage, which by way of emancipating them, is to chain individuals to soils, except of the single circumstance of enchainment? Of what description they are in the Colonies has been stated. Their condition I may lament, though I may not respect their motives. The numbers are indeed small of these speculators and therefore distressed, of these distressed and therefore speculators in agriculture, in general and Colonial policy, in all things. Still less do I respect the motives of those in Great Britain, who with similar views possess not similar means of judging.

West India slavery is in fact already as nearly as may be, that species of villeinage in gross which all have agreed to consider as the least degrading, least oppressive to individuals. The proposal is to change it for and into that other, of attachment to the worst soils, and to services the most base.

The question of English villeinage is between WHITE MEN alone ; of West India slavery, between WHITE MEN and NEGROES. Before the systems can be compared, the persons must be assimilated, identified in species and in colour. One entire class must be changed. Until the leopard change his spots, or the Ethiopian change his hue, this *sliding* system may not be contemplated,—not as likely to attain its purposed end even in 550 years, the period of English villeinage, by that association and union into one homogeneous body composed of these smaller parts. The everlasting distinctions of nature may not be so controuled and surmounted.

No commixture, personal or social, leading to it, can be contemplated without alarm and apprehension at the consequences of thus confounding all things, and sacrificing the smaller number of persons delivered over to the greater, disarmed of those artificial defences of differing institutions, habits, manners, conditions, persons, by which, in all societies, the few maintain against the multitude those rights or possessions which fanciful, specious, and perverted opinions have claimed, and even now claim for all.

Should the voice of humanity inquire how then may the slavery be terminated ? How may its evils be redressed ? Reserving the latter, to the former question I answer, certainly by none of the modes proposed ; and further, that I see no display of adequate intelligence or accurate information in the proposers, no proper general consideration of the subject in all its parts and relations, to justify any expectation of any thing better from prejudices and personal interests which require rather to be maintained by agitating unceasingly all sorts of questions to support a misplaced popularity, and to gratify sordid motives of lucre and ambition.

I have given throughout my life the most earnest

and constant attention to the subject, and confess freely, that with the most anxious desire to effect whatever is practicable and safe, I have not been able to satisfy myself.

The course of reasoning and of reflections through which I have passed, I will put down for my own justification, for the elucidation of the subject, and for the information of others, of men who from pure motives respect, and would secure to all, the rights of liberty and of humanity.

Is this slavery to be perpetual? Often as has this question presented itself to my consideration, it has always been preceded or accompanied by the following train of reflections.

In considering the state of British society, British institutions, establishments, and orders of persons, there is no consideration which has to my heart been such a source of exultation and triumph, as the power which every man, the child of every man possesses, of arriving at the first places of honour and distinction in the government and country. Against any exclusions, but of demerit, against any patrician or plebeian distinctions, or disqualifications, I would for ever contend, zealous to shed my blood and to sacrifice my life in the sacred cause. This privilege I will not submit to any calculate of individual beneficial chances to ascertain its value. Like a gem it is to be estimated, not by its sordid use, but by the sense of distinction and of possible attainment which it confers.

Apply this feeling to the state of slavery, and let the question be repeated—Is it to be perpetual? This question must be distinguished as applied to the condition, or to the individual. The British question so applies itself. All cannot arrive at the first honours of Great Britain—some will. The access is open to all, but almost all will retain their original relative condition in the great political body.

A state of slavery, from which no personal merit or exertion could raise the individual would indeed be terrible. There is no such slavery in the Colonies. Access to the first stations in society is indeed restrained by bars of policy, of nature, and of manners. The road is however open which leads from slavery to a state of comparative distinction, and of all the rights of British freemen, and the possibility and the frequency of thus raising himself into a higher class may be compared and estimated for the slave, and for the British labourer; and I question whether the chance of the one is so very far superior to that of the other.

If the individual were a white man, as in Roman slavery and English villeinage, the full power of enjoyment would be superadded to the possession of these rights. Changing his political, the negro cannot put off his natural condition, and this may be considered as only one more impediment, one of those chances contained in the calculate which we rejected, which professed to estimate, and which would have reduced almost to extinction in the white, as does his condition absolutely in the negro, the chances and consequent value of the privilege of rising to the first stations.

The individual therefore may raise himself above his servile condition. How may the servile condition itself be exalted into one purely social. If the slavery was of whites no difficulty would remain. I should be anxious to anticipate the English period of 550 years by all the means that could possibly be devised. That this period will be shortened even for negro slavery I most confidently trust and hope. In the mean time how it may be accelerated I have not been able to devise. For them, as could only be done for whites, who if they were slaves would of necessity, await the progressive changes of tim and circumstance, every thing that is possible should be effected by a continued supervision of the governing authorities, whilst the servile state continues, to secure to them the possession and enjoyment of all those rights and benefits to which free labourers in Great Britain are entitled, which they could obtain by the same labour, and which constitute all the property and happiness of nine-tenths of British freemen.

All that a good man can desire or propose to himself is to secure to those, the rights of labour in these, and that the slavery of the Colonies, as are their laws, should be agreeable as near as may be, the climate and other things considered, to the servitude and laws of Great Britain. In both, the Colonies will not shrink from the comparison, or from the provisions necessary.

Not to exclude the class of coloured freemen by law from general or legal, or political rights—to secure to the class of slaves the perception of these their just and indefeasible rights of labour, and of protection against the abuse of powers—both these objects are within the power and province of the royal prerogative. The first may easily be effected by that negative controul which of ordinary right belongs to it. The second by an active exercise of its powers under the direction of good men, practically and personally conversant in Colonial affairs, who to liberal education and natural intelligence add a knowledge of the subject obtained by actual residence and inspection, and who have not disqualified themselves for ever by their courses, their prejudices, their motives, their objects—men of independent, enlightened, unprejudiced minds, of information acquired by having contemplated the scenes and the states and the persons in their natural and actual, and local condition and existence, men capable of moving through a moral or a social medium without imbibing any of its impregnations or taints,—men of feeling without prejudice, of no personal motives, no sordid objects, no malignant feelings,—men who know men, and to whom nothing that is human is unknown, *nihil humani alienum.* With the power secured to individuals of rising above the servile condition, with a due conservation of rights to all who continue in the servile classes—without injury to property, without violation of persons, without destruction of national establishments, of commerce, and of power—time discovering and working out for all interests compensations, by changes effectual, but gradual—to Providence may be left the final consummation of this state of things, to be effected according to the dispensations of that wisdom and goodness which direct and order all things.

On reviewing what is past, it appears that the Registry Bill may be considered as disposed of upon a total failure of proof that there exists any fact, circumstance, or necessity to support it as a parliamentary measure, if not rejected *in limine* by a dignified proceeding on the part of the British Parliament refusing to interfere in matters entirely within the province of Colonial Legislation.

The points which remain, and remain I trust for ever settled, respect the right of the Imperial Parliament internally to legislate for Colonies possessed of duly and fully constituted Legislatures, and the emancipation of Colonial slaves considered in its modes and consequences.

Nothing can be more clearly and constitutionally established than these points; that after by the King, in whom primarily the power is by the prerogative vested, or by Parliament, in whom the King is included and by his own assent alone concluded, a British constitution and laws are established in any Colony, the power of internal regulation antecedently in the King, and all power of internal legislation in the Parliament, is ended:

That emancipation cannot immediately and never can be directly accomplished without compensations for the property taken or rendered of no value, without a sacrifice of commerce and navigation, and of naval power dependent upon these, which the nation would for ever feel, without evils and injury incalculable even to the slaves themselves.

Although the power of internal legislation for the Colonies is not in Parliament, yet for and over the whole empire Parliament possesses powers to be exercised for the good of all, specially for the good of the United Kingdom. To these powers we now resort, humbly invoking of Parliament the aid, and the display and exercise of all its energies, to protect the rights of the Colonists, and in them the rights of the whole empire. To Parliament we commit the care of these rights, which should be, and indeed are, and are to them as their own.

We intreat Parliament to watch over the antient Colonies, to preserve them, and with them the antient Constitutions under which the Colonies have in all times past thriven, and continue to thrive; to apply all their energies to a consideration of the unconstitutional state in which the British conquered and ceded Colonies are retained; over all mismanagements and abuses, which beginning in the Colonies and extending themselves every where by their influence and example, may affect the general interests of the empire, to exert their continued vigilance and controul for the sake of British interests primarily, finally for the good of all.

Let me again and again warn the British Government and Ministers with respect to the whole course of measures and proceedings into which a self-interested faction would lead them, and by which they may incur a fearful responsibility to the nation, and to posterity.

Let me exhort all ministers, governors, judges, and officers to aid these energies of Parliament, to shorten as much as possible the duration of these intermediate states of foreign despotism and royal regulation in Colonies now British, and whenever called to apply and enforce the laws of tyrannous establishments, to confine themselves in practice within the pale of British law and British feeling, and to prescribe to themselves as a general rule, never to do that which British law, and freedom, and manners, would reject and reprobate.

Let me warn all, by the examples herein adduced, against committing themselves personally or politically to these agents of African traffic and trade. I warn public men returning from the Colonies against the insidious practice of introducing persons and tracts to their consideration, and the flattery which appears to consult, whilst it intends to betray; and I warn the Colonist himself against all hypocritical greetings and notices to which he may find himself exposed, against the self-complacency thus excited in himself, by which, combined with his own manly regret respecting the evils of a state he cannot change, he may unwarily be led to mix himself with men whose objects and feelings are not in unison with his own.

I again return to and to warn Parliament against the impropriety of any corporation, company, association or institution proceeding as such beyond the principles and powers of creation and existence appertaining to each. Beyond these they are not known, are not to be received. Organized and constituting themselves judges of things beyond themselves, or assumed to belong to themselves, they expect to influence, perhaps to overawe, Parliament, as clubs have done in other countries, being like clubs, always conducted and moved by a few inferior agents with the power and *momentum* of the whole body; and I claim from its magnanimity and justice declarations and the adoption of measures which shall secure the liberties, properties, and lives of the Colonists from all question or danger of invasion, by which they are daily threatened, and may be suddenly destroyed.

On the 26th of February this Work was sent to the press; on the 25th day of this instant, (March) it comes forth. In the mean time printed declarations and admissions have been made of persons and transactions which would give the credit of divination to what is herein written.—" What I have written I have written." I feel considerable satisfaction in being able to refer the Trinidad Letter to its proper source. This I was anxious to do in the text, to separate what was of office from the person of the noble writer, and to refer the things which were most invidious, as well as those which were not duly founded, only to those to whom they were then, and it now appears truly ascribed, to those who were permitted "*to advise on the Constitution and Laws to be given to that Colony.*" The voice was indeed Jacob's voice, the hand appeared to be the hand of Esau. I cannot however applaud the prudence of employing prejudiced and unqualified persons to advise in these cases. The letter will be read by every Colonist with feelings which a Government should never excite. These in me were severe, so as almost to be remembered with regret.

By feelings like these are the sons of the Colonies urged irresistibly to come forward in their own defence. The British Colonies have never wanted men, their sons, to vindicate their characters and assert their rights, whenever occasion has demanded, or excitement urged. Nothing less than the meditated invasion of these could now have excited me. Among these sons my desire is to stand the most humble in consideration, among the most ardent in defence of all. The Colonies possess and will always possess sons equally zealous, more powerful, constantly ready to march to the *pomœrium* of their rights, liberties, and establishments, and by all the arms and arts of policy, prudence, and science to resist all aggression.

RESOLUTIONS

OF THE

HOUSE OF ASSEMBLY OF BARBADOS,

READ AND PASSED UNANIMOUSLY,

JANUARY 17, 1816.

1st. *Resolved.*—That this House having received from its agent in London the copy of a Slave Registry Bill lately introduced into the House of Commons, conceives itself most urgently called upon to protest against the infringement which this Bill attempts on the rights of our Colonial Legislature.

2d. *Resolved.*—That the allegation contained in the said Bill, namely, that there is an illicit importation of Slaves into the West Indies, as far as it respects this Island, is totally void of foundation; this House feeling the most thorough conviction that the only Africans imported here since the abolition of the Slave Trade have been either brought in as prize to his Majesty's navy, or for the purpose of recruiting his army.

3d. *Resolved.*—That although the ostensible object of the Bill is to obtain a Registry of Slaves, it obviously proposes to obtain that by imposing a tax upon every slave proprietor within the Colony in manifest violation of that sound and just principle of the British Constitution, that representation and taxation are inseparable.

4th. *Resolved.*—That the sole right of imposing taxes on the inhabitants of this Island, or of passing laws for internal regulation, is now and hath been for a length of time past vested in the House of Assembly, with the consent of the Council and of the King, or his representative here for the time being, a right which can never be safely or advantageously exercised by those who are utter strangers to these Colonies, and must necessarily want that local information which is so essential to the important work of Legislation.

5th. *Resolved.*—That although there is an Act at present in force in this Island which requires under a heavy penalty the annual return upon oath of the slaves of each proprietor; yet to evince the cordial desire which this House feels to co-operate in any measure deemed necessary for carrying into effect the Acts of the Imperial Parliament for abolishing the Slave Trade, it declares that it is most willing to adopt by any Act of the Legislature of this Island such parts of the Registry Bill as are compatible with the legitimate rights and local circumstances of the inhabitants of this Island, and which may be more adequate to ascertain the slave population.

6th. *Resolved.*—That the Committee of Correspondence be requested to instruct our agent in England to give every opposition in his power to the Registry Bill now pending in the Imperial Parliament, and by the earliest opportunity to transmit to him the address prepared by the joint Committee of the Honourable Board of Council and of this House.

By Order of the House of Assembly,
JOHN BECKLES,
Speaker.

(Copy)

TO

HIS ROYAL HIGHNESS

GEORGE PRINCE REGENT.

The humble Address and Petition of the Council and Assembly of Barbados:

MAY IT PLEASE YOUR ROYAL HIGHNESS,

We, his Majesty's most faithful subjects, Members of the Council and of the General Assembly of this his antient and loyal Colony of Barbados, in approaching your Royal Highness, at a moment to us of just alarm, hope we may be permitted to condole with your Royal Highness on that melancholy affliction of Providence, which deprives us of the paternal protection of our most gracious Sovereign, and to entreat your Royal Highness's favorable attention to these our humble supplications.

Yielding to none of our European fellow-citizens in zeal and affection to your Royal Highness's illustrious house, and attachment to the glory and interests of the United Kingdom and its dependencies, we beg leave, with all due deference, to claim, in a spirit strictly accordant with these professions, for ourselves, our constituents, and our posterity, all the acknowledged and well-known rights and privileges of British subjects.

It is not without serious concern, therefore, that we have noticed the introduction into the House of Commons of a Bill "for " more effectually preventing the unlawful Importation of Slaves, " and the holding free persons in slavery in the British Colonies," which, were it to receive the sanction of the Legislature, would, in many of its enactments, be entirely subversive of that most vital and fondly-cherished principle of our Constitution, that

"Taxation and Representation are inseparable," the inhabitants of this Colony, as your Royal Highness must be aware, having neither Representative nor influence in the Imperial Parliament.

Allow us, without offence, to call to your Royal Highness's recollection, that the darkest cloud which ever obscured the brightness of the present glorious and happy reign, originated in unjustifiable and impolitic attempts to establish the doctrine against which we now contend, and which is, we are confident, no less incompatible with the well-known liberality of your Royal Highness's sentiments than with the enjoyment of those rights and liberties, which we have ever been taught to esteem as the most valuable possession of freemen.

We pray your Royal Highness to reflect how probable it is, that all endeavours to frame provincial laws, by a body of men, four thousand miles distant from the scenes of their attempted regulations, will fail of their desired effect, as it is impossible that the best understandings and the purest motives can supply the want of that local knowledge so essentially necessary to the important work of Legislation.

We most solemnly assure your Royal Highness of our firm conviction, that in this Colony, there never has been, nor is ever likely to be, any evasion of the Slave Trade Abolition Act, a measure which has always been considered by us equally honorable to the mother country, and conducive to the prosperity of this Island, abounding as it does in a large and increasing population of Creole Slaves, which will, we trust, in a short time, be amply competent to the task of cultivating the whole of its productive soil.

Could any plan, nevertheless, be devised by the parent state, not inconsistent with the exercise of our undoubted political rights, to give the completest effect to that law, it would be received by us with gratitude, and furthered with alacrity and zeal.

We challenge any the strictest scrutiny that can be made into the state and condition of the Slaves of this Colony, confident that the result of it would be highly creditable to the character of the Colony, and soothing to the feelings of our fellow-subjects

CONSIDERATIONS

No. 2.

ON THE

Abolition of Negro Slavery,

AND

THE MEANS

OF

PRACTICALLY EFFECTING IT.

BY

J. F. BARHAM, ESQ.

THE SECOND EDITION.

LONDON:
PRINTED FOR JAMES RIDGWAY, PICCADILLY.
1823.

PREFACE.

Every one, who addresses the public, must wish, that what he has to offer may be received without any prejudice arising from a misconception of his former opinions and conduct. On this account I am desirous to correct two misstatements, which have been made respecting myself.

I have been represented by some, as having been originally a defender of the Slave Trade, though afterwards a convert to its abolition. This is not so. I have never, at any time, viewed the Slave Trade without the strongest feelings of disapprobation; nor have I ever done an act, nor have I ever spoken a word, which, according to my judgment, had a tendency to support it. The first occasion on which I ventured to address the House of Commons on a public subject was in support of the Bill, which was introduced in 1794, for the purpose of abolishing the Trade for supplying Foreign Colonies. It is true, that being thoroughly convinced, that, under the circumstances of that day, it would be impossible to enforce, practically, *a direct and general prohibition;* and that the attempt would only create a contraband trade of equal extent, worse character, and more difficult cure; I very unwillingly opposed that measure; recommending, in lieu of it, *as much gradual restriction, as it might be found, from time to time, practicable to enforce*: but no sooner had the revolution of St. Domingo, and the disappearance of every flag but the British from the West-Indian Seas opened a chance, as I thought,. of really and practically abolishing the

Trade throughout, than I joyfully added my best assistance to those who ultimately accomplished the abolition.

I have also lately been represented as hostile to the improvement of the Slaves. This imputation has surprised me (since my exertions in their favour had not always been unnoticed); but I suppose it may have arisen from the opposition I made to the Registry Bill. It is with reluctance that I advert to a measure, which again divided me from many whom I respect; but I must claim from them that candour, which I am willing to show. They introduced the Bill, doubtless, because they believed, that a contraband trade existed, or would arise: I resisted it, because I was satisfied, that no such trade existed, or, *under the changed situation of the Colonies*, was at all likely to arise. They supported the Bill, because they thought it would be beneficial to the

Slaves: I opposed it, because I thought, that, without being of any use to the Slaves, by being *misunderstood*, it would lead them into mischief and danger. Whether there have been any reasons to suspect, that I was not wholly wrong, I shall not here inquire.

To improve the condition of the Slaves, in every safe and practicable way, I have ever deemed the first duty of the master; nor have I ever contemplated such improvement, without viewing at the end of my perspective, as its ultimate object and consummation, *their capacity for, and their possession of* FREEDOM.

That the process to this point must, under the present circumstances, be exceedingly slow, has always, to me, been a most painful consideration; and my chief motive, in presenting these pages to the public, is to point out, that the present moment offers an opportunity, which never has occurred before, and which may never occur again, of altering those circumstances so, as to render an accelerated progress of improvement both safe and practicable.

ON

THE ABOLITION

OF

Negro Slavery.

THE nation, as with one voice, has called on its legislature to adopt speedy and decisive measures for the abolition of Slavery in our Colonies—Government has accepted the call, and demanded that the task be committed to itself—Expectation is everywhere alive, and deeply painful will be the general feeling if it should be disappointed.

It would be uncandid to suppose, that government had taken the matter into its own hands merely to get rid of a temporary embarrassment; and without meaning really to effect the object. But even if this were so, it would make no difference in the end. Those, who have awakened the public feeling on this subject, will know how to arouse it again; the public voice will be heard in a yet louder tone; and the danger is, that government will thus be forced on measures, which, if due preparation be not made for them, will involve both the Slaves and the Colonies in common ruin.

The nation does not indeed expect that emancipation can be effected by any immediate act, for, until the Slaves can be fitted for freedom, it is acknowledged, that emancipation would be injurious even to themselves: but what the nation does expect, is this—*that the most energetic measures shall be forthwith employed to bring them into that state, in which freedom may be granted to them with benefit and safety.*

To judge correctly with regard to these measures is *the* important point, both for government and the nation. For, if, on one hand, by too much precipitation the greatest mischief and danger may be produced; so, on the other hand, if there be not sufficient decision, the object will remain at a distance most unsatisfactory to the public feeling, and unjust towards those, whose wrongs we want to redress with all possible speed.

In considering this difficult subject, our first question will naturally be to ask, What is the *actual* condition of the Slaves, and what has it hitherto been? Has it improved? Is it improving, or is it stationary? The answer cannot be disputed. In physical respects it has much improved, and little is left to do. The Slave is now in most physical circumstances better off than the labouring class of other countries*. This it was in the power of the master to accomplish, and it is done. But in civil and moral respects, his condition is not materially changed. Some improvement may have been made, and some may be in progress (more perhaps in reality than appearance, and more by custom than by law); but still we must confess, that his civil rights are yet hardly definable, and his moral improvement is almost yet to be begun.

That progressive improvement, however slow, must arrive at the desired point at last, will of course be admitted. But if the question be asked, will it, under the present process, arrive at the point of emancipation within the *time* that the nation expects?—the answer must be, *decidedly no.* At the present rate of improvement, generations must pass before freedom could be safely or beneficially imparted to the Slaves.

If again it be asked, whether by such measures as have been now recommended

---

* Let it not be understood as if it were meant to place physical good in any competition with the blessings of liberty, moral improvement, or religion. It is merely meant to state the fact as it is.

to the Colonies, the progress of improvement will be rendered satisfactory?—the answer must be again, *decidedly no*. Some good they may do: some branches of the evil they may lop off, but they go not to its root: they may somewhat relax the bonds of the Slave, but they will not practically *much* advance *that*, which, if ever he is to be free, must precede his freedom; *namely, his moral improvement*.

Moral improvement is the hinge on which every thing must turn. When that is sufficiently advanced, civil rights may be freely granted, and emancipation will have no danger. But moral improvement will not be accomplished by vain recommendations to the Colonies to do what they have not the means of effecting.

Nothing indeed could be easier than for the Colonies to pass specious laws, which would remove every reproach from their statute book; but if, from existing circumstances, these laws could not have any practical effect, it were better that the evil should remain open to public view, than that it should be thus disguised.

Nothing could be easier for them, than to introduce Christianity *in name*. For the most insignificant reward, the Slaves would universally accept baptism. Without reward, they would rather doze at a monthly sermon, than work during the time. But such feeble means of conversion would not change them: it were better that they should remain as they are, than that a people, whose religion (if indeed it can be called such at all) continuing in fact as it is, should be regarded as Christians.

Nothing could be easier than to comply with the constant requisition, that the evidence of a Slave should be *admissible* in a court of justice; but no one has yet contended, that, till he can feel the obligation of an oath, till you have at least found some symbol fairly to swear him by, his evidence shall be regarded as *credible*. What will the Slave then have gained? The mockery of being produced not to be believed. Better for him that he should remain as he is, than exchange a technical disability for a public exhibition of his incompetence.

Nothing could be easier than to abolish the use of the whip; but those, who call for this abolition, always end by proposing some other means of coercion, some other instrument of punishment; less decried perhaps, but which is to be equally effectual. What again will the Slave gain by this? It were better that his chains should appear in their full deformity, than that they should be gilded over*.

---

* One exception must, however, be made here. The recommendation lately sent out, to prohibit the use of the whip towards women, is most important in a *moral* point of

One of the measures recommended to the Colonies is the facilitating individual emancipation; and certainly it is desirable, that there should be no impediment in the way of those, who are disposed to give freedom to their Slaves*, as a reward, or from kindness; but no error could be more pernicious than to suppose, that general emancipation can arrive by

view. Degradation of the female is everywhere the prominent feature of barbarism; and to distinguish their women by any mark of respect cannot fail to raise them in the estimation of the Slaves, and to lead towards every virtue.

* It does not appear, that any law has passed with the *view* of discouraging individual emancipations, nor indeed is it conceivable, that a policy of this nature could be entertained by any owner of Slaves, for the plain reason, that the fewer Slaves there are besides, the more valuable must be his own. Could one-fourth of the Slaves be emancipated this year, the income of the Colonies would be quadrupled in the next, for the redundant produce, which depresses the market, would disappear. The laws, which impose some difficulty on emancipations, had another object. In part it was a humane one. The owner of Slaves is now by law obliged to furnish them annually with a fixed quantum of clothing, food, &c. Now to escape from this obligation, some persons were base enough, when their Slaves were past work, to emancipate them, and these became the most miserable objects imaginable. To prevent this, and to protect the parishes from the burthen of maintaining these poor people, laws were passed, requiring, that when a Slave was emancipated, some security should be given for his future sustenance.

multiplying individual emancipations. The case of the Negro has by some been compared to that, which once existed in our own and most other countries, where (as has been justly said) Slavery was at last extinguished by the enfranchisement of the last Slave. But the cases differ essentially. When the European Slave was enfranchised, he passed into the general mass of the free population. Not thus is it with the Negro: when he is enfranchised, he passes not into the condition of the free community, but forms a separate class of his own; and (as we see in every Colony) the most wretched class of the whole population. The reason of this is evident; namely, that *he is not yet in that state of moral improvement, in which freedom is a good.*

It will perhaps be said, that the case will become different when the number of emancipated Negroes becomes greater; but experience does not warrant this opinion. We do not observe, that the free Blacks are more improved where they are more numerous: we can hardly discern anywhere, that one step has ever been taken by them voluntarily towards civilization; nor ever will there, till their whole character be previously changed. But as they become more numerous they will become more dangerous; and, be where it may, whenever they become sufficiently strong, unless altered in character, they will drive out the Whites, and make the remaining Blacks slaves to themselves*.

Of all the projects that have ever been imagined, that of declaring all the children free, who shall be born after a certain time, is the one which would bring with it the most *certain ruin*. Indeed, we may fix the date at which that ruin would arrive: this would be (if it did not happen sooner) at the first moment when this generation had reached maturity.

Those, who expect that this generation would resemble the free labourers of other countries, are strangely deceived. Let men conclude what they will, *from cases of exception*, we know that the Negro race is so averse to labour, that without force we have hardly anywhere been able to obtain it, even from those who had been trained to work; and now we are to expect it from those who have been trained to idleness!

* There is nothing of which a Negro Slave has such horror as that of becoming the Slave of a free Negro, for these are generally found to be the severest of masters. I would not willingly undervalue the virtues of the Slaves (and attachment to their masters, when kindly used, they certainly have in an eminent degree), but I imagine, that to the fear of being made Slaves to other Negroes we must in some degree attribute that adherence to their masters, which the Slaves have often manifested in cases of insurrection.

No—if ever general emancipation is to come without general ruin, it must come, not by emancipating *Slaves*, but by emancipating *Slavery*; by gradually extracting from the condition of Slavery all its ingredients, till at last the whole mass of Slaves shall at once glide, as it were, into freedom. From the former course we could expect only an idle and vicious population; in the latter, every step we take is good in itself, and leads to good. In the former process, the farther we go the greater is the danger; in the latter, every day would bring additional security.

But what, then, are the means, by which this desirable change could be so accelerated as to give us some *near* view of the object we aim at? The answer is painful, but it is of no use to disguise the truth—*at present they exist not; nor can they be created, unless we can remodel the whole frame of our Colonial establishments.*

This, therefore, we must either boldly determine to undertake, or we must be content to await the slow progress of such improvement as time may gradually produce.

Persons, who have given but slight consideration to the subject, or who have trusted false information as to facts, will be surprised at this statement, having hitherto believed, that, if the Colonial assemblies and proprietors were in earnest, they could speedily effect whatever was desired; but such will not be their opinion if they examine the subject more closely.

The assemblies may pass what laws they will; but here are customs, manners, and opinions to be entirely altered; deep prejudices to be rooted out, both in the White and Black population; here is the character of a *people* to be changed; above all, some stimulus is to be discovered, and brought into action, by which those are to be induced to labour, who have no wants, and those to submit to moral institutions, who have no moral feelings. If to change the character of a people by law be in any case the most difficult problem in political science, what must it be in that strange anomaly of human society, which the Colonies now present to our view?

The owners of Slaves may labour for the same object as much as they will, and many have thus laboured all their lives, but have laboured nearly in vain. Nor are the causes of this failure out of sight. The changes to be wrought are not within the scope of a master's *mandate;* and his *influence* with the Slaves, as to many things, is less, exactly because he *is* their master. To any thinking mind this will convey no paradox: the fewer rights a man retains, the more tenacious he is of them. All here depends on opinion: the opinion of the Slave at present acknowledges the right of his master to his labour, because he bred and feeds him: he acknowledges the right to enforce that labour by punishment: but of any interference with his domestic life or pleasures he acknowledges not the right, and is exceedingly jealous of any approach to it, in the shape of advice or influence.

Nothing can betray more ignorance of the subject, than when persons blame the master for not enforcing marriage amongst his Slaves. By persuasion and reward, sometimes, a *seeming* acquiescence in this institution has been obtained from a few Slaves; but nothing would sooner excite their open resistance than any exertion of authority on the subject.

Let it not be supposed for a moment, that this representation of the difficulties to be overcome proceeds from a wish to discourage the purpose: it proceeds from the very opposite motive. The first step to overcome a difficulty is to ascertain its full extent; and he, who would undervalue, is not the most likely to surmount it. To represent a thing easier than it is, may indeed lead men more readily to the attempt, but it is likely to place them farther from the execution of any thing that requires persevering exertion.

Of exceeding difficulty is indeed the object we aim at; but from nothing that has been said does it follow, that it is unattainable. It follows not, that, because in the present condition of the Colonies improvement *must* be extremely slow, changes might not be made in that condition, which would render a rapid improvement both safe and practicable.

Of what nature those changes must be, will best appear by a review of the principal obstructions which now exist against improvement.

OF THE
CHIEF OBSTRUCTIONS TO IMPROVEMENT,
AND
THE MEANS OF REMOVING THEM.

I. The chief obstruction is *fear of the Slaves.* In physical force, they are tenfold superior to their masters; but, from their state of ignorance, they are not able to devise, and, from their close confinement, they are not able to execute, any plan of concert, or combination. Now, to improve them, we must enlighten their minds, and relax their confinement. But the more we succeed in these objects, the more we increase our own danger. Knowledge is strength, and freedom from confinement is opportunity. Suppose the assemblies to be as liberally disposed as possible, you cannot expect them to be divested of those feelings, which govern the rest of mankind, and self-preservation will ever be the first law of human nature.

To judge what would best remove this obstruction from fear, it will be well to examine from what point the danger chiefly arises. The Slaves know pretty well, that, besides the power of their masters, there is another power over the water, which is stronger than they. Their notions are indeed not very distinct on the subject, but they have occasionally heard, that this power over the water is sometimes disposed to side with them against their masters; and in proportion as this notion prevails more or less among them, so is naturally the danger greater or less of their resistance and insurrection. The way, then, to diminish, or rather to do away the danger at once, would be *to let them see that there was but one authority, from which there was no appeal, and against which all resistance would be vain, namely, that of the King,* for under such title would the authority of Great Britain be regarded. In the mind of the Slave resistance to the King of England would appear in a very different light, than resistance to the local powers; and, if this change could be brought about, many an improvement, which *now* would be hazardous in the extreme, would be free from all danger. In fact, the danger would then become less, in proportion as the knowledge of the Slaves became greater; for such knowledge would the more convince them of their inability to cope ultimately with the power of Great Britain.

II. The *next obstruction* to improvement is the absence of all wants, that would stimulate a free Negro to labour in the West Indies. What they may have done in other countries or climates proves nothing. Nor will any minute cases, which are brought forward (and which one has no means of examining), have much weight. A few Negroes under peculiar circumstances may have laboured for hire, but the evidence of all the Colonies in the West Indies (in some of which there are abundance of free Negroes, and abundance of people who would gladly hire them) proves, that, constituted as he now is, the Negro will not work but under coercion. Hayti proves it — Africa proves it*.

* The cultivation of Hayti seems to be now confined to the raising of provisions, which requires very little labour, and to the gathering of coffee and cotton from the trees already planted. As to Africa, even though in one particular part there should be a class of men, who will undertake temporary jobs for hire, and even though there may be some symptoms of voluntary labour at Sierra Leone, produced by moral improvement, yet such exceptions destroy not the general evidence of that vast continent. Indeed, the latter case rather confirms our statement. It is far from our meaning, that by moral improvement any change may not be effected; what we mean to say is, that till such improvement shall have taken place, the Negro will only work by coercion. A curious proof of this will be found in Mr. John Hay's Narrative of the Grenada Insurrection, published by Ridgway, page 106. This gentleman was some time detained at Guadaloupe, then under the government of Victor Hugues. Punishment by the whip had been then totally abolished; but instead of it a military tribunal had been established, consisting of five whites and blacks, who made a tour of the Island once a month, in order to try and punish such Negroes as had neglected their work. *They were condemned to be*

But indeed we hardly need to appeal to experience for the proof. By the clearest conclusions from facts, that cannot be disputed, we may assure ourselves, *a priori*, that it *must* be so. The labour of a few days builds as good a habitation as the Negro desires, and the labour of a few more supplies him with food for the year. Clothing he hardly wants, and artificial desires he has none so strong as the desire to pass his time in idleness. By what then but force can he be brought to work? We must here call, with the Greek mathematician, for ground to stand on. Ground there is none; and we might as soon expect to put a machine in motion by a power, which should be weaker than the power that resists, as we might expect the free Negro to labour for hire, till some adequate want shall impel him. To teach him artificial wants must be a work of time and uncertainty; and the case is hopeless unless we can bring him under the same impulse, which acts on the free labourer everywhere else. All the world over, this is neither more nor less than the want of food; and if the Negro is to work, that stimulus must

chained by the middle and ancle for five to fifteen years. The more refractory were shot, which very frequently happened. Mr. Hay relates this incidentally, and not for the purpose of founding any argument upon it.

be applied to him, or he must remain under the whip; for as to confinement or disgrace, he would hardly feel them as a punishment.

Such are not the most pleasing views of human condition, but we must not shut our eyes to them, unless we would grossly deceive ourselves. The Slave probably would prefer his present state under the whip, to that into which we would thus lead him; and no doubt, that physically he suffers less in his present state, than he would then do *at first*; but the process is unavoidable; and if you would convert him into a free labourer, there is no other way to teach him.

But how may the thing be effected? Half an acre is sufficient for his cottage and his food; the kind of land he wants is of little value, and is divided amongst proprietors so numerous as to render a combination impossible. Sooner than let their land lie waste, these proprietors would underbid each other, and the Negro would thus obtain what land he wants at a rent, which the labour of a week, perhaps, would procure him. Another week would serve for its cultivation, and the remaining fifty weeks he would remain idle. It does not seem, that any law could reach this case, nor could it be prevented, unless *all the land were in one proprietor*, who might require a reasonable quantum of labour to pay for it. If this could be effected, the situation of the free Negro would become similar to that of the free labourer everywhere else, whose constant work is requisite for his constant food: some would then labour more and more successfully than others; artificial wants would gradually supervene, and thus we should have obtained the ground to stand on, by which we might raise a due proportion of these people into the different degrees of social order.

III. A *third obstruction* to improvement arises from the impossibility of obtaining any general concert amongst the numerous proprietors, which now exist. To produce the effect we want on the moral condition of the Slaves, it is indispensible, that some *general and uniform plan* should be everywhere instituted and followed up. Now this could not be accomplished by law, and must in great part, as matters stand, depend on the voluntary exertions of the proprietors and managers. But these (even if we suppose them unanimous as to the *object*) cannot be expected to be unanimous as to the *means* of pursuing it. According to their different notions, one man will aim at improvement one way, while his neighbour aims at it another, and thus the endeavours of all will be lost.

This obstruction could obviously only be removed by bringing *all the Slaves under one government.*

IV. A *fourth obstruction* to moral improvement is the want of adequate means in the Colonies to form the establishments it would require.

The chief means of moral improvement are *religion and education.* Religion we know may do any thing; but it depends not on man to ensure its acceptance and diffusion, especially amongst those, who are past the age of education.

Education must therefore go hand in hand with religion; and perhaps it would be best expressed thus, *we must have the means of religious education first, and of religious observance afterwards.* If we would produce the effect speedily, these institutions must be so extensive, that every child shall be thus educated, and that the means of religious instruction and worship shall be within the reach of every Slave. Partial attempts may do *individual good,* but *our* object they would not attain*; whereas if the thing were done every-

---

* It was the opinion of Mr. Burke (who at one time honoured the author by much communication on these subjects), that the moral improvement of the Slave would only be effected by a *general* diffusion of religious instruction *at once.* He said, that the point must be carried at first by a *sort of force,* and that partial impressions would often be

where at once, we may calculate the day on which Slavery may be finally abolished; for that day will have arrived when we shall have obtained a generation thus educated.

Now, establishments of this extent it is out of the power of the Colonies to command, either in regard to the pecuniary means, or those of ob-

obliterated as fast as they were made. But let it not be thought, that partial attempts are here undervalued. Infinite is the merit of those, who have made them, and great, in some cases, has been their success. The United Brethren (commonly called Moravians) have led the way, and their mode of teaching is peculiarly adapted to impress the minds of the Slaves. But neither their number nor their pecuniary means enable them to extend their missions as much as might be desired. The Methodists have also had considerable success; but they are viewed in the Colonies with some jealousy. I am inclined to believe, that this jealousy is in general unwarranted, though, perhaps, there have been some instances of particular persons (perhaps not authorized, but calling themselves Methodists) acting with considerable indiscretion. If in nonessentials they could adapt their forms a little to the circumstances of the case, their zeal might be highly useful. The Established Church has not hitherto been very active in this work; but it appears, that, under the patronage of the Lord Bishop of London, a society, having for its object the conversion of the Negroes, is now about to enter on the task with energy worthy of its object. Should the diffusion of religious instruction among the Slaves not be made a national concern, certainly, those who are prompted by humane views towards them, or a desire for the abolition, could in no way so well promote that object as by contributing to the means of converting them to Christianity.

taining the requisite teachers and ministers. At present, schools there are none, and the established clergy are barely sufficient for the white population. To furnish education and religious instruction to eight hundred thousand slaves, dispersed as they are, would require so many teachers and ministers as to induce a fear, that the thing could hardly be accomplished; especially as we know, on one hand, the indisposition of men to risk their health in those climates, and, on the other, the expenses of living there. Yet, as this is the *turning point* of the whole, let us not abandon it till we find it quite unattainable.

A calculation of the requisite number of these establishments must at present rest on very uncertain data, and much depends on the denseness of the population in the different Colonies. In the Appendix (No. I) an attempt has, however, been made to calculate that number and their expense, which it is supposed would not be less than two hundred and fifty thousand pounds per annum; though afterwards it might perhaps be reduced. But even this supposes, that a considerable concentration of the population had been previously effected. At present, if education and religion are to reach all the Slaves, a much larger establishment and expense would be requisite.

The means then of removing this obstruction

must be either to furnish an establishment such as has been stated; or, if the population be left in its present dispersed state, to furnish a much larger establishment. To alter the state of the population is obviously impossible, while the property remains in the hands of different proprietors; and this brings us again to the same point, the advantage, or necessity of *vesting it all in one proprietor, or at least placing it under one direction.*

V. The last obstruction, that need be enumerated, is the apprehension, which the present proprietors entertain, that though *all* Great Britain demands the abolition of Slavery, yet that *all* the price of obtaining it would be cast upon them. Such apprehension is probably unfounded; but when their all is at stake, men are not easily cured of their fears; and till these are entirely removed, it cannot be expected, that the proprietors should act as they would, if perfectly assured, that they were to bear whatever loss may ensue, *only in just proportion* with the rest of the nation.

The remedy here would of course be to give them that assurance, either by some *solemn declaration of the legislature,* or, what would be better (if practicable), by *some immediate indemnity.* But as this leads to a subject of much importance and extent, it may be well to consider it separately.

OF COMPENSATION.

Compensation should be considered in two points of view; its *necessity* and its *justice*.

Of the Necessity of Compensation.

It is *necessary*, because without it our object (the abolition of Slavery) cannot be attained. Doubtless it is in the power of Great Britain to abolish Slavery by its own decree, to enforce that decree on the Colonies, or to leave the Slaves to enforce it for themselves. Nothing could be easier or shorter than this process. The free condition of Hayti can everywhere be attained in a week. But if we want to retain the Colonies as possessions of any value* after the abolition, we *cannot enforce* it on the proprietors and resident white population; *for the very first application of force on them, that be-*

---

* No man's opinion deserves more weight on most subjects than that of Mr. Baring; but particularly on this, on which his knowledge must be great, though not himself a Colonial proprietor. Mr. Baring declared to the House, that if the Slaves were emancipated, we must take leave of the Colonies as a productive possession. Doubtless this gentleman would admit the condition, "*unless the character of the Slaves can be previously changed.*"

comes visible to the Slaves, will be the certain signal for general insurrection, and the fate of the Colonies is decided without recal.

Let me here adjure those whom it may concern, to take care what they are about in this respect. One wrong step, and their regret may be eternal. Let them do else what they will. If they cannot else be satisfied, let them resume the charters, and abolish the present legislatures of the Colonies: it will be better for the Colonies, and better for the Slaves, than that they should be openly controlled, and yet suffered to exist; for they will be consigned, not only to inefficacy and contempt, but to plunder and death. In whatever shape local authority appears to the Slaves, whether in that of a governor only, or as it is now composed; for their *own* sake, and for the sake of those who are entrusted with the authority, it should appear to the Slaves (while in their present state) to be *absolute.*

But will the white inhabitants put it to this issue? Will they expose themselves to certain ruin, rather than comply with the terms required of them? The answer is perilous; but so much is certain, that they will not accept the assurance of persons here (who, as they think, know little of their situation), that abolition will do them no harm. Many of them believe, that abolition will be fatal to their existence and that of their families; and seeing ruin equally in compliance and resistance, in some quarter or other violent councils will prevail. To produce the catastrophe, it needs not that there should be a general resistance, any spark may be sufficient to light the flame.

To predict this conduct, on the part of the Colonies, is not attributing to them any inveterate determination to maintain a bad system, it is attributing to them only the common feelings of mankind. If it were proposed, *at the separate expense* of any county in England, to remedy an evil which had been established by the *nation at large,* does any one suppose that such county would tamely acquiesce? Yet how infinitely weaker would that case be than the one we have been considering!

Let not the pride of Great Britain be here offended. The same blood flows in the veins of the Colonist as in those of the people of England. They have dared much for their country in forming those Colonies: they have often suffered much for their country: and they will in any case act as their countrymen would. They will be ready to share with their country all the cost of abolishing Slavery; but if it is attempted to make them bear *more than their share,* they will not acquiesce—and your Colonies are gone.

Compensation is therefore necessary, if we will have Colonies as well as abolition. But it were most desirable, for the speedier attainment of the object, not only to have the acquiescence, but the willing co-operation of the white inhabitants; for if that population were merely to be passive, and do nothing, it would not be easy to find *all* the necessary agency by which to effect our purpose.

That co-operation we may have; and we may have it on the fair terms of doing that also ourselves, which we call on others to do, and of paying our proportion of the debt, which we as well as they have contracted.

Of Compensation, as required by Justice.

But is it really so, as we have affirmed, that the people of Great Britain are equally liable for the debt, we would now pay to humanity and justice, as the inhabitants of the Colonies and the owners of Colonial property? The question is most important; and, before it can be safely answered, we must inquire *how this debt arose, by whom, and for whose benefit it was contracted?*

That debt arose by the Slave Trade; and that trade was established by, and for the benefit of, the *nation at large.*

To say, that Great Britain formed the plan,

and that the Colonies executed it—to say, that Great Britain made the laws, and that the Colonies availed themselves of those laws—would be greatly understating the share, which Great Britain had in *the origin of the Slave Trade, and in the consequent system of Slavery that now exists.* But many persons have been so used to charge all the odium of that system on those, who by accident happen to be the present owners of Slaves, that they will be surprised to learn how much larger a share Great Britain has had, than the Colonies, in the *formation, maintenance, and present extent of Slavery.*

The following historical facts will clear up this point a little.

Great Britain established the Slave Trade in the reign of Queen Elizabeth, who personally took a share in it.	The Colonies did not then exist.

Great Britain encouraged it in the successive reigns of Charles I, Charles II, and James II, by every means that could be devised. But it was William III who outdid them all. With Lord Somers for his minister, he declared the Slave Trade to	The Colonies, all this time, took no share in it themselves, merely purchasing what the British merchants brought them; and doing therein what the British government invited them to do, by every means in their power.

be "*highly beneficial to the nation:*" and that this was not meant merely as beneficial to the nation through the medium of the Colonial prosperity, is demonstrated by the Assiento Treaty, in 1713, with which the Colonies had nothing to do; and in which Great Britain binds herself *to supply* 144,000 *Slaves, at the rate of* 4,800 *per annum*, to the Spanish Colonies. From that time, till within a few years of the present time, our history is full of the various measures and grants, which passed for the *encouragement* and protection of the trade.

So much as to those who created and fostered the trade: and now let us see, who it was that first marked it with disapprobation, and sought to confine it within narrower bounds.

The Colonies began in 1760. South Carolina (then a British colony) passed an act to prohibit further importation; but	Great Britain rejected this act with indignation, and declared, that the Slave Trade *was beneficial and necessary to the mother country.* The governor, who passed it, was repri-

manded; and a circular was sent to all other governors, warning them against a similar offence.

The Colonies, however, in 1765, repeated the offence; and a bill was twice read in the assembly of Jamaica, for the same purpose of limiting the importation of Slaves; when	Great Britain stopped it, through the governor of that island, who sent for the assembly, and told them, that, consistently with his instructions, he could not give his assent: *upon which the bill was dropped.*
The Colonies, in 1774, tried once more; and the assembly of Jamaica actually passed two bills to restrict the trade; but	Great Britain again resisted the restriction. Bristol and Liverpool* petitioned against it. The matter was referred to the Board of Trade, and that Board reported against it.
The Colonies, by the agent of Jamaica, remonstrated against that report, and pleaded against it on all the grounds of justice and humanity; but	Great Britain, by the mouth of the Earl of Dartmouth, then president of the Board, answered by the following declaration: "We cannot allow the Colonies to check or discourage, *in any degree*, a traffic so beneficial to the nation." And this was in 1774!

---

* The conduct of this town, with regard to the Slave

It is presumed, after this, not many persons will be disposed to contend, that Great Britain has not had at least an equal share in establishing Slavery with those who happen now to be the actual owners of Slaves.

But still there are some points to be closely examined before we shall venture to pronounce, that the claim for compensation rests on the strictest grounds of justice.

To make that claim *absolute*, it must be shown, that the thing which is required to be

Trade and Slavery, is too curious to pass without remark. Within a very few years of the present time, Liverpool was the great Slave Trader of all. Liverpool invented and clung to all the enormities of the middle passage. Liverpool defended the trade to the last moment, not as a necessary evil, but as a good thing in itself. The sense of the nation, however, prevailed, and the trade was abolished. Still Liverpool would not give up the topic of Slavery, and its voice is still heard more than any other on that subject: but (oh the miracle!) it has suddenly changed sides, and the ultra advocate of the Slave Trade has become the ultra declaimer against Slavery! How is this to be accounted for? Self-interest is pretty generally worshipped, but seldom in so public a way. But something still more extraordinary has been reserved for this most mercantile town. It has not only changed sides diametrically within a very few years on this subject, but it is able at this moment to view the same thing in both ways at once. An ingenious merchant of that place has invented a glass, by which, if directed to the West, Slavery is seen as a monster of such frightful magnitude, that, in order to destroy it instantly, you ought to destroy all your Colonies; but which same glass, if directed to the East, shows the same Slavery in a form perfectly diminutive and inoffensive.

surrendered is not merely *a system*, which afforded the means of prospective gain, but that it is absolutely *a property in possession*, and held by the same right by which all other property is held—*the law*. Closer than this it does not seem possible to draw the line; and here lies the distinction between the present claim, and that which was made at the time the Slave *Trade* was abolished. The claim then made (but which was urged much more strenuously by the British Slave merchant than the planter) was not a claim for *property in possession*. The Slave *Trade* could not be property, though it might be the means of creating property. The right to trade had been permitted by law, but no engagement had been made, that it should be permitted for ever. Those, who trusted to its continuance, trusted at *their own risk*, and when it was prohibited, what they lost was not a *vested property*, but the chance of contingent gain; whereas what will be taken here is, that which the law has sanctioned as property for ever.

A very respectable author (Mr. Clarkson) contends against this claim of property upon a ground, which it is not necessary here to dispute. His argument seems to be, that such property cannot be created even by law, since it is contrary to the first principles of our nature (which are anterior and superior to all law) that one man should have property in another man. Be it so, but what then? This would justify the Slave in regaining his liberty by any means he could employ, since he had been unjustly deprived of it. But in the question of compensation the Slave is no party. That question lies wholly between the proprietor and the legislature, which has constituted the property. *The law must be binding, at least on those that made it.* If the legislature, with a view to national advantage, has committed injustice, and now, with a view to national justice, would repair the wrong, it is for the nation to pay the price of its wrong, and not for the individual, who acted in conformity to the law. To fix on the present proprietor the cost of redeeming the acts of the nation at large would be concluding a series of injustice to Africa by an act of injustice to a portion of your own subjects, with regard to whom your first laws would have been a fraud, and your last would be a robbery.

It has been often repeated, that evil must not be done that good may come out of it: that the end can never sanctify the means: that injustice may not be committed even for the purposes of justice; and certainly there is no principle of morality which it is more important to keep inviolate than this, though there often appears much temptation (even from good motives) to swerve from it. But here we are in no such distressing alternative. We are not to choose between injustice to the Slave, and injustice to his owner; but we are to choose between injustice to the owner, and that justice which we have it in our power to do him.

If the people of Great Britain, by their general call on the legislature to abolish Slavery, meant to say, that they were so deeply sensible of its injustice, that they would pay whatever it cost to abolish it; there is not a passage perhaps in any history, which does more honour to a national character, for it must have appeared to them that the sacrifice would be great.

But if by that call was meant, that it should be abolished by taking from others the property which they (the nation) had constituted such for their own benefit, and of which they had received the benefit, then there are no words which would adequately express the contempt they would deserve for their hypocrisy and injustice. It may be, that some few have signed petitions in that view; it may be, that many have signed them without much consideration of the consequences; but he must have a vile opinion indeed of his country, who could attribute a view like this to any considerable portion of its inhabitants.

It is however said by some, that no compensation will be due, since there will be no loss; that when the Slaves are set free they will work for hire like labourers everywhere else; and that such hire will be cheaper than the present cost of maintaining them. These assertions, it is not necessary either to admit or deny; for, be they true or be they false, it is quite clear, that common sense, as well as common justice, demands, that the experiment should be made at the risk of those who predict its success, and demand its execution; and not at the risk of those who apprehend its failure, and protest against it. If the former be not altogether insincere in the opinions they express, and dishonest in their purposes, they cannot hesitate to encounter a risk, which they say is nothing, and accept a gain, which they say will be great.

But in what way can it be contrived, that this risk shall fall, as it ought, on the nation at large? In what way can the due compensation be appreciated while one party maintains, that emancipation will be a benefit, and the other, that it will be ruin to the owner? If the former be in the right, the smallest sum, that the people of Great Britain were made to pay, would be an act of injustice to them; and if the latter party be in the right, the largest sum, if less than the whole, would be an act of injustice to the proprietor.

To say, that this may be settled afterwards, according as matters turn out, will not do, because the result may remain in suspense for an indefinite period, and when it arrives its cause may be disputed. We know how compensations are made after the event, when the same party is to make the estimation and pay the price. No men will agree to what they fear may be their ruin first, and then take their chance for what may be given them afterwards. It would be neither wise nor honourable for Great Britain to desire it. It would not be wise, for the expectation would be disappointed; it would not be honourable, for, instead of an open display of justice and magnanimity, it would exhibit a narrow and equivocating spirit, which no man would honour, and no man ought to trust.

One way there is to get out of this difficulty, and there is but one. It is obvious. Let the *nation at once assume to itself all colonial property, and make moderate but just compensation to the proprietors for the whole.* Let the nation then do, on its own account, what it desired the present proprietors to do. Then, if there be risk, it will be incurred, *as it ought*, by the nation, which demanded the change; if there be loss, it will fall, *as it ought*, on the nation; and, if there be gain, it will be, *as it ought to be*, the gain of those who incurred the risk.

Justice will be done to the Slaves, for they will be placed in a way in which, with the least possible delay, they may arrive at freedom.

Justice will be done to the proprietor, for he will receive, as proprietor, exactly what was due to him, and, *as one of the nation*, he will pay exactly his due proportion of whatever loss may ensue.

Justice will be done to the people of Great Britain, for in no case will they pay more, or receive less, than *exactly what they ought*.

When, in common life, a man, finding himself in a difficult case, of doubtful and seemingly conflicting duties, has had the virtue and courage to turn away from all inferior considerations, and to follow the plain path of strict justice, it will ever be found in the end, that he has taken not only the *honestest* but the *wisest* course, though the consequences, that prove it such, may not always be immediately apparent. In this case they *will* be apparent, for the same measure, which does justice to all parties, will be found not only to remove every one of the obstructions that have been enumerated against improvement, but to facilitate our object in a degree as yet perhaps hardly expected. It will farther be found, that those measures, which in the hands of the Colonists would be inefficient, would, in the hands of government, be efficacious; and that what with the former would be accompanied with great danger, with the latter might be undertaken with perfect security. Finally, it will appear, that what to the individual proprietor would be probable ruin, to the state would bring, instead of loss, certain and considerable gain.

But let us first review the existing obstructions to improvement, in order to see whether they would be really removed.

The first was the danger of the Slaves being led to resist local authority, by the hope of protection from without. This danger would disappear, when they were told, that they were no longer Slaves of any private master, but that they belonged to the King himself; and not only would all thoughts of resistance be at an end, but a very salutary change would be wrought in their own ideas, and their estimation of themselves.

The *second* obstruction arose from the want of means to induce a Negro to work, otherwise than by direct coercion. Such means would now be furnished by the possession of all the soil from which he can derive a subsistence.

The *third* obstruction was the difficulty of obtaining any general concert among the proprietors, as to the modes of improvement that should be adopted. These modes would now be determined on by collective wisdom, and introduced by uniform direction.

The *fourth* obstruction consisted in the want of adequate funds to form the necessary establishments, and the want of power to produce the desirable concentration of the population. The former would now be defrayed by the public, which could not be unwilling to improve *its own* estate, and which, possessing the whole, would naturally draw the population into the more favourable districts, abandoning such as were least profitable.

The *fifth* obstruction arose from the unwillingness, which the present white inhabitants feel to co-operate in that, from which they apprehend their own ruin. Such apprehensions would now be at an end, and, for their own sakes, they would assist in producing an order of things, which must render their future residence both more agreeable and more secure.

OF THE

PRACTICABILITY OF THIS PLAN.

But are we, after all, contemplating a vision? And is not that, which is now proposed, as impracticable as any of those things which we have shown to be so? Does it not contain evils as great as those we would remove, or risks as formidable as those which we have refused to encounter?

These are questions which ought to be fully canvassed, and the answers ought to be satisfactory. No objection should be deprecated, that can be distinctly and specifically stated; but what may be fairly deprecated is this; that, if all such objections shall be satisfactorily answered, the plan may not be rejected, from some *undefined and undefinable notion, that it will not do.*

That most men will at first be startled by the magnitude of the proposal is expected; and some will, on this account alone, be disposed to dismiss the subject without further examination. There is, in some minds, a quality which refuses to contemplate any thing that is extensive, and leads men to regard, as impracticable, that which, if they would summon a little courage and industry to their aid, they would discover to be, not only not impracticable, but not even of difficult execution. If we have hitherto stated facts correctly, and reasoned fairly upon them, it is, perhaps, not asking too much of such persons, when we call on them for a little farther patience and attention.

It may be, that, as we proceed, difficulties, which at a distance appear insurmountable, may vanish as we approach them; and that new, and as yet unperceived facilities may arrive to our aid. The difficulty of a measure is not always commensurate with its extent. It is sometimes easier to do the whole than a part; and generally cheaper to rebuild than repair, when there is an original fault in the construction. We will conclude nothing rashly. But if it has been shown, that the plan proposed affords the best chance of obtaining an object of deep interest; if it shall be shown, that the means of its execution contain nothing of insuperable difficulty, or paramount objection, it is not too much to say, that such plan deserves very serious consideration.

That a measure like this should be free from all difficulties, and exposed to no objection, is not to be expected; all that can justly be expected is; that such difficulties and objections should be less than those which exist in our present state, or which would accompany any other plan to amend it. We hope, however, that something more than this will appear, and that the measure will be found to be practicable with no great difficulty; and, if liable to any objections that cannot wholly be removed, yet that such objections, as compared with the object to be attained, are deserving of very little weight

OF

THE MEANS OF EXECUTION.

We are now to show, first, in what way the present proprietor may be compensated for the property which we call on him to surrender; secondly, how that property can be conveniently taken possession of on behalf of the nation; and, thirdly, how it may be *beneficially* administered in future.

The first process would be simple and easy. A fair estimate would be made of all Colonial property, and a stock to that amount might be created, which would afterwards be apportioned amongst the several proprietors, by separate valuation of their respective properties.

A sufficient number of commissioners might be appointed, who, having first fixed the principles of their valuation, would simultaneously proceed to the Colonies; the average price of a Slave having been fixed already, nothing would remain respecting them, but to observe how much above or below that average each particular lot of Slaves may be. The land, with its appendages, on which the Slave is employed, is currently considered in value as equal to that of the Slaves, and the same observation would take place with regard to that part of the property. Such valuations are very frequent in the West Indies: and, if we may judge by the celerity with which they are made, the whole of this great work might be accomplished in a very short time.

It is next to be shown, how possession could be conveniently taken of this property on behalf of the state: here again there would be no difficulty. A day might be fixed (which ought to be the day on which the crop was concluded), on which each transfer would take place, and a certificate might be delivered to each proprietor for the price that had been fixed upon for his property. Previously to this, a certain number of persons might have been selected in each district for the *immediate* management of property in that district; these would be amenable to a more general authority in each Colony, at the head of which one or more commissioners would for the present remain, and who would correspond with a supreme authority to be created at home. In what shape that authority should be created it may perhaps be deemed here unnecessay to discuss, but we shall suppose it to be formed pretty much on the model of that which governs our Indian empire—a board of direction and a board of control. These would gradually form the most suitable plans of future management; persons duly educated would be sent out for that purpose; and one complaint would be speedily remedied, namely, that the Slaves are now governed too much by inferior persons, who are unfit to be trusted with power.

We are, thirdly, to show, that this administration of the property would be beneficial, or, in other words, that the state need not make a losing bargain.

That all the benefits, which are to flow from this change, would arise immediately, cannot be expected; since many of the alterations from which they are to arise must be gradually introduced. But some of these benefits would be immediate, and sufficiently show, why the same property, which, in the hands of individuals, had been unprofitable, must be highly profitable, when in the hands of one proprietor.

OF THE

INCREASED PECUNIARY PROFITS

THAT WOULD

IMMEDIATELY ARISE.

These will be derived, first, from the price of Colonial produce, which, instead of fluctuating, as it has hitherto done, from extremes that alternately distress the consumer and the proprietor, may henceforth be fixed at a point, equitable and advantageous to both.

Secondly. They would arise by a diminution in the expense at which the market is now supplied.

OF THE PRICE.

That whosoever can regulate the supply can command the price, it must be unnecessary to argue. It would be a monopoly. But let not the odium, which is often attached to that word, be applied here. It is not a monopoly of one person, or a company, imposing an unreasonable price on the people. It is the people's own monopoly, imposing on themselves that fixed price, which they deem just, and which they are willing to pay for the object they desire. Within a few years they have frequently paid 80s., 90s., and even 100s. per cwt. for raw sugar. These prices gave unreasonable gains to the producer; but they distressed the people, and hurt the consumption. At present, the average price is about 60s.; a price, which distresses the producer, and would ultimately ruin the production. It seems, that it would be no bad bargain for the consumer, if the price were fixed at 72s. (which is about 2s. below the average of the last nine years). But if any one should choose to contend, that this would be a tax on the people, be it so. This rise of price from its minimum (which cannot be long maintained) would cost the consumer about $1\frac{1}{4}d.$ per lb.; and, perhaps, with the additional charges of retail, $1\frac{1}{2}d.$

This then would be the total contribution of the people towards the abolition of Slavery. The other objects—their security against a higher price—their security against the loss of the Colonies, with all the important interests dependent on them—nay, the satisfaction of acting equitably to the proprietor shall be thrown in—this $1\frac{1}{2}d.$ per lb. is what they would pay for what they have declared to interest them almost beyond any other object, and would form a sort of gauge by which the world will measure the sincerity of their professions of humanity and justice.

OF EXPENSES, THAT WOULD IMMEDIATELY BE SAVED.

The mercantile expenses, namely, those which arise between the loading of the vessel and the delivery to the first purchaser, and which come under the various heads of freight, insurance, commission, brokerage, &c. &c., amount to about 11s. per cwt. Of these, the freight of 5s. per cwt. could, perhaps, not be lowered (though some advantages would arise to the shipping interest from a greater certainty of freight); but the remaining charges might be done away with altogether.

Insurance, which to the individual proprietors is necessary, would have no object when all the importation belonged to one proprietor. The individual insures lest the loss might happen to fall on him separately; but when the whole is concerned, that loss is already deducted, since the import is taken at the amount of its average *arrival*.

Commission, brokerage, &c. &c., would be reduced to very little; and what remains would be fully balanced by a saving of the expense of collecting the present duties, which would be no longer necessary, since they would afterwards merge in the price.

A calculation of these *immediate* profits by price and saving of expenses will be found in Appendix II*, and amounts to 2,880,000*l.* per annum.

* The more important items in all these calculations rest on data, that are capable of being exactly ascertained; but as we have taken general averages for many points, they will not agree with individual cases. It is believed, that every thing has been rather under than overstated. But the principle being obvious, every one, who may differ from the estimator, will be able to apply his own estimates to the general conclusion.

OF PECUNIARY PROFITS THAT WOULD NOT BE IMMEDIATE.

These would arise from a consolidation of properties now held by different owners. As matters now stand, every proprietor must have his separate establishment of buildings, costing him from 500*l.* to 1000*l.* per annum, in repairs, renovation, and interest on the capital so invested. He must also have his separate establishment of manager, overseer, and subordinate agents. Where the property is small, or ill circumstanced, these two items often sweep away the whole of its produce. Now, by consolidation, one establishment (with perhaps a little addition) would often serve for two, and sometimes for three or four properties. In Appendix III will be found an estimation of the saving which might be made in five years (not counting the first) at the rate of 375,000*l.* per annum, till it amounted to 1,500,000*l.* per annum.

These amounts of immediate and gradual increase, united to the present profits, must be the future income of the Colonies. We have, therefore to consider next, what are the actual returns of colonial property; and in doing which it may not be amiss to consider what they have been hitherto, as well as what they are at present.

OF THE PAST AND PRESENT RETURNS FROM COLONIAL PROPERTY.

The returns from Colonial property have been extremely various. They seem to have been larger about seventy or eighty years ago, than they have ever been since. From that date they fluctuated variously till about the year 1789, when they again became very considerable; but about the beginning of this century they received a severe check by the measure then adopted, of withholding a portion of the drawback on exportation; or, in other words, by charging the Continent with a British duty on Sugar. The experiment was plausible. Great Britain was then severely taxed by continental subsidies, which it was not always easy to remit, and Great Britain at that time possessed almost all the Sugar Colonies in the world. But the scheme could in no case have lasted long. Sugar can be produced in too many parts of the world to be made a subject of monopoly in Europe. The attempt stimulated the Americans to seek sugar in India. It set the Brazils and Cuba to work, and these Colonies, having soon after the Slave Market to themselves, in consequence of our abandoning that trade, obtained

Slaves so cheap, that they were enabled to undersell the British planter in every foreign market. Still the balance of import and domestic consumption might have been gradually restored; but it was determined, at the last peace, to retain the Dutch Colonies in South America, the produce of which has, for the present, entirely destroyed it*.

* Why, at the time when the nation was burning with zeal against Slavery, it was thought fit, as our share of spoil at the last peace, to claim, by preference, *Slave* Colonies, it is not easy to guess; but it is not true (as has been said), that the old Colonies acquiesced. They made the strongest remonstrances against it. They contended, that these Colonies could be of no use to Great Britain (which had already more sugar than she could dispose of), while it would be sacrificing the old Colonies to the interest of speculators, who had no right to plead their investments in these Colonies as a reason for retaining them, since a temporary occupation during war had authorized no conclusion, that they would be retained at the peace. They further argued, that these investments would not be lost, either to the proprietor or the nation, if these Colonies were restored; but that the returns would flow into the mass of private and national profit, just as those, from similar investments in the Danish Colonies are known to do. All was in vain. There existed at that moment an unaccountable desire for Slave Colonies. Demerara and Berbice were retained; and those speculators are now making ten per cent. on their capital, while the old Colonies are ruined. This is owing to the superior fertility of Demerara, which is, however, balanced by its great insalubrity, and the danger, that as soon as the various armies, that have been fighting all round it, shall be withdrawn, the

In the earlier part of this history of the Colonial profits, we have not the means of being very accurate; but for the last thirty-four years we can speak with more precision; and, both from general calculations and reference to a great many actual accounts, it appears, that in this period the profits have been at the rate of about 10*l*. per Slave, or something more than six per cent. on the capital, which agrees with the current estimation of that time, that an estate of one hundred slaves produced 1000*l*. per annum, and so in proportion. At present the profits would hardly be taken at more than 3*l*. 10*s*. by any one, or at less than 2*l*. 10*s*. The medium is probably correct (vide Appendix IV), which would make the present returns of

	£
the Colonies to be	2,400,000
This sum, added to the immediate gain of	2,880,000
Would make the returns for the first year	5,280,000
Which, according to Appendix, would increase every year by 375,000*l*. till it had reached (see Appendix V)	6,780,000

Slaves of Demerara, who are almost within hearing of the revolted Slaves of Surinam, will disappear and join them. Since the publication of the first edition, an insurrection has already taken place in this colony.

Such would be the pecuniary results from this plan, in which we have taken no allowance for many new profits, that might be obtained when the whole were under one direction, but which are not within the reach of individual management.

No one has doubted, that new objects of cultivation might be introduced into the Colonies with success; which would relieve the market from that glut of sugar, which is now exported to great disadvantage, together with its proportionate redundancy of rum. Such experiments have not been, nor probably ever will be, made by individual proprietors. When the prices of the *present* productions are high, the proprietors have no motive for changing them, and when those prices have become low, they have not the means. It is proverbial, that whoever first embarks in a new speculation is likely to be ruined (even though it should turn out profitable afterwards), and therefore no one will begin. Such would not be the case when it were national property. To withdraw a proportion of labour from the production of that sugar, which is now so unprofitably exported, would cost little; and experiments of various kinds might be made throughout all the Colonies at a very trifling expense.

Another great advantage would arise. Those

disasters, which have so often ruined individuals, and even whole colonies, would now lose their terrors. No hurricane has ever affected all the Colonies at once; and therefore the loss, in any particular part, being in future spread over the whole, would be as nothing, since it is the average production which has been taken as the basis of all the calculations.

We must here, also, notice an advantage, that would not exactly be pecuniary, but which would be of no small importance, as a means of checking our rivals in the Slave Trading Colonies; and which would perhaps do more good in this respect than our negociations have done. We have, at present, a surplus of fifty thousand tons for export. This surplus, remaining in the market, is the cause of the present depression. But, if the whole importation belonged to the nation, the surplus would be exported at once*, and, wherever it were directed, would overwhelm every competitor, who would thus find himself much embarrassed in continuing his Slave Trading speculations.

* Here lies exactly the difference. This surplus remaining in the market, the depreciation falls on the whole, but if exported, it would fall only on the fourth part, and thus enable us to undersell the foreign producer.

OF THE AMOUNT OF COLONIAL CAPITAL NOW EXISTING.

This capital consists in Slaves, in land, buildings, stock, &c. The cost of a Slave formerly depended on the price at which he could be imported, with the cost of maintaining him till he became habituated to labour. Since the importation has ceased, it must depend on the cost of rearing him, which, according to Appendix VI, will be found to be about eighty pounds. It has been usual to estimate all other capital equal to the value of the Slaves. The actual cost of this has indeed been much greater. Colonial capital would then be estimated thus:—

	£.
800,000 Slaves, at 80*l*.	64,000,000
Other Capital	64,000,000
	£128,000,000 *

* Vide Appendix VII.

OF THE AMOUNT OF COMPENSATION.

What the amount of compensation for this property ought to be, it is not necessary here to inquire; and as it is not necessary, the task is willingly avoided; since whatever were proposed would probably by some be thought too much, and by others too little. It is the principle, rather than the scale upon which that principle is to be adopted, that we are anxious to establish; and for our purpose it is sufficient to have shown, that the income obtained by the public will be amply sufficient, not only to cover any reasonable claim for compensation, but to defray all establishments for improvement, and to leave a large surplus applicable to any national object. So much, however, may be observed respecting the proper amount of compensation, that on the one hand the proprietor ought not in his estimate to look to profits, such as he has heretofore had; and, on the other, that the public ought not to look to his present moment of depression; first, because it has been caused, not by his own acts, but those of the public; secondly, because there are events, not improbable, that would remove it; and, thirdly, because, as the nation at any rate will gain much by the very thing for which it was willing to pay much, it ought not to seek to make those gains still greater, by unduly depreciating the value of a forced purchase.

OF A NEW ADVANTAGE IN FACILITATING EMANCIPATION.

Having now disposed of the pecuniary gain, and other collateral benefits, that would arise from this plan, we return to the subject with which we began, *emancipation*, and the means of accelerating it.

There yet remains to be stated an advantage, which will be gained for that object — one, that is perhaps more important than any which has been yet considered, and which perhaps alone were sufficient to justify our adoption of the measure proposed.

It is an indisputable fact, that, at the present moment, at least *one-third* of all the labour in our Colonies is absolutely *wasted and thrown away*, by its being unavoidably employed on land unfit for the productions that are cultivated. The individual proprietor has little means of helping this. Both he and his Slave are fixed to the spot, if not by law, at least by the extreme difficulty of removal. Thus, one proprietor employs a numerous body of Slaves on a soil, that makes the poorest return; while another, possessing a fertile tract of land, is obliged to let the greater part lie waste for want of labourers. This evil, which in a country of free labourers cannot exist, may be said almost to predominate in the Colonies; and there are whole islands in this situation. Now this evil would be speedily removed. The individual owner can hardly ever command the capital necessary to purchase and form large establishments elsewhere, and in small bodies the Slaves are most averse to be moved. But when all shall be one property, no capital will be requisite for the purpose, and the Slaves would have no objection to be removed to a better place, when they could be accompanied by all their connections.

Four or five years would be sufficient to place all the Slaves in the places where they might most profitably be employed; and thus we should have at our disposal all the labour, that was wasted before.

Here, then, we have obtained a fund, for as much individual emancipation as we may deem proper, and for as much relaxation of labour as we may think fit to impart. Here we have an engine of such power, as was hardly ever possessed by the rulers of any people; and it is not too much to say, that here we have the means, if we choose so to use them, of accomplishing one-third of the abolition almost immediately.

Let us now recapitulate the positions on which the plan proposed has been founded.

1. The first was, That Slavery must be abolished, at whatever cost.
2. That it cannot be safely or beneficially abolished, till the Slaves shall be brought into a fit state to receive freedom.
3. That this can only be effected by moral improvement.
4. That moral improvement is advancing at a very slow rate.
5. That the Colonial assemblies and proprietors have not the means of materially accelerating this process.
6. That the attempt to force them on measures, to which they are unequal, would, under their present circumstances, produce probable ruin, both to the Colonies and Slaves.
7. That therefore abolition must be deferred to a very remote period, or that some such change must be made in the form and constitution of the Colonies, as would render more practicable the improvement, that must precede abolition.
8. That the obstructions to improvement are, fear of the Slaves — the want of means to induce them to voluntary labour — the impossibility of

producing the necessary concert among the proprietors—the want of adequate means to form the necessary establishments for education and religion—and, finally, the impossibility of obtaining the necessary co-operation of the proprietors and white inhabitants, unless they shall be previously secured against the ruin they apprehend.

9. That all these obstructions would be removed by the measure proposed.

10. That justice, as well as the necessity of the case, demands, that due compensation should be made to the present owners of the Slaves.

11. That there is no mode in which such compensation could be made, without the danger of either wronging the proprietor or the public, unless the public shall assume the whole property, and make compensation for the whole.

12. That this measure would obviate every difficulty, and do complete justice to every party.

13. That there is every reason to believe, that it would be profitable instead of being expensive to the nation; but that, whether profitable or expensive, the profit would accrue, and the expense would fall, where it ought.

14. That there is nothing of paramount difficulty in, or objection to the measure.

15. And that, therefore, unless an equally good, or better measure can be proposed for the purpose, this is a measure, which the legislature owes to the Slaves, to the Colonial Proprietors, and to the People of Great Britain.

CONCLUSION.

Whether the opinions that have thus been submitted to the public be well-founded or no, at least they are not of recent formation; and, if erroneous, they have all the demerit of deliberate error. That the Colonial legislatures and proprietors have *not* the means of accomplishing what is expected of them I have ever contended, both in public and in private; nor has any thing ever induced me to waver in that conviction. It was, undoubtedly, a painful one; for there seemed no chance of bringing about that unity of power and action which were indispensable for success. The plan of vesting the direction of Colonial concerns in the hands of a company, and that which has now been suggested, seemed to afford the only means of effecting it; but, in times of prosperity, no proprietor would have consented to part with the management of his property, or much less to surrender it without such a price as could not have been paid. On the other hand, not till the present moment would the people have endured any thing that *seemed* like taxing them, in order to obtain abolition. Such were the reasons that have hitherto deterred me from venturing on the subject.

But the case is now changed in both respects. On one hand, the Colonial proprietor is so depressed, that he would accept a price to which he would not have listened before; and, on the other hand, the nation, by calling as it has done for abolition, has committed itself to pay its due proportion of the price, should price be necessary.

It has been remarked, that the co-existence of two evils may sometimes furnish the means of removing both: so it is here. Those evils are, the state of Slavery in our Colonies, and their present great depression. The same measure will cure both these evils; but, had they not existed simultaneously, neither could have been cured. But for the present depression, the Colonies would not have consented to this measure; nor would the nation have consented to it, but for the Slavery they wish to abolish. This concurrence of circumstances is so extraordinary, that deep would be, and ought to be, our regret, if, when too late, we should discover, that we had let the opportunity go by, when we could have at once abolished Slavery, and established the future prosperity of our Colonies.

Let those, who are most averse to entertain the project, reflect, that they have not the option to choose between this (or some equivalent) plan, and stopping where they are: the nation will not stop: *Slavery must and will be abolished:* and the question is now only, whether or no some attempt shall be made to prevent that abolition being accompanied by ruin to the Slaves, ruin to the Colonies, and ruin to many of the most important interests of Great Britain.

POSTSCRIPT.

To anticipate the objections that may be made to this plan will perhaps seem premature; yet some having been suggested as probable, it may not be amiss to offer here some reasons that perhaps may remove them.

OBJECTION I.

It will perhaps be said, that to take property from the owner for a public purpose, and to fix its price, not by the intervention of a jury, but by the estimation of those who take it, is vicious in principle, and without precedent.

Now as to precedent, it may be answered, that the *case* is without precedent; and as to principle, except in the order of the thing, it follows the same principle by which, if injury shall have been done to an individual by the public, compensation is fixed by the legislature, and not by a jury. But after all, if both parties are satisfied, who is to complain? The nation must be satisfied, for it is the legislature that will have fixed the compensation; and that the Colonies would be satisfied with any fair compensation, under their present circumstances, there is no reason to doubt.

OBJECTION II.

It will no doubt be said, that individuals always manage their concerns better than the public, and that the less government has to do with the management of property, the better. As a general maxim this is undoubtedly true; yet there are exceptions, when, for the sake of major interests, the state wisely retains in its own hands concerns of a similar nature. Thus it grows its own timber, it builds its own ships, it manufactures its own arms; and thus, if it will introduce free labour into the Colonies, it must, *for a while*, take them into administration.

Besides, there can be no apprehension that it would manage this property in a more disadvantageous way than the proprietors have done, and indeed are obliged to do. The reason why a government generally manages ill is, because it is obliged to trust to agency throughout. But here, the proprietor, resident in Europe (where all reside, that can), trusts to a *double* agency; first that of his merchant here, who never sees the West Indies, and he trusts to an agent there, who never sees him. As for the proprietor, who resides in the West Indies, he manages still worse; for he seldom resides there but from want, and is therefore wholly disabled from conducting his affairs to advantage.

Others may go farther and say, that government could not manage this property at all; but on what grounds exactly such opinion could rest does not appear. That the concern is exceedingly great is true, but surely those, who have found the means of managing our East-Indian Empire, need not despair of being able to govern eight hundred thousand Slaves. There is, doubtless, in this case a difficulty peculiar to it, since we have to bring these Slaves into a new condition of society. But this difficulty could hardly be balanced against the infinitely greater extent, distance, and various complexities of the other case. Let it be also observed, that the difficulty, *here*, will only be temporary; and when the change has been effected, administration may be at an end, and then the estate may be let for payment in produce, by which all the advantages would be retained of commanding the price, without the trouble or expense of agricultural management.

OBJECTION III.

It may also be said, that this plan would throw a dangerous patronage into the hands of government. But the kind of patronage it would give is not of a dangerous description. Direct influence in parliament it need give very little; since all those, who have appointments at home, might be excluded, excepting one or two for the purpose of giving explanations. The probable shape into which the rest would gradually fall would be, that young men would be educated here, in the necessary qualifications; and being sent out, would generally rise by seniority. The patronage, therefore, would chiefly consist in the original appointments, which ought not to be more valuable than is necessary to obtain proper subjects; and against this must be balanced the suppression of all the places now held for the collection of Colonial duties.

APPENDIX.

APPENDIX I.

Calculation of the Expense of a Church Establishment, and Schools for the Negro Slaves.

If we suppose the eight hundred thousand Slaves to be divided, as nearly as possible, into congregations of two thousand each, and that one clergyman could take on him the charge of two adjoining congregations, it would require two hundred clergymen for the whole; and, farther, it would require fifty supernumeraries to assist those who might be disabled by sickness, and supply the vacancies as they occur. It seems almost indispensible that they should be married men, both for the sake of their own domestic society, and for the sake of furnishing examples to the Slaves, of the married state as it ought to be. The buildings in the plantations, which it is proposed to throw up, would conveniently enough supply habitations and churches; and to each should be allotted a few acres of land for private use, but not enough to allow of any speculations of gain. Their stipends should not be such as to tempt worldly avidity, but sufficient to place them beyond the cares of any reasonable want. Above all, they should be freed from any undue solicitude respecting the families they may leave behind them.

	£.
It does not seem, that a married couple could live in decent comfort in those countries under 300*l.* per annum; this, therefore, would require, per annum	75,000
To each congregation should be attached a Negro clerk, a Slave, selected for his good character and Christian conduct; their pay might be 5*l.* per annum each; and, as it should not be taken from them after they were disabled, the amount might be	5,000
Passages out and home, repairs of churches and dwellings, &c. &c. might be	20,000
It would require one Bishop for Jamaica, and two for the other Colonies; these, besides a suitable residence, could not have less than 4,000*l.* each	12,000
Three Deans, or coadjutors, to assist or succeed them, 2000*l.* each	6,000
Passages, &c. &c.	2,000
Total church establishment	£120,000

Taking the number of children to be educated at forty thousand, and dividing them into schools of fifty each, and supposing each teacher to attend four schools, it would require two hundred teachers, and fifty supernumeraries: as these persons ought to be of a description to assist the clergy as catechists and readers, a stipend of less than

	£.
200*l.* per annum would not be more than sufficient to maintain them, and thus we should want	50,000
Incidental charges would amount to, probably	10,000
	60,000
A sufficient fund for the support of all that were disabled in both services, for their widows and children, might require	70,000
Church establishment, as stated before	120,000
Total for church establishment and schools	£250,000

APPENDIX II.

Calculation of the immediate *Profits that would arise (in addition to the present profits), if the whole belonged to one Proprietor.*

	£.
Taking round numbers, we state the consumption of Great Britain and its dependencies to be one hundred and fifty thousand tons of sugar, the increase on which, at 12*s.* per cwt., from 60*s.* to 72*s.*, is 12*l.* per ton	1,800,000
Mercantile expenses saved thereon, at 6*l.* per ton	900,000
Gain on sugar	2,700,000

		£
Gain on sugar (brought forward)		2,700,000
A proportionate rise of one-fifth on rum, from 10*l.* to 12*l.* per puncheon, on 30,000 puncheons, home consumption	£. 60,000	
A proportionate saving of expenses .	30,000	
Gain on rum		90,000
All other articles* being supposed equal to rum, a similar gain on these would be . .		90,000
Total gain.	£	2,880,000

N. B. There would also be a saving on produce exported, a great part of which is subject to all the mercantile expenses that would be no longer necessary; there are not data for ascertaining the exact amount, but it is supposed that it might be little short of 300,000*l.*

---

* Exact data for this item are not to be found, but it is generally supposed, that these articles, as coffee, cotton, &c. &c. are in value equal to rum.

APPENDIX III.

Calculation of additional Profits, that would gradually arise by Consolidation of Properties.

The outgoings on Colonial property, calculated on the Slaves at so much per head, is generally rated at 6*l*., independently of what may be furnished from one property to another, as cattle, &c., and which would not, therefore, come into the general account. It is supposed, that at the least one-third of this would be saved by consolidation.

From the eight hundred thousand slaves, we must here deduct fifty thousand not employed in agriculture, and on whom no saving would be made; but a saving of 2*l*. each on seven hundred and fifty thousand slaves would be £1,500,000

This saving would begin on the second year, and be complete at the end of the fifth year, thus:—

	£.
On the first year	—
On the second	375,000
On the third	750,000
On the fourth	1,125,000
On the fifth	1,500,000

APPENDIX IV.

Estimate of the present Profits of the Slave Colonies, taken from totals.

	£
Two hundred thousand tons of sugar, at 22*l*. net	4,400,000
One hundred thousand puncheons of rum, at 10*l*. net	1,000,000
All other articles taken as equal to rum	1,000,000
Forty thousand Slaves*, not agricultural, as domestic servants, artizans, &c. &c., 20*l*.	800,000
	7,200,000
Deduct 6*l*. per head expenses on eight hundred thousand Slaves	4,800,000
	£ 2,400,000

* In Appendix III, the Slaves, not agricultural, were taken at fifty thousand. They are now reduced to forty thousand, in consequence of a suggestion, that the former might be too large a number; and as there are no *direct* data, on which to calculate, it is preferred to take the lowest estimate. For reasons, however, which will be found in Appendix VIII, it is believed, that in fact the number considerably exceeds even fifty thousand.

APPENDIX V.

Calculation of Future Income.

First year:—
                £
  Present income, as before 2,400,000
  Immediate increase, as per Appendix II 2,880,000
               £ 5,280,000

Second year:—
  Income as last year 5,280,000
  Gradual increase by consolidation, as
    per Appendix III 375,000
               £ 5,655,000

Third year:—
  Income as last year 5,655,000
  Increase as before 375,000
               £ 6,030,000

Fourth year:—
  Income as last year 6,030,000
  Increase as before 375,000
               £ 6,405,000

Fifth year, and subsequent years:—
  Income as last year 6,405,000
  Increase as before 375,000
               £ 6,780,000

Calculation of Future Income, made in another way.

Sugar, home consumption, at 72s. (less duty 27s., and freight at 5s.) = 40s. is 40*l.* per ton, on one hundred and fifty thousand tons .		£ 6,000,000
Fifty thousand tons exported at present, price 22s. net, or 22*l.* per ton		1,100,000
Rum, thirty thousand puncheons, home consumption, at 13*l.*		390,000
Seventy thousand puncheons exported, at 10*l.* . .		700,000
All other articles taken as equal to rum* . . .		1,090,000
Profit on forty thousand Slaves, not employed in agriculture, at 20*l.* each		800,000
		9,980,000
Deduct reduced expenses on seven hundred and sixty thousand Slaves, at 4*l.*	3,040,000	
Expenses on the other forty thousand, at 6*l.*	240,000	3,280,000
		£ 6,700,000

* As there is no general enumeration of the Slaves employed in each separate production, it is difficult to speak with certainty on their separate profits. But it is not necessary for our purpose. *The account we rely on,* for a correct view of the profits, contains but three items. The first is the net sales. Secondly, the profits not arising from sales. And, thirdly, the expenses. All these, taking them in general, may be stated with tolerable accuracy. See Appendix IX with regard to the expenses; the other items have been discussed before.

APPENDIX VI.

The cost of rearing a Slave to the age of fourteen, when first his Labour begins to exceed the cost of his Maintenance, has been calculated thus:—

1. Loss of the mother's labour before and after, allowance being made for the cases in which the child is born dead, or dies immediately £10
2. Medical attendance, &c., with insurance on mother's life, allowance being made as before 5
3. Interest on the above two sums for fourteen years . 15
4. Maintenance of the child (beyond the value of any labour) for fourteen years, at two per cent., with interest 40
5. Insurance on the life of the child to the age of fourteen years 10

£80

APPENDIX VII.

It has been remarked, that, previous to the abolition, the value of a Slave depended on the cost of importing, as it does now on that of breeding him. During the discussions respecting the abolition, there was exaggeration on both sides, on this subject. The abolitionists represented the cost of importing to be so much less than that of breeding, that the planter absolutely discouraged breeding; while those, on the opposite side, represented the cost of breeding to be less than that of importing. The truth was, that the cost of breeding was always greater than that of importing; but the Slaves, bred in the country, were of considerably greater value than the Slaves imported. Nearly the whole of the Slaves may now be considered as bred, and, therefore, will warrant a greater average value than will be found in old valuations. As to all the other property, it is said to be now currently taken as equal to the present estimate of the Slaves. Formerly it was rated higher, and Bryan Edwards puts it at double the former estimation of the Slaves. Thus an estate of one hundred Slaves was, according to him, worth 5000*l.* for the Slaves, and 10,000*l.* for the rest. According to our estimate, the Slaves would be 8000*l.*, and the rest 8000*l.*; making 16,000*l.* instead of 15,000*l.* But the difference, that now almost all would be Creole Slaves, whereas, at the time he wrote, the greater part would be Africans, makes his the higher valuation of the two.

APPENDIX VIII.

By Slaves not agricultural is meant all those, the profit of whose labour is not included in that of the agricultural productions. All servants requisite for those, who are employed in conducting the plantations, and artificers belonging to, and working on those plantations, should *be* counted as agricultural. But all servants or artificers *let out for hire* are not agricultural, as their profits arise from an independent source. Again, artificers *hired* to work for the plantation from without are not agricultural, since their hire is charged in the expenses of the estate.

There are no *direct* data, from which to calculate the number of these non-agricultural Slaves; but it may be estimated in two ways: first, by deducting from the whole number, that number, which we judge to be requisite for producing all the agricultural returns, the remainder being of course the number we seek. Secondly, we may compute, from the best grounds we have, what those other objects must require; and should both these processes lead to nearly the same conclusion, we may infer, that it is tolerably correct.

Now, if we take $6\frac{3}{4}$ cwt. as the average produce of a Slave employed in Sugar alone (and probably no one would put it lower), it will require about six hundred thousand Slaves to produce the whole 4,000,000 cwt., which also tallies exactly with the profits and charges, which we have fixed for Slave labour. The total price of sugar and rum, *viz.* 5,400,000*l.* less 3,600,000*l.* (the expenses on six hundred thousand Slaves, at 6*l.* per head) being 1,800,000*l.*; which is exactly the clear value of the labour of six hundred thousand Slaves. We may, therefore, pretty safely assume this to be the number employed on Sugar. With respect to the number of Slaves employed on other agricultural produce, we cannot go by quantities, since we cannot get exactly at those quantities; but we may see how many Slaves it would require to produce the 1,000,000*l.*, which they are said to amount to; for at 9*l.* each (3*l.* profit, and 6*l.* expenses) about one hundred and eleven thousand Slaves would furnish produce enough to sell for 1,000,000*l.* Thus we have seven hundred and eleven thousand Slaves for agricultural produce, and eighty-nine thousand Slaves for other objects.

This will agree pretty well with the computation, which we should make of the number, that was really requisite for those other objects. And, first, we should estimate the number of artificers, independent of those on the plantations, *thus*:—There are considerably more than one thousand five hundred sugar works in the Colonies, which cannot be estimated at less than 4000*l.* each; and the other agricultural buildings, together with the towns, would certainly make a total of 12,000,000*l.* in value. Now only a small part of these is kept up by the plantation Slaves and Whites (say 2,000,000*l.*), leaving 10,000,000*l.* for the non-agricultural Slaves. Now, if we suppose one twentieth of this to be required annually, in repairs and renovation, we shall want twenty-five thousand Slaves, who, at 20*l.* per annum (the price stated), would perform that work. Next, if we suppose ten thousand resident non-agricultural white inhabitants in the Colonies, and allot to each three domestic servants, we shall want thirty thousand more in this capacity. If to these are added all those, who supply the towns with meat, vegetables, poultry, fish, &c., and all those, who breed horses and cattle for sale, not to the plantations, but to others, with all other kinds of employment, it would perhaps not be too much, were we to insist on the full number produced by the other calculation.

APPENDIX IX.

There is no subject, on which people would answer so variously, as they would, if asked, what is the *expense* of Colonial property, estimating it at so much per Slave. It must naturally include, not only the personal expense of the Slave in food, raiment, medical attendance, &c., but it must include the expense of the tools he works with (as far as they are purchased), the expense of those persons, who superintend him, and the expense in repairs (not done by himself) of buildings, requisite for the manufacture of his produce. It ought not, however, to include what is bought from other agricultural establishments, for the profits of these are not *counted separately*, but thrown into the agricultural produce. In the Leeward Islands, these expenses must be rated high, because there almost every thing must be bought from without; whereas, in Jamaica, almost all the cattle and provisions, together with a considerable portion of the lumber, is supplied within the island; nay, in many cases, even a deduction from those expenses should be made, for articles (such as fat cattle) sold from the estates to the towns. The difficulty, in fixing the right sum, lies in forming a true average on property so variously circumstanced. Bryan Edwards seems to have had too much in view, in this respect, the particular part of the country with which he was connected, and most persons form their opinions in a similar way. But according to the broadest average I have been able to form, from the inspection of as many actual accounts as I have been able to obtain a sight of, and from the best calculation, that, with the assistance of the most experienced persons, I have been able to make, of what they ought to be, it seems to me, that 6*l.* per head is a just allowance.

THE END.

AN APPEAL

No.3.

TO THE

RELIGION, JUSTICE, AND HUMANITY

OF

THE INHABITANTS

OF THE

BRITISH EMPIRE,

IN BEHALF OF THE

NEGRO SLAVES IN THE WEST INDIES.

BY

W^M WILBERFORCE, ESQ., M.P.

Woe unto him that buildeth his house by unrighteousness, and his chambers by wrong; that useth his neighbour's service without wages, and giveth him not for his work.   JEREMIAH.

Do justice, and love mercy.   MICAH.

LONDON:

FOR J. HATCHARD AND SON,
187, PICCADILLY.

1823.

AN

APPEAL,

&c. &c.

———

To all the inhabitants of the British Empire, who value the favour of God, or are alive to the interests or honour of their country — to all who have any respect for justice, or any feelings of humanity, I would solemnly address myself. I call upon them, as they shall hereafter answer, in the great day of account, for the use they shall have made of any power or influence with which Providence may have entrusted them, to employ their best endeavours, by all lawful and constitutional means, to mitigate, and, as soon as it may be safely done, to terminate the Negro Slavery of the British Colonies; a system of the grossest injustice, of the most heathenish irreligion and immorality, of the most unprecedented degradation, and unrelenting cruelty.

At any time, and under any circumstances, from such a heavy load of guilt as this oppression amounts to, it would be our interest no less than our duty to absolve ourselves. But I will not attempt to conceal, that the present embarrassments and distress of our country—a distress, indeed, in which the West Indians themselves have largely participated—powerfully enforce on me the urgency of the obligation under which we lie, to commence, without delay, the preparatory measures for putting an end to a national crime of the deepest moral malignity.

The long continuance of this system, like that of its parent the Slave Trade, can only be accounted for by the generally prevailing ignorance of its real nature, and of its great and numerous evils. Some of the abuses which it involves have, indeed, been drawn into notice. But when the public attention has been attracted to this subject, it has been unadvisedly turned to particular instances of cruelty, rather than to the system in general, and to those essential and incurable vices which will invariably exist wherever the power of man over man is unlimited. Even at this day, few of our countrymen, comparatively speaking, are at all apprised of the real condition of the bulk of the Negro Population; and, perhaps, many of our non-resident West Indian proprietors are full as ignorant of it as other men. Often, indeed, the most humane of the number, (many of them are men whose humanity is unquestionable,) are least of all aware of it, from estimating, not unnaturally, the actual state of the case, by the benevolence of their own well meant, but unavailing directions to their managers in the western hemisphere.

The persuasion, that it is to the public ignorance of the actual evils of West Indian Slavery that we can alone ascribe its having been suffered so long to remain unreformed and almost unnoticed, is strongly confirmed by referring to what passed when the question for abolishing the Slave Trade was seriously debated in 1792. For then, on the general ground merely of the incurable injustice and acknowledged evils of slavery, aggravated, doubtless, by the consideration that it was a slavery forcibly imposed on unoffending men for our advantage, many of the most strenuous and most formidable opponents of the immediate abolition of the Slave Trade charged us with gross inconsistency, in not fairly following up our own arguments, and proposing the gradual extinction also of slavery itself. "If," they argued, "it is contrary, as you maintain, to the soundest principles of justice, no less than to the clearest dictates of humanity, to permit the seizure, and transportation across the Atlantic, of innocent men to labour for our benefit, can it be more just, or less inhuman, to leave the victims of our rapacity to a life of slavery and degradation, as the hopeless lot of themselves and their descendants for ever? If, indeed, it had been true, as was alleged by the African merchants, that the slaves were only the convicts of Africa, condemned after a fair trial, or that they were delivered by the mercy of their British purchasers from becoming the victims of a bloody superstition, or of a relentless despotism, or of cruel intestine wars,—in short, if, as was urged in defence of the traffic, the situation of the slaves in Africa was so bad that it was worth while, even on the plainest principles of humanity, to bring them away, and to place them in a Christian community, though at the price of all the sufferings they must undergo during the process of their deliverance, yet even then our detaining them as *slaves* longer than should be necessary for civilizing them, and enabling them to maintain themselves by their own industry, would be indefensible. But when, as we maintained, all these pleas had been proved to be not merely gross falsehoods, but a cruel mockery of the wretched sufferers, how much more strongly were we bound not to desert them so soon as they should be landed in the West Indies; but to provide as early as possible for their deliverance from a bondage which we ourselves declared to have been originally unjust and cruel. But whatever shadow of a plea might have existed for reducing the imported Africans to slavery, surely none could be urged for retaining, in the same hopeless state, their progeny to the latest generation."

Such was, I repeat it, the reasoning of many of our greatest and ablest opponents, as well as of some of our warmest friends. Such more especially was the argument of our most powerful antagonist in the House of Commons; and, on these grounds, he, thirty years ago, proposed, that in less than eight years, which of course would have expired at the beginning of the present century, not only should the Slave Trade cease, but the extinction of slavery should itself commence. He proposed that from that hour every new-born Negro infant should be free; subject only, when he should attain to puberty, to a species of apprenticeship for a few years, to repay the owner for the expence of maintaining him during the period of infancy and boyhood. Can I here forbear remarking, that if the advocates for immediate abolition could have foreseen that the feelings of the House of Commons, then apparently so warmly excited, and so resolutely fixed on the instant extinction of the Slave Trade, would so soon subside into a long and melancholy apathy; and had they in consequence acceded to these proposals, the slavery of the West Indies would by this time nearly have expired, and we should be now rejoicing in the delightful change which the mass of our Negro Population would have experienced, from a state of ignominious bondage to the condition of a free and happy peasantry.

And by whom was this proposal made? Was it by some hot-headed enthusiast, some speculative votary of the rights of man? No, by the late Lord Melville, then Mr. Dundas, a statesman of many great and rare endowments, of a vigorous intellect, and superior energy of mind; but to whom no one ever imputed an extravagant zeal for speculative rights or modern theories. And let it be taken into account in what character he suggested this measure. In that which seemed to give a pledge not only for its justice but for its expediency;—that of the partizan and acknowledged patron of the West Indian body; and at the very moment when he was most conversant with all their affairs, and naturally most alive to all their interests. If any emotions of surprise, therefore, should be excited by my present appeal, it should be, that it has been so long delayed, rather than that it is now brought forward; that previously to our commencing our endeavours for the mitigation, and ultimate extinction of slavery, we should have suffered twenty-two long years to elapse, beyond that interval for notice and preparation, which even the advocate of the West Indians himself had voluntarily proposed, as what appeared to him to be at once safe and reasonable.

It is due also to the character of the late Mr. Burke to state, that long before the subject of the Slave Trade had engaged the public attention, his large and sagacious mind, though far from being fully informed of the particulars of the West Indian system, had become sensible of its deeply criminal nature. He had even devised a plan for ameliorating, and by degrees putting an end both to the Slave Trade and to the state of slavery itself in the West Indies. He proposed, by education, and above all, by religious instruction, to prepare the poor degraded slaves for the enjoyment of civil rights; taking them, in the mean time, into the guardianship and superintendence of officers to be appointed by the British government. It scarcely needs be remarked, in how great a degree Mr. Burke was an enemy to all speculative theories; and his authority will at least absolve those who now undertake the cause of the Negro Slaves, from the imputation of harshly and unwarrantably disturbing a wholesome and legitimate system of civil subordination.

But if such were the just convictions produced in the mind of Mr. Burke, though very imperfectly acquainted with the vices of the West India system — still more, if it was conceded by many of those who opposed the immediate abolition of the Slave Trade, more especially by that politic statesman, Mr. Dundas, that a state of slavery, considered merely as a violation of the natural rights of human beings, being unjust in its origin, must be unwarrantable in its continuance — what would have been the sentiments and feelings produced in all generous and humane minds by our West Indian slavery, had they known the detail of its great and manifold evils?

The importance of proving, that the alleged decrease of the slaves arose from causes which it was in the master's power easily to remove, led the abolitionists of the Slave Trade, in stating the actual vices of the West Indian system, to dwell much, and too exclusively, perhaps, on the slaves being under-fed and overworked, and on the want of due medical care and medical comforts. These evils, which are indeed very great, must, of course, be aggravated where the planters were in embarrassed circumstances, notoriously the situation of the greater part of the owners of West Indian estates. But, speaking generally, there exists essentially, in the system itself, from various causes, a natural tendency towards the maximum of labour, and the minimum of food and other comforts. That such was the case in general, whatever exceptions there might be in particular instances, was decisively established by the testimony even of West Indian authorities; and it was fatally confirmed by the decrease of the slaves in almost all our settlements. No other satisfactory explanation could be given of this melancholy fact; for it is contrary to universal experience as to the Negro race, not in their own country only, where they are remarkably prolific, but in the case of the domestic slaves, even in our sugar Colonies. The free Negroes and Mulattoes, and also the Maroons*, in the island of Jamaica, the Charaibs† of St. Vincent, and the Negroes of Bencoolen were all known to increase their numbers, though under circumstances far from favourable to population; and, above all, a striking contrast was found in the rapid native in-

* The descendants of the Negro slaves who fled into the woods, when Jamaica was taken by Venables and Vernon, under Oliver Cromwell, and who, about eighty years ago, were settled in separate villages as free Negroes.

† The descendants of the crew of an African ship which was wrecked on the island about a century ago.

crease of the Negro slaves in the United States of America, though situated in a climate far less suited to the Negro constitution than that of the West Indies. There alone, in a climate much the same as that of Africa, it was declared impossible even to keep up their numbers, without continual importations. This fact alone was a strong presumptive proof, and was raised by various concurrent facts and arguments into a positive certainty, that the decrease of the slaves arose in no small degree, not only from an excess of labour, but from the want of a requisite supply of food, and of other necessaries and comforts. The same phenomena, I fear, are still found to exist, and to indicate the continuance of the same causes. For unless I am much misinformed, there is still a progressive decrease by mortality in most of our Colonies; and if in a smaller ratio to their whole population than formerly, it is to be remembered that the enormous loss, in the seasoning of newly imported Africans, now no longer aggravates the sad account.

But though the evils which have been already enumerated are of no small amount, in estimating the physical sufferings of human beings, especially of the lower rank, yet, to a Christian eye, they shrink almost into insignificance when compared with the moral evils that remain behind — with that, above all, which runs through the whole of the various cruel circumstances of the Negro slave's condition, and is at once the effect of his wrongs and sufferings, their bitter aggravation, and the pretext for their continuance,—his extreme degradation in the intellectual and moral scale of being, and in the estimation of his white oppressors.

The proofs of the extreme degradation of the slaves, in the latter sense, are innumerable; and, indeed, it must be confessed, that in the minds of Europeans in general, more especially in vulgar minds, whether vulgar from the want of education, or morally vulgar, (a more inwrought and less curable vulgarity,) the personal peculiarities of the Negro race could scarcely fail, by diminishing sympathy, to produce impressions, not merely of contempt, but even of disgust and aversion. But how strongly are these impressions sure to be confirmed and augmented, when to all the effects of bodily distinctions are superadded all those arising from the want of civilization and knowledge, and still more, all the hateful vices that slavery never fails to engender or to aggravate. Such, in truth, must naturally be the effect of these powerful causes, that even the most ingeniously constructed system which humanity and policy combined could have devised, would in vain have endeavoured to counteract them : how much more powerfully then must they operate, especially in low and uneducated minds, when the whole system abounds with institutions and practices which tend to confirm and strengthen their efficiency, and to give to a contemptuous aversion for the Negro race, the sanction of manners and of law.

It were well if the consequences of these impressions were only to be discovered among the inferior ranks of the privileged class, or only to be found in the opinions and conduct of individuals. But in the earlier laws of our colonies they are expressed in the language of insult, and in characters of blood. And too many of these laws still remain unrepealed, to permit the belief that the same odious spirit of legislation no longer exists, or to relieve the injured objects of them from their degrading influence. The slaves were systematically depressed below the level of human beings.* And though I confess, that it is of less concern to a slave under what laws he lives than what is the character of his master, yet if the laws had extended to them favour and protection instead of degradation, this would have tended to raise them in the social scale, and operating insensibly on the public

* An act of Barbadoes, (8th Aug. 1688,) prescribing the mode of trial for slaves, recites, that "they being brutish slaves, deserve not, for the baseness of their condition, to be tried by the legal trial of twelve men of their peers, &c." Another clause of the same act, speaks of the "barbarous, wild, and savage natures of the same Negroes and other slaves," being such as renders them wholly unqualified to be governed by the laws, practices, and customs of other nations." Other instances of a like spirit might be cited in the acts of other colonies.

mind, might, by degrees, have softened the extreme rigour of their bondage. Such, however, had been the contrary effects of an opposite process, on the estimation of the Negro race, before the ever-to-be-honored Granville Sharpe, and his followers, had begun to vindicate their claim to the character and privileges of human nature, that a writer of the highest authority on all West India subjects, Mr. Long, in his celebrated History of Jamaica, though pointing out some of the particulars of their ill treatment, scrupled not to state it as his opinion, that in the gradations of being, Negroes were little elevated above the oran outang, " that type of man." Nor was this an unguarded or a hastily thrown out assertion. He institutes a laborious comparison of the Negro race with that species of baboon; and declares, that "ludicrous as the opinion may seem, he does not think that an oran outang husband would be any dishonor to a Hottentot female." When we find such sentiments as these to have been unblushingly avowed by an author of the highest estimation among the West India colonists, we are prepared for what we find to have been, and, I grieve to say, still continues to be, the practical effects of these opinions.

The first particular of subsisting legal oppression that I shall notice, and which is at once a decisive proof of the degradation of the Negro race, in the eyes of the whites, and a powerful cause of its continuance, is of a deeply rooted character, and often productive of the most cruel effects. In the contemplation of law they are not persons, but mere chattels; and as such are liable to be seized and sold by creditors and by executors, in payment of their owner's debts; and this separately from the estates on which they are settled. By the operation of this system, the most meritorious slave who may have accumulated a little peculium, and may be living with his family in some tolerable comfort, who by long and faithful services may have endeared himself to his proprietor or manager,— who, in short, is in circumstances that mitigate greatly the evils of his condition—is liable at once to be torn for ever from his home, his family, and his friends, and to be sent to serve a new master, perhaps in another island, for the rest of his life.

Another particular of their degradation by law, which, in its effects, most perniciously affects their whole civil condition, and of which their inadequate legal protection is a sure and necessary consequence, is their evidence being inadmissible against any free person. The effect of this cannot be stated more clearly or compendiously than in the memorable evidence of a gentleman eminently distinguished for the candour with which he gave to the Slave Trade Committee the result of his long personal experience in the West Indies,—the late Mr. Otley, Chief-justice of St. Vincent's,—himself a planter:—" As the evidence of slaves is never admitted against white men, the difficulty of legally establishing the facts is so great, that white men are in a manner put beyond the reach of the law." It is due also to the late Sir William Young, long one of the most active opponents of the abolition, to state, that he likewise, when Governor of Tobago, acknowledged, as a radical defect in the administration of justice, that the law of evidence " covered the most guilty European with impunity."

The same concession was made by both houses of the legislature of Grenada, in the earliest inquiries of the Privy Council. The only difficulty, as they stated, that had been found in putting an effectual stop to gross and wanton cruelty towards slaves, was that of bringing home the proof of the fact against the delinquent by satisfactory evidence; those who were capable of the guilt, being in general artful enough to prevent any but slaves being witnesses of the fact. " As the matter stands," they add, " though we hope the instances in this island are at this day not frequent, yet it must be admitted with regret, that the persons prosecuted, and who certainly were guilty, have escaped for want of legal proof."

It is obvious that the same cause must produce the same effect in all our other slave colonies, although there has not been found the same candour in confessing it.

The next evil which I shall specify, for which the extreme degradation of these poor beings, in the eyes of their masters, can alone account, is the driving system. Not being supposed capable of being governed like other human beings, by the hope of reward, or the fear of punishment, they are subjected to the immediate impulse or present terror of the whip, and are driven at their work like brute animals. Lower than this it is scarely possible for man to be depressed by man. If such treatment does not find him vile and despised, it must infallibly make him so. Let it not however be supposed, that the only evil of this truly odious system is its outraging the moral character of the human species, or its farther degrading the slaves in the eyes of all who are in authority over them, and thereby extinguishing that sympathy which would be their best protection. The whip is itself a dreadful instrument of punishment; and the mode of inflicting that punishment shockingly indecent and degrading. The drivers themselves, commonly, or rather always slaves, are usually the strongest and stoutest of the Negroes; and though they are forbidden to give more than a few lashes at a time, as the immediate chastisement of faults committed at their work, yet the power over the slaves which they thus possess unavoidably invests them with a truly formidable tyranny, the consequences of which, to the unfortunate subjects of it, are often in the highest degree oppressive and pernicious. No one who reflects on the subject can be at a loss to anticipate one odious use which is too commonly made of this despotism, in extorting, from the fears of the young females who are subject to it, compliances with the licentious desires of the drivers, which they might otherwise have refused from attachment to another, if not from moral feelings and restraints. It is idle and insulting to talk of improving the condition of these poor beings, as rational and moral agents, while they are treated in a manner which precludes self-government, and annihilates all human motives but such as we impose on a maniac, or on a hardened and incorrigible convict.

Another abuse which shews, like the rest, the extreme degradation of the Negro race, and the apathy which it creates in their masters, is the cruel, and, at least in the case of the female sex, highly indecent punishments inflicted in public, and in the face of day, often in the presence of the gang, or of the whole assembled population of an estate. From their low and ignominious condition it doubtless proceeds, that they are in some degree regarded as below the necessity of observing towards others the proper decencies of life, or of having those decencies observed by others towards them.

It is no doubt also chiefly owing to their not being yet raised out of that extreme depth in which they are sunk, so much below the level of the human species, that no attempts have been made to introduce among them the

Christian institution of marriage, that blessed union which the Almighty himself established as a fundamental law, at the creation of man, to be as it were the well-spring of all the charities of life — the source of all domestic comfort and social improvement, — the moral cement of civilized society.

In truth, so far have the masters been from attempting to establish marriage generally among their slaves, that even the idea of its introduction among them never seems to have seriously suggested itself to their minds. In the commencement of the long contest concerning the abolition of the Slave Trade, it was one of a number of questions respecting the treatment of slaves in the West Indies put by the Privy Council, — " What is the practice respecting the marriage of Negro Slaves, and what are the regulations concerning it?" In all instances, and from every colony, the answers returned were such as these: "They do not marry." "They cohabit by mutual consent," &c. " If by marriage is meant a regular contract and union of one man with one woman, enforced by positive institutions, no such practice exists among the slaves, and they are left entirely free in this respect, &c."

Let me not be supposed ignorant of some acts of the West Indian Legislatures, the perusal of which might produce an opposite impression on the uninformed and credulous as they gravely require all owners, managers, &c. of slaves, under a penalty, to *exhort* their slaves to receive the ceremony of marriage as instituted under the forms of the Christian Religion: they even profess " *to protect the domestic and connubial happiness of slaves.*" But in direct contradiction to the impression that would naturally be produced by these laws, the Privy Council, but a year after their enactment, was informed, in express terms, that in the very island in which these laws had been passed, there was no such thing as marriage, except that sometimes it existed among the Roman Catholic slaves. This neglect of marriage is the more extraordinary, because the owners of slaves are powerfully called upon by self-interest, no less than by religion and humanity, to make the attempt to promote it. With one concurrent voice they have spoken of the licentiousness of the slaves, and of the numerous bad consequences which follow from the promiscuous intercourse so generally prevalent between the sexes. To this cause, indeed, they chiefly ascribed that inability to keep up the numbers of their slaves which they credibly professed to lament most deeply. How strange, then, that the very institution with which the Almighty associated the primeval command, " Increase and multiply," seems not even to have presented itself to their minds. I have scarcely found a solitary instance in which the want of marriage is regretted, or specified as in any degree instrumental in preventing the natural increase of slaves, which was desired so earnestly. I recollect not a word having been seriously stated on the subject, until long after the charge of neglecting the marriage institution had been strongly urged against the slave owners by the abolitionists. Then, indeed, it was stated in the meliorating act of the Leeward Islands of 1798, that it was unnecessary, and even improper, to enforce the celebration of any religious rites among the slaves, in order to sanctify contracts, the faithful performance of which could be looked for only by a regular improvement in religion, morality, and civilization. To those who know any thing of the public mind in our West Indian colonies, this passage speaks very intelligible language. It plainly intimates the very position I have been laying down, that the slaves are considered as too degraded to be proper subjects for the marriage institution. A striking corroboration of this position was afforded but a few years ago, when a very worthy clergyman, in one of our Leeward Islands, having obtained the master's leave, proposed to solemnize the marriage of a slave according to the forms of the Church of England. The publication of the banns produced an universal ferment in the colony: the case was immediately referred to the highest legal authorities upon the spot; nor was the question, as a point of law, settled, until it had been referred to his Majesty's legal advisers in this country.

I have dwelt the longer, and insisted the more strongly on the universal want of the marriage institution among the slaves, because, among the multiplied abuses of the West Indian system, it appears to me to be one of the most influential in its immoral and degrading effects. It should, however, be remarked, that though the prevalence of promiscuous intercourse between the male and female slaves is nearly universal, yet mutual and exclusive, though rarely permanent attachments between two individuals of different sexes frequently take place; and as the Africans notoriously have warm affections, the regard is often very strong, so long as it continues. On the mother's side also the instincts of nature are too sure not to produce great affection for her children, some degree of which also will often be found in the father. But how far are these precarious connections from producing that growing attachment, that mutual confidence, which spring from an identity of interest, from the common feeling for a common progeny, with all the multiplied emotions of hope and even of fear, of joys and even of sorrows, which bind families together, when mutually attached to each other by the indissoluble bonds of a Christian union? Alas! the injustice with which these poor creatures are treated accompanies them throughout the whole of their progress; and even the cordial drops which a gracious Providence has elsewhere poured into the cup of poverty and labour, are to them vitiated and embittered.

It must also be observed, that licentiousness thus produced is not confined to the Negroes. The fact is perfectly notorious, that it has been the general policy to employ instead of married managers and overseers, single young men as the immediate superintendents of the gangs; and hence it too naturally follows, that they who, from their being the depositories of the master's authority, ought to be the protectors of the purity of the young females, too often become their corrupters.

It is a farther important truth, pregnant with the most serious consequences, that the extreme degradation which is supposed to render the slaves unfit to form the marriage contract, belongs not merely to their situation as slaves, but to their colour as Negroes. Hence it adheres not only to those who are for ever released from slavery, but to those also who, by having one European parent, might be presumed to be raised highly above the level of the servile race. Such is the incurable infamy inherent in what still belongs to them of African origin, that they are at an almost immeasurable distance in the scale of being below the lowest of the whites.* The free women of colour deem an

---

* The extreme degradation of the coloured race, as it affects their marriage relations, is strikingly illustrated by a passage in one of the many pamphlets published

illicit connection with a white man more respectable than a legal union with a coloured husband; while the Mulatto males, as Mr. B. Edwards de-

---

against the Registry Bill, in 1816, by a gentleman some time resident in Barbadoes. He speaks with real humanity of the free coloured people, and strongly recommends their being invested with civil and political rights. Such is the uncommon enlargement of his mind, that he even suggests a plan, through the medium of a moral union of the sexes among the coloured people in the colonies, for the gradual emancipation of the slaves; yet he very strongly deprecates any attempt to introduce any such connection between them and the white inhabitants: and he owns that the West Indian prejudice is sufficiently implanted in his own mind, to render such a connection not only repugnant to his feelings, but " contrary to his idea of morals, religion, and polity." Observe here, that this West Indian prejudice is only against a *moral* union and connection, for he actually informs us that the *immoral* connection with this degraded class of the female population is almost universal, prevailing, with scarcely an exception, among the married no less than the unmarried men. He states, and it is abundantly confirmed by Mr. Edwards, that prostitution is unhappily now the only portion of the coloured women; and that the white men who form connections with them, purchase them of their owners, and in many instances of their own parents. But against the *moral* union he declares that he would guard, by advising that the laws should be made to attach the *heaviest pains and penalties of a felonious act* upon the parties so intermarrying. The opinion of a single individual, however respectable, would scarcely have sufficient weight to entitle it to so much notice in any general argument concerning the treatment of the Negroes; but it becomes of real importance, when, as in this instance, an advocate for the West Indian cause bears his testimony to the generally prevailing sentiments and practices in one of the largest and most ancient of our West Indian colonies.

clares with great feeling, are unhappily in too low a state of degradation to think of matrimony. Well may he then remark, that their spirits seem to sink under the consciousness of their condition.* Thus a fatal looseness of principle and practice diffuses itself throughout the whole community. A licentious intercourse between the white men and the coloured females was confessed by Mr. Long to be general in his day; and Mr. B. Edwards, whose History was published so recently as 1793, while he expresses himself with great pity for the wretched victims of this dissoluteness, acknowledges that the general morals were then little, if at all improved, in this particular.

Nor let this be deemed a consideration of subordinate importance. A most sagacious observer of human nature, the late Dr. Paley, states, " It is a fact, however it be accounted for," that " the criminal commerce of the sexes corrupts and depraves the mind and moral character more than any single species of vice whatsoever." " These indulgences," he adds, " in low life, are usually the first stage in mens' progress to the most desperate villanies; and in high life, to that lamented dissoluteness of principle which manifests itself in a profligacy of public con-

* Can I forbear adding, that Mr. Edwards states, that to the Negroes, these poor degraded Mulattoes are objects of envy and hatred, for the supposed superiority of their condition? How low then must the former be sunk in the scale of being!

duct, and a contempt of the obligations of religion and moral probity." This cannot be surprising to any considerate mind. The Supreme Ordainer of all things, in his moral administration of the universe, usually renders crime, in the way of natural consequences, productive of punishment; and it surely was to be expected that he would manifest, by some strong judicial sanction, his condemnation of practices which are at war with the marriage institution, — the great expedient for maintaining the moral order and social happiness of mankind.

In my estimate of things, however, and I trust in that of the bulk of my countrymen, though many of the physical evils of our colonial slavery are cruel, and odious, and pernicious, the almost universal destitution of religious and moral instruction among the slaves is the most serious of all the vices of the West Indian system; and had there been no other, this alone would have most powerfully enforced on my conscience the obligation of publicly declaring my decided conviction, that it is the duty of the legislature of this country to interpose for the mitigation and future termination of a state in which the ruin of the moral man, if I may so express myself, has been one of the sad consequences of his bondage.

It cannot be denied, I repeat, that the slaves, more especially the great body of the field Negroes, are practically strangers to the multiplied blessings of the Christian Revelation.

What a consideration is this! A nation, which besides the invaluable benefit of an unequalled degree of true civil liberty, has been favoured with an unprecedented measure of religious light, with its long train of attendant blessings, has been for two centuries detaining in a state of slavery, beyond example rigorous, and in some particulars worse than pagan darkness and depravity, hundreds of thousands of their fellow creatures, originally torn from their native land by fraud and violence. Generation after generation have thus been pining away; and in this same condition of ignorance and degradation they still, for the most part, remain. This I am well aware is an awful charge; but it undeniably is too well founded, and scarcely admits of any exception beyond what has been effected by those excellent, though too commonly traduced and persecuted men, the Christian missionaries. They have done all that it has been possible for them to do; and through the divine blessing they have indeed done much, especially in the towns, and among the household slaves, considering the many and great obstacles with which they have had to contend.

I must not be supposed ignorant that of late years various colonial laws have been passed, professedly with a view to the promoting of religion among the slaves: but they are all, I fear, worse than nullities. In truth, the solicitude which they express for the personal protection, and still more for the moral interests, of the slaves, contrasted with the apparent forgetfulness of those interests which so generally follows in the same community, might have appeared inexplicable, but for the frank declaration of the Governor of one of the West Indian islands, which stood among the foremost in passing one of these boasted laws for ameliorating the condition of the slaves. That law contained clauses which, with all due solemnity, and with penalties for the non-observance of its injunctions, prescribed the religious instruction of the slaves; and the promoting of the marriage institution among them; and in order "to secure as far as possible the good treatment of the slaves, and to ascertain the cause of their decrease, if any," it required certificates of the slaves' increase and decrease to be annually delivered on oath, under a penalty of 50$l.$ currency. His Majesty's government, some time after, very meritoriously wishing for information as to the state of the slaves, applied to the governor for some of the intelligence which this act was to provide. To this application the Governor, the late Sir George Prevost, replied as follows: "The act of the legislature, entitled 'An act for the encouragement, protection, and better government of slaves,' appears to have been considered, from the day it was passed until this hour, as a political measure to avert the interference of the mother country in the management of slaves." The same account of the motives by which the legislatures of other West Indian islands were induced to pass acts for ameliorating the condition of the slaves, was given by several of the witnesses who were examined in the committee of the House of Commons in 1790 and 1791.

In all that I state concerning the religious interests of the slaves, as well as in every other instance, I must be understood to speak only of the *general* practice. There are, I know, resident in this country, individual owners of slaves, and some, as I believe, even in the colonies, who have been sincerely desirous that their slaves should enjoy the blessings of Christianity: though often, I lament to say, where they have desired it, their pious endeavours have been of little or no avail. So hard is it, especially for absent proprietors, to stem the tide of popular feeling and practice, which sets strongly in every colony against the religious instruction of slaves. So hard also, I must add, is it to reconcile the necessary means of such instruction with the harsh duties and harsher discipline to which these poor beings are subjected. The gift even of the rest of the Sabbath is more than the established œconomics of a sugar plantation permit even the most independent planter to confer, while the law tacitly sanctions its being wholly withheld from them.

Generally speaking, throughout the whole of our West Indian islands, the field slaves, or common labourers, instead of being encouraged or even permitted to devote the Sunday to religious purposes, are employed either in working their provision-grounds for their own and their families' subsistence, or are attending, often carrying heavy loads to, the Sunday markets, which frequently, in Jamaica, are from ten to fifteen miles distant from their abodes.

These abuses confessedly continue to prevail in despite of the urgent remonstrances, for more than the last half century, of members of the colonial body, and these sometimes, like Mr. B. Edwards, the most accredited advocates for the interests and character of the West Indians.

The insensibility of the planters, even to the temporal good effects of Christianity on their slaves, is the more surprising, because, besides their having been powerfully enforced by self-interest, as I have already stated, in restraining a licentious intercourse between the sexes, they were strongly recommended, especially in the great island of Jamaica, by another consideration of a very peculiar nature. The Jamaica planters long imputed the most injurious effects on the health and even the lives of their slaves, to the African practice of Obeah, or witchcraft. The agents for Jamaica declared to the privy council, in 1788, that they "ascribed a very considerable portion of the annual mortality among the Negroes in that island to that fascinating mischief." I know that of late, ashamed of being supposed to have punished witchcraft with such severity, it has been alleged, that the professors of Obeah used to prepare and administer poison to the subjects of their spells: but any one who will only examine the laws of Jamaica against these practices, or read the evidence of the agents, will see plainly that this was not the view that was taken of the proceedings of the Obeah-men, but that they were considered as impostors, who preyed on their ignorant countrymen by a pretended intercourse with evil spirits, or by some other pretences to supernatural powers. The idea of rooting out any form of pagan superstition by severity of punishment, especially in wholly uninstructed minds, like that of extirpating Christianity by the fire and the faggot, has long been exploded among the well-informed; and it has even been established, that the devilish engine of persecution recoils back on its employers, and disseminates the very principles it would suppress. Surely then it might have been expected, that, if from no other motive, yet that for the purpose of rooting a pagan superstition out of the minds of the slaves, the aid of Christianity would have been called in, as the safest species of knowledge? and it was strange if the Jamaica gentlemen were ignorant of the indubitable fact, that Christianity never failed to chase away these vain terrors of darkness and paganism. No sooner did a Negro become a Christian, than the Obeah-man despaired of bringing him into subjection. And it is well worthy of remark, that when in the outset of our abolition proceedings, His Majesty's Privy Council, among a number of queries sent out to the different West India islands, concerning the condition of the slaves, had proposed several concerning the nature and effects of this African superstition, of which the Privy Council had heard so much from the agents for Jamaica, the Council and Assembly of the Island of Antigua, in which, through the successful labours of the Moravian and Methodist missionaries, great numbers of the slaves had become Christians, resented, as an imputation on their understandings, the very idea of their being supposed to have considered the practices of the Obeah-men as deserving of any serious attention. Surely then we might have expected that regard for the temporal well-being of the slaves, if not for their highest interests, would have prompted their owners to endeavour to bring them out of their present state of religious darkness into the blessed light of Christianity? But even self-interest itself appears to lose its influence, when it is to be promoted by means of introducing Christianity among the slaves.

If any thing were wanting to add the last finishing tint to the dark colouring of this gloomy picture, it would be afforded by a consideration which still remains behind. However humiliating the statement must be to that legislature which exercises its superintendency over every part of the British Empire; it is nevertheless true, that, low in point of morals as the Africans may have been in their own country, their descendants, who have never seen the continent of Africa, but who are sprung from those who for several successive generations have been resident in the Christian colonies of Great Britain, are still lower. Nay, they are universally represented as remarkable in those colonies for vices which are directly opposite to the character which has been given of the Africans by several of the most intelligent travellers who have visited the interior of their native country. In proof of this assertion, I refer not to any delineations of the African character by what might be supposed to be partial hands. Let any one peruse the writings of authors who opposed the abolition of the Slave Trade, more especially the Travels of Mr. Parke and M. Golberry, both published since the commencement of the Slave Trade contest. It is not unworthy of remark, that many of the Africans in their own country are raised, by not being altogether illiterate, far above the low level to which the entire want of all education depresses the field slaves in the West Indies. It is stated by Mr. Parke, who took his passage from Africa to the West Indies in a slave-ship, that of one hundred and thirty slaves which the vessel conveyed, about twenty-five of them, who, as he supposes, had been of free condition, could most of them write a little Arabic. The want, however, of this measure of literature is of small account: but compare the moral nature of the Africans, while yet living in their native land, and in all the darkness and abominations of paganism, with the character universally given of the same Africans in our West Indian colonies. He will find that the Negroes, who while yet in Africa were represented to be industrious, generous, eminent for truth, seldom chargeable with licentiousness, distinguished for their domestic affections, and capable at times of acts of heroic magnanimity, are described as being in the West Indies the very opposite in all particulars; selfish, indolent, deceitful, ungrateful, — and above all, in whatever respects the intercourse between the sexes, incurably licentious.

And now, without a farther or more particular delineation of the slavery of the British colonies, what a system do we behold!! Is it too much to affirm, that there never was, certainly never before in a Christian country, a mass of such aggravated enormities?

That such a system should so long have been suffered to exist in any part of the British Empire will appear, to our posterity, almost incredible. It had, indeed, been less surprising, if its seat had been in regions, like those of Hindostan, for instance, where a vast population had come into our hands in all the full-blown enormity of heathen institutions; where the bloody superstitions, and the unnatural cruelties and immoralities of paganism, had established themselves in entire authority, and had produced their natural effects in the depravity and moral degradation of the species; though even in such a case as that, our excuse would hold good no longer than for the period which might be necessary for reforming the native abuses by those mild and reasonable means which alone are acknowledged to be just in principle, or practically effectual to their purpose. But that in communities formed from their very origin by a Christian people, and in colonies containing no Pagan inhabitants but those whom we ourselves have compulsorily brought into it,— inhabitants too, who, from all the circumstances of their case, had the strongest possible claims on us, both for the reparation of their wrongs, and the relief of their miseries,— such a system should have been continued for two centuries, and by a people who may, nevertheless, I trust, be affirmed to be the most moral and humane of nations, is one of those anomalies which, if it does not stagger the belief, will, at least, excite the astonishment of future ages.

But it may naturally and perhaps not unfairly be asked of the abolitionists — You professed to be well acquainted with the state of things in the West Indies when you moved for the abolition of the Slave Trade — if you then thought the system to be at all such as you now state it to be, how could you rest contented with restricting your efforts to the abolition of the traffic in slaves, contrary, as you confess, to the wishes and even the endeavours of many friends of your great cause, and of some even of its enemies?

It is true, that the evils of the West Indian

system had not passed unnoticed; and we would gladly have brought forward a plan for ameliorating the condition of the Negroes, but that the effort was beyond our strength. We found the adversaries of the abolition far too numerous and too powerful for us, and we were perfectly sure that we should greatly add to their number and vehemence by striking also at the system of slavery. But farther I will frankly confess, that we greatly deceived ourselves by expecting much more benefit to the plantation Negroes from the abolition of the Slave Trade than has actually resulted from that measure. We always relied much on its efficiency in preparing the way for a general emancipation of the slaves: for let it be remembered, that, from the very first, Mr. Pitt, Mr. Fox, Lord Grenville, Lord Lansdowne, Lord Grey, and all the rest of the earliest abolitionists, declared that the extinction of slavery was our great and ultimate object; and we trusted, that by compelling the planters to depend wholly on native increase for the supply of their gangs, they would be forced to improve the condition of their slaves, to increase their food, to lessen their labour, to introduce task-work, to abolish the driving system, together with degrading and indecent punishments, to attach the slaves to the soil, and, with proper qualifications, to admit their testimony as witnesses — a necessary step to all protection by law; above all, to attend to their religious and moral improvement, and to one of the grand peculiarities of Christianity, the marriage institution. By the salutary operation of these various improvements, the slaves would have become qualified for the enjoyment of liberty; and preparation would have been made for that happy day, when the yoke should be taken off for ever, when the blessed transmutation should take place of a degraded slave population into a free and industrious peasantry.*

* It is the more necessary to state that the views of the abolitionists were always directed towards the extinction of slavery, after preparing the black population for the enjoyment of it; because, from some statements which were made in the Register-bill controversy, we may expect that our opponents will renew the charge they then brought against us, that we had originally disclaimed all views of emancipating the slaves actually in the islands, confining ourselves exclusively to the prohibition of all future importations of Negroes. Our explanation is clear and short. Our opponents imputed to us that our real intention was, *immediately*, to emancipate the slave population of the Colonies: they were aware that there were many who felt themselves bound by the most urgent principles of justice and humanity at once to put an end to a system of crimes, which was so falsely called a trade in Negroes, who yet would oppose all endeavours to emancipate the slaves without those previous and preparatory measures that would be requisite for enabling them to render the acquisition of liberty either safe for their owners or beneficial to themselves. We, in consequence, declared, that although we certainly did look forward ultimately to the emancipation of the slaves, yet that the object we were then pursuing was only the abolition of the Slave Trade, of which it was one grand recommendation, that by stopping the further influx of uncivilised Africans, and by rendering the planters sensible that they must in future depend on the native increase for

We were too sanguine in our hopes as to the effects of the abolition in our colonies; we judged too favourably of human nature; we thought too well of the colonial assemblies; we did not allow weight enough to the effects of rooted prejudice and inveterate habits — to absenteeship, a vice which, taken in its whole extent, is perhaps one of the most injurious of the whole system; to the distressed finances of the planters; and, above all, to the effects of the extreme degradation of the Negro slaves, and to the long and entire neglect of Christianity among them, with all its attendant blessings.

True it is, that from the want of effectual Register acts, the experiment has not been fairly tried; as the abolition is in consequence known to be a law that may easily be evaded. For,

---

keeping up their slave population, it would tend powerfully to prepare the way for the great and happy change of slave into free labourers. Our adversaries, however, continuing artfully to confound abolition and emancipation, our efforts were often employed in distinguishing between the two, and in distinctly and fully explaining our real meaning; nor am I conscious of any occasion, on which we disclaimed the intention of emancipation, without accompanying the disclaimer with the clear explanation that it was immediate, not ultimate emancipation, which we disclaimed. Not to mention declarations without number of our real meaning, various illustrations might be referred to of the chief speakers in those debates, which would prove that the emancipation of the slaves was the ultimate, though not the immediate object, of all those who took the lead as advocates for the abolition of the Slave Trade.

let it be ever borne in mind, that the ground of our persuasion was, that the absolute prohibition of all future importation of slaves into the colonies, provided means were adopted for insuring its permanent execution, would exercise a sort of moral compulsion over the minds of the planters, and even of their managers and overseers, and induce them, for the necessary end of maintaining the black population, to adopt effectual measures for reforming the principal abuses of the system : but it is manifest, that such compulsion could not arise from a law which they had power to elude at pleasure. I am willing, however, for my own part, to admit that this foundation-stone of our hopes may have rested on sandy ground; for what has since passed has proved to me how little prudence and foresight can effect in opposition to the stubborn prejudices, and strong passions, and inveterate habits that prevail in our West Indian assemblies. With one single exception in favour of the free coloured people in Jamaica, the admission of their evidence, which, however, only placed them in the situation which they had always before occupied in most of our other islands, I know not any vice of the system that has been rooted out, any material improvement that has been adopted. Not only the abuses which had been pointed out by the abolitionists are still existing in all their original force, but some of those reforms which had been urged on the colonial legislatures by their warmest friends, and most approved advocates, remain to this hour unadopted in every island. Mr. B. Edwards, for instance, near thirty years ago, in his History of the West Indies, recommended the introduction, wherever practicable, of the system of task-work, accompanied of course with a law for securing to the slave his little peculium. He recommended also, though with less confidence, a plan for instituting among the slaves a sort of juries for the trial of petty offences — a measure which, he added, he had heard had been tried successfully in two instances in Jamaica, and which a humane proprietor of Barbadoes, the late Mr. Steele, introduced, and for many years maintained with great advantage on his own estate. Another measure, which, as he truly stated, was of less doubtful efficacy, was strongly enforced by him; namely, the duty of rendering the Sabbath a day of rest and religious improvement, by suppressing the Sunday markets, which he justly declared to be a disgrace to a Christian country. But above all the rest, he pressed the reform of what he represented the greatest of all the Negro's grievances, and which he afterwards brought to the notice of the British Parliament. This was the liability of the slaves to be sold by creditors, under executions for the payment of debts. This grievance he alleged to be upheld and confirmed, though not originally created, by a British Act of Parliament, 5 Geo. 2. cap. 7., which, he contended, it was necessary to repeal, in order to enable the colonial legislatures to do away with the practice altogether. He declared it to be a grievance, remorseless and tyrannical in its principle, and dreadful in its effects; a grievance too, which it could not be urged occurred but seldom. "Unhappily," he added, "it occurs every day; and, under the present system, will continue to occur, so long as men shall continue to be unfortunate. Let this statute then," said he, "be totally repealed. *Let the Negroes be attached to the land,* and sold with it." He even arraigned the abolitionists as eminently criminal for not having solicited the repeal of that "execrable statute," as he termed it, though of its operation and even existence nineteen-twentieths of them perhaps were utterly ignorant. With no little pomp and circumstance did this gentleman introduce and carry through Parliament, an act for repealing the statute complained of; and he had the cordial and unanimous support of all the abolitionists. This measure seemed to pledge the assemblies in the most effectual manner to follow up the principle of the repealing act, by repealing also their own laws which supported, and had, in fact, first introduced the cruel practice: and this experiment on their humanity was tried, it must be admitted, under the most favourable circumstances; for Mr. B. Edwards's proposal of attaching the slaves to the land was strongly recommended to their adoption by the Duke of Portland, then secretary of state for the colonies, a nobleman well known to be peculiarly acceptable to them, in a circular letter to the Governor. Yet of all our colonial legislatures, then thirteen in number, not one has in any degree reformed the grievance in question, much less, followed the suggestion of Mr. Edwards, by attaching the slaves to the plantations. The House of Assembly of Jamaica contemptuously declined giving any answer at all to the Governor's message upon the subject; and the slaves are still everywhere subject to that "*remorseless and tyrannical grievance*," which above three-and-twenty years ago was so feelingly denounced to, and condemned by, the British Parliament.

Other mitigations of slavery have as long been recommended to the assemblies, even by their own most respected advocates in this country; but not one has been effectually adopted. The laws which the various legislatures have passed for such purposes, still precisely answer the description given by Mr. Burke in his letter to Mr. Secretary Dundas, in 1792, of such colonial statutes: " I have seen," said he, after the passing of the celebrated consolidated Slave Laws of Jamaica, and of other islands, " I have seen what has been done by the West Indian Assemblies. It is arrant trifling; — they have done little, and what they have done is *good for nothing, for it is totally destitute of an executory principle.*" Taking into consideration all the circumstances that accompanied and followed the enactment of those laws, it is difficult to suppose that they were not passed on the views stated in the memorable letter before noticed of the Governor of Dominica, and which, indeed, seemed to have been virtually recommended to them in the year 1797 by the West Indian committee; as the objects suggested to them by that body were " the joint purposes of opposing the plan of the abolitionists *," (*i. e.* the abolition of the Slave Trade,) "and establishing the character of the West Indian body." One grand class of such laws, passed, indeed, at a considerably later period, — the acts of the colonial assemblies for registering the slaves, with a view to prevent illicit importation, — are shown, by a report of the African Institution, to be wholly and manifestly ineffectual to their purpose. But the case, in several of the islands, is still more opprobrious; new laws have been passed, which so far from even exhibiting any show of a wish to alleviate the pressure of the yoke of slavery, have rendered it more dreadfully galling, and less tolerable, because even more than before hopeless. The individual manumission of slaves by their masters, which has been provided for, with so much sound policy as well as true humanity, by the laws in force in the Spanish colonies, and has there been found productive of such happy effects; those individual manumissions which,

---

* It is, in the original, "the plan of Mr. Wilberforce." See papers of 1804. St. Vincent's, I. 7.

while slavery prevailed here, the English law assiduously encouraged and promoted, have been cruelly restrained. They were long since, in one or two of our islands, subjected to discouraging regulations; but were, in most of our colonies, wholly unrestrained till within the last thirty years. Can it be conceived possible, that even since the mitigation of slavery was recommended from the throne, in consequence of addresses from Parliament, several of the colonial legislatures have for the first time imposed, and others have greatly augmented, the fines to be paid into their treasuries on the enfranchising of slaves, so that in some colonies they amount nearly to an entire prohibition? Such acts may be truly said to be more unjust in their principle, and more cruel and dangerous in their effects, than almost any other part of the dreadful code of West Indian legislation. The laws of England, ever favourable to manumissions, progressively rooted out the curse of slavery from our native land; but it is the opposite and opprobrious tendency of these colonial laws to make the barbarous institution perpetual.

I press these topics the more earnestly, because there has prevailed among many of our statesmen, of late years, a most unwarrantable and pernicious disposition to leave all that concerns the well-being of the slaves to the colonial legislatures. Surely this is a course manifestly contrary to the clearest obligations of duty. The very relation in which the Negro slaves and the members of the colonial assemblies, which consist wholly of their masters, stand towards each other, is of itself a decisive reason why the imperial legislature ought to consider itself bound to exercise the office of an umpire, or rather of a judge between them, as constituting two parties of conflicting interests and feelings. And this, let it be remembered, not merely because, knowing the frailty of our common nature, and its disposition to abuse absolute power, we ought not to deliver the weaker party altogether into the power of the stronger; but because in the present instance there are peculiar objections of great force, some of which have been already noticed. In truth, West Indians must be exempt from the ordinary frailties of human nature, if, living continually with those wretched beings, and witnessing their extreme degradation and consequent depravity, they could entertain for the Negroes, in an unimpaired degree, that equitable consideration and that fellow-feeling, which are due from man to man; so as to sympathise properly with them in their sufferings and wrongs, or form a just estimate of their claims to personal rights and moral improvement.

The fact is, that though the old prejudice, that the Negroes are creatures of an inferior nature, is no longer maintained in terms, there is yet too much reason to fear that a latent impression arising from it still continues practically to operate in the colonies, and to influence the minds of those who have the government of the slaves, in estimating their physical claims, and still more those of their moral nature. The colonists, indeed, and the abolitionists, would differ as to facts, in speaking of the sufficiency of the slave's supply of food, and of his treatment in some other particulars. But on what other principle than that of the inferiority of the species, can it be explained, that, in estimating what is due to the Negroes, all consideration of their moral nature has been altogether left out? When it is undeniable that they have no more power of giving their testimony against any white ruffian by whom they may have been maltreated, than if they were of the brute creation; that they are worked like cattle under the whip; that they are strangers to the institution of marriage, and to all the blessed truths of Christianity; how, but from their supposed inferiority of nature, could we nevertheless be assured by the colonial legislatures, with the most unhesitating confidence, that whatever defects there might formerly have been in their treatment, they are now as well used *as can reasonably be desired?* If such be indeed their opinion, whether that opinion proceeds from the views here intimated or not, it would still suffice to show the criminality, of our committing to them the destiny of the slaves. For let it be observed, there is not in this instance any difference as to the facts of the case; nor do the colonists affirm what we deny, as to the moral degradation of the slaves. Both parties, for instance, agree that promiscuous intercourse between the sexes, and Pagan darkness, are nearly universal among them; and yet the colonists contend that the slaves are as well treated and governed as they need to be. Can then the members of the British Parliament conscientiously devolve the duty of establishing such religious and moral reforms, as I trust it must be the universal wish of every member of the empire to introduce among the Negroes, upon those, who, to say nothing of the extremity of personal degradation, consider marriage and Christianity as unworthy of their regard, in estimating the condition of their fellow creatures?

Indeed, the West Indians, in the warmth of argument, have gone still farther, and have even distinctly told us, again and again, and I am shocked to say that some of their partizans in this country have re-echoed the assertion, that these poor degraded beings, the Negro slaves, are as well or even better off than our British peasantry,—a proposition so monstrous, that nothing can possibly exhibit in a stronger light the extreme force of the prejudices which must exist in the minds of its assertors. A Briton to compare the state of a West Indian slave with that of an English freeman, and to give the former the preference! It is to imply an utter insensibility of the native feelings and moral dignity of man, no less than of the rights of Englishmen!! I will not condescend to argue this question, as I might, on the ground of comparative feeding and clothing, and lodging, and medical attendance. Are these the only claims? are these the chief privileges of a rational and immortal being? Is the consciousness of personal independence nothing? are self-possession and self-government nothing? Is it of no account that our persons are inviolate by any private authority, and that the whip is placed only in the hands of the public executioner; Is it of no value that we have the power of pursuing the occupation and the habits of life which we prefer; that we have the prospect, or at least the hope, of improving our condition, and of rising, as we have seen others rise, from poverty and obscurity to comfort, and opulence, and distinction? Again, are all the charities of the heart, which arise out of the domestic relations, to be considered as nothing; and, I may add, all their security too among men who are free agents, and not vendible chattels, liable continually to be torn from their dearest connections, and sent into a perpetual exile? Are husband and wife, parent and child, terms of no meaning? Are willing services, or grateful returns for voluntary kindnesses, nothing? But, above all, is Christianity so little esteemed among us, that we are to account as of no value the hope, " full of immortality," the light of heavenly truth, and all the consolations and supports by which religion cheers the hearts and elevates the principles, and dignifies the conduct of multitudes of our labouring classes in this free and enlightened country? Is it nothing to be taught that all human distinctions will soon be at an end; that all the labours and sorrows of poverty and hardship will soon exist no more; and to know, on the express authority of Scripture, that the lower classes, instead of being an inferior order in the creation, are even the preferable objects of the love of the Almighty?

But such wretched sophisms as insult the understandings of mankind, are sometimes best answered by an appeal to their feelings. Let me therefore ask, is there, in the whole of the three kingdoms, a parent or a husband so sordid and insensible that any sum, which the richest West Indian proprietor could offer him, would be deemed a compensation for his suffering his wife or his daughter to be subjected to the brutal outrage of the cart-whip—to the savage lust of the driver—to the indecent, and degrading, and merciless punishment of a West Indian whipping? If there were one so dead, I say not to every liberal, but to every natural feeling, as that money could purchase of him such concessions, such a wretch, and he alone, would be capable of the farther sacrifices necessary for degrading an English peasant to the condition of a West Indian slave. He might consent to sell the liberty of his own children, and to barter away even the blessings conferred on himself by that religion which declares to him that his master, no less than himself, has a Master in heaven—a common Creator, who is no respecter of persons, and in whose presence he may weekly stand on the same spiritual level with his superiors in rank, to be reminded of their common origin, common responsibility, and common day of final and irreversible account.

But I will push no farther a comparison which it is painful and humiliating to contemplate: let it however be remembered, that it is to those who have professed insensibility to this odious contrast that the destiny of the poor slaves would be committed, were we to leave them to the disposal of the colonial legislatures.

There is another consideration, which, on a moment's reflection, will appear perhaps not less decisive. The advocates for the Negroes declare without reserve, as from the first they declared, that the reforms they wish to introduce are intended, by preparing the slaves for the possession of self-government, for the purpose of gradually and safely doing away slavery altogether, and transmuting the wretched Africans into the condition of free British labourers. Now, let it never be forgotten, the West Indian legislatures, and almost all the colonists, with one concurrent voice, declare that the emancipation of the slaves, within any period except that to which an antediluvian might have looked forward, would be their utter ruin. Shall we then devolve the duty of introducing into the West Indian system the moral reforms which, once effected, would render it manifestly impossible to detain the slave in his present degrading bondage, on those who plainly tell us that his being delivered from it would be productive of their utter ruin? Can *they* be expected to labour fairly in producing reforms, the ultimate object of which they do not merely regard as superfluous, but dread as most pernicious and destructive? Should we act thus in any parallel instance? All comparisons on this subject are weak; but suppose that, through a criminal inadvertency, we had administered some poisonous substance to a fellow creature, who had a special claim to our protection and kindness; that we had deeply injured his constitution, and that the comfort of all his future life, or probably his life itself, should depend on his being immediately put under a course of the ablest medical treatment. Supposing also—surely in such a case no unnatural supposition—that we felt the deepest distress of mind from the consciousness of the wrong we had done to this poor sufferer, and were prompted, alike by conscience and feeling, to use our utmost possible endeavours to restore him to ease and health—should we be satisfied with committing this patient into the hands of some medical practitioner, whom otherwise we might have been disposed to employ, if he were to state to us, contrary to our plain knowledge of the fact, "The man has taken no poison—his health has sustained no injury—he is already as sound and well as he needs to be, and requires no farther medical care." But we may put the case still more strongly:—Supposing there were a declared opposition of interest between the patient and this same medical practitioner, and that the latter conceived that the recovery of the patient would prove fatal to his own future fortunes—could we then, as honest and rational men, commit the case to his uncontrouled management alone? If we did, who would not pronounce our alleged sorrow for the injury we had done, and our earnest wish to repair it, to be no better than hypocritical affectation.

Let me not be conceived to dwell on this topic with unreasonable pertinacity. In truth, practically speaking, the fate of the Negro slaves, so far at least as a safe and peaceable reform of the system is in question, hinges entirely on this point. Of this the colonists themselves are well aware; and, wise in their generation, they therefore take their principal stand on the ground of objecting to the interference of the imperial legislature for the protection of the slaves, though this is an objection which did not even so much as present itself to the inquiring mind of Mr. Burke, when in the year 1780 he drew up his plan for the reformation of the Negro system; or in 1792, when he communicated it to his majesty's ministers. For we cannot suppose that had it suggested itself to his mind, as an obstacle to the introduction of his plan, he would have left it quite unnoticed. Few, if any, are bold enough to claim for the assemblies an exclusive jurisdiction on these subjects as their right. They only tell us of the *delicacy* of Parliamentary interference in such matters of internal legislation. This delicacy, however, was not felt, I repeat it, by Mr. Burke. As little was it felt by Mr. Dundas, the avowed advocate of the Colonies, when, in 1792, he brought forward his plan of emancipation. We may therefore certainly conclude, that no such objection occurred to that experienced statesman, who, as a minister of the crown, was called on for great circumspection, especially in regard to measures proposed by himself; but who, like Mr. Burke, never condescended to notice any such objection to the plan which he laid before the House of Commons.

To persons not conversant with the state of things in the West Indies, it may appear plausible to say, that the assemblies and their constituents are the most competent, in point of information, to the important work of reform; and many are apt, perhaps, to be misled by a supposed analogy between the relations of master and slave in the West Indies, and those of the owner or occupier of land and his labourers in this country. But there is in fact no just analogy between them; nor are the colonial legislatures composed of such men as the West Indian proprietors whom we are accustomed to see in this country; many of whom are personally strangers to their estates, and to the crimes and miseries of the system by which they are governed. Nor is the moral state of the whites resident in the West Indies, less different from that of the corresponding classes of our countrymen in their native land. It has been most truly remarked by Mr. Brougham, in his able work on colonial policy, that the agriculture of the West Indies has always been of a nature nearly allied to commercial adventure; and the spirit of adventure, as he justly observes, is, in such circumstances, unfavourable to morals and to manners. Mr. B. means of course, as the context shews, not such commercial enterprise as belongs to the mercantile character in its proper element, but that of which man is the subject, in the gaming agricultural speculations of a sugar colony. He means, that it gives none of the proper virtues of the industrious European merchant, and still less of those steady local attachments which belong to the landed proprietor here, and make him the natural patron of the labouring class, settled on his hereditary property. " The object of a West India resident speculator," he observes, " is not to live, but to gain ; not to enjoy, but to save ; not to subsist in the colonies, but to prepare for shining in the mother country." This I am well aware will be an offensive, as I am sure it is to me a painful topic ; but it ought not on that account to be left out of view ; and any one who wishes to form a just notion of the effects of these causes will find them stated in the work above-mentioned, with the accustomed force of that very powerful writer.* Even in the French islands, where there have been always far more resident proprietors than in our own, the same causes are stated by Mr. Malonet, himself a colonist, to operate powerfully, and to produce in a considerable degree similar bad effects.

And is it to societies consisting of such elements as these, that a humane and enlightened legislature can conscientiously delegate its duties

* Mr. Brougham must be understood to intend to state only the tendency and general effects of the causes he has been enumerating. When individuals manifest that they are exceptions to the rule, it is so much the more to their honour. " A colony," he remarks, " composed of such adventurers, is peopled by a race of men all hastening to grow rich, and eager to acquire wealth for the gratification of avarice or voluptuousness." " The continuance of the members in this society is as short as possible " " What," they may be supposed to say to themselves, " what, though our conduct is incorrect, and our manners dissolute? We shall accommodate them to those of our European countrymen when we return." " Such I fear is the natural language of men in those circumstances. But their manners are affected also by other peculiarities in their situation. The want of modest female society, the general case on the plantations remote from the towns, while it brutalizes the mind and manners of men, necessarily deprives them of all the virtuous pleasures of domestic life, and frees them from those restraints which the presence of a family always imposes on the conduct of the most profligate men. The witnesses of the planters' actions are the companions of his debaucheries, or the wretched beings who tremble at his nod, while they minister to the indulgence of his brutal appetite; and impose no more check upon his excesses than if they wanted that faculty of speech which almost alone distinguishes them from the beasts that surround them."

as to religious and moral reforms; reforms too, as has been already shewn, which the colonists not only slight as frivolous, but condemn as ruinous. Let it be further taken into account, that the formation of laws and regulations for the slaves is not left to the uncontrouled sentiments and feelings of the more affluent, and consequently, it may be presumed, more liberal of the resident land-owners. For the colonial house of assembly, which answers to our House of Commons, is chosen by the resident white proprietors at large, and must necessarily be governed in great measure by their general sentiments and feelings. Nor can it be supposed to be uninfluenced by what is here called the popular voice, but which, in the West Indies, is the voice of the white colonists only, and these too of the lower order, among whom the *esprit de corps* is peculiarly strong. These borderers on the despised coloured race are naturally the most hostile to them, and the most tenacious of those complexional privileges which constitute their own social elevation. The voice, therefore, of the populace in the West Indies, or what may be called the cry of the mob, is always adverse to the humane and liberal principles by which the slavery of the blacks should be mitigated, and by which they should be gradually prepared for the enjoyment of freedom.

These considerations are of no trifling moment; and they may be, in some measure, illustrated by some transactions which took place not long ago in the largest, except Jamaica, and the longest settled of all our colonies, the island of Barbadoes; though there are in that colony more resident proprietors than in any other, in proportion to the whole population. The facts I here allude to may have the more weight, because they are not liable to the objection, which has been sometimes urged against the abolitionists when they have quoted laws and transactions of an old date, that they formed an unfair test of the opinions and feelings of the present generation; for they took place so recently as the latter part of 1804.

It had long been a reproach to Barbadoes, that the murder of a slave by his owner, instead of being a capital crime, as in most of our other West Indian colonies, was, in that colony, punishable only by a fine of 15l.* Lord Seaforth, the governor, therefore, himself a West Indian proprietor, wishing to wipe off the blot, sent a message, in the common form, to the house of assembly, recommending that an act should be passed to make the murder of a slave a capital

* The murder of another man's slave was punished more severely, the penalty being then 25l. to be paid to the public treasury, and double the slaves value to the owner. But to subject the criminal to any punishment, the murder was to have been committed " of wantonness, or only of bloody mindedness or cruel intention:" and lest there should be any disposition to visit the crime too severely, it was specially enacted, that " if any Negro or other slave under punishment by his master or his order, for running away, *or any other crimes or misdemeanors towards his said master, unfortunately shall suffer in life or member, which seldom happens, no persons whatsoever shall be liable to any fine therefore.*"

felony. There seems every reason to believe that the council, or colonial house of lords, would gladly have assented to the proposition. But strange as it may appear to those who are unacquainted with West Indian prejudices, notwithstanding the time and manner in which the proposition was brought forward, the house of assembly absolutely refused to make the alteration.

If the bare statement of this fact must shock every liberal mind, how much will the shock be increased, when it is known under what circumstances it was that this refusal took place. For it had happened very recently, that several most wanton and atrocious murders had been committed on slaves; and some of them accompanied with circumstances of the most horrid and disgusting barbarity. Lord Seaforth felt all the horror likely to be produced by such incidents in a generous and feeling mind. He writes thus to Lord Camden, then the Secretary of State for the Colonies. " I inclose the Attorney-general's letter to me on the subject of the Negroes so most wantonly murdered. I am sorry to say, *several other instances of the same barbarity* have occurred, with which I have not troubled your Lordship, as I only wished to make you acquainted with the subject in general." It is due to Mr. Beccles, the Attorney-general, and to Mr. Coulthurst, the Advocate-general, to state, that they also felt and expressed themselves on the occasion just as persons in

the same rank of life would have done in this country. Lord Seaforth also thus described the official papers he transmitted, as to the murders he had mentioned in some former letters, " they are selected from *a great number*, among which there is not one in contradiction of the horrible facts. The truth is, that nothing has given me more trouble to get to the bottom of, than this business, *so horribly absurd are the prejudices of the people*. However, a great part of my object is answered by the alarm my interference has excited, and the attention it has called to the business. Bills are already proposed to make murder felony in both the council and the assembly, but I fear they will be thrown out for the present in the assembly : the council are unanimous on the side of humanity. *
Lord Seaforth's prediction was but too fully

---

* The letter from the Attorney-general of Barbadoes to Lord Seaforth throws so much light on the popular feeling of the lower class of white men in Barbadoes, that it ought not to be suppressed, although it is a humiliating and disgusting recital : — " Extract of a letter from the Attorney-general of Barbadoes to the Governor of the Island : — " A Mr. ————, the manager of a plantation in the neighbourhood, had some months before purchased an African lad, who was much attached to his person, and slept in a passage contiguous to his chamber. On Sunday night there was an alarm of fire in the plantation, which induced Mr. ———— to go out hastily, and the next morning he missed the lad, who he supposed intended to follow him in the night, and had mistaken his way. He sent to his neighbours, and to Mr. C. among the rest, to inform them that his African lad had accidentally strayed from him;

verified;—the assembly threw out the bill, and the law against wilful murder remained in its pristine state.

---

that he could not speak a word of English, and that possibly he might be found breaking canes, or taking something else for his support; in which case, he requested that they would not injure him, but return him, and he, Mr. ——— himself, would pay any damage he might have committed. A day or two after the owner of the boy was informed that Mr. C. and H. had killed a Negro in a neighbouring gully, and buried him there. He went to Mr. C. to inquire into the truth of the report, and intended to have the grave opened, to see whether it was his African lad. *Mr. C. told him, a Negro had been killed and buried there; but assured him it was not his, for he knew him very well, and he need not be at the trouble of opening the grave. Upon this the owner went away satisfied.* But receiving further information, which left no doubt upon his mind that it was his Negro, he returned, and opened the grave, and found it to be so. I was his leading counsel, and the facts stated in my brief were as follows: That C. and H. being informed that there was a Negro lurking in the gully, went armed with muskets, and took several Negro men with them. The poor African, seeing a parcel of men coming to attack him, was frightened; he took up a stone to defend himself, and retreated into a cleft rock, where they could not easily come at him: they then went for some trash, put it into the crevices of the rock behind him, and set it on fire: after it had burnt so as to scorch the poor fellow, he ran into a pool of water close by; they sent a Negro to bring him out, and he threw the stone at the Negro; upon which the two white men fired several times at him with the guns loaded with shot, and the Negroes pelted him with stones. He was at length dragged out of the pool in a dying condition, for he had not only received several bruises from the stones, but his breast was so pierced with the shot, that it was like a cullender. *The white savages ordered the Negroes to dig a grave, and whilst they were dig-*

I should be glad to be able to refer the conduct of the assembly, in this instance, altogether to the influence of the lower orders over their minds. This, doubtless, we may hope, had some

---

ging it, the poor creature made signs of begging for water, which was not given to him, but as soon as the grave was dug, he was thrown into it, and covered over; and there seems to be some doubt whether he was then quite dead. C. and H. deny this; but the owner assured me that he could prove it by more than one witness; and I have reason to believe it to be true, because on the day of trial C. and H. did not suffer the cause to come to a hearing, but paid the penalties and the costs of suit, which it is not supposed they would have done had they been innocent.

" I have the honour to be, &c."

The same transaction, with another far more dreadful murder, in which there was a deliberate ingenuity of cruelty which almost exceeds belief, but of which I will spare my readers the recital, is related, with scarcely any variation as to circumstances, by the Advocate-general, who, as well as the gentleman of whose estate the criminal was the manager, and who was at the time absent, expressed their most lively indignation against such horrid cruelty. It may be proper to remark, that the story of the poor boy strikingly shews that such protection as the Negro slave occasionally receives from the laws, is too often to be ascribed rather to the master's care of his property, than to any more generous motive. The master, in this case, when he had only reason to believe that *a* Negro had been killed and buried out of the way, and not that it was his own slave, goes away satisfied. Is there a human being who in this country would have so done? Again, it is a suggestion which the circumstances of the story enforce on us, that the crowd which was now collected, instead of being shocked at such barbarity, were rather abettors of it; and then we hear the white savages, (as the Attorney-general justly styles them,) order the Negroes who were present to dig a grave for their wretched country-

share in producing the effect; though considering that in their circumstances it was peculiarly their duty to set the tone of public judgment and feeling to the bulk of the community, this would not be a very creditable plea. But it is due to truth to remark, that there is no hint to this effect in the papers laid before the House of Commons: on the contrary, in the Assembly's answer, there is an expression of resentment against the Governor, and an intimation of the danger of interfering between master and slave.

This incident will exhibit to every considerate reader a striking specimen of the state of the public mind in the West Indies, at least so recently as 1805, in regard to the African race: and it may serve in some degree to shew the error into which we should fall, by conceiving that the bulk of the white population in our colonies, in estimating the proper conduct to be observed towards the slaves, would think and feel like ourselves. Even in this land of liberty and humanity, acts of atrocious cruelty have been perpetrated. We have heard of an apprentice being starved to death by her mistress; and, more recently, the British Governor of an African settlement caused the death of a soldier by exces-

---

man. They knew their state too well to refuse; and accordingly, with a promptitude of obedience which, with all our ideas of their sunk and prostrate spirits, must surprise us, they immediately executed the order.

sive punishment. But what was the effect on the public mind? In both cases it was difficult to prevent the populace from anticipating the execution of the sentence of the law. In Barbadoes, on the contrary, the proposal to punish such enormities by more than a small fine, was just as unpopular as it would be in this country, to inflict a punishment which should be utterly disproportionate to the crime — such as hanging a man for petty larceny. Except among the highest and best educated classes, the natural sympathy was reversed; and the most horrible murders, some of them attended with circumstances too shocking for recital, instead of exciting any just commiseration for the Negro race, had actually worked in the opposite direction. And is it to assemblies subject to the influence of such popular prejudices as these, and sitting in the bosom of such communities, that we can commit the temporal and eternal interests of many hundred thousands of these despised fellow creatures?

If this case itself suggests to us a useful distrust of the colonial assemblies, in what relates to the Negroes, the sequel of it will not perhaps be less useful in enabling us to judge of their probable conduct, even when they may profess a disposition to conform to our wishes. Whether it was that the influence of the higher members of the Barbadoes community worked at last upon the minds of the assembly, or that the effect likely to be produced in the English Parliament led to a change of conduct, so it was that the assembly ultimately gave way, and it was supposed, that by the new law of Barbadoes, no less than by that of the other islands, the wilful murder of a slave was made a capital offence. Such, indeed, was the statement made afterwards by more than one advocate for the West Indians, in the controversy in 1816, concerning the Registry Bill; and the abolitionists were reproached with having referred to a period when the law had been different, as if it had been of an antiquated date. Yet, when the statute book itself was examined, (which, I confess, not doubting the accuracy of the statement, I did not look into for several years,) it was found that the alleged reformation of the law is highly problematical at least, if not clearly and totally evasive; for instead of simply declaring the well-defined crime of wilful murder to be a capital felony when perpetrated on a slave, the enacting words are, " if any person shall hereafter wilfully, *maliciously, wantonly,* and WITHOUT PROVOCATION kill and murder any slave, &c." If, hereafter, any of those " *White Savages,*" so justly termed such by the Attorney-general of Barbadoes, in wreaking their vengeance on the wretched subjects of their tyranny, should actually murder any of their slaves, or the slaves of others, would there be a hope, even if all the scarcely superable obstacles arising from the absolute rejection of Negro testimony were to be overcome, of a conviction under the terms of this act? What offender could be unable to prove, to the satisfaction of a Barbadoes jury, that there had been *some provocation?* Yet this is the amended, — this, I suppose, the ameliorating law passed in April, 1805, entitled, " An act for *the better protection* of the slaves of this island."*

Surely, with these and the many other evidences we have had of the state of mind respecting Negroes, which prevails in the Colonies, we should be more culpable than they, if we were still to commit implicitly to their legislatures the task of devising and carrying into execution such physical and moral reforms as humanity demands in the slavery of the West Indies. More culpable; I say it advisedly; for, though it is no praise to us, but to the good providence of God, we are exempt from the influence of the harsh prejudices to which they, in some degree by our concurrent fault, have been subjected.

The information also which we now possess, as to the African character, would aggravate our criminality. For though the day, I trust, is gone by for ever, in which the alleged inferiority of intellect and incurable barbarity of the African race were supposed to extenuate their oppression, yet it ought not to be left unnoticed, that the notions which formerly prevailed to their prejudice, in these respects, have of late

---

* See papers entitled Colonial Laws respecting Slaves, 1788 — 1815, ordered by the House of Commons to be printed, 5th April, 1816.

years been abundantly refuted, not only by authority but experience. It may be confidently affirmed, that there never was any uncivilised people of whose dispositions we have received a more amiable character than that which is given of the native Africans by Parke and Golberry, both of whom visited those districts of Africa from which victims for the Slave Trade were furnished; and whose testimony in their favour will naturally be admitted with less reserve, because neither of them could be biassed by any wish to discountenance the Slave Trade, they having evidently felt no desire for its abolition.

But it is at Sierra Leone, that long despised and calumniated colony, that the African character has been most effectually and experimentally vindicated. The first seeds of civilization which were sown there by the Christian philanthropy of Mr. Granville Sharpe nearly perished from the unkindly soil to which they had been committed, but they were saved from early destruction, and cultured at length successfully, under the fostering care and indefatigable attention of the late excellent Mr. H. Thornton, and by other good and able men, who both at home and in the colony, co-operated with him; by one living benefactor especially, who will be hereafter venerated as the steady, enlightened, and unwearied, though unostentatious friend of Africa. It is at Sierra Leone that the great experiment on human nature has been tried; and there it has appeared, that the poor African barbarians, just rescued from the holds of slave-ships, are capable, not merely of being civilized, but of soon enjoying, with advantage, the rights and institutions of British freemen. In truth, to have formed any conclusions against the Negroes from the experience we had of them in their state of bondage, was not less unphilosophical than unjust. It was remarked by M. Dupuis, the British consul at Mogadore, that even the generality of European Christians, after a long captivity and severe treatment among the Arabs, appeared at first exceedingly stupid and insensible. " If," he adds, " they have been any considerable time in slavery, they appear lost to reason and feeling; their spirits broken, and their faculties sunk in a species of stupor, which I am unable adequately to describe. They appear degraded even below the Negro slave. The succession of hardships, without any protecting law to which they can appeal for any alleviation or redress, seems to destroy every spring of exertion or hope in their minds. They appear indifferent to every thing around them; abject, servile, and brutish." *

If the native intelligence and buoyant independence of Britons cannot survive in the dank and baleful climate of personal slavery, could it be reasonably expected that the poor

* See Quarterly Review for January 7. 1816.—Article, *Tombuctoo.*

Africans, unsupported by any consciousness of personal dignity or civil rights, should not yield to the malignant influences to which they had so long been subjected, and be depressed even below the level of the human species? But at Sierra Leone, they have resumed the stature and port of men, and have acquired, in an eminent degree, the virtues of the citizen and the subject. Witness the peace, and order, and loyalty which have generally prevailed in this colony, in a remarkable degree; especially under the present excellent Governor, Sir Charles Macarthy. Still more, these recent savages, having become the subjects of religious and moral culture, have manifested the greatest willingness to receive instruction, and made a practical proficiency in Christianity, such as might put Europeans to the blush. Not only have they learned with facility the principles of the Christian faith; but they have shewn, by their mutual kindnesses, and by the attachment and gratitude to their worthy pastors and superintendents, that they have derived from their knowledge of Christianity its moral and practical fruits.

The same testimony as to the progress of the Negro children, in common school learning, has been given by all the masters who have instructed them in the Island of Hayti; and the missionaries, in our different West Indian islands, testify, with one consent, the gratitude and attachment which the West Indian, no less than the Sierra Leone Negroes feel to those who condescend to become their teachers.

Again, the impression so assiduously attempted heretofore to be made, that the *indolence* of the Negro race was utterly incurable, and that without the driving whip they never would willingly engage in agricultural labour, has been shewn to be utterly without foundation. Mr. Parke relates, that the Africans, when prompted by any adequate motives, would work diligently and perseveringly both in agricultural and manufacturing labours. And there is on the African coast a whole nation of the most muscular men and the hardiest labourers, who, from their known industry, are hired both for government service, and by the European traders, as workmen, both on ship-board and on shore.

Nor have instances of a similar kind been wanting even in the West Indies, whenever circumstances have been at all favourable to voluntary industry. Since the dissolution of the black corps, (a measure which the abolitionists are scarcely, I fear, excusable for not having opposed, though prompted to acquiesce in it by unwillingness to thwart, when not indispensably necessary, the prejudices of the colonists) many of the disbanded soldiers have maintained themselves by their own agricultural labours, and have manifested a degree of industry that ought to have silenced for ever all imputations on the diligence of their race.

But another still more striking instance has been lately afforded in Trinidad. There many hundreds of American Negroes, at the close of the late unhappy war with the United States, were, by the humane policy of Sir Ralph Woodford, received into Trinidad, to the no small alarm of the planters. These were slaves enfranchised by desertion, yet instead of becoming a nuisance to the community by idleness and dissolute manners, as prejudice loudly foretold, they have maintained themselves well, in various ways, by their own industry and prudence. Many of them have worked as hired labourers for the planters with so much diligence and good conduct, that they are now universally regarded as a valuable acquisition to the colony; and it is supposed, that a large addition to their number would be very gladly received.

Are all these important lessons to be read to us without producing any influence on our minds? Ought they not to enforce on us, as by a voice from heaven, that we have been most cruelly and inexcusably degrading, to the level of brutes, those whom the Almighty had made capable of enjoying our own civil blessings in this world, not less clearly than he has fitted them to be heirs of our common immortality?

But while we are loudly called on by justice and humanity to take measures without delay for improving the condition of our West Indian slaves, self-interest also inculcates the same duty, and with full as clear a voice. It is a great though common error, that notwithstanding we must, on religious and moral grounds, condemn the West Indian system, yet, that in a worldly view, it has been eminently gainful both to individuals and to the community at large. On the contrary, I believe it might be proved to any inquiring and unprejudiced mind, that taking in all considerations of political economy, and looking to the lamentable waste of human life among our soldiers and seamen, raised and recruited at a great expence, as well as to the more direct pecuniary charge of protecting the sugar colonies, no system of civil polity was ever maintained at a greater price, or was less truly profitable either to individuals or to the community, than that of our West Indian settlements. Indeed, it would have been a strange exception to all those established principles which Divine Providence has ordained for the moral benefit of the world, if national and personal prosperity were generally and permanently to be found to arise from injustice and oppression. There may be individual instances of great fortunes amassed by every species of wrong doing. A course, ruinous in the long run, may, to an individual, or for a time, appear eminently profitable; nevertheless, it is unquestionably true, that the path of prosperity rarely diverges long and widely from that of integrity and virtue; or, to express it in a familiar adage, — that honesty is the best policy.

It ought not to be necessary to assert such

principles as these in an age in which it has been incontrovertibly established by the soundest of our political economists, — that the base and selfish, though plausible views, which formerly prevailed so widely among statesmen, and taught them to believe that the prosperity and elevation of their country would be best promoted by the impoverishment and depression of its neighbours, were quite fallacious; and when we have now learned the opposite and beneficent lesson, — that every nation is, in fact, benefited by the growing affluence of others, and that all are thus interested in the well-being and improvement of all. At such an enlightened period as this, when commerce herself adopts the principles of true morality, and becomes liberal and benevolent, will it be believed that the Almighty has rendered the depression and misery of the cultivators of the soil in our West Indian colonies necessary, or even conducive, to their prosperity and safety? No, surely! The oppression of these injured fellow-creatures, however it may be profitable in a few instances, can never be generally politic; and in the main, and ultimately, the comfort of the labourer, and the well-being of those who have to enjoy the fruits of his labour, will be found to be coincident.

As for the apprehensions of ruin, expressed by the West Indians, from the instruction and moral improvement of their slaves, or from the interference of the Imperial Legislature, we have been taught by experience in the Slave

Trade controversy, that their apprehensions are not always reasonable, either in degree, or in the objects to which they are directed. How confidently did all the Slave Traders predict their own ruin, together with that of the West Indies, and also of the town of Liverpool, from the regulations of the bill for limiting the number of slaves to be taken in ships of given dimensions, while the trade should be tolerated, and for requiring certain particulars of food and medical attendance! yet, after a few years, the regulations were allowed, not merely to be harmless, but to have been positively and greatly beneficial. The total ruin of the sugar colonies was still more confidently foretold by the planters, the assemblies, and their agents, by their parliamentary advocates, and the West Indian committee, as a sure consequence of abolishing the Slave Trade; and yet there is not, I believe, an intelligent West Indian who will not now confess, that it would have been greatly for the benefit of all our old colonies, if the Slave Trade had been abolished many years sooner; and that if it had continued some years longer, it must have completed their destruction.

Mr. Dundas, in 1792, did not hesitate to ridicule the vain terrors of the parties whose battle he was fighting, and, by their own selection, as their commander-in-chief, though emancipation itself was the object. In illustration of the apprehensions which many entertained of the consequences of changing their slaves into free labourers, he stated that some years before, in certain districts of Scotland, the persons who la- -boured in the salt-works and coal-mines were actually slaves; and that a proposal being made to emancipate them, instantly the owners of the works came forward, declaring that if their vassals were to be raised to the condition of free labourers, they themselves would be utterly ruined; for that such was the peculiarity, such the unpleasant nature of those species of labours, that they could not depend on hired service, as in other instances. "But at length," added Mr. Dundas, "the good sense of the age obtained the victory.— The salters and colliers were changed into free labourers, and all the terrors of the owners ended in smoke."

While thus alive to imaginary dangers, or rather while thus assiduous in endeavouring to inspire alarm in the mother country, to prevent her listening to the claims of justice and mercy, our planters appear blind to the new and real dangers that are accumulating around them. Providence graciously seems to allow them a golden interval, which, duly improved, might prevent the dreadful explosion that may otherwise be expected. But they neglect it with a supineness and insensibility resembling infatuation. With a community of near 800,000 free blacks, many of them accustomed to the use of arms, within sight of the greatest of our West Indian islands; with a slave population in Cuba and Porto Rico, which has been of late so fearfully augmented with imported Africans, as, according to all received principles, to produce, even in pacific times, and much more in the present æra of transatlantic convulsions, the utmost extremity of danger; with the example afforded in many of the United States, and in almost all the new republics of South America, where Negro slavery has been recently abolished, — is this a time, are these the circumstances, in which it can be wise and safe, if it were even honest and humane, to keep down in their present state of heathenish and almost brutish degradation, the 800,000 Negroes in our West Indian colonies? Here, indeed, is danger, if we observe the signs of the times, whether we take our lesson from the history of men, or form our conclusions from natural reason or from the revealed will of God.

But raise these poor creatures from their depressed condition, and if they are not yet fit for the enjoyment of British freedom, elevate them at least from the level of the brute creation into that of rational nature — dismiss the driving whip, and thereby afford place for the developement of the first rudiments of civil character — implant in them the principle of hope — let free scope be given for their industry, and for their rising in life by their personal good conduct — give them an interest in defending the community to which they belong — teach them that lesson which Christianity can alone truly inculcate, that the present life is but a short and uncertain span, to which will succeed an eternal existence of happiness or misery — inculcate on them, on the authority of the sacred page, that the point of real importance is not what is the rank or the station men occupy, but how they discharge the duties of life — how they use the opportunities they may enjoy of providing for their everlasting happiness. Taught by Christianity, they will sustain with patience the sufferings of their actual lot, while the same instructress will rapidly prepare them for a better; and instead of being objects at one time of contempt, and at another of terror, (a base and servile passion, which too naturally degenerates into hatred,) they will be soon regarded as a grateful peasantry, the strength of the communities in which they live, — of which they have hitherto been the weakness and the terror, sometimes the mischief and the scourge.

To the real nature of the West Indian system, and still more to the extent of its manifold abuses, the bulk even of well-informed men in this country are, I believe, generally strangers. May it not be from our having sinned in ignorance that we have so long been spared? But ignorance of a duty which we have had abundant means of knowing to be such, can by no one be deemed excusable. Let us not presume too far on the forbearance of the Almighty. Favoured in an unequalled degree with Christian light, with civil freedom, and with a greater measure of national blessings than perhaps any other country upon earth ever before enjoyed, what a return would it be for the goodness of the Almighty, if we were to continue to keep the descendants of the Africans, whom we have ourselves wrongfully planted in the western hemisphere, in their present state of unexampled darkness and degradation!

While efforts are making to rescue our country from this guilt and this reproach, let every one remember that he is answerable for any measure of assistance which Providence has enabled him to render towards the accomplishment of the good work. In a country in which the popular voice has a powerful and constitutional influence on the government and legislation, to be silent when there is a question of reforming abuses repugnant to justice and humanity, is to share their guilt. Power always implies responsibility; and the possessor of it cannot innocently be neutral, when by his exertion moral good may be promoted, or evil lessened or removed.

If I may presume to employ a few words on what belongs more particularly to the writer of these lines, I can truly declare, that an irresistible conviction that it is his positive duty to endeavour to rouse his countrymen to a just sense of the importance and urgency of our duties towards the Negro Slaves, has alone compelled him reluctantly thus to come forward again in such an arduous cause as this, and at a period of life when nature shrinks from a laborious contest. He can but too surely anticipate from experience, that the grossest and most unfounded calumnies will be profusely poured out against him; but he nevertheless proceeds, animated by the wish, and, he will add, the confident hope, that the cause of our African brethren will deeply interest the public mind, and that the legislature will be induced to adopt the course prescribed to us by the strongest obligations of moral and religious duty.

Before I conclude, may I presume to interpose a word of caution to my fellow-labourers in this great cause, — a caution which I can truly say I have ever wished myself to keep in remembrance, and observe in practice: it is, that while we expose and condemn the evils of the system itself, we should treat with candour and tenderness the characters of the West Indian proprietors. Let not the friends of the Africans forget that they themselves might have inherited West Indian property; and that by early example and habit they might have been subjected to the very prejudices which they now condemn. I have before declared, and I now willingly repeat, that I sincerely believe many of the owners of West Indian estates to be men of more than common kindness and liberality; but I myself have found many of them, as I have had every reason to believe, utterly unacquainted with the true nature and practical character of the system with which they have the misfortune to be connected.

While, however, we speak and act towards the colonists personally with fair consideration and becoming candour, let our exertions in the cause of the unfortunate slaves be zealous and unremitting. Let us act with an energy suited to the importance of the interests for which we contend. Justice, humanity, and sound policy prescribe our course, and will animate our efforts. Stimulated by a consciousness of what we owe to the laws of God and the rights and happiness of man, our exertions will be ardent, and our perseverance invincible. Our ultimate success is sure; and ere long we shall rejoice in the consciousness of having delivered our country from the greatest of her crimes, and rescued her character from the deepest stain of dishonour.

THE END.

A REVIEW

No. 4.

OF

SOME OF THE ARGUMENTS

WHICH ARE COMMONLY ADVANCED

AGAINST PARLIAMENTARY INTERFERENCE IN BEHALF OF THE NEGRO SLAVES,

WITH

A STATEMENT OF
OPINIONS WHICH HAVE BEEN EXPRESSED
ON THAT SUBJECT

BY MANY OF OUR MOST DISTINGUISHED STATESMEN,

INCLUDING,

EARL GREY,
EARL OF LIVERPOOL,
LORD GRENVILLE,
LORD DUDLEY AND WARD,
LORD MELVILLE,
MR. BURKE,
MR. PITT,

MR. FOX,
MR. WINDHAM,
MR. WILBERFORCE,
MR. CANNING,
MR. BROUGHAM,
SIR S. ROMILLY,
MR. WARRE,
&c. &c. &c.

LONDON:

Printed by Ellerton and Henderson,
Gough Square, Fleet Street;

SOLD BY J. HATCHARD AND SON, PICCADILLY;
AND J. & A. ARCH, CORNHILL.

1823.

A REVIEW,
&c.

THE subject of Colonial Slavery being about to be brought before Parliament, it may not be unseasonable to take a brief view of some of the arguments which will probably be advanced against the proposed legislative interference with that system. In replying to those arguments, it is my intention to have recourse, not so much to my own reasonings as to the recorded opinions of some of our most distinguished statesmen, who, during the last thirty-five years, have been led to employ their powerful minds in considering the subject.

Throughout the whole progress of the controversy respecing Slavery and the Slave Trade, one main argument of the Colonial party against public discussion has been THE DANGER OF INSURRECTION. From the year 1787, to the present day, it has been their uniform policy (and that policy has to a certain extent succeeded, especially with the timid and the ignorant,) to excite alarm on this point, whenever questions touching any part of their system have been publicly agitated.

In the year 1788, a bill was brought into Parliament by Sir William Dolben for regulating the African Slave-Trade, and preventing those horrors of various kinds which had hitherto accompanied the Middle Passage.

The bill was opposed by the united influence of the Slave-traders of Great Britain and the Planters of the West Indies. The absolute ruin of that invaluable branch of commerce, the Slave Trade, and the entire loss of the immense capital embarked in the West Indies, were confidently and clamorously predicted as the certain result even of that measure of regulation. The alarm of insurrection was at the same time sounded throughout the land. And here it is curious, and not a little edifying, to observe the identity of the very expressions which were then employed to stigmatize this harmless and beneficent measure—as a measure of cruelty and blood—as pregnant with devastation and massacre—with those which now fill the mouths of the holders of Slaves whenever they allude to the approaching discussion on the subject of Slavery. A single instance may suffice.

While Sir W. Dolben's bill was before the House of Lords, on the 25th June 1788, the Duke of CHANDOS produced a letter which had been addressed by a gentleman in Jamaica to Mr. Fuller, then agent for that island, informing him, that, " in consequence of what was doing in Parliament, the Negroes expected that an end was to be put to their slavery; that there was the greatest reason to fear they would rise in consequence ; and that *the island was in a state of great alarm and apprehension.*" The Duke added, that " he had many more corresponding accounts with which he would not then trouble the house ; but as often as *the bill* was agitated he should think it his duty to warn their Lordships of the danger that ANY *agitation of such a subject* was liable to." (The Duke, be it remembered, was speaking of a proposal not to emancipate the Slaves, but to regulate the Middle Passage). "The universal massacre," he went on to say, " of the Whites might be the consequence. He must be permitted to know rather more of the West-India Islands than most of their Lordships ;

and it was his duty to lay the result of his acquaintance with the customs of these islands before their Lordships. *The Negroes read the English newspapers as constantly as the ships from England came in; and,* FROM WHAT WAS THEN DOING, *they would conclude their final emancipation was at hand**."

By such assertions and arguments did the Colonists of that day endeavour to prevent the Parliament of England from taking a single step to abate the atrocities, and lessen the wholesale murders, of the Middle Passage, or to alleviate, in however small a degree, the mass of misery which was crowded within the holds of Slave-ships. It is unnecessary to say, that the apprehensions then expressed proved utterly vain, and that not the slightest disturbance of any kind occurred in the West Indies to justify them. But to say this, is to give a very inadequate idea of the gross imposition on Parliament and the Public, which such a statement involved. During the year 1788, and for several years both before and after that period, the whole of our West-India possessions continued in a state of the most profound tranquillity. Not only did no insurrection occur, but not the very slightest tendency to insurrection was manifested, in any one of our colonies; a fact which may be attested by persons who resided in the West Indies during these years, and who never heard of a single occurrence which was capable even of being perverted to the purposes of alarm †. Then comes the bold and confident statement of the noble Duke, grounded on the assumption of his superior acquaintance

* Hansard's Parliamentary History, 1788-9, pp. 646, 647.

† The insurrection in Grenada did not occur till March 1795; and this was caused *in no degree* by parliamentary discussion, but by the intrigues of Victor Hugues, operating on the French planters and Slaves (who were very numerous) in that island.

with West-Indian habits and customs, that "*the Negroes read the English newspapers as constantly as the ships from England came in.*" In making this statement, the Duke was doubtless deceived; but whoever might be its author, the profligate contempt of truth which it necessarily involved, could only be paralleled by the grossness of that ignorance which could be deluded by it. To every man who had resided in the West Indies, it must have been known not only to be false, but to be as absolutely absurd and preposterous as it would be to hear a Jamaica legislator gravely affirming, in the House of Assembly of that island, that the horses in England read the Jamaica newspapers. I can think of no parallel which will more aptly describe the case. The Slaves in Jamaica were universally just as ignorant of letters as the horses are in England.

Similar alarms of danger were sounded during every succeeding stage of the abolition controversy, and with as little foundation in truth as that just alluded to; and on this alleged ground of danger, not only the abolition of the *British* Slave-Trade, but even that of the *Foreign* Slave-Trade carried on in British ships, was uniformly opposed, for many successive years, by the West Indians.

In 1791, we find Mr. J. STANLEY, a West-Indian agent, threatening the Parliament with *the horrors of insurrection* for agitating the question of abolition *.

In 1792, Mr. BAILLIE, agent for Grenada, affirmed, that the " *West-India Islands were filled with emissaries and inflammatory publications by the friends of the abolition* †."

In 1794, when Mr. WILBERFORCE moved for leave to

---

* Hansard's Parliamentary History, vol. xxix. p. 315.
† Ib. p. 1079. None of those emissaries were ever named, nor were any of those publications ever produced.

bring in a bill to abolish the Slave Trade *for the supply of foreign colonies,* it was opposed by the West Indians generally *. Sir W. YOUNG and others represented the proposal as " *dangerous* in point of time and experiment;" and Mr. JENKINSON, now Lord LIVERPOOL, also thought *such a bill* " *highly dangerous* †."

In 1795, Mr. WILBERFORCE was again opposed on

* Only one West Indian, a Mr. VAUGHAN, was of a contrary opinion. He thought it extraordinary, and extraordinary it doubtless was, " that any British colonists should be anxious to raise up rivals to supplant themselves." The West-Indian body, however, turned a deaf ear to this friendly remonstrance, and continued to oppose the abolition of the Foreign as well as of the British Slave-Trade, until they had verified Mr. Vaughan's prediction, and had seen themselves actually supplanted by the rivals they had themselves thus raised up. Even in 1806, Jamaica petitioned against the abolition of the Foreign Slave-Trade; and this, notwithstanding the loud warning which had been addressed to the West Indians on this subject by Mr. Stephen, in a work published in 1804, entitled The Opportunity. It may not be without its use to quote in this place a passage from Mr. Wilberforce's Letter to his Constituents in 1806, to the same effect, viz.—

" What but party-spirit could cause them to support the continuance of that branch of the Slave Trade, which consisted in supplying foreigners with Slaves; and still more, what else could prevent their even strenuously and eagerly anticipating the efforts of the Abolitionists for stopping the supply for the cultivation of the immeasurable expanse of the South-American continent." " The proprietor in our old islands will not deny that these continental settlements have not only injured him by greatly increasing the quantity of colonial produce in the market; but that enjoying very decided advantages over our older islands, from a more fertile soil, from being exempted from hurricanes, from the opportunity of feeding their slaves more plentifully and at a cheaper rate; they have been to him the cause of great loss and embarrassment. Had this evil been suffered to advance, the ruin which must have followed from it, though gradual, would have been sure and complete."—1st Ed. p. 284.—3d Ed. p. 133.

† Hansard's Parliamentary History, vol. xxx. pp. 1446, 1447.

similar grounds, in an attempt to abolish the Foreign Slave-Trade *.

In 1796, the renewal of the motion for the general abolition was represented by Mr. JENKINSON and Mr. DENT, as *endangering the safety* of the West-India Islands; and Mr. BARHAM affirmed, that if carried, it would create *universal rebellion in the islands* †.

In 1798, Sir W. YOUNG desired the House to reflect what *calamities* might happen if the motion was carried ‡; and in 1799 he represented the mischiefs of discussion as " *obvious and fatal. The effect would be to deluge the islands with blood* §."

Again in 1807, to pass over the intermediate discussions, we find the enemies of the Abolition using the same language. Lord REDESDALE believed " it would be the means of producing in the West Indies *all the horrors of insurrection* ||." Mr. BROWN, the agent of Antigua, dwelt on " the alarming danger to the lives of our fellow-subjects from the Abolition. He viewed it with fearful anxiety as *necessarily leading to a fatal paroxysm of insurrection and revolutionary horror*. When the Negroes in the island shall learn what has been done, it will be sufficient to animate them to a spirit of discontent and a desire of redress, from which a scene of misery and horror may be expected equal to that which has disgraced France."

Nor were these alarming views of danger confined to the warmth of parliamentary debate; they formed a prominent topic in all the petitions presented to the Legislature on the subject, from the beginning to the end of the controversy, by the West-Indian Assemblies and

* Hansard's Parliamentary History, vol. xxxi. p. 1330.
† Ibid. vol. xxxii. p. 740.   ‡ Ibid. vol. xxxiii. p. 1402
§ Ibid. vol. xxxiv. p. 528.] || Ibid. vol. viii. p. 701.

their agents. Even so late as the year 1807, the petitions on this subject continued to speak the same language. They all professed to view with " *peculiar alarm*" the very DISCUSSION of the subject, as *necessarily leading to scenes of horror and blood.* And at a still later period, in 1815, when Mr. Wilberforce brought forward his bill for establishing a registry of slaves in the West Indies, similar denunciations of danger were renewed in still louder and more vehement tones than had ever been heard before; although it was not very easy to perceive what connection existed between a Registry Bill and insurrection. That they had in reality no connection, excepting what was attributed to them by the policy of some West Indians, and the blind passion of others, is perfectly obvious from what has since taken place. The different Colonial Legislatures have since passed Registry Acts for themselves; and Parliament, (with the vain view of giving force and efficacy to these crude, imperfect, and inconsistent enactments,) has also passed a general law of the same kind. And all this has been done without the least agitation, or pretext of agitation among the slaves. The subject excited no more interest or attention among them than a turnpike bill would have done; and but for the indiscreet, and clamorous, and misplaced opposition of the West Indians themselves, in 1816, the measure would have passed then as quietly as it afterwards did at a somewhat later period.

The best answer which can be given to those menaces of insurrection, by which the proposal to abolish slavery is now opposed, seems therefore to be, our past experience of the utter falsehood of similar alarms created for a similar purpose. And upon that ground the matter might be safely left to the good sense of the country. It may not, however, be inexpedient to bring forward some authorities on the subject to which it will be felt that no inconsiderable weight is due.

The general feeling, indeed, of our eminent statesmen was in strict unison with that of the Marquis TOWNSEND, who stated in 1788, that he would " not be influenced by such reports, when he was doing a right thing as a legislator, and that he could not be made to believe that the Negroes would be induced to rise *because* Parliament was intent on granting them relief*." Who, indeed, ever heard of an attempt on the part of prisoners to break from confinement by force, and at the hazard of their lives, when there was a fair hope of early and peaceful relief? Such a proceeding on the part of the slaves would also be contrary to all experience and to all analogy. No instance can be produced to justify the apprehension of it. But innumerable instances may be brought forward of a contrary kind; instances, that is to say, which prove that the fair hope of relief, by peaceable means, would extinguish even the desire to rebel, in those who had ground to expect such relief †.

But it may be further demonstrated, that the West Indians, when they sounded, in former times, those alarms of danger from public discussion which they are now repeating, had really no faith in their own representations. Let us hear on this point the statement of Earl GREY, in 1807.

"We are told," says his Lordship, "that the West Indies will be put into a state of revolt if we agree to

---

* Hansard's Parl. Hist. 1788-9, p. 647.

† See on this subject a work which has just appeared from the pen of the venerable champion of this cause, Mr. Clarkson, entitled Thoughts, &c.

the abolition;—and the preamble of the Bill, which states that the Slave Trade is contrary to justice and humanity, is in this view particularly complained of. But is it necessary to tell the Negro, torn from his native land, his wife, his children, his friends, that the act of violence which tears him from all the former endearments of life, is contrary to humanity? If he cannot see it in the wounds inflicted on the back of his fellow-sufferer; if he cannot hear it in the cries of his fellow-slave, are we to suppose that he will read it in the preamble of an act of Parliament? But the West Indians themselves do not believe the argument. If they did, never was the conduct of men more imprudently regulated. After twenty years, during which the question has been agitated, is the House to be told, that all the debates, motions, resolutions, and reports which have gone forth, declaring Slavery to be contrary to humanity, have had no effect in producing that conviction, and that this preamble is to produce it? Has not THE JAMAICA GAZETTE, on various occasions, stated the *very means by which insurrection might be excited, and plans of revolt organised and carried into effect?* And yet, is it not notorious that there never were so few insurrections amongst the Negroes," (indeed there had been none, if we except the revolt caused by the French in Grenada,) " as in the last twenty years, during which an abolition of this infamous traffic has been under discussion?*"

In 1816, Mr. BROUGHAM adopted the same line of reasoning, and produced to the House THREE JAMAICA GAZETTES, in which it was openly and vehemently asserted, that *Registration was only a cloak for emancipation* †.

Again, in 1818, Sir SAMUEL ROMILLY, who had

---

* Hansard's Debates, vol. viii. p. 951.
† Ibid. vol. xxxiv. p. 1213.

brought before the House some cases of cruelty which had occurred in the West Indies, was led to remark;—
"We are told that such discussions have no other effect than to excite disorder and insubordination, and to break the chain which bound the slave to his master. This goes, however, to prevent all discussion. Are we then, under such a pretence, to allow slaves to undergo the most rigorous treatment without inquiry? It was the custom to attribute every insurrection among the Slaves to those who took an active interest in their condition. The charge was unfounded. Revolts were much more frequent before the abolition than they had been since, as may be seen from Long's History of Jamaica. It was merely a cry set up by the island newspapers, and by those interested in continuing the abuse*."

* Hansard's Debates, vol. xxxviii. p. 854.

It may be expected, that some allusion should be here made to the BARBADOES INSURRECTION, as it is called, of 1816. Of this alleged insurrection it may be sufficient to say, that for some cause or other, the whole of the circumstances attending it have been most cautiously suppressed by Government, as well as by the Colonial authorities. Not a single official document respecting it has been allowed to see the light. All we know is, that *the alleged insurgents made no attack: they were the party attacked. No White man appears to have been killed or even wounded by the Blacks, while from one to two thousand Blacks are said to have been hunted down, and either put to death without resistance, or summarily tried and executed. Into this bloody transaction, Parliament has made no inquiry whatever!* Why have not the West Indians called for such inquiry? Until this is done; until the whole of this most mysterious affair is placed in the light of day, it will be impossible for them to use it as an argument against discussion. Neither Parliament nor the country can forget the utter contempt of Negro life which prevailed among the Whites in Barbadoes, as displayed both in their statute-book, and in the ferocious acts of wanton barbarity communicated by Earl Seaforth in 1805; and both will require proof, before they decide that the real cause of this enormous waste of human life, was an insurrection produced by public discussion in this country. Had the different details on

The reader will probably be satisfied, by what he has read, that the alleged danger of insurrection from parliamentary discussion, though it may have proved a very convenient topic of argument, in resisting every successive attempt to abolish the Slave Trade, was wholly without any foundation in fact. In the present case, therefore, after the uniform experience of thirty-five years, the presumption must be admitted to be very strongly adverse to the reality of the alleged peril. Indeed if the representations of the West-India party are worthy of credit, THE STATE OF THE NEGROES IS ONE OF SUCH HAPPINESS AND COMFORT as would, of itself, render abortive every attempt to excite them to insubordination, and would seem to preclude on their parts all desire of change. And this has been the uniform language of the Colonists:—

"I have lived," said Mr. BAILLIE, the agent of Grenada in 1792, "sixteen years in the West Indies; and I declare, in the most solemn manner, that *I consider the Negroes in the British West-India Islands to be in as comfortable a state as the lower orders of mankind in any country of Europe. They are perfectly contented with their situation* *."

Mr. BARHAM affirmed, in 1796, that "*the* SLAVES

---

this subject been favourable to the Barbadian Colonists; or could *they* have exhibited clear proof of *designed* revolt and insurrection on the part of the Slaves; and, above all, could they have connected such revolt with the discussions respecting the Registry Bill in England, the public would have been satiated with statements on the subject: nothing could have availed to suppress them. But not a syllable has been officially published, either in England or in Barbadoes, which can throw light on these dark and sanguinary occurrences;—nothing to shew the guilt] of the Blacks, or the lenity and forbearance of the Whites. This deep and deathlike silence speaks volumes.

* Hansard's Parl. Hist. vol. xxix. p. 1079.

were *better fed and clothed, and enjoyed more of the comforts of life, than the generality of the labouring class throughout Europe.*"

Mr. CHARLES ELLIS, in 1797, repelled the charges brought against the West-Indian system, of an *excess of labour and deficiency of food, and bestowed the highest praise on the consolidated Slave-law of Jamaica**.

In 1798, Sir WILLIAM YOUNG affirmed, that "*the Negroes on the islands had* NOTHING *to complain of. They enjoyed* COMPLETE PROTECTION: *their property was* BETTER SECURED *than our own†.*"

And to omit innumerable assertions of the same kind, Earl ST. VINCENTS, in 1807, asserted, that " he was enabled to state that *the West-Indian islands formed* PARADISE ITSELF *to the Negroes, in comparison with their native country* ‡."

The statements of the present day are no less strong and sweeping. But then they are generally accompanied by an observation which goes far to discredit all the earlier panegyrics pronounced on the system of Negro Slavery; namely, that *very great improvements have taken place, of late years, in the treatment of the Slaves.* One would naturally have supposed, from those previous statements, that there had been little or no room for improvement.

In 1788, the Marquis TOWNSEND, after having listened to some such sweeping affirmations of the superior comfort and happiness of the West-Indian Slave,

---

* Ibid. vol. xxxiii. p. 251. This law, however, requires only to be read, in order to shew how little it merited such an encomium.

† Ibid. vol. xxxiv. p. 558. And yet, at a later period, when he was Governor of Tobago, he acknowledged, that the law of evidence was such as almost necessarily " covered the most guilty European with impunity," whatever oppressions or cruelties he might have committed towards slaves.

‡ Hansard's Debates, vol. viii. p. 670.

as have been quoted above, got up and remarked, that "if it were true, as was alleged, that the Negroes were *twice* as happy as the English labourers, Parliament ought to sit all the summer, in order to put the English yeoman on a footing with the West-India slave*.

But in reply to all the glowing descriptions which have, at any time, been given of the happiness of the Negro slave, it might be sufficient to adduce the decided testimony borne, by some of the most distinguished of the West-India Planters, to the NECESSITY OF PARLIAMENTARY INTERFERENCE, in order to meliorate their condition. Mr. BRYAN EDWARDS, and others, have painted, in the most affecting colours, the wretchedness which results from the principle of law, universally recognised in the British West Indies, that SLAVES ARE CHATTELS, and have dwelt on *the immense benefits they would derive from being attached to the soil.* Mr. CHARLES ELLIS took the same view of the subject, when, in 1797, he moved an address to the Crown, that the different Colonial Legislatures might be called upon " to adopt such measures as should appear to them best calculated to obviate the causes *which have hitherto impeded the natural increase of the Negroes already in the islands,*" and " particularly with a view to the same effect, to employ such means as may conduce to *the moral and religious improvement of the Negroes,* and secure to them, throughout all the British West Indies, the *certain, immediate,* and *active protection of the law.*" And in the speech which accompanied the motion, he dwelt on the necessity of affording to the Slaves *moral instruction* and *education.*

Now there must have been, in the mind of Mr. Ellis and his friends, a strong persuasion that in 1797 much,

* Hansard's Parl. Hist. 1788-9, p. 646.

very much remained to be done by the Colonial Legislatures to improve the condition of the slaves. It is for them to shew what steps have been taken, during the twenty-six years which have since elapsed, to realize any of those improvements which were so admitted, by the whole body of the West-Indians in Parliament, (all of whom supported the address) to be then greatly needed. *The Slaves have not yet ceased to be* CHATTELS. *No means of education have yet been provided for them. No effective steps have yet been taken for their religious improvement; nay, they are to this hour denied the Sabbath as a day of repose and religious observance.* So far have the Colonial Legislatures been from removing the impediments to the natural increase of the Slaves, that that work is still to be commenced, the marriage tie being still unknown among them. And so far are the Slaves from being CERTAINLY, IMMEDIATELY, *and* ACTIVELY PROTECTED *by* LAW, *that*, BY LAW, *at the present moment, every slave, male or female, in the Colonies, may be punished by their owner or overseer, without his being required to give any reason for so doing, not only with any length of confinement he may think proper, but with thirty-nine lashes of the cartwhip on the naked body; and may also be compelled to labour, willing or unwilling, without wages, by the impulse of the same cruel instrument.*

The West Indians boast that their Slaves are as happy as the peasantry of England. But, let us suppose a state of things in this country, in which every bailiff of an estate should be armed with a power of driving the labourers, both men and women, to their work, by means of the lash, and should be also at liberty to use his entire discretion as to the infliction of punishment, by confinement to *any* extent, and by the cartwhip to the extent of *thirty-nine lashes on the* *bare body*, for any conduct which he might construe into an offence. What, I ask, would, in this case, be the condition of our English peasantry? And can we regard the overseers of the West Indies as safer depositaries of such tremendous powers than English bailiffs would be; especially when we consider all the circumstances of degradation arising from colour, and other peculiarities attaching to Negro bondage? Or are indeed the overseers of the West Indies angels, and not men, that there is no risk of their abusing the authority thus reposed in them? Mr. BROUGHAM is well known to have deeply considered the subject of Colonial manners. Whoever reads his work on Colonial Policy, or his Speech on the Registry Bill in 1816, will see how little he thought these men qualified for the due exercise of so momentous a trust*

But it was not only in 1797, that the necessity of parliamentary interference was admitted by the West Indians. Again, in 1816, the same necessity was implied in the motion of Lord Holland in the House of Lords, and of Mr. Palmer in the House of Commons, praying his Majesty " to *recommend*, IN THE STRONGEST MANNER, to the local authorities in the respective colonies, *to carry into effect every measure which may tend to promote the moral and religious improvement, as well as the comfort and happiness of the Negroes.*" But why this STRONG *recommendation* from Parliament (proposed too by West Indians), if it were true that the state of the Slaves was what it ought to be; was, in short, as happy as that of British labourers?

To all this the West Indians may, and probably will reply—" To such parliamentary interference as this we do not object. What we object to is ANY ATTEMPT

---

* Hansard's Debates, vol. xxxiv. p. 1217.

ON THE PART OF PARLIAMENT TO LEGISLATE FOR THE COLONISTS; as such an attempt would be a violation of the sacred rights of the Colonies, *whose local legislatures* ALONE *ought to make laws for their internal government.*"

Had the previous references made by Parliament to the Colonial Legislatures been attended with beneficial effects, such a plan might have been more deserving of attention. But this is notoriously not the case. On the point of RIGHT, however, what has been the opinion of our most distinguished statesmen?

Mr. BURKE, it will be recollected, (himself the great opposer of the taxation of the North-American Colonies,) *framed a plan for ameliorating the condition of the Slaves, which was to be enacted and enforced by* THE IMPERIAL PARLIAMENT ALONE, *without the intervention or even recognition of the Colonial Legislatures.*—Mr. DUNDAS, afterwards Lord MELVILLE, followed, in this respect the general plan of Mr. Burke. He professed to have in view " *the total annihilation of hereditary Slavery.*" " And he should suggest (he said) the manner in which he thought this might be accomplished. The planter who was the owner of the father, in his opinion, should take away the child from the moment of his birth; take care to have him inspired with a sense of religion; and when he had attained to a certain age, the boy in return should serve him for so many years, till he had repaid him the expense of his education. The consequence of this must be visible. Thus nurtured in the principles of religion, he would be filled with a just sense of duty and gratitude. If his master was a humane man, he would feel a consolation in what he had done. *The parents would also turn with gratitude to their owner, and* FORGET THEIR MISERIES *in the prospects of the happiness of their offspring.* The rising generation, thus trained and *conducted in the paths of piety,* would be attached to the island, and, of course, in the hour of danger spring forward in the defence of it. Was this visionary? He trusted not. *He was well convinced that the heart of the African was susceptible of the finest impressions of gratitude, as experience had evinced; and that it was also susceptible of the tenderest emotions of love.* He most earnestly solicited all the gentlemen interested in the question to support his modification : he would sooner see all the lands in the West Indies cultivated by freemen than by slaves.'

" To illustrate the topic of discussion, he referred to an instance of the abolition of Slavery in the northern parts of the kingdom. Alluding to the parliamentary proceedings in 1775, he stated, that, at that period, the coalliers, salters, and those employed under ground, were in a state of Slavery; and that *when it was proposed to acknowledge them* AS FREE CITIZENS, *a clamour was excited that those concerned in the coallieries would be ruined; that the slavery of these poor people was a necessary evil; and that to grant them freedom would raise the price of coals beyond the capacity of their fellow-citizens.* THESE ASSERTIONS, HOWEVER, PROVED NUGATORY: THE PROPERTY WAS NOT INJURED, *and the idea of an advance in the price of coals vanished in smoke* *."

Mr. WINDHAM appears to have viewed this matter in the same light with these two statesmen. In 1798, we find him saying, " I am inclined to trust for a while to the Colonial Assemblies *by way of experiment.* Had I no hopes of considerable advantage by doing so, I own I should be inclined to the plan of the late Mr.

---

* Clarendon's Parliamentary Chronicle, vol. iv. p. 530.

Burke; a man who left no part of the interests of mankind unexamined, and who brought with him more wisdom in discussing every subject he attempted to investigate than any man I ever knew. His idea was *to take much of the power of legislation on this subject out of the hands of the Colonists, and to make many regulations within ourselves by which to meliorate the condition of the Negro**."

Earl GREY, in 1807, looked forward to " *the abolition of Slavery, encouraged and assisted by such regulations as the wisdom of Parliament should think fit to adopt* †."

Lord GRENVILLE, in 1817, declared, "that he never could admit that by any address to the Crown," (alluding to that of the preceding year mentioned above,) "*a million of British subjects should be withdrawn from the control of the Imperial Parliament* ‡."

In 1818, Mr. WILBERFORCE observed,—" When it is known that the recommendation of such men as Mr. Ellis and Mr. Barham had failed to make any impression on the Colonial Assemblies, he could place no firm dependence, *except on the legislation of the mother country, and could put his trust in no other guarantee. It was their duty to watch over the interests of a million of beings at length recognised as fellow-creatures* §."

On the same occasion, Sir S. ROMILLY remarked, that " it had been said that this country had not the power of legislating for the Colonies. It was needless for him to state, that *it had been already done in numerous instances.* He might only mention, that it had been done by the act by which Colonial property was made liable as assets for debt. No man could for a

* Hansard's Parl. Hist. vol. xxxiii. p. 1413.
† Hansard's Debates, vol. viii. p. 954.
‡ Ibid. vol. xxxv. p. 1205.
§ Ibid. vol xxxviii. p. 295.

moment imagine that the British Constitution could apply to these colonies. That constitution should be taken as a whole. It held, that *all men stood in a state of equality* IN THE EYE OF THE LAW. *The moment an individual set foot on British soil, he became free.* What then could be more inconsistent than to talk of establishing that constitution in the West Indies ? For there its principles would be reversed and destroyed ; and under the auspices of British liberty, Slavery would be rendered worse than under arbitrary governments. Arbitrary governments, indeed, did make laws for their Colonies. But how is that principle of the British Constitution to be applied to such Colonies as ours, that no man could be bound by laws to which he had not consented. In Dominica, for instance, it was enacted, that a free Man of Colour, coming hither from another island. became a slave, if he had not a certain certificate, and did not pay a tax of 35*l*. This was the enactment of those who talked of the British Constitution ! A Slave once landed on the British coast became a freeman ; but a free Man of Colour, the instant he touched the soil of Dominica, became a slave !—In short, the whole of these laws were founded on a principle diametrically opposite to that which formed the basis of the British Constitution. And, with respect to those laws which looked so well on paper, which appeared so well calculated to benefit the Slave Population, they not only were not executed, but were never *intended* to be carried into effect. But though these unfortunate beings were the slaves of their masters, they were also THE SUBJECTS OF THE KING. THEY OWED HIM ALLEGIANCE, AND HE WAS BOUND TO AFFORD THEM PROTECTION. THEY WERE AS MUCH SUBJECTS AS ENGLISHMEN WERE *."

* Hansard's Debates, vol. xxxviii. pp. 302—304.

Mr. J. H. Smith then stated, that "when he considered that in none of the Colonies any steps had been taken to encourage the manumission of slaves; when be considered the treatment to which, in all the Colonies, they were still subject; that the cartwhip was still resorted to as an instrument of discipline; that the slaves were still discredited as witnesses; and that their evidence could not be taken in a Court of Justice;—he could not help thinking it the duty of Parliament to protect those who might thus be exposed to oppression.

Mr. Warre contended that it was absurd to suppose that any real good could be effected for ameliorating the condition of the slaves, unless discussions were raised in that House. It was by such discussions that every thing hitherto done had been effected *.

But by far the most decisive statement made on this subject came from Mr. Canning. A speech of his, in 1799, is given at great length in Hansard's Parliamentary History of that year, from which I shall take the liberty of making some extracts:—

Alluding to the Address moved by Mr. C. Ellis, in 1797, Mr. Canning said, The point to be ascertained was, " *whether or not the Colonial Assemblies were,* in fact, *taking such steps as evinced a sincere desire to fulfil the expressed purpose of that motion.*"—He then proceeded to animadvert on a petition of the Assembly of Jamaica, in which they asserted the right *of obtaining labourers from Africa*. " Never," observed Mr. Canning, "even in the practical application of that detested and pernicious doctrine of the *rights of man*, had the word right been so shamefully affixed to murder, to devastation, to the invasion of public independence, to the pollution and destruction of private hap-

* Hansard's Debates, pp. 308—852.

piness, to gross and unpalliated injustice, to the spreading of misery and mourning over the earth, to the massacre of innocent individuals, and to the extermination of unoffending nations, as when THE RIGHT TO TRADE IN MAN'S BLOOD* *was asserted by the enlightened government of a civilized country."*

In a preceding part of the debate, Sir W. YOUNG had expressed much displeasure with Mr. Wilberforce, for having said that the laws of our islands did not even equal those of the French *Code Noire*. Mr. Canning made the following observations in reply: "The Hon. Bart. felt the utmost indignation that the laws by which the colonies of a free country were regulated should be compared with any body of legislation emanating from an absolute monarchy. He might refer to the papers upon the table, to prove that, be the *Code Noire* of France as bad as the Hon. Bart. was desirous it should be thought, the laws in the English islands had been found at least as susceptible of amendment. He might refer the Hon. Bart. to the maimings and mutilations, the scourges and spiked collars, the use of which was prohibited or regulated by the papers on the table. But, wishing to avoid invidious topics, he would only ask, in point of fact, whether he had never found, in the whole extent of his various reading, in ancient and modern history, that *the Colonies of a free country were in general worse regulated and worse administered than those of more absolute governments? That this was a truth all history shewed."* "But," says the Hon. Bart., "it cannot be that a code framed by a despotic government should be superior or equal to the laws enacted by the government of a free country. Was he then prepared to argue that there was something in the nature of the relation between the despot and his slave, which must

* The very question now at issue.

vitiate, and render nugatory and null whatever laws the former might make for the benefit of the latter?" " Was this his argument? He thanked him for it. He admitted its truth to any extent the Hon. Bart. pleased. And let the House, and the Hon. Bart. mark how it bore on the question before them. The question is, whether, in what is to be done towards alleviating and finally extinguishing the horrors of the Slave Trade, the proper agent was the British House of Commons, or the Colonial Assemblies. The Hon. Bart. contended that the Colonial Assemblies, and not the British House of Commons were the agents most proper to be employed. But what was his argument? 'Trust not the masters of slaves in what concerns legislation for Slavery. However specious their laws may appear, depend upon it they must be ineffectual in their application. *It is in the nature of things that they should be so!*' Granted. LET THEN THE BRITISH HOUSE OF COMMONS DO THEIR PART THEMSELVES. *Let them not delegate the trust of doing it to those who, according to the Hon. Bart., cannot execute that trust fairly. Let the evil be remedied by an assembly of freemen, by the government of a free people, and not by those whom he represents as utterly unqualified for the undertaking, nor by the masters of slaves. Their laws*, the Hon. Bart. avowed, *could never reach, would never cure the evil.*" " There was something in the nature of absolute authority, in the relation between master and slave which made despotism, in all cases, and under all circumstances, an incompetent and unsure executor even of its own provisions in favour of the objects of its power." Again—" A man's strongest permanent interests were liable to be overborne by his passions. Look at the laws on the table, and see what sort of evils they are intended to remedy. Besides, the interest of a proprietor resident on the island, unencumbered with debt, and looking to his estate as a permanent provision for his family, is one thing;—that of the absentee proprietor, who wishes to lay the foundation of a fortune elsewhere—that of the embarrassed proprietor, who wishes to discharge his encumbrances—and that of the overseer, anxious to realize a sum of money to purchase an estate, are interests of a very different kind indeed from that steady and permanent interest, which, contenting itself with moderate returns, would ensure mild and considerate treatment to the labourers, whose work was to produce them. All these might require increased labour and rapid produce: all these might, in the nature of things, be less solicitous about the eventual exhaustion of the soil, or of the workers of the soil, than about the extent of present profit. And when the proportion of these classes to that of the resident and unembarrassed proprietors was considered, what became of the general statement that the interest of the owner must, in all cases, secure the good treatment of the slaves? He hoped the slaves were well treated, but that they must be so from any necessitating and unalterable cause he could not agree*."

Again, on the 19th June, 1816, Mr. CANNING observed, that " it was far from him to doubt the omnipotence of Parliament; but he thought that the question should not be stirred unless interference became absolutely necessary. *When that necessity arose, his voice should be fearlessly raised in its favour.*" " He had known, in some cases, instances of obstinacy in the Colonial Assemblies, which left that House no choice but of direct interference. Such conduct might now call for such an exertion on the part of Parliament; but all he pleaded for was, that *time should be granted.* The address (Mr. Palmer's) could not be misunderstood. *It said to the assemblies, You are safe for the present from the interference of Parliament, on the belief that you will do yourselves what is required of you. The Assemblies might be left to infer the consequences of refusal, and* PARLIAMENT MIGHT REST SATISFIED WITH THE CONSCIOUSNESS THAT THEY HELD IN THEIR HANDS THE MEANS OF ACCOMPLISHING THAT WHICH THEY HAD PROPOSED*."

Enough has probably been said on this subject. Let us now advert to another. It is alleged, that the Abolitionists have acted in bad faith towards the Colonists; that throughout the Slave-Trade controversy, they professed to have no view to any object but that of the abolition of the *Trade*, and disclaimed any ulterior design of aiming at the EMANCIPATION OF THE SLAVES; but that now, the emancipation of the Slaves was their declared and settled purpose.

To judge correctly of the fairness of this imputation, it will be necessary to take a review of what was all along avowed upon the point in question by those who took a prominent part in advocating the cause of abolition.

The language both of Mr. PITT and Mr. FOX was very unequivocal. In April 1791, we find the latter laying down the following general principle on the subject, from which he never deviated.

" *Personal freedom must be the first object of every human being; and it was a* RIGHT *of which he who deprives a fellow-creature is absolutely criminal in so depriving him, and which he who withholds when it is in his power to restore, is no lesss criminal in withholding* †."

No less decisive was the language of Mr. PITT, in

* Hansard's Debates, vol. xxxiv. p. 1220.
† Hansard's Parliamentary History, vol. xxix. p. 534.

April 1792. " It is within the power of the Colonies," he remarked, " and is it not their indispensable duty, to apply themselves to the correction of the various abuses by which population is restrained. The most important consequences may be expected to attend Colonial regulations for this purpose. With the improvement of internal population, the condition of every Negro will improve also : his LIBERTY *will advance, or at least he will be approaching to a state of liberty.* NOR CAN YOU INCREASE THE HAPPINESS OR EXTEND THE FREEDOM OF THE NEGRO, WITHOUT ADDING IN AN EQUAL DEGREE TO THE SAFETY OF THE ISLANDS AND OF ALL THEIR INHABITANTS. *Thus, Sir, in the place of slaves, who naturally have an interest directly opposite to that of their master, and are therefore viewed by them with an eye of constant suspicion, you will create a body of valuable citizens and subjects forming a part of the same community, having a common interest with their superiors in the security and prosperity of the whole.* Gentlemen, talk of the diminution of labour. But *if you restore to this degraded race the true feelings of men ; if you take them out from among the order of brutes, and place them on a level with the rest of the human species, they will then work with that energy which is natural to men, and their labour will be productive in a thousand ways above what it has yet been, as the labour of a man must be more productive than that of a brute* *."

Mr. Pitt then proceeded to illustrate his argument by referring to the answers which had been given by the Grenada Assembly to certain queries put to them by the Privy Council ; and in which it was affirmed, that the Negroes did twice as much work when employed

---

* Hansard's Parliamentary History, vol. xxix. p. 1138.

for their own benefit, as they did when labouring for their masters. The whole of the passage, indeed the whole of that splendid speech, is most highly deserving of attention.

Again, in 1804, Mr. Pitt affirmed, that " *it was for the interest of the planters, and for the benefit of all the islands, (and those who look at the subject with reference to the principles of general philosophy would admit, that the system of restraint was as unprofiable as it was odious); that the labour of a man who was conscious of freedom, was of much more value than of him who felt that he was a slave* *."

Lord GRENVILLE'S views were perfectly coincident with those of Mr. PITT and Mr. FOX. " *Personal freedom,*" observed his Lordship, in 1806, "*was a blessing granted by God, and could not with justice be violated.*" "In the course of Mr. Pitt's discussions of the subject, his calculations on the comparative value of the labour of freemen and slaves, were luminous and convincing. *One of the incontrovertible results was, that the labour of slaves was not so profitable by much as that of freemen* †."

Again: " It is of great consequence that we should look attentively to that period, *when the disgrace of slavery, in any form, shall no longer be suffered within the territories of this free country.* While we are advocates for the liberties of Europe, while we raise the standard of freedom against the common enemy of order, virtue, and humanity, *it behoves us peculiarly to preserve that freedom unpolluted within the pale of the British empire.* I recommend this measure as the most safe and effectual means of *the ultimate emancipa-*

---

* Hansard's Debates, vol. ii. p. 550.
† Hansard's Debates, vol. vii. pp. 803, 804.

tion *of the Slaves in the West Indies.* By this expedient you will abundantly ameliorate their condition, *so that they may be fitted for the enjoyment of that liberty which in every region of the earth* IS THE COMMON RIGHT OF HUMAN NATURE *."

Nor was Earl GREY less decisive on this point. In 1807, he thus expressed himself:

" We have been told, that if this be considered as a measure of justice, we do not follow up our own principles; for if slavery be in itself unjust, we ought to abolish it altogether. I think it sufficient to say that *the result of this measure will, I trust, lead to the abolition of slavery,* ENCOURAGED AND ASSISTED BY SUCH REGULATIONS AS THE WISDOM OF PARLIAMENT MAY AFTERWARDS THINK FIT TO ADOPT. I trust, that by this measure, slavery will gradually wear out without the immediate intervention of any positive law; in like manner as took place in the states of Greece and Rome, and some parts of modern Europe, *where slaves have been permitted to work out and purchase their own freedom, and that such regulations may be adopted as have been adopted in some of the Spanish and Portuguese colonies. In some of the states of America, measures of gradual emancipation have been adopted; and I would ask whether any instance can be pointed out, of insurrections and revolutions in consequence of such measures, or whether th y have not, in such states been peaceable and orderly* *?"

It seems wholly unnecessary to quote the frequent declarations of Mr. WILBERFORCE to the same effect. He often declared his strong desire " to convert the Slaves into a free and happy peasantry, capable of de-

* Debates on Slave Trade, for 1807, pp. 27, 28.
† Hansard's Debates, vol. viii. pp. 954, 955.

fending the islands which they inhabited, instead of endangering them by their presence*." It may be of still more weight in the argument, to refer to the memorable declaration of Mr. WARD, now Lord DUDLEY and WARD, himself a large proprietor of slaves, whose numbers have continued regularly and rapidly to increase under his benign and paternal management. " It was a fact," he observed, " which needed no evidence to support it, *that the human race was prevented by nothing but* ILL TREATMENT, *from multiplying as fast in the West Indies as in every other country where the bounty of nature was not cramped by mischievous institutions.*" " The reasons which applied to the termination of the Slave Trade," he was of opinion, " applied as well TO THE TOTAL ABOLITION OF SLAVERY " as to that of the Slave Trade; " *and if I did not believe,*" added he, " *that this measure would ultimately tend to the emancipation of the Negroes, I should be inclined to oppose it as an improper compromise between the British Parliament and the West-India planters* †."

But even if the Abolitionists had heretofore been silent on this subject, the principles on which the abolition of slavery is now called for would not have been affected by such a circumtance. For it cannot be denied, that the very same principles which led to the condemnation of the Slave Trade by the British Legislature, as immoral, inhuman, and unjust, must lead to the very same sentence on the Slavery which has been produced by it, whenever that system comes under the serious review of Parliament. Nor is this any new opinion. It is an opinion which was clearly and une-

* See Hansard's Debates, vol. xxxv. p. 775.
† Debates on the Slave Trade for 1807, p. 167.

quivocally expressed in 1807, by two of his Majesty's present Cabinet Ministers, who were then hostile to the measure of abolition.

The Earl of WESTMORELAND observed, that "*if the Slave Trade was contrary to justice and humanity, it was also contrary to justice and humanity to keep the Negroes who had been procured by means of the trade in a state of perpetual slavery* *."

And it was the Earl of LIVERPOOL's opinion, that "The same principle on which the noble Lord condemned the Slave Trade applied with equal force to the state of slavery itself †."

The language of Mr. WINDHAM, in 1806, was still more full and decisive. "That the Slave Trade," he said, " is contrary to justice, humanity, and sound policy, nobody can doubt; and I would add, slavery too; for that is the first character of slavery. Slavery is that which every one must wish to see abolished. *And certainly I had rather see it abolished by law, than wait for the process of civilization. What gentlemen say of the Slave Trade, I say of slavery, that it is a great evil;* they are each *malum in se*. Although slavery has so long subsisted, I have no hesitation in saying, it is a state not fit to subsist, because it gives to one human being a greater power over another than it is fit for any human being to possess. Man is not fit to have so much power over his fellow-creatures ‡."

It is not, of course, the intention of this pamphlet to enter into the general question of Negro Slavery. On that subject I must refer to the various publications

---

* Hansard's Debates, vol. viii. p. 702.
† Ibid. vol. vii. p. 805.
‡ Debates on the Slave Trade, for 1806, pp. 70, 71.

which have recently appeared*, and which prove that the state of *slavery* existing in the British Colonies, no less than the Slave Trade from which it sprung, *is contrary to justice, humanity, and sound policy; inconsistent with the principles of the British Constitution; and repugnant to the spirit of the Christian religion; and that it ought to be abolished at the earliest period, which is compatible with a due attention to the various interests involved in the measure.*

If the reader concurs in this proposition, he will probably find in the preceding pages enough to satisfy him, that the British Parliament alone is competent to carry that proposition into effect, and that it may do so without any apprehension of those dangers which, it has been so confidently affirmed, must follow from parliamentary interference.

* See particularly Mr. Wilberforce's " Appeal," and a pamphlet entitled " Negro Slavery."

FINIS.

Printed by Ellerton and Henderson,
Gough Square, London.

The Report

No. 5.

OF THE

Committee of the Legislature

OF

DOMINICA,

APPOINTED TO ENQUIRE INTO AND REPORT
ON CERTAIN QUERIES

RELATIVE TO THE

Condition, Treatment, Rights & Privileges

OF THE

NEGRO POPULATION

OF THAT ISLAND.

JUNE, 1823.

PRINTED BY CHARLES M. WILLICH,
No. 8, PICKETT STREET, TEMPLE BAR, LONDON.

DOMINICA.

THE REPORT of the Committee of the Legislature appointed to enquire into, and Report on certain Queries relative to the Condition, Treatment, Rights and Privileges of the Negro Population of this Island.

Your Committee beg leave to state to your Honorable House, that, though the pressure of the important subjects submitted to their consideration, has not allowed them to devote to their examination, so much time and attention as they deserve, they nevertheless have been enabled to procure from the most respectable and authentic sources, a mass of information, which completely establishes that every care and attention is paid to the happiness and comforts, as well as to the moral and religious instruction of the Slaves.

From many individuals possessing, from others having the superintendance and care of the largest Estates, belonging to resident and absent Proprietors, from the Clergymen of the different religious persuasions, from medical gentlemen of high character and extensive practice, from the Register of Slaves, from the Records of the Courts of Justice and from the Laws of the Island, they have procured a body of evidence upon which they have founded their report, to the truth of which they challenge the severest investigation.

Your Committee beg leave to state to your Honorable House, that the general and individual condition of the Negroes is such as to secure to them every comfort and enjoyment consistent with their situation in the country.

The state of Slavery, established, not by the laws of the colonies, but by those of Great Britain, is soothed and ameliorated by the kindness and humanity of the West Indian Proprietor. Amply provided by the care of his owner (enforced by the authority of the law) with every necessary and comfort of life, the Negro can never feel the hardships of want, is never distressed by the cares of a starving family, and secure in the possession of a comfortable house, can never know the misery of seeing his family and children driven from the shelter of his roof, by the cruelty of a creditor or the hardships of the times, nor doomed to depend on charity for the support of a wretched existence.

In sickness he is provided with medical attendance and every attention and care is bestowed npon him which his situation requires. That this is not a vain, but effectual provision of the law and strictly attended to, your Committee refer to the annexed certificates of three medical gentlemen who attend the greater number of estates in this Island.

Your Committee declare that punishments have greatly decreased, that the use of the cart whip has very generally been laid aside, for which the cat used in the army has been substituted, that for the greatest offences the number of thirty-nine stripes never is, and cannot, by an express law of the Island, be inflicted, for much less offences than which, a soldier would be condemned to the horrible and disgusting punishment of two or three hundred lashes; and the cat in use, is much smaller than the one used in the army.

By a law of the Island, the various provisions of which are enforced by severe penalties of fine or imprisonment, every Proprietor of Slaves is compelled to provide for his Negroes sufficient and wholesome food, with a comfortable house, and in sickness medical attendance with wine and every necessary indulgence which the physician may direct. If the Proprietors prefer it, they also may allot a sufficient piece of land not less than half an acre to each Negro, for his provision ground, with time for the proper cultivation. In addition to which they are allowed to cultivate as much land as they please without any restriction whatsoever, and it is the particular duty of the manager and overseer to see that the time allowed by law for cultivating their grounds is properly applied to that purpose. It is a notorious fact that many industrious Negroes from the produce of their grounds have obtained their own freedom as well as that of their families, and some have even purchased, and are actually owners and possessors of other Negroes; and for the truth of this statement, your Committee refer to the accompanying certificates from the Register of Slaves, by which it will appear that their owners have returned Slaves, not as their own property, but as that of these Negroes, thereby furnishing evidence against themselves and in favor of the Negro Proprietors.

Their property of every kind is secured to them by the law, and any person guilty of depriving a Negro of his property, is compelled by summary process to appear before a Magistrate to be fined for such offence, and the Magistrate is authorized to direct such fine to be paid to such Slave.

In the moral character of the Country, they have even a stronger protection, in the execration and contempt with which any individual of the community will be followed, who shall presume to deprive a Negro of any part of his property. Slaves are competent under certain restrictions, to give evidence in Courts of Justice, and on reference to the records, it will be found that the property and persons of this class have enjoyed equal protection with that of the white inhabitant. At this moment there are two informations on the files of the Court of Chancery, one on behalf of a poor Negro boy named John, by His Majesty's Attorney General, and another on behalf of seven Slaves claiming their freedom, and which suits are conducted free of any expence whatever, as will appear by the annexed certificate of the Register of that court. In the last of these suits, the plaintiffs claim their freedom absolutely on an account of rents and profits of a Negro which they claim as their own, for the purpose of purchasing their manumission.

By the law, religious instruction is strictly enjoined, and it will appear by reference to the accompanying certificates of the Catholic and the Wesleyan clergymen, that the greater part of the Negro population enjoy the blessings of religion to the fullest extent.

Your Committee call the attention of this

House to the fact that a public school has been lately established for the purpose of religious instruction, for the support of which many of the first and most respectable individuals in the Colony have contributed. For further information on this head, your Committee refer to the accompanying papers, which have been furnished by Mr. Dawes the church missionary and director pro tempore of the school, and to the letter of that gentleman to Mr. Henry Glanville, one of your Committee.

With regard to discipline, the law specially provides for the protection of the Negro from severe punishments. The owner of a Slave cannot inflict more than thirty-nine lashes, the manager is limited to twenty, and the overseer cannot exceed five.

Any person accused of cruel treatment, must submit to be examined before a magistrate upon oath; and in case of his refusal to answer, his contumacy is taken as an admission of guilt: an anomalous precedent in British jurisprudence in favor of the Slave, by which the party accused is compelled to furnish evidence against himself; and power is given to the court to order the Slave to be taken from his owner to prevent the possibility of his again becoming the victim of a cruel master—an instance of which, actually occurred in the case of the Negro Thornton, who by the order of the Court of King's Bench, was transferred from his owner to another master.

Your Committee further state, that the baptism of Negroes is directed and enjoined by the law, and the increase of late has been very considerable, as will appear by the returns of the Protestant and Catholic clergymen, and of the Wesleyan Methodist Missionary accompanying this report—the reason why the two latter so much exceed the former, is that the mass of the Negro population are Catholics, and those who are not, adhere principally to the Wesleyan missionaries.

On the subject of marriages, your Committee beg leave to observe, that they have lately increased, but not so much as is to be desired; that this however, is not to be attributed to any defect of the law, nor to any impediment offered by the planters, who encourage and promote matrimony amongst such Slaves, as have a just idea of its moral obligation, and only object to it on occasions when the character and conduct of the individual shews him incapable of estimating the duties and advantages of the married state.

With regard to the transfer of Negroes, your Committee report that it is the universal practice to dispose of Negroes in families, and it is so evidently the interest of the Planter, that scarcely one would be found so blind to their own advantage as not to purchase them in families; in addition to which, the law specially provides that no child under twelve years of age shall be sold without the mother.

With regard to manumissions, the Colonial Tax is trifling, not exceeding seven guineas; but the Negro who has purchased his manumission is totally free from the power of his master, even before payment of the tax, and the tax is not for the purpose of revenue, but to secure a provision for poor free persons, many of whom are on the pension list of the Colony; the number of manumissions since January 1821, amounts to one hundred and eight: and the free persons enjoying pensions from the Colony, in a list of twenty-seven individuals, amount to ten, as will appear by the annexed return under the hand of the public treasurer.

Your Committee feel convinced that the condition of the Negroes has much improved, and is daily improving; that their wants and comforts in health and sickness are carefully attended to; that punishments are proportioned to offences and have greatly decreased; that they enjoy the benefits of religious instruction, possess the means of acquiring property and freedom; and your Committee feel no hesitation in saying that the generality of the Negroes are happy and contented, and will so remain if their minds are not excited and inflamed by the delusive hopes of emancipation.

JOHN LAIDLAW,
WILLIAM BLANC,
HENRY J. GLANVILLE,
JOSEPH COURT,
ROBERT BURT.

DOMINICA.

Certificate of Dr. Greenway.

I do hereby certify, that for upwards of thirty years past, I have had the medical care of several of the largest plantations in this Island, and that during that period, I have in general found every attention paid to the comforts of the Negroes, in providing them with wine, medicines, and every other necessary; and that my instructions in regard to their proper diet have been strictly attended to, and have witnessed the greatest solicitude for their recovery. And I do further certify, that for several years past, the situation of the Negro population as far as they come within my knowledge, has been gradually much ameliorated in every respect.

Given under my hand at Roseau, this 5th day of June, 1823.

JOHN GREENWAY,
Surgeon and Practitioner of Physic.

DOMINICA.

CERTIFICATE OF DR. SPALDING.

I do hereby certify, that for upwards of three years past, I have had the medical attendance of several plantations in this Island, and that during that period, I have in general found every attention paid to the comfort of the sick, in providing them with medicines, wine, and every other necessary, and that my instructions in regard to their proper diet have been strictly attended to. And I do further certify, that the Negro population as far as they have come within my knowledge are comfortably lodged and furnished with every thing that relates to the necessaries and conveniences of life.

Given under my hand at Roseau, this 6th day of June, 1823.

JOHN SPALDING, Surgeon.

DOMINICA.

Certificate of Dr. Johnstone.

I do hereby certify, that I have resided in this Colony thirty-two years, and that during the greatest part of that time, I have had the medical care of a number of large estates in different parts of the Island; that for the last six years, I have had the care of all the principal estates in the quarter of St. Joseph's; and that I always found the proprietors and attornies of the different properties anxious that every attention should be paid to the comfort of the sick Negroes, by allowing them wine, and every article of nourishment necessary for their situation; and that my directions respecting their medicines and diet, have been uniformly attended to.

I do further certify, that the condition of the Negroes generally, in this quarter, has been very much ameliorated in every respect during the six years that I have resided in it.

St. Joseph's, June 8th, 1823.

James Johnstone, M. D.

Certificate of Registration.

Treasury Office, Roseau, Dominica, June 12*th*, 1823.

I do hereby certify to all whom it may concern, that the following Slaves, viz:—

Victoire, a female, black, 46 years, an African, Rosalie, ditto, ditto, 2 ditto, a Creole, Have been duly recorded in my office by R. Burt, Esq. as the joint property of Moise, Jude and Harriet, Slaves on the Resource Estate, the property of Burt and Charrarier, conformable to law, and that the foregoing is a true and accurate description of said Slaves, faithfully extracted from the Original Slave Registry of this Island.

For JAMES CORLET, Treasurer,

W. H. REDMAN.

Certificate of Registration.

Treasury Office, Roseau, Dominica, June, 12*th* 1823.

I do hereby certify to all whom it may concern, that the following Slave, viz:—

Francoise, female black, 46 years old, an African; hath been duly recorded in my office, as the property of Veronique, a Slave on Geneva Estate, the property of the Honorable I. P. Lockhart, and purchased by herself, conformably to law, and that the foregoing is a true and accurate description of said Slave, faithfully extracted from the Original Slave Registry of this Island.

For JAMES CORLET, Treasurer.
W. H. REDMAN.

DOMINICA.

CERTIFICATE OF THE REGISTER OF THE COURT OF CHANCERY.

I do hereby certify that on the 7th day of May, in the present year, an information was filed in the Court of Chancery, by Mr. Henry Glanville, Barrister at Law, and Solicitor in the cause; in the name of His Majesty's Attorney General, on behalf of John, an indigent Negro Boy, praying the establishment of his freedom.

Also, that a bill was filed on the 11th day of November last past, by Mr. Henry Glanville, on behalf of Pauline, an indigent Negro Woman, her five children and grand child; praying that their freedom might be established, by their next friend Ellinor; that the said bill was afterwards withdrawn at the suggestion of the court, that an information might be filed on their behalf, by His Majesty's Solicitor General, Mr. Henry Glanville, to enable them to prosecute their suit free of expence; and that Mr. Henry Glanville, as Solicitor General, has this day filed an information accordingly.

June 19th, 1823.

HENRY B. TULLOH,
Act. Register in Chancery.

DOMINICA.

CERTIFICATE OF THE REV. JAMES CATTS.

I do hereby certify that full liberty is granted at present, to the Wesleyan Missionaries to visit the Estates where the Slaves are not Roman Catholics, for the purpose of imparting religious instructions, by all the Proprietors, or their representatives to whom application has been made.

JAMES CATTS,

Superintendant of the Wesleyan Missionaries.

June 5th, 1823.

DOMINICA.

CERTIFICATE OF THE CATHOLIC PRIEST.

I do hereby certify that since my arrival in this Island, in the year one thousand eight hundred and nineteen, every facility has been granted by the proprietors of estates, to enable the Negroes to attend divine service on Sundays, and the holidays, at the Roman Catholic Church.; and that the attendance of the Negroes is so great, that the Church is crowded to excess; and that every attention is paid to their religious instruction, and that hardly a Sunday passes without the communion being administered to Slaves.

Given under my hand at Roseau, this 11th day of June, 1823.

JEAN DE LA HOS XIMENO, Curé.

LETTER OF MR. DAWES.

Roseau, Dominica, 6th June, 1823.

SIR,

In compliance with your request, that I would furnish you with a statement of my experience of the disposition evinced by the community of this Island, toward the instruction of the lower orders in the doctrines and duties of the christian religion, I herewith present you with a few printed copies of an account of the formation of a Dominica Auxiliary Church Missionary Society, which took place in February last, in consequence of a representation from myself, (as agent to the Church Missionary Society, instituted in London,) to His Excellency, the Earl of Huntingdon, Governor, and as many of the most respectable characters in the community, as I could meet with in town.

This account, I conceive, Sir, speaks almost as forcibly to the purpose as can be desired. It may not, however, be irrevelant to add, that in making the representation, I was much gratified by obtaining the signatures, to a written paper on the subject, of thirty one persons *in succession,* among whom were His Excellency the Governor; the Honorable the Chief Justice, and all the other Members of the Council then in the Island; the Honorable the Speaker, and ten other Members of the Assembly; the Rev. the Rector of the Parish of St. George; one gentleman of the legal profession; a fourth, resident in the Country, has since become a subscriber, and five of the most respectable merchants, two of whom have been since elected into the assembly. A society was in consequence formed on the 14th February; but the opening of the school, was unavoidably delayed, from the want of a suitable teacher, until the 3rd May, when a young gentleman with respectable testimonials, having been appointed,* a school room, kindly lent to the society by Charles Court, Esq. was opened in form by the Rev. H. C. C. Newman, the Rector, when His Excellency and suite, with several other gentlemen and some ladies attended, and a very appropriate and impressive prayer, composed for the occasion, was put up by the rector. A gentleman having the care of many estates in the Island, the second time I met him on the business in question, expressed his readiness to receive a teacher, whenever a suitable one could be procured on one estate, which is centrical to two others, for the exclusive purpose of affording instruction to the Slaves; to allow him a house and sufficient salary. The school above mentioned, is situated in this town, and has now twenty seven scholars, which number is rapidly encreasing. The scholars are in general, tractable, and making as good progress as can reasonably be expected. A sufficient supply of school books has been furnished by me, on account of the Church Missio-

* With a Salary of £150 per annum.

nary Society; and some bibles and testaments, by the Antigua Auxiliary Bible Society. If you conceive that I may be able to afford any further information on this truly interesting subject, it will give me pleasure to do so.

I am Sir, your obedient Servant,

WILLIAM DAWES,
Agent and Director of Schools in the West Indies, for the Church Missionary Society.

HENRY I. GLANVILLE, ESQ.

FORMATION OF A DOMINICA AUXILIARY CHURCH MISSIONARY SOCIETY.

At a meeting of several of the principal Inhabitants of the Island of Dominica, held at Mrs. Anderson's Tavern, in the Town of Roseau, on Friday, the 14th of February, 1823, for the purpose of considering of and adopting the most effectual mode of affording instruction in Reading and Christian knowledge to the lower orders of the community.—

The Honourable Archibald Gloster, Chief Justice, in the Chair;

The following Resolutions were unanimously passed :—

First Resolution, moved by the Hon. William Anderson, seconded by Frederick H. Garraway, Esq.

" That the views and objects of the Church Missionary Society established in London, have the most cordial approbation of this Meeting."

Second Resolution moved and seconded by the same.

" That therefore, for the effectual promotion of these views and objects, an Auxiliary Society, to be designated " The Dominica Auxiliary Church Missionary Society," be now formed."

Third Resolution, moved by the Hon. the Chief Justice, seconded by Alexander Dalrymple, Esq.

" That the Hon. Robert Reid be elected President of the Society."

Fourth Resolution, moved by Henry Trew, Esq. seconded by Edward Dowdy, Esq.

"That the Hon. Archibald Gloster, President of the Council, and the Hon. William Anderson, Speaker of the Assembly, be elected Vice-Presidents of the Society."

Fifth Resolution, moved by the Hon. Robert Garraway, seconded by Alexander Dalrymple, Esq.

"That James Corlet, Esq. be elected Treasurer of this Society for the ensuing year."

Sixth Resolution, moved by Lieut. Col. Lodington, seconded by Edward Dowdy, Esq.

"That the Hon. Robert Garraway and William Blanc, Ralph Ashton, John Lodington, Edward Dowdy, Alexander Dalrymple, Frederick H. Garraway, Henry Trew, Henry Glanville, and Adam Patterson, Esqrs. be appointed a Committee for managing the affairs of this Society for the ensuing year."

Seventh Resolution, moved by the Hon. William Blanc, seconded by Ralph Ashton, Esq.

"That a Deputation, consisting of the President, Vice-Presidents, Treasurer, and two other Members of the Committee, do wait on

His Excellency the Right Hon. the Earl of Huntingdon, and most respectfully solicit the favour of his countenance and support by becoming the Patron of this Society."

Eight Resolution, moved by the Rev. C. C. Newman, seconded by James Corlet, Esq.

"That the existing state of the lower orders of this community is such, as to demand the utmost exertions of all its powers to be exclusively directed to the instruction of such individuals as need it, in reading, so as to enable them to peruse the Holy Scriptures, and to affording them such other instruction in the principles of the Christian religion as is not inconsistent with the Articles, Homilies, and Liturgy of the united church of England and Ireland. This Society however, does not, in its present infant state, feel competent to offer any contribution to the funds of the Parent Society, but will thankfully avail itself of any assistance, with respect to Bibles, Testaments, School Books, or otherwise, which that Society may think proper to afford."

Ninth Resolution, moved by Ralph Ashton, Esq., seconded by Henry Glanville, Esq.

" That the following be adopted as the standing Laws and Regulations of this Auxiliary Society."

1st. That this Institution shall be designated " The Dominica Auxiliary Church Missionary Society," and shall consist of a Patron, a President, two Vice Presidents and a Treasurer, and also of Life and Annual Members, together with such other officers as may be deemed necessary for conducting the affairs of the Society.

2nd. Every person subscribing annually the sum of two pounds ten shillings and upwards shall be deemed a Member of this Society, during the continuance of such subscription.

3d. Every person giving a benefaction of twenty five pounds and upwards shall be a Member for life.

4th. Every clergyman subscribing one pound five shillings annually shall be considered a Member during the continuance of such subscription.

5th. The Committee shall have the power of

appointing such persons as shall have rendered essential services to the Society Members for life.

6th. The annual meeting of the Members of the Society shall be held in Roseau, on the third Friday in January, when the proceedings of the foregoing year shall be reported by the Committee, the accounts presented, and a Treasurer and a Committee chosen for the ensuing year.

7th. A special general meeting of the Members of the Society, at which not less than ten shall constitute a quorum, shall be called at any time, at the requisition of the Committee, or of any seven Members, on addressing a letter to the Secretary, specifying the object of the meeting. Ten days notice shall be given in the newspaper of any such intended meeting, and of the purpose for which it is called, which shall be deemed sufficient publicity.

8th. At all general meetings, and at those of the Committee, the Patron, or in his absence the President, or in his absence one of the Vice-Presidents; should neither of the Vice-Presidents be present, the Treasurer, and in his absence such

Member as shall be voted for that purpose, shall preside at the Meeting.

9th. None of the Rules of the Institution shall be repealed or altered, or any new one established but at the annual meeting, or at a special meeting called for that purpose.

10th. An anniversary Sermon shall be requested to be preached in the Established Church in Roseau, and a collection made at the doors of the Church for the purpose of this Institution.

11th. The Committee shall consist of ten Members, exclusive of the Patron, President, Vice Presidents, Treasurer, and of all such clergymen as are Members of the Society, and it shall meet at least once in three months, on the third Friday in January, April, July and October, for the dispatch of any business which may be brought before it, and any five of the Committee shall be a quorum.

12th. The Patron, President, Vice-Presidents, and Treasurer shall be ex-officio Members of the Committee,

13th. When any vacancy shall happen in the

Committee, by death or absence, the remaining Members shall have power to supply such vacancy from among the Members of the Society, until the next general meeting, provided that no Member of the Committee shall be considered as having vacated his seat until he shall have been absent from the Island six months.

14th. A secretary and collector, in one person, shall be chosen by the committee, who shall attend all meetings of the committee, and general meetings. He shall collect all subscriptions and donations within the town of Roseau, and pay them regularly every Friday, into the hands of the treasurer.

15th. The business of the committee shall be to enquire for, and appoint teachers; to fix the station where they are to act; to order, through the depositary,* the distribution of lessons, books, &c. to the different schools, of which the principal teacher in each school, is to have the charge; to receive from the secretary, the

* The office of depositary, is usually additional to that of treasurer.

monthly reports of the teacher; and when necessary, to appoint a superintendant, or any other officer, which it may deem requisite, or to adopt any other measure, subject to the approbation of the next general meeting, which it may deem promotive of the objects of this society.

16th. The teachers shall be persons of good religious and moral character. They shall be competent to teach their scholars to read the holy scriptures fluently, and to explain to them the meaning of such words, as may not be in common use among the lower orders; but more especially of those passages of scripture, which particularly enforce the performance of the relative duties of persons in their humble station. They shall not, on any pretence, admit into their respective schools, any book, lesson, or printed paper, but such as shall be delivered to them, or sanctioned by the committee; nor shall they extend their teaching than that to which they may be appointed in their respective schools. In short, they must consider it their bounden duty, to use their utmost endeavours to instil into the minds of their scholars, the genuine doctrines of the gospel; the practice of which, will, by the blessings of God, insure them the favour and approbation of all good men while they live, and through the merits of a Redeemer, eternal and unspeakable felicity in the Kingdom of Glory!

17th. The principal teacher in each school, shall keep a regular journal, according to a prescribed form, and deliver a copy thereof monthly to the secretary, for the inspection of the committee at their next meeting. He shall also keep a register, by which the attendance, proficiency, conduct and disposition of each scholar may be seen; and deliver the same to the secretary, on the day previous to each quarterly meeting of the committee for its inspection.

18th. A friendly intercourse shall be maintained with other Protestant Societies, engaged in the same benevolent design, of propagating the knowledge of the christian religion.

19th. It is recommended to every member of the society, to pray to Almighty God for a blessing upon its designs, under a full conviction, that unless he "prevent us in all our doings with his most gracious favor, and further us with his continual help," we cannot reasonably hope that its endeavours will be crowned with the desired success.

Then the following Resolutions were passed unanimously:—

Tenth Resolution, moved by the Honorable William Blanc, seconded by Ralph Ashton, Esq.

"That the thanks of this Meeting are most cordially given to William Dawes, Esq. for the zeal, temper, and ability he has manifested in the promotion of an Institution so highly important and desirable as that which has this day been established."

Eleventh Resolution, moved by Henry Glanville, Esq, seconded by the Honorable William Blanc.

"That the thanks of this Meeting be given to His Honor the Chief Justice, for his conduct in the chair, in countenancing and promoting the objects of this Institution."

Twelfth Resolution, moved by Lieut. Colonel Lodington, seconded by Edward Dowdy, Esq.

"That the proceedings of this Meeting be printed in the Dominica Chronicle."

ARCHIBALD GLOSTER, Chairman.

The Meeting being adjourned, the Chief Justice waited on his Excellency the Earl of Huntingdon, to know when it would suit his convenience to receive the deputation, when his Lordship was pleased to appoint the next day, at eleven o'clock.

Saturday the 15th, the deputation consisting of the following members: the Honorable the Chief Justice; the Honorable William Anderson, Speaker of the Assembly; the Rev. H. C. C. Newman; James Corlet, and F. H. Garraway, Esqs.; waited on His Excellency according to appointment, when the Chief Justice addressed his Lordship as follows:—

"My Lord,

"A Society was yesterday established in this Colony, as Auxiliary to the Church Missionary Society of London; whose views and objects are, to contribute to the instruction of the poorest classes in reading the Holy Scriptures, and to afford them such other information in the Christian Religion; as the Articles, Homilies, and Liturgy of the Church of England warrant. Of this Society, we are a deputation, and are directed to solicit your Lordship, as Governor of this Island, to honor the Institution by becoming its Patron."

To which his Lordship replied,—

"Gentlemen,

"It was with the greatest pleasure I heard of the unanimity which prevailed at your Meeting yesterday; but where the object is charity and instruction to the poor, every hand and heart will unite. I cheerfully accept the honor of becoming the Patron of the Auxiliary Church Missionary Society of Dominica."

The Chief Justice then resumed as follows:

"In the name of this Society, I beg to thank your Lordship for your condescension in accepting this appointment.

"As the representative of a most gracious and benevolent Sovereign, we looked to your Lordship's acquiescence in our request; independant of your established character for piety and charity, which must always excite your Lordship to take a deep interest in the progress of christianty, and the education of the poor.

"Under your Lordship's fostering care and protection, we trust the labours of this Society will prosper, and that it may receive, as it proceeds, an increasing degree of public regard."

His Lordship most graciously concluded in the following words of reply:

"I cannot suffer the deputation to depart, without further expressing a hope that our best thanks may be given to **Mr. Dawes**, the worthy agent of the Church Missionary Society, for his unwearied attention. Every assistance possible, in my power, will be at all times afforded to the Society."

William Dawes,
Secretary pro tempore.

Letter of the Rev. H. C. C. Newman.

Sir,

Agreeably to the Governor's requisition, I send you, for the information of the House of Assembly, the enclosed return of the baptisms and marriages of Slaves.

I am, Sir,
Your obedient humble Servant.
H. C. C. Newman.

30th May, 1823.

Return of baptisms and marriages of Slaves solemnized by me, for the last two years.

                                       H. C. C. NEWMAM.
30th May, 1823.

During the Year 1821 .... None
               1822 .... 6 Baptisms.
               1822 .... 2 Marriages.
               1823 .... 6 Baptisms.

Return of baptisms of Slaves performed by the Roman Catholic Clergyman, in the Island of Dominica.

From 1st, January, 1821 to 1st. January, 1822 ..323
      1st, January, 1822 to 1st. January, 1823 ..325
      1st, January, 1823 to 24th. May, 1823 ..146
                                        Total.... 794

I do hereby certify that the above is a correct return of Slaves baptized by the Roman Catholic Clergyman, as appears by the register.

                JEAN DE LA HOS XIMENO, Curé.

Return of marriages of Slaves celebrated by the Roman Catholic Clergyman, in the Island of Dominica.

From 1st. Jan. 1821 to 1st. Jan. 1822 .. 15 Marriages
1st. Jan. 1822 to 1st. Jan. 1823 .. 17 Ditto
1st. Jan. 1823 to 7th. June 1823 .. 5 Ditto

Total.... 37

I do hereby certify that the above is a correct return of the marriages of Slaves, celebrated by the Roman Catholic Clergyman, as appears by the register.

JEAN DE LA HOS XIMENO, Curé.

Baptisms of Slaves performed by the Wesleyan Missionaries, from the 1st. of January, 1821, to May 30th. 1823.

PLACE, ESTATE, OR OWNER'S NAME.
ROSEAU.

Mary Cowes..........	1 Baptized
——— Rainey	1 ditto.
Canefield Estate......	1 ditto.
Macancherie	4 ditto.
Carried over	7

Brought over ..	7 Baptized
Clarke Hall	5 ditto.
Hillsborough	4 ditto.
Sugar Loaf	5 ditto.
Point Round	11 ditto.
Bell Hall	2 ditto.
College	5 ditto.
Picard	1 ditto.
Clifton	2 ditto.

PORTSMOUTH TOWN.

——Kirwan	1 ditto.
J. A. Nisbet	1 ditto.
—— Rosette	1 ditto.
—— Home	1 ditto.
Mr. Johnson	1 ditto.
Hatton Garden Estate ..	28 ditto.
Melville Hall	12 ditto.
Eden	8 ditto.
Mr. Noble	1 ditto.
Total	96

JAMES CATTS,
Wesleyan Missionary.

Marriages performed between Slaves by the Wesleyan Missionaries, from the 1st January, 1821, to the 30th of May, 1823.

ROSEAU.

Miss Clarke, Owner	1 Couple married.
Hon. A. Gloster ......1 Female ———— Bostick ....1 Man	1 ditto.
Canefield Estate	1 ditto.
J. P. Lockhart's Estate, Grand Bay.	1 ditto.
Hillsborough Estate	8 ditto.
Clarke Hall	4 ditto.
Sugar Loaf	1 ditto.
Ditto .... 1 Man*	
Picard .... 1 Woman*	
Bell Hall .... 1 ditto*	
Ditto .... 1 Man*	
Point Round Estate	3 Couple.
Hatton Garden	1 ditto.
Melville Hall	9 ditto.
Eden	1 ditto.
Total....	35

JAMES CATTS,
Wesleyan Missionary.

* The other party did not belong to the same property.

Letter of Mr. Catts to H. Nisbet,

Private Secretary of the Governor.

Dear Sir,

I send you enclosed the Account of Baptisms and Marriages of Slaves performed by the Wesleyan Missionaries for the two last years, according to your request. I have set down those who have been baptized or married since the 1st of February, 1821, to the present time. It may be proper for me to remark, that in November and December, 1820, a great number were baptized, and also a great number were married, and this, I judge, is one reason why the number since that period is comparatively small.

Your's respectfully,

JAMES CATTS.

May 30, 1823.

Return of Slaves who have been manumitted from the 1st of January, 1821, to the 1st of June, 1823.—Total, 108. Number of free persons, formerly Slaves, receiving pensions from the Colony,—Total, 10.

Total number of white and free persons—27.

JAMES CORLET,
TREASURER.

Treasurer's Office,
June the 10*th,* 1823.

FINIS.

A REPORT

No.6.

OF A

COMMITTEE

OF THE

COUNCIL OF BARBADOES,

APPOINTED TO INQUIRE INTO THE

ACTUAL CONDITION OF THE SLAVES

IN THIS ISLAND;

WITH A VIEW TO REFUTE CERTAIN CALUMNIES RESPECTING THEIR TREATMENT; AND ALSO TO TAKE INTO CONSIDERATION CERTAIN MEASURES AFFECTING THE WEST INDIES, WHICH HAVE BEEN LATELY AGITATED IN THE HOUSE OF COMMONS.

" And I would recommend to your serious consideration whether it
" be prudent to form a rule of punishing people, not on their own acts
" but on your conjectures. Surely it is preposterous at the very best.
" It is not justifying your anger by their misconduct, but it is convert-
" ing your ill-will into their delinquency."—BURKE.

London:

PUBLISHED BY W. SIOR, 12, SOUTH ROW, NEW ROAD.

1824.

PREFACE.

THE following Report was presented to the Council upwards of six months ago, as the date implies; the publication has, however, been delayed to the present time by unavoidable causes. It must be obvious that some occurrences will have taken place in the interval, which in some measure change the aspect of certain subjects adverted to in the Report: wherever these occurrences materially affect the argument, it has been deemed most advisable to allude to them in a short note without altering the original argument. This, as well as certain other deviations from form, with which the Council are conscious their Report is chargeable, the candid and impartial Reader will forgive, on account of the peculiarity of their situation as distant Colonists singularly obnoxious to misrepresentation. And if it be objected to the Report that it is too controversial for a paper of the kind, let it be remembered that the main object of the undertaking is to counteract the mischievous impression which has been made on the public mind by misrepresentation.

BARBADOES,
January 1, 1824.

A REPORT,

&c. &c.

The following Report was presented by Mr. HAMDEN *from the Committee of the Council appointed to inquire into the condition of the Slaves, &c. &c.; and being adopted by the Board, was ordered to be published.*

BARBADOES COUNCIL-CHAMBER,
Tuesday, July 22, 1823.

YOUR Committee find that a party in England, who have been for a long time the avowed enemies of the West Indies, have at length explicitly declared their determination to bring about a Revolution in the state of society in these Colonies; and that, in furtherance of these views, they have, by means of exaggeration and misrepresentation, exhibited a picture " of the grossest injustice; of " the most heathenish irreligion and immorality; " of the most unprecedented degradation, and un- " relenting cruelty*"—in short, such a picture as must fill with horror and disgust " all who have

* Wilberforce's Appeal.

"any respect for justice, or any feelings of humanity:" and this they declare to be a faithful picture of West Indian Slavery.

Calumny can only be repelled by facts. In order to give the stamp of authenticity to the facts on which our defence must be founded, we have thought proper to obtain from His Excellency the Governor, a Commission authorizing us to examine on oath all such persons as we may have occasion to call before us.

Having to contend against prejudices of no ordinary force, and prejudices which we freely confess are founded in some of the best feelings of our nature, we have been very circumspect in the selection of the witnesses whom we have examined as to the treatment and condition of the Slaves. In a community constituted as this is, it is impossible to find many persons in no respect interested in the issue of the question to which their examinations refer, and who have had opportunities of making observations on the state of Slavery. Some such persons, however, we have fortunately met with—gentlemen, in whom the common and natural claim to credit, resulting from perfect disinterestedness, is fortified by that refined and high-toned sense of honor which is peculiarly the characteristic of the profession to which they belong. To obviate all suspicion of collusion, we beg to remark, that we have been directed in the choice of these witnesses by a regard to the official situations which they fill, without any reference to the private opinions of individuals. By looking to the Appendix it will be seen, that Sir Edmund Williams is Commandant of the Garrison, Lieut.-Col. Berkeley the head of the Adjutant-General's department, Lieut.-Col. Popham the head of the Quarter-master's department, Dr. Tygart the chief of the Medical Staff, Major Cruttenden the Major of Brigade, and Capt. Spink attached to the Staff of the Commander of the Forces.

Certain details, however, connected with the domestic economy of the Plantations, could only be obtained from persons connected with property; but, in all such cases, care has been taken to select gentlemen whose established reputation for integrity places them above the suspicion of being seduced from the straight path of honor and truth, by considerations of self-interest.

We are fully sensible of the disadvantages under which we enter upon this field of controversy. Inveterate prejudices, interested views, blind fanaticism, even amiable feelings (abused by falsehood) are enlisted against us. The very imputation of guilt, especially the guilt of base and sordid vices, covers the party accused with an odium, which makes even virtuous minds unconsciously reluctant to admit a conviction of innocence; and those who stand most in need of candour and indulgence, are sure to obtain the the smallest allowance of it. Such is human nature! But truth is omnipotent, and will triumph in the end.

We do not stand forth as the willing advocates of Slavery in the abstract; for although we know that it is not condemned by Divine authority, and has been sanctioned by the example of all ages, from the remotest periods to which history reaches down to the present time; yet it cannot be thought that a system which subjects man to the absolute power of his fellow-man is a desirable state of society. Our object is to shew, that Slavery does not necessarily imply such injustice, cruelty, and moral debasement, as have been ascribed to it by our enemies; and that the representations of West Indian Slavery which have been given by them, bear no more resemblance to the actual state of things in this country than a caricature commonly does to the object which it is meant to ridicule.

We beg that it may be steadily kept in mind, that our case rests on the testimony of honourable men, delivered under the solemn sanction of an oath—some of them interested we admit; but when it is considered, that these gentlemen are delivering their testimony in the presence of a community thoroughly acquainted with all the facts to which it refers, to suppose them capable under such circumstances of departing from the truth, would be to attribute to them a degree of profligacy and barefaced depravity which is rarely met with. Throughout the world the sense of shame is stronger even than the love of virtue. Whereas, on the other hand, the charge of our adversaries rests on the vague statements of anonymous writers, or the more than questionable assertion of interested persons, lying under strong temptation to misrepresent the truth. This we pledge ourselves to prove, and we shall also do a little more; we shall shew that some of these accusers are not honourable men, and not worthy of the confidence of the public. This is a part of our task which we would willingly forego, were it not indispensible to our vindication; but how often does it happen that the innocence of the accused, can only be established by exposing and discrediting the witnesses of the accuser.

Before we proceed farther, there are certain obstructions which the Goliath of our adversaries has judiciously thrown at the very threshold; these must first be removed, in order that truth may be let in.

Mr. Wilberforce no doubt calculated very justly that his mottoes, taken from the sacred volume, would have great effect in strengthening his alliances. There are many pious people in England, who, whatever doubts they may previously have entertained about the sinfulness of Slavery, would cease to doubt when they are told that it is expressly condemned by Scripture.

Now, really, among the many things in Mr. Wilberforce's pamphlet which we have found it difficult to reconcile with that gentleman's reputation, this is not one of the least striking. That a person so well acquainted with the Bible as Mr. Wilberforce is said to be, should resort to that volume for a motto to a tract written in reprobation of Slavery, seems to us not quite consistent with candour and fair dealing. He must have known that the Scriptures abound with texts clearly available to the advocate of Slavery: the very text he has chosen by no means condemns such a system as Mr. Wilberforce and his coadjutors have represented West Indian Slavery to be.

They all assert incidentally, and some of them have written books to prove, that the expense which we are at to maintain our Slaves greatly exceeds what would be the wages of labour, were Slavery abolished. With what justice, then, can it be said of the West Indian Slave-owner, that " he useth his neighbour's service without wages, " and giveth him not for his work." It matters not whether the wages be paid in money, or in those things which money must be exchanged for, as food, clothing, houses, medical attendances, &c. it is equally the reward of labour.

In Leviticus, chap. xxv., there is the most distinct recognition of Slavery as a lawful state of society which words can express:—" Moreover
" of the children of the strangers which do so-
" journ among you, of them shall ye buy, and of
" their families which are with you, which they
" begat in your land: and they shall be your
" possession. And ye shall take them as an in-

" heritance for your children after you, to inherit
" them for a possession; they shall be your bond-
" men for ever." Nor is it less clearly sanctioned
by the divine Author of our Religion; *vide* Saint
Luke, chap. xii. v. 47-48.

In St. Paul's Epistles there are many passages indicating that he does not condemn Slavery as unlawful—*vide* Corinthians, chap. vii. 21-24; and we may learn from his affectionate Epistle to Philemon (a Slave-owner), and from the terms in which he speaks of Onesimus the Slave, that he did not think with the modern Saints, that Slavery necessarily produces a moral debasement of both Master and Slave*.

Having driven in the enemy's picquets, we may now advance. We beg, in the first instance, to direct your attention to the annexed examinations, referring to the treatment of the Slaves. You will there find it proved, by the concurrent testimony of Sir Reynold Alleyne, Mr. Clarke, and Mr. Sharpe, that the Slaves on the Plantations

* As it will perhaps be said by our antagonists, that Slavery amongst the ancients was much more mild and lenient than West Indian Slavery, we beg to refer to Hume's Essay on the populousness of Ancient Nations, for an account of the Slavery under the Greeks and Romans.

are regularly furnished with a daily allowance of food more than sufficient for their personal uses, which enables them to raise, with the superfluity, pigs, poultry, &c.; by the sale of which, they provide themselves with certain luxuries in dress, and other little comforts which are not afforded by the master.

These allowances never vary under any circumstances; and it is one striking peculiarity in the condition of the Slave, that he is in a great measure exempt from the contingencies of inclement seasons, short crops, and scarcity; for although these causes do sometimes occasion great embarrassment to the master, they are never deemed a sufficient justification for withholding or diminishing the allowances of the Slaves, except in cases of such extreme exigency as very rarely occur even partially, and when food really cannot be had for money.

The raising of a sufficient crop of provisions, being considered a matter of primary importance in the economy of a plantation, there is generally a surplus quantity produced in those parts of the island which are most favourable to the growth of corn; and in periods of scarcity, these accumulations becoming diffused by the high scarcity price, are generally found sufficient to relieve the distress. When the scarcity becomes general, it is sometimes found necessary to assist the domestic granaries by importation; and although these calamities may exhaust the proceeds of the Sugar Crop, the Slave has hitherto seldom felt any ill consequences from it. Of this fact many of us have had bitter experience during the two years immediately preceding the last. There was a total failure of crops in certain districts of the island from unfavorable seasons; nevertheless, the owner contrived, by the aid of other resources, or by credit, to procure the usual supplies for his Slaves.

Nor is the Slave less exempt from the hopeless sufferings inseparable from age, infirmity, and sickness, among the labouring classes of free men; for as Mr. Clarke has very properly expressed it, after enumerating the various allowances, comforts, &c. which are afforded to the labouring Slaves, he adds, " all these allowances are *of course* " continued to the aged and infirm until their " death;" and it must be acknowledged as one of the redeeming privileges of Slavery, that the poor man does not cease to enjoy the moment he ceases to labour.

Every family has a comfortable cottage built at the expense of the estate, generally of stone wall and thatched.

You have it proved to you also, on the same authority to which we have already referred, and confirmed by the testimony of three highly respectable and regularly educated medical men, that in sickness the Slave is received into a wholesome well-arranged hospital, where he is regularly attended by a medical practitioner, and where all the necessaries and comforts which his case may require are abundantly supplied. Every Member of this Board knows that chocolate, animal food, Madeira wine from the master's own cellar, in short every thing that the practitioner may think proper to direct for his patient, is freely given. Does the Slave require the more costly aid of a physician, surgeon, or accoucheur, the same person who would be employed to attend a member of the master's family in a similar case, is always called in; so that it is really no exaggeration to say, that the Slave enjoys many of the solid comforts, and is only excluded from the *luxuries* of wealth.

But, exclaims Mr. Wilberforce, in the fervor of his enthusiasm, " I will not condescend to argue "the question on the ground of comparitive feeding, and clothing, and lodging, and medical attendance. Are these the only claims? Are these the chief privileges of a rational and immortal being?"—Assuredly not. Nevertheless they are claims, and they are privileges, which those to whom they are but too frequently denied, appreciate more highly, than the spoiled child of Fortune, nursed in the lap of Luxury, can well conceive.

The homely topics of food, raiment and shelter, appear sordid and contemptible indeed, when compared with the brilliant themes of civil liberty and the rights of man: but although they be not so well adapted to the purposes of declamation, nor so well calculated to excite enthusiastic emotions, we beleive they are found to be not less indispensable to the purposes of solid happiness; and when we have stripped *free poverty* of the adventitious ornament with which the eloquent declaimer has invested it, and cease to be dazzled by the false gloss with which he has artfully covered its asperities, we shall find it allied to much abject toil, great misery, and all the external evils of servitude. Who ever went into a manufactory of almost any description in England, without being struck with the squalid, unhealthy looks and comfortless condition of the people employed in it. And although you should succeed in giving to the emancipated Slave " the " feeling of independence without the danger of " licentiousness," it would require but short experience to convince him that he had purchased the blessings of freedom, by the sacrifice of benefits of no small value.

But, say our adversaries, " the Slave is subject " to the brutal outrage of the cart-whip." This is the chosen theme of exaggeration amongst our calumniators: upon this topic they have out-heroded Herod. It is necessary therefore to go into much detail upon it.

Mr. Clarke, who has a greater number of Slaves under his directions than any other gentleman in the Island, declares on oath, " that the driver is " allowed at no time to give more than six stripes " with a cat. If the obstinacy or unruly conduct " of any Negro require a greater punishment, he " is reported to the Manager; and that he knows " of no other punishment but moderate flogging " with a cat, or solitary confinement; that the " female Slaves are never exposed when punish-" ed; that the cow-skin or cart-whip is never

" used upon the Estates under his care; and that
" he believes it is generally laid aside as an instru-
" ment of punishment.*"

Mr. Sharp swears " that the driver is not
" allowed to give more than six stripes on his
" own authority, and that the Negroes are encou-
" raged to complain against him if he abuses his
" power, and in general they are very ready to
" do so: that the under white servants have very
" little power, their business being to observe and
" report the ill-conduct of the Negroes to the
" manager, who if his conduct be not regulated
" by higher principles, is checked in the abuse
" of his power by self-interest, for the strong
" voice of public opinion is against his using
" tyrannical measures.†" " The community in
" general," he adds, " look with detestation on a
" man who has once obtained a character for
" severity, and if he be dependant on his profes-
" sion, he is ruined, for he cannot get employ-
" ment. The usual way," he says, " of inflicting
" punishment, is with rods or a cat of five or six
" strands applied over the shoulders, and the
" women are *never* indecently exposed."

* Appendix H. † Appendix I.

The Planters who have been examined, have given a very circumstantial account of the means pursued for encouraging and promoting the increase of the Slave Population. For particular information on this head, we therefore refer to the Appendix, but we think it right to notice here, the general result of this system.

By the second registry return, it is shewn that the number of births exceeded the number of deaths by 1698. The books for the last registration are not yet made up, but from the increase which appears in the returns of the seven parishes which have been completed, there is reason to expect that the result of this registration will not be less gratifying than the last. Dr. Richards and Dr. Lacock swear, " that they " never did have a patient under their care who " was suffering from the effects of severe punish- " ment, and that as they visit the estates under " their care daily, did such cases occur, they must " necessarily have come under their notice*." Where is the resemblance between these descriptions on oath and the loathsome pictures of Messrs. Wilberforce, Macauley, and Co. That

* Appendix K and L.

there are "White Savages" in this community as well as in all others, we do not pretend to deny; and that cruel punishments are sometimes inflicted by these wretches, we admit. But do not such acts of cruelty render the master infamous in the estimation of the public? Is he not stigmatised as a brute, and detested by all respectable men?

The military gentlemen who have been examined, all declare with one concurrent voice, that " they firmly believe that a cruel Slave-" owner would be held in the same abhorrence in " this Island as he would be in England." We invite you particularly to remark in the Appendix, the decided peremptory tone in which all these gentlemen reply to the question on this subject. They will be allowed to be impartial witnesses. If they were capable of being influenced by sinister motives, it is obvious that they would find their account in taking the popular and fashionable side of the question.

The Philanthropists will perhaps say,—" still we have reason to fear that the West Indian and the European standard of humanity do not exactly coincide, and that when we descend to particulars, our opinions as to what constitutes an act of cruelty, will be found to differ widely." To be more explicit then, your Committee mean distinctly to condemn as cruel, all punishments which occasion lacerations in any degree. Punishments may be improperly severe even without producing these effects, but it is impossible accurately to define the boundary. However it is very well known to this Board, that it is almost exclusively for the purpose of checking vice or enforcing subordination, that these punishments are administered. Flogging for a deficient quantity of work so rarely takes place on a well regulated estate, that it scarcely deserves to be mentioned.

Yet it is asserted with a confidence calculated to silence all doubt, that the drivers " are usually " the strongest and stoutest of the Negroes*." That is to say, the person capable of inflicting the heaviest blows. There is a degree of malignity in this remark which can hardly be forgiven. Happily it is the property of malice to defeat its own ends. This assertion carries contradiction upon the face of it: the office of Driver, which, as Mr. Sharp has said, would be more properly

* Wilberforce's Appeal.

denominated " Overseer of the Work," is one which requires sagacity, judgment, and thought beyond every other on a Plantation; therefore, to select a man for this situation without reference to these qualities, and simply on account of his bodily strength, would be about as wise, as to choose a general to command an army because he was a good swordsman.

There is no passage in this very disingenuous production, which we think a man with just notions of honour would be more ashamed to have written than this. How desperate must be the the hate, that would seek to gratify its revenge at the expense of truth and common sense.

We turn with pleasure from contemplating such a frame of mind as this, to exhibit the triumph of truth and honour over prejudice and calumny. With feelings of honest pride and self-gratulation, every good man in this community will read the examination of the military officers taken before the Committee.

Sir Edmund Williams confesses that he came to this Island with a mind deeply imbued with prejudices against our institutions; expecting no doubt to find every Master a tyrant, and every Slave the victim of oppression and wrong. What are his sentiments now that those prejudices have been chastened and corrected by personal observation?—That from the alacrity and vivacity exhibited in the deportment of the Slaves, " he " should really think them a happy race of people; " that generally speaking he firmly believes they " are better off than the poor in England; that " he has been particularly struck with the kind " and feeling manner in which he has heard large " gangs of Negroes salute their Master when he " has visited them at their work, inquiring par- " ticularly after the rest of his family*." Does this look like oppression and misery?

Colonel Popham is equally strong in expressing his entire approbation, of the treatment of the Slaves generally, as the result of eight year's observation, during which period he has visited every part of the Island. He particularly notices " the great attention paid to the rearing of " children, and the kindness and care which the " old and infirm receive." He also is of opinion that " in regard to comforts, the Slaves in this " Colony are better off than the lower classes in " England, having no care or thought for to-

* Appendix A.

" morrow, feeling confident that all their ne-
" cessary wants and comforts will be provided
" for.*"

Colonel Berkeley has not had frequent opportunities of observing the condition of the Slaves on the Plantations, and can only speak positively of the treatment of the Negroes on one Estate, where he had seen something of the interior detail; and of that Estate he declares, that in his opinion, the system established was, as far as the preservation of discipline required, too lenient; and, he adds, that he has no doubt the same system very generally prevails among the respectable classes of Owners. †

Mr. Tygart, Inspector of Hospitals, acknowledges that " he came to this country preposses-
" sed that the Negroes were very harshly used,
" from what he had heard and read on the sub-
" ject, but he now finds that it is not so; and he
" believes that they are generally kindly treated;
" that they appear to him to be better off than
" the labouring people are in his own country,"
(Ireland;) " that he has observed on several of
" the Estates which he has seen, that the Hospi-

---

* Appendix B. † Appendix C.

"tals are very well conducted for the care of
"the sick.*"

Major Cruttenden says, that "that he has been
"ten years in the Colony; that he has spent
"weeks and months on certain Estates; that he
"has ever observed the kind treatment the Slaves
"invariably receive, and the cheerfulness with
"which they perform their duty; that he never
"was witness to an act of cruelty or oppression
"during the period he has been in the island.†"

Captain Spink asserts, that "he has frequent
"opportunities of observing the general treat-
"ment of the Slaves, from which he is convinced
"that great humanity and kindness is shewn to
"the Slave Population in this Colony; that they
"are generally cheerful and happy, and appear
"to be sensible of the great care taken of
"them.‡"

Upon the sworn testimony of these disinterested witnesses we rest our defence. To the assertions without proof, and opinions contrary to reason, of our calumniators, we oppose a mass of evidence, distinct, positive and consistent; obtained from a number of persons of different habits, dif-

* Appendix D. † Appendix E. ‡ Appendix F.

ferent pursuits, and in some respects of different interests—all concurring to prove that the Slaves in this Colony are treated with kindness and humanity; that they themselves are sensible of it, and that they are, in consequence, cheerful, happy and contented.

Nevertheless, exclaim the pseudo-philanthropists, they ought not to be happy! Their cheerfulness and contentment is the evidence of their degradation! And we owe it to the sacred rights of man to dispel the delusion by which these mistaken people are cheated into happiness. Then comes the ready " appeal to the feelings," by which, let it be remarked, " such wretched " sophisms as insult the understanding" are more frequently *supported* than exposed. A Slave and happy!—base, servile thought! " What, an utter " insensibility to the native feelings and moral " dignity of man!" Better ten thousand times that the victims of this delusion be hurried into anarchy and bloodshed, than longer endure such ignominious happiness! All this may be very fine, but we must be allowed to pronounce it very wicked.

When the professors of the rights of man endeavour to argue the people of England out of their feelings, and to persuade them, that as all men are born with the same natural rights, *subordination* necessarily implies *usurpation*, the attempt is denounced as wicked and seditious, and the philosophers are stigmatised as traitors; but when the same doctrines are applied to other countries, where the interests of even the teachers themselves are not involved in the consequences of their doctrines, it becomes sound Philosophy and pure Religion*, and the teachers are hailed as Saints.

The National Convention were at least consistent, in decreeing the enfranchisement of the Slaves at Cayenne. They wished to impart to the Colonies the blessings of the same equalizing principles which they deemed salutary at home, and which they had actually adopted in their domestic government.

This controversy furnishes many edifying examples of the influence of *self* on the moral perceptions of men; which serve to shew how differently the same conduct is regarded when it

---

* " It is nothing to know on the express authority of Scripture, that the lower classes instead of being an inferior order in the creation, are even the preferable objects of the love of the Almighty."—WILBERFORCE.

is likely to affect ourselves, and when it can only affect the interest of others, for whom we have no concern. One of the most conspicuous examples of the kind is afforded by Mr. Cropper, a quaker, of Liverpool. This upright East India merchant has had the audacity formally to propose a plan for the express purpose of ruining the West Indies, *professedly* as the most certain means of accomplishing the object of his party. Now should any unprincipled man have the hardihood to promulgate a scheme avowedly for the purpose of ruining any class of men in England, who under the sanction and special encouragement of the government and the nation, had fairly and honourably invested large capitals in a speculation which had happened to get out of favour and fashion, would he not run some risk of being pelted by the mob for his perfidy? But Mr. Cropper's apology is, that he is largely engaged in the East India free-trade, which he finds unprofitable, and that his private interest would be essentially advanced by the desolation of the West India Colonies, which would give to the East India sugar-dealer (of whom he is one) the monopoly of the home market. So this gentleman, with all his scruples, has no hesitation in recommending a measure which would inevitably bring hundreds of thousands of happy people to the most abject wretchedness and despair, and may possibly light up a flame in the Colonies which shall only be extinguished by the blood of every white person in them!—But we trust that the people of England are not to be led by those " blind guides who " strain at a gnat and swallow a camel."

Having now, we trust, proved to the satisfaction of all who will suffer themselves to be convinced, that " the physical evils of our Colonial " Slavery are" *not* " cruel and odious;" that on the contrary the physical wants of the Slaves are more regularly and more abundantly provided for, than the wants of the labouring class are or can possibly be in any country in the world where Slavery does not exist; and also that the punishments, generally speaking, are as mild and as rare as is consistent with the preservation of necessary discipline, and that we have been most cruelly slandered in this matter; we shall proceed to another branch of the inquiry, on which we regret to say, we shall not have the satisfaction of exhibiting so favourable a picture of the condition of the Negroes as we have done on the points already discussed. We allude to the state of Religion among them.

" It cannot be denied," says Mr. Wilberforce, " that the Slaves, more especially the great body " of the field Negroes, are practically strangers " to the multiplied blessings of the Christian Re- " ligion." Candour compels us to acknowledge that there is some foundation for this charge; but we are not prepared to admit that this confession justifies the virulent invective with which it is ushered in; much less, that it justly subjects us to the heavy pains and penalties denounced against us for the dereliction of duty implied by it.

That it is the duty of every man having a firm faith in the Christian Dispensation, to endeavour by all the means in his power to impart the hopes and comforts of that faith to all who stand in need of his assistance, and to diffuse the light of Revelation as widely as possible, cannot be denied. But it is not less true that there is no important duty more generally neglected than this, and that nine hundred and ninety-nine Christians out of every thousand content themselves with taking care of their own souls. That we are peculiarly obnoxious to this reproach, and that considering the relation of Master and Slave, a lukewarmness and indifference about religious instruction is more culpable in us than in ordinary cases, we cannot deny and will not attempt to extenuate. But that there is a deliberate opposition to the efforts of pious men, and that " the tide of popular feeling and practice sets " strongly in every Colony against the religious " instruction of the Slaves," we most positively and peremptorily assert to be false.

It is true that there does exist among the Planters a deep rooted, and, we think, well-founded prejudice against the sectarian Missionaries. The reluctance to patronize the efforts of these persons is founded upon various reasons. In the first place, it is known by experience, that the Scriptures have often been perverted to favour the views of men hostile to the existing state of society in this country.

The case of Mr. Tallboys so fully exemplifies these remarks, that we would relate it at length had it not been already before the public. It is sufficient for our present purpose, simply to state that it was reported to General Hislop, the Governor, that he was preaching Doctrines to the

Slaves which were highly inflammatory and dangerous. The Governor upon inquiry found these representations so fully confirmed, that he subjected him to certain restrictions; a remonstrance was made to Government by the friends of Mr. Tallboys, and the Governor was called upon to justify his conduct, which he did by sending home the Petitions and communications upon which his conduct had been founded, and they were deemed quite satisfactory by Government.

Religion was employed by the leaders of the late conspiracy at Charleston in South Carolina, as a powerful engine to work upon the minds of the Slaves. The chief conspirator*, it is said, " ren-
" dered himself perfectly familiar with all those
" parts of the Scriptures which he thought he
" could pervert to his purpose, and would readily
" quote them to prove that Slavery was contrary
" to the laws of God; that Slaves where bound
" to attempt their emancipation however shock-
" ing and bloody might be the consequences, and
" that such efforts would not only be pleasing to
" the Almighty, but were absolutely enjoined and

* We do not mean to insinuate that the leader of this conspiracy was a Methodist Preacher.

" their success predicted in the Scriptures. His
" favorite texts when he addressed his own colour
" were, Zechariah, chap. xiv. 1, 2, 3, and Joshua,
" chap. iv. 21, and in all his conversations he
" identified their situation with that of the Israel-
" ites.*" The knowledge of these things must
naturally warn us to beware of the persons to
whom we confide the religious education of our
Negroes: and it is well known, that the Methodist
Preachers have not always been remarkable for
discretion in their instructions.

But independently of political considerations, if it be intended to inculcate a Religion which addresses itself to the understanding as well as to the heart, it cannot be supposed that teachers who dwell almost exclusively upon the mysteries and the denunciations of Religion, are the fittest to instruct ignorant, unenlightened Heathens. That there are things hard to be understood in Christianity, the most orthodox believer admits: but these surely are not the doctrines most likely to interest the curiosity, or captivate the feelings of persons, whose understandings have not been much exercised by thought, and whose morals

* Original Report of Negro Plot at Charleston.

have not been much disciplined by restraint: and there is reason to apprehend that the wild flights of enthusiasm (in which these preachers too often indulge) are more likely to make the Negroes consider Religion a bugbear, than a source of comfort and hope.

There is yet another consideration which induces the Planter to decline all intercourse with this class of men. They are the systematic calumniators of the West Indian Societies, and no wise man will cherish a serpent in his bosom.

Upon this topic we find it necessary to expatiate at some length.

We have said at the commencement of this Report, that in our own defence we shall be constrained to discredit the witnesses of our accusers, amongst whom are known to be the Methodist Missionaries, and this must be our apology for what follows.

In a pamphlet entitled *A Defence of the Wesleyan Methodists' Missions in the West Indies*, we find the following passage,—" Where no per-
" secuting laws have existed, they" (meaning the Methodists) " have often been attacked by mobs
" (chiefly of whites or those under their imme-
" diate control) and in many cases without being

" able to obtain redress from the Colonial Ma-
" gistracy. In Barbadoes the only redress which
" could be obtained in case of riot and an at-
" tempt to *pull down the Chapel*, was an observa-
" tion from a Magistrate, that the offence was
" committed against Almighty God, and therefore
" he could take no cognizance of it."

The following is an extract from the records of the Court at which the case above alluded to was tried, certified by the clerk of the Court.

" William Brooks and John Gibson were ar-
" raigned upon an indictment found against them
" for a misdemeanor, which said Indictment set
" forth and charged, that James Whitworth on
" the eleventh day of February in the fifty-third
" year of the Reign of our Sovereign Lord George
" the Third of the United Kingdom of Great Bri-
" tain and Ireland King, etc., and long before,
" was and now is a teacher or preacher of the
" Gospel to a Congregation of Protestants called
" Methodists, who assemble and meet in and for
" religious worship, in a certain house called and
" known by the name of the Methodist Chapel,
" in Bridge Town, in the parish of Saint Michael,
" and Island aforesaid. And further, that after-
" wards, to wit, on the said eleventh day of

" February, in the said fifty-third year of the
" reign of our said Lord the King, about the hour
" of seven in the afternoon of the same day, a
" Congregation of Protestants called Methodists,
" of which the said James Whitworth was the
" teacher or preacher, were assembled for the
" worship and service of Almighty God in the
" House or Chapel aforesaid, and that one William Brooks, late of the Parish of Saint Michael
" and Island aforesaid, yeoman, and one John
" Gibson, late of the same Parish and Island
" aforesaid, yeoman, not regarding the laws of
" this realm, afterwards, to wit, on the same
" eleventh day of February, in the said fifty-third
" year of the reign of our said Lord the King,
" with force and arms at the Parish aforesaid, in
" the Island aforesaid, willingly and of purpose,
" maliciously and contemptuously did come into
" the said Congregation, and disturb and disquiet
" the same Congregation during the time of
" divine service, by then and there talking and
" laughing with a loud voice, and also by talking
" with a loud voice to the said James Whitworth,
" the said James Whitworth then and there being
" in the pulpit, the doors of the said Meeting-
" house and place called the Methodist Chapel

" where the said Congregation were so assembled
" not being then locked, barred or bolted, to the
" example of all others in the like cases offending,
" and against the peace of our said Lord the
" King, his crown and dignity. To which In-
" dictment the said Brooks and Gibson pleaded
" Guilty. The Reverend James Whitworth, the
" Prosecutor, was then sworn, and related the
" circumstances of the case, and after addressing
" the Court, recommended that the mildest pu-
" nishment should be inflicted on the said defend-
" ants. The Court then ordered the said William
" Brooks and John Gibson to pay a fine of five
" pounds each, and be discharged."

Certified per ROBT. B. CLARKE,
Clk. Coron. et Pacis.

This case needs no comment.*

* With feelings of deep mortification, we have now to allude to a disgraceful transaction which has occurred since this Report was drawn up. We allude to the destruction of the Methodist Chapel. We freely acknowledge that we consider the conduct of Mr. Shrewsbury, the resident Missionary, in giving such a false and calumnious representation of the state of Society here, *highly culpable*, and we do not think that had we seen his Report earlier, we should have given him the praise which is bestowed upon him in our Report. We are willing, also, to make all due allowance for the exasperated feelings of the people, and for the influence which recent occurrences in Demerara were calculated to have, in heighten-

It is too notorious in this country that we have not always found these preachers of the Gospel men of such pure lives and correct morals, as those who take upon themselves the office of public censors ought in reason and consistency to be.

Of Mr. Cooper, the Missionary, we know nothing personally—we do not know to what denomination of Christians he belongs. Nor do we know more of his writings than what can be gathered from the *Edinburgh Review* and Sir Robert Wilson's speech. These extracts, however, exhibit abundant internal evidence that the author is not above the mean vice of " bearing false wit-" ness against his neighbour." The scene of the chamber candle and young woman he may possibly have acted a part in; such a thing may have happened; but to hold up a solitary instance, or even a few rare cases as *instar omnium*, a specimen of the depravity of a whole community, indicates a frame of mind which is detested and abhorred among Slave-owners, what-

ing the prejudices and inflaming the passions of the populace against all sectarian Missionaries. Nevertheless we can never cease to condemn, in the most unqualified manner, such an outrageous violation of all law and order, and deplore it as a lasting stigma upon the Colony.

ever may be thought of it in more enlightened societies. Who has not heard of the infamous orgies celebrated by persons of no mean rank in England. But is it to be inferred from a few isolated facts of this kind that the English are a people lost to all sense of decency, and sunk in profligacy and vice?

As to his assertion that he never saw a Slave whose back was not marked by the lash of the whip, if he means to insinuate that most Slaves are so marked, it would be nothing less than a vile fabrication if applied to this Colony, and we have no reason to suppose that there is more humanity among us than among onr neighbours. Surely it is not upon the authority of such men as these, that the character of large communities is to be consigned to execration and infamy.

We do not mean to follow the bad example of our adversaries and stigmatize any body of men for the crimes of individuals. We know that there are among the Methodist Clergy in England men of distinguished piety, exemplary virtue, and great learning. And no doubt there have been some good men among the Methodist Missionaries who have visited the West Indies. The Missionary now resident in this Island, Mr.

Shrewsbury, we have heard spoken of as a gentleman of cultivated understanding and correct morals. But even of such persons we would say, that they, in common with all who write upon the state of society in the West Indies, lie under a strong temptation to mislead the public.

An overweening solicitude about the approbation of the public is the universal and natural vice of authorship. It is not to be wondered at, that he who writes a book should endeavour to fall in with the taste and prejudices of the people by whom he expects his book to be read. The application of this remark to all publications on West India subjects is obvious. The Popish plot was never a better stalking horse than Negro Slavery is at the present day. The arrantest nonsense, written in a style of the most bloated fustian, shall be abundantly read and praised, provided it be duly seasoned with abuse of the West Indians. A deep-toned lament over the miseries of the Slave, or a lofty declamation on the tyranny of the Master, shall be a sufficient passport even for such a book as Doctor Pinckard's Notes on the West Indies.

Besides this ambition of literary fame, there is another craving desire which would urge an author to take the *Wilberforcean* side of the question, namely, the desire of place. It is a very general opinion in the West Indies, that Mr. Wilberforce's party, or what is called the *Saints*, have considerable influence in the disposal of places, nominations to *Commissions*, and so forth, especially in the Colonies: and whether this opinion be well founded or not, the belief that it is so, will be sufficient to determine the hungry candidate for favour.

Of course we do not mean to charge the Methodists with being the only vilifiers of the West Indies. A great deal of the information about the state of society here, which certain gentlemen so liberally impart to the British public, is obtained from persons actually employed by the African Institution as spies among us. The worthiness of the agents will be inferred from the dignity of the employment. " By their works ye shall know them." A salutary lesson we had hoped was read to the credulous Philanthropists of England by the case of the *King versus Hatchard,* for a libel against certain gentlemen of the Island of Antigua. The African Institution very naturally refused to give up the name of their correspondent, feeling convinced that persons employed in dirty work must be effectually protected, or none would be found to undertake it. Where there is no glory there should be impunity. However we believe it is very well known in the West Indies who this gentleman was. A certain person so vain of his classical acquirements, that he would even thrust his Greek upon us, in the newspapers in this Island. This spy then was a scholar, from which we are to infer that however " elegant learning may soften the manners" it does not purify the heart.

But to return from the digression into which the subject of Methodist Missionaries has led us. We beg to refer to the examination of the Rev. Mr. Hinds, who is now principal of Codrington College, for a refutation of the charge that the Masters oppose the religious instruction of their Slaves. This gentleman is the first Clergyman of the established Church, who has been employed as a Missionary in this Colony.

Mr. Hinds says that " he made many applica-
" tions to the proprietors and overseers of estates
" for liberty to instruct their Slaves in Religion,
" and without any exception all his applications
" were favourably received, and in several in-
" stances great zeal and earnestness was mani-

" fested in the cause in which he was engaged.
" That he has known the proprietor himself read
" prayers, and explain the Scriptures to his
" Slaves." He concludes a most clear and satisfactory examination with this remark. " In short,
" from the inquiries which I made, as well as
" from my own observations, the impression left
" upon my mind is, that the general sense of the
" proprietors is in favour of the religious instruc-
" tion of the Negroes, whenever undertaken by
" ministers of the Church of England."

This testimony is sufficiently favourable as to the willingness of the owners of estates to have their Slaves instructed in Religion. A higher praise than this we must confess we do not merit. However, the following extract from a pamphlet published in this Island some years ago, will serve to shew that there are other persons in the Colonies who have a concern for Religion, besides " *a few Missionaries.*" It was written by a proprietor, at that time resident in Barbadoes, addressed to the people of Barbadoes, and its circulation confined to Barbadoes; so that it cannot be said of this tract, as it is generally said whenever a liberal sentiment is expressed, or a liberal measure proposed in the West Indies, that

it is meant to gull the people of England, and
" as a political measure to avert the interference
" of the mother-country in the management of the
" Slaves."

" But let us not forget that there is another
" class of society which claims our regard on
" better grounds than as fellow citizens, by a still
" closer connexion as our Slaves. Next to the
" natural tie between the parent and his offspring,
" is that which binds the Master to his Slave.

" As to the responsibility attached to these
" relations, the difference is still less between the
" parent and the master. If we are bound by a
" law of GOD, implanted in our hearts to protect
" and cherish our offspring, we are also bound by
" the principles of justice and gratitude (which,
" though in an inferior sense, may be considered
" laws of nature), to protect and cherish those
" who serve and obey us, and contribute most
" essentially to the comfort of our lives. If we
" are responsible for the performance of our
" several duties as parents towards our offspring,
" because they are in our power and dependent
" on us, we are also responsible for the perform-
" ance of our duties as master on the very same
" principle.

"I would forbear as much as is consistent with my present purpose, to inquire whether the institution of Slavery is sanctioned by the law of God or not:—whether it is consonant with the principles of Christianity, or justifiable on the plea of necessity:—such an inquiry may lead to a discussion no less unseasonable than injudicious. Unseasonable, because the abolition of Slavery under existing circumstances would be the subversion of this and every other neighbouring community, and because these remarks are founded on the presumption that Slavery is admitted; it would be injudicious, because such discussions are sometimes productive of mischievous effects, and have a tendency to defeat the very purpose which I am anxious to promote.

"Not that I would be deterred from expressing my sentiments if I conceived it my duty to do so, or if I thought that it would answer any good purpose. But it can never be a duty to relax the bonds of society, or to propagate the doctrine of resistance to lawful authority.

"It would answer any but a good purpose, to endanger the peace and security of one part of the community, by sowing the seeds of sedition

"and discontent among the other. Still, if I
"could by pronouncing the freedom of such a
"number of my fellow creatures, pronounce them
"at the same time civilized and happy, I would
"do so with all my heart, and without a moment's
"hesitation. This is what every friend of huma-
"nity must wish, but it must be the work of time,
"and must be accomplished by better means than
"human wisdom can devise, so as to render jus-
"tice to one without taking it from the other.

"Since then we cannot thus establish their
"freedom, we should do all in our power to pro-
"mote their happiness,—we should endeavour to
"civilize them,—to make them Christians. This
"I think would be the proper beginning of a
"work, calculated ultimately to place them in
"that state of enlightened civil liberty, to which
"the Supreme BEING seems to advance all his
"creatures by various means, and by almost im-
"perceptible gradations. Some theorists have
"doubted whether GOD has destined all his
"creatures to be free, but none who are guided
"by his revealed WORD can doubt, that he willeth
"all to be civilized and happy, or, that they
"should 'be converted and live.' This is a work
"in which we may dare to be instrumental; it is

" the very work which our Lord has given us to
" do; which he has expressly commanded us.
" It is the most important, the most essential
" duty of a master. We must allow that the
" responsibility of a master is such as a man of
" reflecting mind does not willingly undertake;
" but if we have it in our power to make so many
" of our fellow creatures miserable, we also have
" it in our power, in a great measure, to make
" them happy. In the present state of things,
" any man may reconcile it to his conscience to
" be a Master of Slaves, as long as he performs
" the duties of one,—as long as he considers his
" Slaves as his fellow citizens and friends, to
" whom he is bound by the closest ties and by
" the strongest obligations; and above all, if he
" make their slavery the means of their conver-
" sion; the road to a more exalted state of
" existence in this world, and to everlasting hap-
" piness in that which is to come*."

These were the sentiments of a resident proprietor. It is not our intention to flatter our
countrymen or to deceive others, therefore we
cannot quit this subject without confessing that

* Remarks on various subjects connected with the Church
establishment of Barbadoes.

the work of conversion is as yet scarcely begun*; and that the attempts to wipe off this stigma from the character of the country have hitherto been only partial †.

We are aware that this confession will draw down upon us a torrent of obloquy from our adversaries. We beg leave, however, to make one exception here in favour of that candid, impartial, and liberal journal, the *Edinburgh Review*. We will do the gentlemen who conduct that Review the justice to declare our firm conviction, that though it should be proved that there is a total destitution of religious instruction among the Slaves, this journal would never, on *that account*, have recommended, as they have done, that our throats should be cut by our Slaves. *The liberal*

---

* Appendix, G and H.

† By the delay which has occurred in the publication of this Report, we are now enabled to speak in a much more satisfactory manner on this important subject. An Association has recently been formed for promoting the religious instruction of the Slaves, which comprehends a very large proportion of the proprietors and overseers of the Island; and from the zeal which is manifested in the cause, and the progress that has already been made in the undertaking, it would seem that "the "fulness of the Gentiles is now come." At the same time, we do not think it consistent with candour to suppress any thing that we said upon the subject six months ago, and which was true at that time.

journal!! We have no doubt this is the very acme of liberalism, being a flight above the reach of ordinary minds. Perissent plutot nos Colonies que de deroger un seul instant à nos principes, was the sentiment of Robespierre.

Mr. Wilberforce, as he justly says, has dwelt with " so much pertinacity" on the marriage of the Slaves, that your Committee feel themselves called upon to make a few remarks on that topic, although really after reading what Mr. Wilberforce has written about it, it is difficult to contemplate the subject with the sedate, composed feelings, which as a religious institution it ought to be regarded. Can this gentleman be serious in what he has written about the marriage of Slaves? Can he really mean to recommend that " destitute of all sense of religion and incorrigibly " licentious," as he (however unjustly) has represented them to be, they should be forced to contract the solemn obligations of matrimony, under the awful sanction of vows addressed to heaven? Does he think that there is any mystical charm in that combination of words which forms the ritual of the marriage ceremony, that shall in an instant purify their hearts from all licentious passions, and fill their minds with a just sense of moral responsibility? Must not every reflecting man, whose reason is not warped or obscured by enthusiasm, consider such an attempt as a downright mockery of Religion? We are convinced that all cool thinking persons will concur in the following sentiment, upon which Mr. Wilberforce so loudly cries shame; " That it is unnecessary and even improper to enforce the celebration of any religious rites among the Slaves in order to sanctify contracts, the faithful performance of which, could be looked for only, by a regular improvement in Religion, morality, and civilization." To promote their improvement in these important objects by all *rational* and practicable means, every respectable man in this community would give his hearty co-operation; but we cannot consent blindly to adopt every wild project of visionary enthusiasts.

Polygamy was imported by the Negroes from their native country, where it is a sort of privilege of rank; the richest and the greatest man enjoys the largest number of wives; and in these Colonies they no doubt consider a plurality of wives the privilege of their colour. A more effectual way of giving them a distaste for Christianity, could not well be devised, than to tell them in the *first instance,* that it required a surrender of this their highly valued privilege.

We suppose that it will give great pleasure to the friends of the Blacks to learn from good authority, that these objects of their anxious care have been sadly traduced, and that they are by no means so sunk in depravity and wickedness as they have been represented to be. That chastity is not classed among the cardinal virtues by the Blacks is most true, but a violation of it, even in a woman not contracted to a husband, is visited by the ridicule of the gang when it is detected, and in women who are wives, want of fidelity is considered disgraceful. As we do not wish to defile our pages by quoting the remarks of the Rev. Mr. Cooper and the *Edinburgh Review* upon this subject, we must refer for their refutation to the annexed examinations*.

It is now time to direct your attention to the state of the laws for the government and protection of the Slaves. This topic has been made a fertile source of obloquy and abuse against us. Our pious enemies, in literal compliance with the

* Appendix G, H, and I.

divine command, to visit the sins of the fathers upon the children, are not content to reproach us with the existing defects of our criminal code, but call up in judgment against us, laws passed in the infancy of the Colony, which have either been virtually repealed by change of manners and circumstances, or expressly repealed by subsequent enactments. " In the earlier laws of our " Colonies," says Mr. Wilberforce, " the opinions " of the legislature are expressed in the language " of insult, and in characters of blood. And too " many of these laws still remain unrepealed to " permit the belief that the same odious spirit " of legislation no longer exists, or to relieve the " injured objects of them from their degrading " influence."

Your Committee feeling themselves unequal to the task of vindicating the conduct of the Colony in this particular by reason or argument, have endeavoured to discover whether wiser and better people have not also incurred the guilt implied in this heavy charge, and if the folly and cruelty of old and obsolete laws are to be taken as evidence of the ignorance or depravity of the present generation. The following remarks will perhaps have some influence in mitigating the severity of the sentence to be passed upon us poor Colonists.

An eloquent modern writer thus expresses himself upon the penal code of England.

" It seems a strange incongruity that the offence
" of counterfeiting foreign coin, legitimated by
" Proclamation, should work a corruption of
" blood, which is saved by special proviso in the
" offence of counterfeiting the current coin of the
" kingdom. Again, it is a clergyable felony by
" our law to destroy or damage the bridges of
" Brentford or Blackfriars, but it is death to
" commit the same offence on the bridges of
" London, Westminster, or Putney. There is
" a similar unaccountable distinction between
" prison-breakers convicted of perjury, or com-
" mitted for entering black-lead mines with in-
" tent to steal, and such as are convicted of, or
" committed for, any other offence within Clergy.
" God forbid that I should insinuate a necessity
" to drag all this variety of discordant instances
" to the same bloody line of uniformity! Their
" cruelty appears to me equal to their incon-
" sistency; and it would not, perhaps, be dif-
" ficult to prove their folly equal to their cruelty."

" Persons," he adds, " carrying subjects out

"of the northern counties, or giving black mail for protection; jailers forcing prisoners to become approvers; masons confederating to prevent the statutes of labourers; purveyors in certain cases, though purveyance is abolished, are all capital offenders. The alterations in our government have rendered these particular provisions totally ineffective, but there are other obsolete statutes which exist, the possible instruments of mischief in the hand of tyranny*."

Under these numerous instances of absurd and cruel statutes, we may hope to screen our delinquency; but, at the same time, we fully agree with the same learned author, that " obsolete and useless statutes should be repealed, for they debilitate the authority of such as still exist, and are necessary. Neglect on this point is well compared by Lord Bacon to the cruelty of Mezentius, who left the living to perish in the arms of the dead."

There are undoubtedly many laws in our own statute book which disgrace it, and although many of them have been repealed, and had indeed

* Principles of Penal Laws.

become a mere dead letter for years before they were repealed, it is due to the character of the country, no less than to the interests of humanity and justice, to recast this crude mass, and purify it from the foul materials which debase it. We know with what extreme lenity the laws for the government of the Slaves are administered, but the existence of bad laws, or the want of good ones, is nevertheless a stigma on the Legislature, and exposes a very vulnerable point of attack to the malice of our enemies.

This subject naturally recalls to our recollection an address made to the Legislature in 1818, by our late highly esteemed governor, Lord Combermere. There is a striking coincidence of thought between this address, and the language of the enlightened author of *The Principles of Penal Laws.* It also contains a very favourable testimony of the kindness and humanity of masters in this country, which makes it peculiarly applicable to the present purpose. We shall, therefore, make no apology for extracting the following passages:

"A sincere desire to promote the honour and
"interest of this Island, induces me to press
"upon your attention the consolidation of your

" Slave laws, and the abolition of those clauses
" which have long ceased to be enforced, whilst
" their being retained among your statutes has
" had no other effect than to enable those op-
" posed to the present system of Colonial policy
" to degrade the West Indian proprietors in the
" eyes of their European countrymen.

" During my visits to the other West India
" Islands as Commander of the Forces, I have
" taken great pains personally to inform myself
" respecting the actual treatment of Slaves: and
" it was with the most sincere pleasure and gra-
" tification that I observed, almost universally,
" the greatest attention paid by Planters to the
" domestic comforts and proper regulation of the
" labours of their Slaves; but in no Colony which
" I have visited, do I conceive the regulations for
" the feeding of the Negroes so well laid down
" and acted upon as in this Island, owing to the
" judicious plan which has been adopted here in
" raising provisions for them, instead of depending
" on foreign supplies; and the excellent system
" of giving them daily dressed meals in addition
" to the ration of raw food.

" Under these circumstances, and fully aware
" that it is the anxious wish and desire of all the

" well-meaning inhabitants of this Colony, that
" the laws should be in unison with the practice
" of the country, I feel convinced it will meet
" your views to have those clauses repealed which,
" although become nearly obsolete, might at any
" time screen from the just rigour of the law,
" persons guilty of crimes at which humanity
" would shudder."

Confident in the integrity of his mind and the uprightness of his conduct, Lord Combermere feared no reproach, and dared to vindicate a much injured and calumniated class of men. He never thought whether by expressing his decided approbation of the conduct of the Planters, he was likely to provoke the hostility of a powerful party in England—he thought only of doing justice*.

We must all acknowledge the propriety of his Lordship's remarks on our Slave code, and although some of the obnoxious clauses have been since repealed, much yet remains to be done: other enactments for giving more effectual protec-

---

* The character of this nobleman cannot fail to give great weight to his testimony, we could not therefore deny ourselves the benefit of it; but, at the same time, we have reason to believe that the Governors of this Colony have been our friends—indeed there is strong ground to suspect that even Lord Seaforth's despatches have been unworthily garbled.

tion to the Slave against the cruelty or caprice of the Master are loudly called for by the change of sentiment and manners. We grant that this change has already done much for the cause of amelioration; but we must not suppose, because public opinion has preceded legislation in the march of reform that it can supersede it: laws are required to govern bad men who do not partake of the good feelings of the general society.

Nothing we are convinced has tended more to obstruct the progress of improvement in this branch of legislation, than the indiscreet zeal of the false friends of the Blacks. We remember to have heard measures for the better protection of this class opposed on this ground: " Be cautious
" how you furnish our enemies with more han-
" dles of attack. We know that acts of bar-
" barity very seldom occur, yet they do occur
" sometimes; if you make all these matters of
" record, our enemies will be perpetually re-
" proaching the community at large with them.
" Crimes in the Colonies are not judged of as
" crimes committed in any other part of the
" world; the most wanton cruelties, the most
" atrocious murders, happening in England, bring
" disgrace and detestation upon the guilty indivi-

" dual alone, but the same acts occurring among
" us, shall cover the whole community with in-
" famy; until we receive fair play it cannot be
" expected we should give it." This to be sure
is very bad reasoning, but we mention it to shew
in what various ways the red-hot enthusiasts defeat the very object they profess to have in view.

As the first step towards affording effectual
protection to the Slave, it would appear to be
highly expedient to give him the benefit of his
testimony, under certain circumstances and subject to certain restrictions. This we admit is a subject beset with numberless difficulties. It will
require the utmost circumspection and judgment
to guard the privilege in such a way as to prevent
it from becoming a scourge to the community,
and a dangerous trap to those for whose benefit
it had been conferred. All who are conversant
with the Negro character, know from experience
that there is no moral obligation so little respected
by these people as truth. Honesty is by no means
a rare virtue, particularly in the domestic servants;
but an exact attention to veracity is scarcely ever
met with, even among the worthiest of the class;
nor is this fact extraordinary. A love of truth
may be considered above all others, the virtue of

refinement; and perhaps it may be laid down as a broad rule, that truth is only respected by people among whom the point of honour is recognized. With the crude and imperfect notions of religion which the Negroes unfortunately at present possess, it is impossible to aid the moral sense by the sanction of an oath*.

And although the Slaves of this Colony are a mild, tractable set of people, by no means addicted to violent resentments, and, generally speaking, love and respect the Master more than any other man in the world, yet when it is considered that the occasions upon which they will be chiefly called upon to exercise the privilege in question, will be occasions when revengeful feelings must have been excited, it will be allowed to expose them to a fearful trial of integrity. These are

* A curious scene occurred a few years ago at the Court of Grand Sessions, which may help to illustrate the folly of administering the rite of baptism to ignorant pagans, without following it up with a course of religious instruction. An African soldier appeared at the bar of the court as a witness, and being asked if he had been christened, he replied in the affirmative. The next question was, " Do you believe in the Lord?" A wild and vacant stare denoted that this Christian did not exactly comprehend the nature of the question; it was accordingly repeated—" Do you believe in the Lord?" " Yes, oh! yes, my Lord Combermere!!"

weighty considerations; nevertheless, if it shall appear that the inadmissibility of Negro evidence against a white man must sometimes " cover the " most guilty with impunity," do we not choose the minor evil by granting a privilege which though peculiarly liable to abuse, seems almost indispensible to the ends of justice and humanity.

It must be the business of the Legislator to impose every possible check which wisdom and experience shall point out, against the abuse of this most questionable privilege. It should be restricted exclusively to matters in which the personal security of the Slave is concerned, and when other evidence cannot be obtained. Neither justice nor humanity require that the testimony of a Slave should be received in questions between free-men. Considering the almost irresistible influence of the Master over his Slave, it is obvious how powerful an engine of injustice and wrong Slave-testimony would become under the control of an unprincipled Master. After all, this, it must be confessed, is the Gordian knot of Colonial legislation, and we do not feel ourselves prepared to give a decided opinion upon it*.

* Since the presentation of this Report, a despatch has been received in this Colony from Lord Bathurst, which,

Other regulations for accomplishing the object in view naturally present themselves. Laws should be enacted imposing heavy penalties on Slave-owners guilty of acts of barbarity, amounting in extreme cases to forfeiture of possession, and absolute incompetency to hold property in Slaves for ever after.

As to the mighty bugbear the Cow's-skin or Cart-whip, we can have no objection to enforce by law that which is almost already accomplished by custom, and abolish the use of this instrument of punishment by legislative enactment. But with regard to certain other restrictions on the Master's power of punishment, at the same time that we earnestly recommend a respectful attention to the suggestions of all parties who we have reason to believe are sincere in the cause of humanity, and especially to the wishes of His Majesty's Ministers, we must not too hastily renounce the right of judging of their expediency, and of profiting

amongst many other regulations for ameliorating the condition of the Slaves, contains some very enlightened suggestions relative to the admission of Slave Testimony; and the Council, willing to profit by his lordship's hints on the difficult task of disentangling this Gordian knot, can now venture to express with greater confidence their willingness to extend this privilege to the Slaves, under the restrictions there proposed.

by that better knowledge of the subject which experience and constant observation cannot fail to give. We believe that it is the sincere and hearty wish of all the respectable proprietors and overseers in this Island, and we have no doubt throughout the West Indies generally, to reduce punishments to the lowest possible standard that is compatible with discipline and subordination. In this country very mild measures are found adequate to that purpose; but there must be power to restrain licentiousness and punish vice, however mild and lenient the exercise of it might be. It is a maxim not to be controverted, that the more absolute and unquestionable that power is, provided it could always be placed in safe hands, the fewer would be the occasions which call for its exertion. All Masters of Slaves of course are not worthy to be trusted with such unlimited power. It is therefore necessary to restrict it; but care should be taken, lest in binding the hands of authority too fast, we do not loosen the bands of society in the same degree.

We do not feel it necessary to go much into detail on this subject, as it would be encroaching on the province of a Committee which is now sitting for the purpose of revising the Slave laws, and suggesting such measures of amelioration as may seem best calculated to promote the happiness of the Slave, without endangering the peace of society or the security of property.

It will be admitted that we have now said enough on the actual condition of the Slave, and on the conduct and feelings of the Master, to convince every person capable of being convinced, that the charges of " gross injustice and unrelent- " ing cruelty" are founded on exaggeration and misstatement. We shall therefore quit this part of our task, after having given one extract as a fair specimen of the exaggerated, hyperbolical tone, in which Mr. Wilberforce always speaks on the subject of his mania. " The Africans," says he, speaking of them in their savage state, " are " represented to be industrious, generous, emi- " nent for truth, seldom chargeable with licen- " tiousness, distinguished for their domestic affec- " tions, and capable at times of heroic acts of " magnanimity." So much for savage life! *Credat Judæus Apella.* Mandeville never went further than this in his fable of the bees. Who that believes this delineation of the unsophisticated purity and lofty virtues of the savage African, can refuse to admit that licentiousness and vice are the attributes of civilization*.

It is by the aid of exaggeration such as this, that our enemies have endeavoured to reconcile the honest people of England to the most unprincipled act of spoliation, the most outrageous violation of the sacred rights of property, and the most disgraceful breach of national faith, that was ever proposed to any Christian people on the face of the earth.

Having effectually, we hope, cleared away the thick cloud of falsehood by which this party have artfully contrived to obscure the moral vision of the British people, we may expect that they will be prepared to contemplate the rights of a West Indian with the same feelings, and appreciate them by the same standard, by which they would judge of the rights of any other class of His Majesty's subjects.

The origin of the Slave-trade is involved in

---

* When it suits the purpose of this party, Africa is represented as "*steeped* in barbarity," and we are told that " a " state of society more miserably dismembered, and in which " the elements seem less capable of combination, can scarcely " be imagined. Europe might be rebarbarized before Africa " could civilize herself."

some obscurity, but it is sufficient for our purpose to shew, that the right of property in Negroes has been sanctioned by various acts of Parliament and orders in Council. We shall only allude to the three following Statutes:—one of them confers the rights of a British subject on a foreigner settled in the West Indies for a given number of years; another invites persons to lend their money on the security of Slaves, and allows a higher rate of interest than that which is permitted to be taken by law in Great Britain; and a third affords the creditor an easy mode of recovering his debts on lands and slaves in the Colonies.

Indeed at one period of our history, the African Slave-trade was in such high favour in the nation, that it was specially honoured by Royal Patronage. The Duke of York, at that time Heir-apparent, and afterwards King James II., thought himself not disgraced by being placed at the head of an Association which was formed for the purpose of promoting that trade. In Jamaica royal grants of land were made only to such persons as were possessed of Slaves.

Is it to be wondered at, then, that seduced by such high example, and encouraged by the approbation of public opinion, some bold enterprising spirits should be tempted by the prospect of honourable gain, to embark in adventures in the Colonies, and unguardedly connect themselves with a system which all the world then approved of, not being able to divine that at some future time a change of opinion was to take place, which would brand as infamous, a pursuit which was then thought fair and honourable, and that they or their posterity were to be the devoted victims of this change of opinion. Indeed we are not called upon to prove, that whatever may be the turpitude of Slavery is the turpitude of the nation. Our bitterest enemies admit it, although they desire that we alone should be the sacrifice to expiate the guilt. Mr. Wilberforce calls it a " National crime:" again, he says, " the people of " England are called upon to do justice to the " descendants of the Africans, whom we (the " nation) have ourselves wrongfully planted in " the western hemisphere.*" In the Liverpool

---

* As our enemies will pervert to our disadvantage every form of expression at all ambiguous, we think it necessary to make a formal confession of faith on the Slave-trade. We are confident in saying, that this traffic is now regarded with the same feelings here as it is in England; and it ought to be recorded, to the credit of this Colony, that at a very early stage of the discussion which led to the abolition, our Agent in England received instructions not to oppose the measure.

declaration, the following passage occurs: "The "time is yet within the memory of persons not "far advanced in life, when this traffic was not "only considered allowable, but was sanctioned "by the voice of the community, and carried on "under public encouragement and legislative au- "thority." Again, at page 7—" This Society "disavow, in the most explicit manner, all idea "of attaching to the Colonial proprietors any "moral impututiòn further than such as attaches "also to the nation at large, which has sanctioned "and encouraged a system of Slavery in its fo- "reign possessions.*"

Notwithstanding these clear admissions that a property in Negroes was fairly acquired under the sanction of law and public opinion, and that, consequently, British merchants, taught to confide " in the mysterious virtue of wax and parchment," have been induced to lend their money on the security of this species of property, it is now

---

* As this is the first time we have had occasion to refer to this little tract, we must take the opportunity to acknowledge the gentlemanly language in which it is written, so different from the low abuse and scurrility with which we are accustomed to be treated, particularly by Messrs. Wilberforce, Macauley, Cropper and Co. We do not remember one opprobious epithet in it.

proposed, without scruple or compunction, to emancipate the Slave, strip a large and valuable class of subjects of their lawful property, and at once to reduce thousands of faithful citizens from comfort and affluence to misery and want.

The learned professors of the rights of man regard prescription, not as a title to bar all claim set up against old possession, but they look on prescription as itself a bar against the possessor or proprietor. They hold immemorial possession to be no more than " a long continued and there-" fore an aggravated injustice.*" These are the mild and reasonable measures which alone are acknowledged to be just in principle and practically effectual to their purpose. Of compensation not one word is said; that would endanger the popularity of the cause, inasmuch as compensation implies taxation.

It is difficult to find language to characterize the profligacy and total destitution of principle implied in this atrocious attempt. The rights of property are so consecrated in the opinions and feelings of the nation, that we should suppose the intentions and conduct of this party need only to

* A Letter to a noble Lord.

be represented in their true colours, to be visited by the execration and detestation of every honest man in the British dominions.

Mr. Justice Blackstone's notions upon the subject of property, will exhibit the schemes of our adversaries in a proper point of view: " The
" third absolute right inherent in every English-
" man is that of property, which consists in the
" free use, enjoyment and disposal of all his ac-
" quisitions, without any control or diminution,
" save only by the laws of the land. The original
" of private property is probably founded in
" nature, as will be more fully shewn in the se-
" cond book of the ensuing Commentaries, but
" certainly the modifications under which we at
" present find it, the method of conserving it
" in the present owner, and of translating it from
" man to man are entirely derived from society,
" and are some of those civil advantages, in ex-
" change for which every individual has resigned
" a part of his natural liberty. The laws of
" England are therefore, in point of honour and
" justice, extremely watchful in ascertaining and
" protecting this right."

" So great, moreover," he adds, " is the regard
" of the law for private property, that it will not

" authorize the least violation of it, no not even
" for the general good of the whole community.
" If a new road, for instance, were to be made
" through the grounds of a private person, it
" might, perhaps, be extensively beneficial to the
" public; but the law permits no man, or set of
" men, to do this without consent of the owner
" of the land. In vain may it be urged, that the
" good of the individual ought to yield to the
" good of the community: for it would be dan-
" gerous to allow any private man, or even any
" public tribunal, to be the judge of this com-
" mon good, and to decide whether it be expe-
" dient or not. Besides, the public good is in
" nothing more essentially interested than in the
" protection of every individual's private rights,
" as modelled by the municipal law. In this and
" similar cases, the legislature alone can, and in-
" deed frequently does, interpose and compel the
" individual to acquiesce. But how does it in-
" terpose and compel? Not by absolutely strip-
" ping the subject of his property in an arbitrary
" manner, but by giving him a full indemnifica-
" tion and equivalent for the injury sustained.
" The public is now considered as an individual
" treating with an individual for an exchange.

"All that the legislature does is to oblige the
"owner to alienate his possessions for a reason-
"able price; and even this is an exertion of
"power which the legislature indulges with cau-
"tion, and which nothing but the legislature can
"perform.*"

These are principles founded in reason and equity, not peculiarly adapted to local circumstances or particular times, but as universal and immutable as truth and justice. They form the very basis of civil association; and the slightest violation of these elementary principles, committed in the remotest corner of the British Empire, cannot fail to give a rude shock to the whole fabric of civil rights; or, as it has been well said by an eminent statesman on a different occasion, " In
" effect we suffer as much at home by this loosen-
" ing of all ties, and this concussion of established
" opinions, as we do abroad."

These are considerations which no doubt have had, and we trust will continue to have, due weight in the Councils of the Nation; but we must be upon our guard not to be deluded into a dangerous sense of security by the hollow and

* Blackstone's Com. vol. I.

treacherous pledges of our adversaries. Of the inconsistency, equivocation, contradiction and tergiversation of the emancipators, we have had ample experience: their shuffling, truckling conduct has been so admirably exposed by Mr. Marryatt, that we shall content ourselves with refering to the second pamphlet of that able defender of West Indian rights, entitled *More Thoughts.*

However guarded, however ambiguous, however vague may be their notions and their speeches, we now know that the emancipation of the Slaves and the ruin of the Owners is their object; and that respect for national pledges and vested rights, will never stand in *their* way when they have a chance of accomplishing it. It requires a much smaller share of political sagacity than is possessed by this party, to discover that there are various ways of bringing about the consummation they so devoutly wish,—the desolation of these Colonies. They have already succeeded but too well in giving a tremendous shock to our credit, the foundation of agricultural, as much as of commercial prosperity. It will be some time before the panic occasioned by the late discussions in Parliament, will cease to manifest itself in the depreciated market value of property, and the difficulty of effecting transfers; for no man in his senses will hazard his money in the purchase of an article which he is in danger of having wrested from his possession by the arbitrary, uncompromising fiat of irresistible power.

It is, no doubt, with a view of sapping the foundation of our institutions, and ultimately effecting our ruin, that the emancipators invoke with such pious fervour the interposition of the Imperial Parliament in the regulation of our internal affairs. They know well from reason and history, if experience had not taught them, that no country can possibly prosper under a system of government, where the governors are three or four thousand miles removed from the theatre of their operations, and where calumny would supply the place of observation, and speculation usurp the province of experience. It is obvious how admirably adapted such a system would be to the views of our foes. We must, therefore, deprecate such interference with the same earnestness, with which these men invoke it. Experience however, has taught us to expect that the British Parliament will always be governed by considerations of political equity, even although partial interests should desire to inculcate that might is right.

As to the absurd notion by which it has been attempted to impose upon the honest part of the nation, that estates would be profitably cultivated by the freed Slaves, we scarcely think it worth our while to advert to it. Not one man who has promulgated this doctrine, from Mr. Cropper up to the most respectable, can possibly believe what he has asserted. Admitting, for the sake of argument, the soundness of M. Say's theory, that the labour of free men is more productive than the labour of Slaves, what is to become of the immense capital already vested in this species of property. And what consideration is it to the merchant who holds mortgages over Slaves *exclusively*, that lands may be still cultivated profitably by them after they are freed. The moment they cease to be property, his mortgage becomes waste paper. Transfer the security to the land, it will, perhaps, be said; but in this Island, and we fear it is the case in most of the neighbouring Colonies, there are a vast number of estates in which both land and Negroes are entirely covered by mortgages. Again it may be replied, if the productions of the land are not diminished by the change, the whole amount of the debt would be liquidated in the same time as it would have been under the old system; but, unfortunately, in these times it often happens that debts, when they are large, cannot be paid by crops, and the creditors can only be satisfied by a sale of the property pledged. Moreover it may happen, and indeed often does happen in the most prosperous times, that a creditor may wish, for the very best reasons, to collect his money; is he to wait upon the precarious fluctuations of crops and prices, which, in in many cases, would never be adequate to satisfy all claims? What would a creditor holding a mortgage over property in England, say to a law which should destroy his right of foreclosure in the property, and compel him to wait for payment out of precarious crops which barely keep down the interest?—it would be quite as unjust as a law which should declare all securities forfeited, allowing the interest only to the original holder; or, in other words, it would be to convert a proprietor into an annuitant upon very *disadvantageous and iniquitous terms.*

This argument is founded on the presumption that our estates really could be profitably cultivated by the emancipated Slaves; a doctrine which we are very far from admitting. At any rate the present generation of proprietors would be ruined before the newly-freed Slave would be convinced " that the necessity of providing for " his subsistence, though less degrading, is not " less imperative than that under which he had " before been compelled to return to his daily " task;" or before he would acquire such settled habits of industry as would ensure to the proprietor of the soil that regular supply of labour which would be necessary to enable him to continue his cultivation. And it seems never to have been noticed in this controversy, that the object of our cultivation, combining manufacture with agriculture, can only be successfully carried on by the united exertions of large numbers of persons, at stated periods, and according to the crop for a long continuance of time.

As we do not pretend to be such acute reasoners as our antagonists, and are by no means so well skilled in the tactics of controversy, we take care never to advance but under cover of a strong battery of facts—we must therefore halt a moment to bring up our artillery.

It appears by an Official Return from the Treasurer's Office, where every Slave and every acre of land are annually given in for the purpose of being taxed, that there are 5206 Owners of Slaves in this island; that of this number, 1535 are Owners of land as well as Slaves: the remaining 3671 Owners of Slaves have no land at all.* What is to be said to these unfortunate people, if the right of property in Slaves be abrogated? They, poor creatures, would not profit one penny by it, though the lands *innocently* cultivated by free people should produce gold instead of sugar. Many of these proprietors it is true have but a few Slaves; but that does not alter the quality of the act. There is as much injustice in robbing a man of small possessions of his all, as in stripping the wealthiest nobleman in England of his princely domains.

Some of the more honest of the party, cannot help manifesting a certain compunction at the thought of beggaring a large class of their fellow subjects in this off-hand way; and as a means of quieting their consciences, or perhaps of saving their credit with the world, they propose to allow the present generation of Slaves to continue in slavery, and only to declare their posterity free:

* Appendix O.

and upon this plan, say they, " there can be no " pretension to a claim of indemnification, for " how can a man expect compensation for the " loss of property which he never possessed?" What sophistry! He would have precisely the same right to compensation that a remainderman or reversioner of an estate in England would have for the violation of his contingent rights by the strong hand of Parliament. In all conveyances of Slaves " the future issue and increase" is as firmly conveyed and secured as the existing property. This prospective right cannot be taken away without materially impairing the value of all securities, and in many instances it would have the effect of totally annihilating their value; as when the debts are so large that the junior creditors cannot expect in the ordinary course of things to be paid out of the crops for twenty or thirty years. Sales of property, we take it for granted, would be totally at an end under the state of things we are contemplating. This would be the effect of the measure on mortgagees and judgment creditors. Its operation on actual proprietors would be to convert an estate in fee into a life estate; for it is obvious, that it makes no difference in fact, whether the term of possession depend upon the life of the owner, or of the Slave, in both cases the proprietorship determines with the life of a certain party. What would the country gentlemen of England say to a Bill, which generously allowed them the undisturbed possession of their estates for some thirty or forty years, and declared them forfeited at the expiration of that period?—for such in effect would be the operation of the measure in question on West India property.

There is yet another point of view in which this plan must be considered, in its effect upon reversionary rights. The rights of persons entitled to estates in expectancy, are equally respected with those of persons in actual possession of property, and the justice and honesty of our laws are admirably displayed by the scrupulous attention with which the vested interests of posterity are regarded. No instance can be produced in our legal history, where the rights of the reversioner or remainderman have been sacrificed upon any speculative notion of the fitness of things. These rights were held to be sacred in a case where the property amounted to a sum almost incalculable. Although in a decision in which these contingent rights were upheld, it was publicly declared to be "a triumph of private vanity "over the whole system of British jurisprudence, " by which the English law would be made " subservient to posthumous avarice, and all the " landed property of the kingdom would be sunk " in mere trusteeship, and the people of England " deprived of all its beneficial enjoyments."

The modern jurists, we are to suppose, consider Justice, as has been said of Religion, " an affair of geography," so that what is right and equitable in Europe is not so on this side of the Atlantic.

This Report has unavoidably swelled to such a bulk already, that your Committee find themselves under the necessity of omitting altogether some topics connected with their inquiry, and of touching very concisely upon others which they had intended to discuss at some length.

This Colony (which seems to be peculiarly the object of Messrs. Wilberforce and Co.'s most rancorous enmity,) is reproached with throwing unnecessary obstacles in the way of emancipation, by attaching penalties to manumission, and according to newspaper reports, one of the party stated in the House of Commons that this penalty amounted to 500*l*. As it happens to be 50*l*. the addition of a nought, we suppose, he considered a matter of no importance. These gentlemen have not had the candour to state that the freed Slave receives an annuity for life, at the rate of eight per cent. on the deposit.

We think it likely that the policy which first dictated this law had a reference to the preservation of that preponderance of the white population over the free people of colour, which was at one time considered essential to the security and stability of property. Experience had in some instances illustrated the wisdom and expediency of this policy. The history of the insurrections at Grenada and Saint Vincent, and even at Saint Domingo, may have been quoted in proof of it. But the fidelity and good conduct of this class of subjects in this island, in the insurrection of 1816, removed all apprehension on that score from the minds of our legislature: and having proved themselves good citizens, they were deemed worthy of a greater extension of civil rights. A law was immediately enacted for the purpose of legalizing their testimony, and as it now appeared that there was no good reason for opposing the increase of their numbers, the deposit on a manumission was reduced to a sum which was thought barely sufficient to prevent unkind and ungrateful owners from ridding themselves of the burthen of maintaining their old and infirm Slaves, and also for the purpose of providing in some measure for the support of the enfranchised Slave. Indeed this law, as it now stands, is constantly evaded by the connivance or rather by the consent of public opinion. At least nine-tenths of the Slaves who have been emancipated during the last six years, have obtained their freedom by virtue of English manumissions, which are deeds of enfranchisement executed by a person in England, to whom the Slaves are conveyed by their owner resident in this Island. These deeds were not originally legalized by any statute of the Island, but their validity has for a series of years been recognized by all our Courts, and they are now considered as good and effectual for their purpose as any other form of manumission.

Another point to which we may be expected to advert, is the propriety of attaching the Slaves to the soil; but we really think that the multiplied evils of such a law, even to the Slaves themselves, have been so fully illustrated and so clearly made manifest in the " Report of the House of Assembly " of Jamaica on the Registry Bill," that those who are not already convinced of the policy of such a law, would not be convinced by any body of evidence which human labour could collect, or by any force of argument which human ingenuity could invent: and as to the fine piece of declamation on this subject in Mr. Wilberforce's pamphlet, we beg him to try whether it will not apply with greater force to the impressing of seamen, or even to the sending soldiers and sailors on foreign service, without consulting their inclinations. But we must not expect to find the principles of this party susceptible of that universal, indiscriminate application, which is at once the criterion and the beauty of sound principles. In every thing we discover that " fanatical irregula-" rity of mind" which characterizes all the doctrines and all the measures of these super-pious men. Their philanthropy is of that eccentric kind, which aims more at giving notariety to themselves than happiness to others; for how shall we reconcile to our vulgar, home-bred notions of philanthropy, the conduct of a gentleman who declares his conviction, that the prosperity of the Master and the comfortable condition of the Slave are inseparable, and nevertheless opposes systematically every measure calculated to rescue the Master from adversity. " These evils," says Mr.

Wilberforce " which are indeed very great, must of " course be aggravated where the Planters are in " embarassed circumstances, notoriously the situ- " ation of the greater part of the owners of West " India Estates." If these are his impressions, in the name of heaven, what became of his benevolence—of his charity—when he lent the aid of his great talents to the support of a motion for equalizing the duties on East and West India sugar? A measure which all the House of Commons except thirty-four members, saw must inevitably bring ruin upon every West Indian proprietor; and of this number, twenty-one were proprietors of East India Stock, and Mr. Wilberforce was one of them.

In any other man, such conduct as this would have some chance of being characterized as highly disgraceful; but, notwithstanding the great name and high reputation of the individual, it cannot fail to make all impartial persons question the purity and integrity of the motives, which actuate him in the splendid career which he has been pursuing; and we must, for a time at least, hesitate in allotting him a station among the virtuous benefactors of mankind, or in placing him in the same class with a Howard or a Boromeo. What toils has Mr. Wilberforce endured? What sacrifices, either personal or pecuniary, has he undergone for the cause of humanity? Such a name and such a station as he enjoys are cheaply purchased indeed by a few splendid orations or well written pamphlets, which cost him little effort, and procure him vast applause.

In the foregoing pages it will perhaps appear that we have been occasionally betrayed into some warmth of expression; but let it be remembered that we write under a sense of the deepest injuries—that the attempt of our adversaries is to rob us of character and fortune. What else on earth is there valuable to man?

The Colonists have been so often annoyed, and are now so heartily disgusted by the reiterated attempts to overthrow their property, and by the distractions and commotions occasioned by those attempts, that we believe the enemies of the Colonial system will find them very ready to co-operate in their views, so soon as arrangements have been made to indemnify them for the losses which they are to sustain by the accomplishment of those views. It cannot be expected that any set of men shall consent to beggar themselves from a deference to certain speculative notions of philanthropy. But the West Indian proprietor we have no doubt will submit to bear a full share, or even more than a just share of the burthen.

Since however it is admitted on all hands, that the criminality of the Slave system belongs to the nation at large, surely the sacrifice for the atonement ought to be co-extensive with the guilt, and fall equally upon every part of the Empire. But should the nation refuse to attest the sincerity of their zeal in this cause, by consenting to such impositions as may be required to indemnify us, let them never again reproach us with the turpitude of Slavery. What principle of political or ethical justice can require that we alone should be the victims to expiate a crime, the guilt of which according even to the admission of our adversaries, attaches to us only in common with the rest of the nation.

No class of His Majesty's subjects has borne a larger share of the burthens of the late war, or bore it with less complaining than the West Indian proprietor. How many of this class are there, who having inherited handsome fortunes, are now reduced to difficulties, not by personal extravagance or by physical calamity, but by the irresistible pressure of duties, and by the depreciation of the value of their staple commodities—the result of certain measures of Government, which though perhaps of sound national policy, have borne with peculiar hardship upon this part of the Empire. And are we now to be denied all those civil advantages, for the sake of which we have resigned so much, and have indured so much? Instead of protection of our property or full indemnification for the violation of it, are we to be rewarded by confiscation and rapine? Or ought we even to be exposed to the apprehension of these things, and to the multiplied evils which must inevitably arise from such an apprehension? These are doctrines which we are well assured His Majesty's Ministers would renounce with disdain. But we do fear that they are not sufficiently impressed with the magnitude of the mischief which is done to us, by the compromising policy which they seem disposed to adopt, in regard to the views of the advocates of rapine.

APPENDIX.

A.

Examination (on Oath) of Sir Edmund Williams, K. C. B.

Query 1. What is your professional rank, and the nature of your connexion with this Colony? How long have you been resident in this Island? During such residence have you, or have you not, had frequent opportunities of observing the general treatment of the Slaves in this Colony? If yea, state what has fallen under your observation relative to their general treatment and condition.

Answer. Examinant saith—that he is a Lieutenant-Colonel in the Army, and at present the Commandant of the Garrisons at Saint Ann's; that he has been resident in this Island upwards of eight months, and that he has had opportunities, having purposely sought them, from an impression when he left England that the Slaves were badly treated in the Colonies; that he has visited gentlemen on their Plantations, and that he has anxiously looked at their Hospitals and other establishments; that he has found their Hospitals particularly attended to, and the young Slaves well fed and treated, and that he firmly believes that generally speaking they are better off than the poor in England.

Qu. 2. From your knowledge of the manners of the inhabitants of this Island, do you, or do you not, think that a cruel Owner of Slaves would be held in the same abhorrence here, as he would be in England?

Ans. Examinant saith—that he firmly believes that a cruel Owner of Slaves would be held in the same abhorrence here as he would be in England.

Qu. 3. From the general demeanor and conduct of the Slaves themselves, would you, or would you not, pronounce them to be a happy and contented, or an oppressed and ill-treated, people? State particularly what has fallen under your own observation in this respect, and your reasons for the opinions which you may have formed on this subject.

Ans. That it is difficult for him to answer that question, because it is impossible to know their feelings, but if he can judge from their singing and amusing themselves when off their, and even when at labour, he should really think them a happy race of people; and that he has observed that every family has a cottage and some poultry, a pig and other things, which they take to market, and make the most of for their families. That he has frequently rode over the Plantations with the Owners, and seen gangs of thirty or forty Slaves speak in the most kind and feeling manner when at work to their Owners, particularly inquiring how the rest of the family were.

(Signed)   EDMUND KEYNTON WILLIAMS.

B.

Examination of Lieutenant-Colonel Popham, (on Oath).

Query 1. What is your professional rank, and the nature of your connexion with this Colony? How long have you been resident in this Island?

During such residence have you, or have you not, had frequent opportunities of observing the general treatment of the Slaves in this Colony? If yea, state what has fallen under your observation relative to their general treatment and condition.

Answer. Examinant saith—that he is a Lieutenant-Colonel in the army, and Deputy Quarter-Master-General; that he has been resident in this Island upwards of seven years; that during such residence he has had several opportunities; that he has reason to suppose from his own observation, that they are generally well treated.

Qu. 2. From your knowledge of the manners of the inhabitants of the Island, do you, or do you not, think that a cruel Owner of Slaves would be held in the same abhorrence here, as he would in England?

Ans. Examinant saith—certainly he thinks so.

Qu. 3. From the general demeanor and conduct of the Slaves themselves, would you, or would you not, pronounce them to be a happy and contented, or an oppressed and ill-treated people? State particularly what has fallen under your observation in this respect, and your reasons for the opinions which you may have formed on this subject.

Ans. Saith—that he verily believes, from personal observation on the estates he has visited, from riding through and passing many others, having been in every parish, they are a contented and happy people, generally speaking; that they appear cheerful in the performance of their work, and that he does not recollect witnessing any severity practised upon them in the field; that they appear to him clothed in general, and in many instances well so; that the greater proportion of the houses of these people appear comfortable, having the advantages of poultry, pigs, and goats, in many instances fruit trees and a little garden; and that the markets held by them on Sunday, clearly demonstrate that they enjoy the benefit arising from the produce and sale thereof; that he has every reason to believe, from frequently seeing medical men riding through the estates, and from inquiries made upon the subject, that they are visited weekly, and oftener if required in particular cases, by a practitioner, who is paid annually for his attendance; that very great attention is paid to the rearing of children, and that the old and infirm receive the kindest attention, as is fully proved by the very few Blacks who are beggars, whereas the white population exhibit frequent instances; thus proving that the Slaves in this Colony are much better off than the lower class in England, having no care or thought for to-morrow, feeling confident that all their necessary wants and comforts will be provided for.

(Signed)   S. J. POPHAM, D. Q. M. G.

C.

Examination of Lieutenant Colonel Berkeley, (on Oath).

Query. 1. What is your professional rank, and the nature of your connexion with this Colony? How long have you been resident in this Island? During such residence have you, or have you not, had frequent opportunities of observing the general treatment of the Slaves in this Colony? If yea, state what has fallen under your observation relative to their general treatment and condition.

Ans. Examinant saith—that he is a Lieutenant-Colonel in the Army, and Deputy Adjutant-General to the Army serving in the Leeward Islands;

that he has been resident, with some interruptions, since the year 1806; that he has not had an opportunity of observing the condition of the Slaves in the Country, from his professional duties confining him to the vicinity of the town.

Qu. 2. From your knowledge of the manners of the inhabitants of this Island, do you, or do you not, think that a cruel Owner of Slaves would be held in the same abhorrence here, as he would be in England?

Ans. Examinant saith—decidedly so.

Qu. 3. From the general demeanor and conduct of the Slaves themselves, would you, or would you not, pronounce them to be a happy and contented, or an oppressed and ill-treated people? State particularly what has fallen under your own observation in this respect, and your reasons for the opinions which you may have formed on the subject.

Ans. Saith—from any thing he could observe, that the Negroes appear to be as contented as any other labouring people in any part of the world; that within the last few months he has had an opportunity for the first time, of seeing something of the interior detail of an estate, and that in his opinion the system established, was, as far as the preservation of discipline required, too lenient, and that he has no doubt that the same system very generally prevails among the respectable class of owners.

  (Signed)   J. H. BERKELEY.

D.

Examination of Dr. Edward Tegart, (on Oath).

Query 1. What is your professional rank, and the nature of your connexion with this Colony? How long have you been resident in this Island? During such residence have you, or have you not, had frequent opportunities of observing the general treatment of the Slaves in this Colony? If yea, state what has fallen under your observation relative to their general treatment and condition.

Ans. Examinant saith—that he is Inspector of Hospitals, that he has been resident in this Island upwards of two years; that he has not had frequent opportunities; that in one estate he looked minutely into their condition, when the great number of Slaves appeared to him to be well managed, and comfortably taken care of; that he has seen several others, but only superficially, when the external appearance gave him reason to think that they were very comfortable; that he has observed that on several of the estates their Hospitals are very well conducted for the care of the sick; that he came to this Island prepossessed that the Negroes were very harshly used, from what he had heard and read on the subject, but he now finds that it is not so, and he believes that they are generally kindly and well treated; they appear to him to be better off than the labouring people are in his own country (Ireland).

Qu. 2. From your knowledge of the manners of the inhabitants of this Island, do you, or do you not, think that a cruel owner of Slaves would be held in the same abhorrence here, as he would be in England?

Ans. Saith—decidedly.

Qu. 3. From the general demeanor and conduct of the Slaves themselves, would you, or would you not, pronounce them to be a happy and contented, or an oppressed and ill-treated people? State particularly what has fallen under your own observation in this respect, and your reasons for the opinions which you may have formed on the subject.

Ans. Saith—that he thinks, generally speaking, they seem very contented.

(Signed) Edw. Tegart.

E.

Examination of Captain Courtenay Cruttenden, (on Oath).

Query 1. What is your professional rank, and the nature of your connexion with this Colony? How long have you been resident in this Island? During such residence have you, or have you not, had frequent opportunities of observing the general treatment of the Slaves in this Colony? If yea, state what has fallen under your observation relative to their general treatment and condition.

Ans. Examinant saith—that he is a Captain in the Royal Artillery, commanding the detachment of that Corps at the Head Quarters in this Island, and Major of Brigade to the Forces in this Island; that he has been resident in this Island ten years; that he has very frequently had opportunities of observing the treatment of Slaves in this Island upon a great number of Estates, where he has resided weeks and months at a time, and that he has ever observed the kind treatment they invariably receive—the cheerfulness with which he has observed them perform their duty, and that he never was witness to an act of cruelty or oppression during the period he has been in this Island; he does declare, what he has frequently asserted, that he considers them a much more happy race, better clothed and enjoying more comforts, than the poor in that part of Ireland (Cork) where he was for a short time stationed.

Qu. 2. From your knowledge of the manners of the inhabitants of this Island, do you, or do you not, think that a cruel Owner of Slaves would be held in the same abhorrence here, as he would be in England?

Ans. Saith—equally so.

Qu. 3. From the general demeanor and conduct of the Slaves themselves, would you, or would you not, pronounce them to be a happy and contented, or an oppressed and ill-treated people? State particularly what has fallen under your own observation in this respect, and your reasons for the opinions you may have formed on this subject.

Ans. Saith—that he thinks he has answered this question in his reply to No. 1.

(Signed)   C. CRUTTENDEN,
Capt. R. Artillery, Major of Brigade.

F.

Examination of Captain Spink, (on Oath).

Qu. 1. What is your professional rank, and the nature of your connexion with this Colony? How long have you been resident in this Island? During such residence have you, or have you not, had frequent opportunities of observing the general treatment of the Slaves in this Colony? If yea, state what has fallen under your observation relative to their general treatment and condition.

Ans. Examinant saith—that he is a Captain in His Majesty's Army, and an Aid-de-Camp to His Excellency the Commander of the Forces; that he has been resident in this Island two years, and has had frequent opportunities of observing the general treatment of the Slaves in the Colony; such observation has led him to form an opinion that great humanity and kindness is shewn to the Slave population of this Colony.

Qu. 2. From your knowledge of the manners of the inhabitants of this Island, do you, or do you not, think that a cruel Owner of Slaves would be held in the same abhorrence here, as he would be in England?

Ans. Examinant saith—that he certainly thinks a cruel Owner of Slaves would be held in the same abhorrence here as he would be in England.

Qu. 3. From the general demeanor and conduct of the Slaves themselves, would you, or would you not, pronounce them to be a happy and contented, or an oppressed and ill-treated people? State particularly what has fallen under your own observation in this respect, and your reasons for the opinions which you may have formed on this subject.

Ans. Examinant saith—that his opinion is, that the Slaves of this Island are a happy and contented people, and that they do not consider themselves an oppressed and ill-treated people; that his reasons for forming this opinion, are, that they are always cheerful and happy, and appear to be sensible of the great care taken of them.

(Signed)   JOHN SPINK, Capt. A. D. C.

G.

Examination of Sir Reynold A. Alleyne, Bart. (on Oath).

Query 1. What is your station in this Colony?

Answer. A Member of Council, and Owner of four properties, two in Saint Andrew's parish, and two in Saint Peter's and Saint Lucy's, the management of which are under my immediate superintendence.

Qu. 2. What is the condition and treatment of the Slaves on the Plantations under your direction, in respect to food, clothing, general comforts, labour and punishments? Is the cart-whip or cow's-skin whip in general used as an instrument of punishment, and is it customary to expose the female Slaves indecently when subjected to punishment?

Ans. The people under my charge have two dressed meals every day. Warm tea in the morning, and from three to four pounds of raw food, in addition to the dressed meals, besides salt-fish and molasses. On my Scotland estate, where there is more moisture, I allow every adult a petticoat and bed-gown of Pennistone, in addition to the Oznabrugs. The children are allowed one suit annually, and wherever I perceive an individual in a ragged style, whether adult or infant, I give an additional suit. Each family has a small cottage provided at the expense of the estate. The Hospital is provided with bed, blankets, and sheets, attended daily by a medical practitioner, without whose sanction no person is allowed to quit the Hospital. I allow no thonged whip to be used even as a symbol of authority; whatever punishment is inflicted, is inflicted by a small cat with about five strands. I never allow the Superintendent, commonly called Drivers, to apply more than three stripes for any one offence, and though it rarely happens that any mark is made on the persons of the Negroes, I have invariably punished the Driver whenever I have perceived it. Females are punished over the shoulders only, and except for very heinous offences, I have never suffered even the jacket to be removed: wherever confinement in a wholesome room could be effected, I have always preferred it, but to this there is an objection, arising occasionally from the large families of females, which would suffer from the confinement of the mother.

Qu. 3. From your knowledge of the habits of Negroes; are you prepared to say whether or not the women get husbands at an early age, and can you undertake to assert with confidence, whether or not they are restrained from contracting engagements of this kind, by their licentious intercourse with the white men on the estates?

Ans. Most of my young women have husbands at a very early period; whenever I have discovered any attempts on the part of the white servants to form connexions with the females of the estate, I have invariably discharged them; and I have pleasure in stating this fact, that in a population of 525 Slaves, I have not a single child the offspring of a white man, since the estates have been in my possession. I took possession of my first estate in the year 1811.

Qu. 4. What are your opinions respecting the religious instruction of the Slaves by Clergymen of the Established Church?

Ans. The Reverend Mr. Harte, the Rector of Saint Lucy's parish, has lately undertaken to give religious instruction to the Slave population of his parish, and I have from the commencement given him every encouragement and support, by giving my people every Saturday afternoon, and sending them to Church, and occasionally attending myself, together with my family.

These Answers are intended to apply equally to the estate of Sir H. Fitzherbert, which is confided to my care.

(Signed) R. A. ALLEYNE.

H.

Examination of Forster Clarke, Esq. (on Oath).

Query 1. What is your situation in life?

Ans. Examinant saith—that he is a Planter owning an Estate, and an Attorney to nineteen others belonging to absentee proprietors, on which there is a population of 4589 Slaves, of which he does not believe that there is at this moment a single one absent, or under disgrace or punishment for any crime.

Qu. 2. What is the condition and treatment of the Slaves on the plantations under your direction, in respect to food, clothing, general comforts, labour and punishments. Is the cart-whip or cow-skin whip in general used as an instrument of punishment, and is it customary to expose the female Slaves indecently when subjected to punishment?

Ans. Examinant saith—he is convinced that the Negroes have a sufficient allowance of food, as they are frequently enabled to sell a part of it; that they are never stinted under any circumstances of scarcity arising from unfavourable seasons or failure of crops, as in that case corn or other food would be provided for them by purchase. The usual allowances on estates under his direction are as follows:—each grown Negro has per day one pint and a half of Guinea-corn, or two pints of Indian-corn, making $4\frac{1}{2}$ or 5 lbs. when dressed, or $4\frac{1}{2}$ or 5 lbs. of roots, and sometimes more when there is any great abundance, as is often the case, of those crops, in addition to which a plentiful meal is provided for every one at dinner. They have all a pint of tea every morning before they set to work, with an allowance of weak diversion, (*i. e.* rum and water sweetened with molasses,) once or twice a day, and a pint of beverage made of molasses and water; they have also a weekly allowance of one pound of fish, one pint of molasses, and half a pint of salt; on festivals they have extra allowances of pork and other provisions. The children have three dressed meals daily, which is served to them under the eye of the manager; the old and infirm people are also provided with dressed meals. That the clothing for every man is a Pennistone jacket, an Oznabrugs shirt and trowsers, and a woollen cap or hat. The women have a full-sized jacket of Pennistone, an Osnabrugs petticoat, a handkerchief and a woollen cap; on some estates they have a check chemise besides, and the children have likewise an annual suit. The quantity of clothing may appear insufficient for a year, but the Negroes, or at least the industrious part of them, have ample means of procuring additional raiment, and they are always observed to be not only decently but comfortably clad. A house is built for each family at the expense of the estate, who have a small piece of ground allotted to them, on which they cultivate for themselves provision and other crops, by the sale of which and the raising of hogs and poultry they are enabled to indulge themselves in dress and other comforts. The superannuated and infirm people have all their allowances continued for life, and often receive extra helps. The hours of work are generally from about six in the morning, or in the long days a little before, till nine, when an hour is allowed for breakfast; they again set to work at ten, and come home to dinner at one; at three they set to work again and work till six, or in the long days, when the sun sets after six, it might be a little after; so that they seldom work more than three hours at a time, and not more than nine hours for the day, at that season of the year when the days are short, and nine hours and a half when the days are long. In the crop time, (which does not last more than one third of the year, if all the days employed in making sugar were put together,) the people employed about the works, amounting on a large estate to about fifteen or sixteen, are detained till eight or nine o'clock at night, and sometimes, but very rarely, later; and then, all of those are not required to remain to the last—they come out the next morning when the other Negroes go to work. It is usual, on most estates, for the Negroes on Sunday mornings to bring up with them a bundle of grass, at eight o'clock, and receive their allowances for that day, after which they are never called upon to do any thing, and Saturday afternoons are very commonly given to them;—that on some estates he has abolished the bringing of grass on Sunday mornings, which, however, occupies a very short time. There is a good Hospital on almost every estate, which is generally a clean well-ventilated building, provided with cabins and other conveniences, and beds for such as are ill to lie on. To the sick, proper and regular nutriment is allowed, and no expense is spared for such articles as the doctor thinks necessary for them: a practitioner attends every day, and a surgeon or physician is called whenever required. From the time the breeding women report themselves with child, they are withdrawn from the large gang, and employed about very light work till delivered;—baby-linen is provided for them, candles and other necessaries sent them, and a midwife paid to attend them, a nurse of their own choice to keep them in for the month, which they are allowed to stay in, and upon coming out they receive a small present of money, and for three months after they do little more than attend to their children. When the children grow a little stronger, the mothers come out at seven o'clock in the morning, leave the children in the nursery, and go to work; they come home at nine, go to work again at ten, and draw off at twelve; in the afternoon, they go to work at three, and draw off at five; they then come home and take their children to their houses. The children are generally weaned at the age of eighteen months. On every estate a proper building for a Nursery is erected, where the infants are kept during the day, under the care of elderly women as nurses, with a sufficient quantity of pap provided to feed them with, in the absence of their mothers.

The Overseers of the field-work, or, as they are often called, Drivers, are permitted at no time to give a Negro more than six stripes with a cat; if the obstinacy or unruly conduct of any Negro require a greater punishment he is reported to the manager. Examinant saith—He knows of no other punishments but solitary confinement, or moderate flogging with a cat; the female Slaves are never exposed when punished, the cart-whip or cow-skin is never permitted to be used upon the estates under his care, and he believes that it is generally laid aside as an instrument of punishment.

Qu. 3. From your knowledge of the habits of the Negroes, are you prepared to say whether or not, the women get husbands at an early age, and can you undertake to assert with confidence, whether or not they are restrained from contracting engagements of this kind, by their licentious intercourse with the white men on the estates?

Ans. Examinant saith—that although he does not think the young women do in general settle themselves very early with husbands, he is not of opinion, that they are often prevented from doing so, by their intercourse with the whites; it can seldom or never be the effect of arbitrary influence, as he attends to the complaints of every Negro, and he believes that most others do the same, and such conduct would ever be resented and punished by the discharge of any white servant, or manager who attempted it; that an illicit intercourse does often exist there can be no doubt, but from the small number of Mulatto children born in estates, it would appear that such connexions were not so often formed as might be expected.

Qu. 4. What are your opinions respecting the religious instruction of the Slaves by Clergymen of the Established Church:

Ans. Examinant saith—that he is willing to give every encouragement to such plans of religious instruction, as he thinks calculated to do any good; and that, although he has not permitted Methodist Missionaries to preach in any of the estates for which he is concerned, he has for some time past, allowed a man of religious habits to attend his own, and some other Negroes under his direction, for the purpose of giving such instruction as they were capable of receiving; that he thinks much good may be done by a safe and efficient plan of religious instruction towards the moral improvement of the Negroes, and that men of good character and moderate acquirements, but sufficiently informed for the undertaking, are best calculated to effect it; and such persons should be employed as subordinate agents under the direction of the Rectors of the parishes, or of principal Missionaries of the Church of England.

(Signed) F. CLARKE.

I.

Examination of William Sharp, Esq. (on Oath).

Query 1. What is your situation in life?

Ans. Saith that he is a Planter and Attorney to three estates.

Qu. 2. What is the condition and treatment of the Slaves on the Plantations under your directions in respect to food, clothing, general comforts, labour and punishments?

Ans. Saith—that the Negroes under his direction have a pint of tea early in the morning, a pint of molasses and water, or half-pint of rum and water sweetened with molasses, in the forenoon, with a plentiful dinner at noon; besides a daily allowance of one pint and a half of Guinea-corn, or two pints of Indian-corn (Guinea-corn yields three pounds of cocoa to a pint, and Indian two pounds and a half)—when roots are served out, it is in the proportion of three pounds to a pint of corn, they are also allowed one pound of fish and one gill and a half of salt per week; and on Festivals and harvest-home, they have one pound of salted pork to each person; children and infirm people have three meals a day cooked for them. The grown people are allowed a small piece of land for a garden, which they cultivate as they like best; they raise a great quantity of pigs, goats, and poultry, with which articles they principally supply the market. Every kind of property which they acquire is held as sacred to them, as their master's to him. The clothing for the men, consists annually of a check and Osnabrugs shirt, two pair of Osnabrugs trowsers, a Pennistone jacket, and a woollen cap or hat. The women have a check shift, Osnabrugs petticoat, a Pennistone jacket, and a cap or handkerchief. The children have one suit each; baby-linen is provided for the infants. Their houses are built of stone and thatched; there is an average number of about four persons inhabiting each house. Good Hospitals are provided for the sick, and a woman of the best character is selected as sick nurse; an Apothecary is employed to attend them every day, and in cases of danger a Physician, Surgeon, or Accoucheur, is called, as the occasion may require. There are also Nurseries in which all the children who are not of an age fit to work are kept under the superintendence of middle-aged women, who are selected on account of their good characters, and are mothers themselves; the children who are nursing are fed with pap during the time their mothers are at work. As soon as the women report themselves pregnant, they are removed from the able gang and put to light work. One month is allowed them for lying-in, and a careful person attends them during their confinement. When the mother brings out her child she receives a dollar, and is instructed to purchase a pig, or any thing else she likes better, for the benefit of the child. They do very little work for two months after they come out, and during the whole time they are nursing, have an indulgence of time in the morning and evening, and return home twice in the forenoon and once in the afternoon to their children, independent of the time allowed for breakfast and dinner. The children are not weaned till the eye-teeth are cut. According to the size of the estate, the gangs are differently classed, using all practical means of separating the weak from the strong. They generally set to work about sun-rise, but if the field in which they are to labour is near their houses, a little earlier; take breakfast at nine o'clock, and resume their work about ten o'clock; at one o'clock they come home to dinner, and are absent from work about two hours; they are drawn off at sunset, and retire to their houses to look after their own concerns; when making sugar, the boilers and stokers, and some of the mill people, which in large estates amount to twelve or fourteen persons, are kept out later, generally till nine or ten o'clock, and the boiling-house sets to work about five o'clock in the morning. Watchmen and cattle-keepers are unavoidably more exposed to the weather than other descriptions of persons on the estates, but on the whole they are not found to be more unhealthy than their fellow labourers;—according to the size of the gang, one or more persons are allowed to bring them water, and any little comforts which they may require whilst at work. On Sunday morning the gangs bring a handful of grass and take their allowance; no work is expected from them on that day, but after they have been assembled in the morning, which is principally done with a view to prevent their rambling on Saturday night, the rest of the day is entirely left to them to dispose of as they think proper.

Qu. 3. Is the cart-whip or cow-skin whip in general used as an instrument of punishment, and is it customary to expose the female Slaves indecently when subjected to punishment?

Ans. Saith—that the Driver (who is also an Overseer, to see the work faithfully performed) is restricted in his authority. He is not allowed to inflict more than six stripes; if greater punishment is necessary, the offender is reported to the Manager, who punishes according to the nature of the offence, either by corporal chastisement or confinement; if the Driver abuses his authority, the gang are encouraged to complain against him, and in general they are very ready to do so, and he is punished in the manner already described. Under white servants have very little authority placed in their hands, their business is to observe and report the ill-conduct of the Negroes to the Manager, who if his (the Manager's) conduct is not regulated from higher principles, he is checked in the abuse of his power by self-interest, for the strong voice of public opinion is against his using tyrannical measures. The community in general look with detestation on a man who has once obtained a character for severity, and if his maintenance depends on his profession, he is left to pine in want of the necessaries of life, because he cannot get employment. The cow-skin whip is carried more as a badge of office, than used as an instrument of correction; the usual way of inflicting corporal punishment, both to men and women, is over the shoulders, with rods or a light cat of five or six strands; the women are never indecently exposed on the estates.

Qu. 4. From your knowledge of the habits of Negroes, are you prepared to say, whether or not the women get husbands at an early age, and can you undertake to assert with confidence, whether or not they are restrained from contracting engagements of this kind, by their licentious intercourse with the white men on the estates?

Ans. Saith—It has not appeared to him that the young Negro women are very remarkable for having husbands at an early age; particular instances do sometimes occur of their getting husbands when very young. Examinant saith, it is hardly necessary for him to remark what is so well known, that they have gallantries amongst their own colour, as well as the fair-complexioned, and a line is drawn, although the marriage ceremony does not take place, between a woman who is the acknowledged wife of a black man, and another who lavishes her favours without settling herself: his answer is to be applied to those who have acknowledged husbands. Examinant saith, he must divide the latter part of your question in two parts—firstly, if you mean to inquire whether arbitrary means are made use of on the estates to restrain the young Negro women from having husbands of their own colour at an early age, he does not believe it exists;—secondly, an illicit intercourse with the whites does sometimes take place, but it is principally confined to the inferior servants on the estates, who are young men whose circumstances in life will not admit of their marrying and supporting a family:—when a connexion of this kind takes place between them and the young black women, it is done by persuasion, and because they have it more in their power to gratify the vanity of the females in their fondness for dress; punishment however awaits the offender when his improper conduct is discovered, for he seldom escapes being turned out of the estates. A Manager's moral conduct is a great recommendation of him: glaring instances of immoral conduct would not be tolerated. Saith—he is of opinion that the illicit intercourse with the whites, has but very little effect in preventing the young women on estates from having husbands at an early age. On two estates which are under his direction, and have upwards of four hundred negroes on them, only two coloured children, descendants of white men, have been born since May 1817 to the present time; and on another which he took over in 1819, with 120 Negroes, there has been no coloured child born.

Qu. 5. What are your opinions respecting the religious instruction of the Slaves by clergymen of the Established Church?

Ans. Saith—that to this question he can answer decidedly, that he has no objection to the religious instruction of the Slaves, but on the contrary, is willing to give all the assistance in his power to promote so desirable an object.

(Signed)   WM. SHARP.

K.

The Examination of George Richards, M.D.
(on Oath).

Query 1. What is your situation in life?

Answer. Examinant saith—that he is a Physician, and a Member of the Royal College of Surgeons in London; that he is in the habit of visiting estates daily, as their regular medical attendant.

Qu. 2. What number of Plantations have you under your care, and do you think there is a proper attention to the means of preserving the health of the Slaves generally, and to the comforts of the sick in particular?

Ans. Examinant saith—that he practises for about eight estates, and other properties, the whole population of which, amount to about

2,500, and that he has also a general practice as Physician and Surgeon, and visits many estates in that capacity; that in all the properties he attends, the Slaves have the greatest attention paid them, and in case of illness they have every allowance that he directs.

Qu. 3. Do you, or do you not, sometimes have patients brought into the Hospital, suffering from the effects of severe punishments; and if such cases do occur, must they not necessarily come under your notice?

Ans. Examinant saith—that he has never seen a single instance of that kind; and if they did occur, they must necessarily come under his notice.

(Signed) G. RICHARDS.

L.

Examination of John H. Leacock, M. D.
(on Oath).

Query 1. What is your situation in life?

Ans. Examinant saith—that he is a Physician, and a Member of the Royal College of Surgeons in London; that he is in the habit of visiting estates daily, as their constant medical attendant

Qu. 2. What number of Plantations have you under your care, and do you think there is a proper attention to the means of preserving the health of the Slaves generally, and to the comforts of the sick in particular?

Ans. Examinant saith—that he has about thirty Sugar Plantations, and many small places, having a population of about four thousand; that there is generally every care taken to preserve the people in health, and every comfort afforded them during sickness. That independant of these estates, he is usually consulted in cases of extreme illness on others, and that he has ever witnessed the same care and attention to the sick.

Qu. 5. Do you, or do you not, sometimes have patients brought into the Hospital, suffering from the effects of severe punishments; and if such cases do occur, must they not necessarily come under your notice?

Ans. Examinant saith—that such cases must come under his notice when they do occur, but that he has never met with such as to require his care and attention.

  (Signed)   JOHN. H. LEACOCK.

Examination of Reynold C. Thomas, M. D. (on Oath).

Query 1. What is your situation in life?

Ans. Examinant saith—that he is a Physician, Surgeon and Accoucheur, and that he has been practising for about 10,000 Slaves in this Island for the last three years. That fifteen years ago, he was engaged in an apothecary's business, containing about 2000 Slaves.

Qu. 2. What number of Plantations have you under your care, and do you think there is a proper attention to the means of preserving the health of the Slaves generally, and to the comforts of the sick in particular?

Ans. He thinks that there has been considerable amelioration in their treatment, and attention to their comforts in every respect, within the last fifteen years; at present their Hospitals are good, and they have every attention in sickness. If the public Hospitals be excluded, he thinks that the Slaves here have considerably more comforts and advantages in sickness, than the labouring poor of England can have.

Qu. 3. Do you, or do you not, sometimes have

patients brought into the Hospital, suffering from the effects of severe punishments; and if such cases do occur, must they not necessarily come under your notice?

Ans. Saith—that he has never attended any Slave who had suffered severe corporal punishment, either while practising as an apothecary or since; and although he does not consider that such cases must necessarily have come under his notice if they had occurred, yet he has every reason to believe, that if the punishment had been so severe as to have been at all dangerous, that they would then have come under his notice.

  (Signed)   R. C. Thomas,

Examination of the Rev. Samuel Hinds, A. M.
(on Oath).

Query 1. What is your station in life?

Ans. A Clergyman, and Principal of Codrington College.

Qu. 2. Did you not officiate for some time in this Colony, as Missionary from the Society for the Conversion of the Negro Slaves; and did you, or did you not, meet with encouragement from the Owners and Overseers of estates, in prosecuting the object of your mission? State particularly the manner in which you were received by the Owners and Overseers of Plantations.

Ans. In 1821, I was appointed Missionary by the Society for the Conversion of Negroes, and held the office for upwards of six months, during which time I made many applications to the Proprietors and Overseers of estates, for liberty to instruct their Slaves in religion, and without any exception, all these applications were received favourably, and in several instances great zeal and earnestness were manifested in the cause in which I was engaged. I have known the Proprietor himself read Prayers and explain the Scriptures to his Slaves. My duties as Curate of Christ Church, prevented me from visiting the estates on Sundays; I was therefore obliged to select some other day for the purpose, and I observed that whenever I visited an estate, generally the Negroes were allowed an afternoon holiday and encouraged otherwise to attend me. It is but justice towards two respectable bodies of men, to state further, that the Agricultural Society and the Planters' Club, each passed a vote approving the object of my mission, and offering their assistance to carry into effect any measures which I might propose, for the general diffusion of Christianity among the Slaves. In short from the inquiries which I made, as well as from my own observations, the impression left on my mind is, that the general sense of the Proprietors of this Island is in favour of the religious instruction of the Negroes, whenever undertaken by ministers of the Church of England.

(Signed)   SAMUEL HINDS.

O.

To The Honble. Renn Hamden, Chairman of the Committee, &c. &c.

BARBADOES, TREASURER'S OFFICE,
8th July, 1823.

Sir,

In compliance with the request of the Committee of the Council appointed " to inquire " into the actual state of Slavery," that I would furnish them from the Treasury Books, with an account of the number of Slave-owners in this Island, " distinguishing the number possessing " land and Slaves, from those possessing Slaves " only," I now have the honour to state, that there are one thousand five hundred and thirty-five possessing land and slaves, of which number three hundred and two are sugar-works; and that there are three thousand six hundred and seventy-one owners possessing Slaves only.

This Account is taken from the Books of 1822, the present year not being made up.

I have honour to be, with the highest respect,
Sir,
Your obedient, humble servant,

(Signed)   CONRADE A. HOWELL,
Treasurer.

NEGRO EMANCIPATION No. 7.

AND

WEST INDIAN INDEPENDENCE,

THE

TRUE INTEREST

OF

GREAT BRITAIN.

BY

JOHN TAYLOR.

Hinc rapti pretio fasces, sectorque favoris
Ipse sui populus; fatalisque ambitus urbi,
Annua venali referens certamina campo:
Hinc usura vorax, avidumque in tempora foenus;
Semina, quæ populos semper mersere potentes.
Lucan.

LIVERPOOL:
PRINTED BY R. ROCKLIFF, DALE STREET,
AND SOLD BY G. AND J. ROBINSON, AND W. GRAPEL; AND BY LONGMAN,
HURST AND CO. LONDON.

1824.

NEGRO EMANCIPATION,

&c. &c.

THE discussion of the policy or impolicy of the continuance of Negro slavery, in the British West Indian Islands, has run to so great a length, that to a man of common capacity the real question seems in danger of being lost in the mass of writing.

The points to determine are, whether the present system be beneficial to the people at large of Great Britain and Ireland, and whether it confer greater happiness on the Negroes than they would enjoy by emancipation. If it do neither of these, then any pecuniary injury which so small a number of persons, as the slaveholders, might sustain, by the abolition of slavery, cannot be considered of sufficient moment to justify delay in the immediate adoption of such measures, as the safety and happiness of the Negroes and of the British people may require.

The question, respecting the amelioration of the state of the Negroes by emancipation, is at once answered, by their well known wish to emancipate themselves. That wish, the unceasing cause of alarm to those who now hold them in bondage, springs from a sense of their sufferings; of which the oppressed, at all times, know the grievance more thoroughly than the actual oppressor, or than the dispassionate bystander. The question has also fortunately received a satisfactory answer, by the experiment made in St. Domingo, where the distress of a few years' war, from 1791 to 1798, and from 1800 to 1802, sustained by the Black people against their inveterate, their natural-born enemies, if ever there were such, the French and English, has been compensated by twenty years of internal peace, prosperity, and happiness. The best informed travellers, who have visited St. Domingo, agree that the condition of that people is greatly better, as to food, raiment, and all the other comforts of life, than that of the Negro slaves in the British West Indian Islands. If there be not so much sugar and coffee exported from St. Domingo as formerly, there is more of these good things consumed there; and this the Black people find quite as well for them.

Without, therefore, going into a particular inquiry as to the grievances which have been and are still suffered by the Black population—the whippings, the brandings, the shootings, the hangings, the beheadings, the burnings alive, which the slaveholders have from time to time found necessary, to the maintenance of their authority; without any such particular investigation, we may safely, from the two plain facts before stated, conclude that there need be no hesitation, as far as the Blacks are concerned, in making an immediate change.

As respects the people of Great Britain, they have suffered, from the continuance of the present West Indian Colonial system, great pecuniary loss, political corruption, and, finally, extreme national weakness.

It is not pretended, even by the planters, that the British market is supplied by them with West Indian produce at so cheap a rate, as it would be if the produce of other tropical countries were admitted to a fair competition; so far from it, that the planters demand the monopoly of the British market, as indispensable to their support.

For whose pecuniary benefit then is this system maintained? Not for that of the British people, nor of the 700,000 Blacks, nor of any great portion of even the 70,000 Whites resident in the Colonies; but for the benefit of a small number of individuals, styling themselves West Indian proprietors and merchants.

If the British people had in return an entire monopoly of the Colonial markets, which they have not, would the supplying of merchandise to 70,000 White persons, and to 700,000 Blacks in a state of poverty and slavery, be an equivalent for the monopoly of the markets of Great Britain and Ireland, in the articles of the greatest consumption after the absolute necessaries of life? The British manufacturers and mechanics are not so far behind those of the rest of Europe, as to need an enforced monopoly for the sale of their goods. All they need and all they wish is the liberty of fair, equal, and voluntary exchange of the products of skill and industry with all men. Every deviation from that they consider as detrimental to them, however cunningly the deceit may be covered.

Neither does the acquisition, nor the preservation of naval power, depend upon the possession of foreign Colonies.

England was a great naval power, before she ever had a Colony; so were the Dutch; and the Spaniards, who possessed the most extensive, the most distant, and the richest Colonies in the world, were unable to withstand either of them on the sea.

Besides, the strength which the number of ships in the West Indian trade may be supposed to confer on Britain, does not depend on the West Indian Islands being in the possession of the British forces, or on their owning allegiance to the British government. The employment, and, consequently, the number of those ships, depend on the people of Great Britain continuing to use the produce of the West Indies. If the British people want sugar, coffee, and rum, and are able to pay for them, in money, or in useful or ornamental commodities, the inhabitants of some of the tropical countries will take care to cultivate them for the British market. Our seamen would have an equal chance for the freight with the seamen of other nations; and the same revenue might be raised on the sale of the sugar, rum, and coffee, from wherever they were brought.

If our seamen should be unequal to a fair competition; if, through excessive taxation, British ships cannot carry freight as cheap as those of other nations, our present navigation laws, if kept in force, would still secure the freight to our own vessels; for it is by the cheapness of their rates of freight, or else by the operation of those navigation laws, that the West Indian trade is now carried on in British ships, and not from any patriotic preference given to them by the proprietors of the West Indian estates.

The whole trade to Columbia, Brazil, Buenos Ayres, Chili, and Peru, has been carried on for fourteen years in British shipping; and from Britain those countries receive the whole of their European manufactured goods; and in a great measure so do the United States of America. None of those countries are bound to Britain by any restrictive treaty. They buy our goods, because we sell them cheap; they sell to us, because we pay for what we buy; and by this voluntary, unconstrained interchange of commodities, our naval power is strengthened, because a demand is thereby created for our ships, and an active and healthy employment is thereby found for our seamen.

The trade to the West Indies is at present confined to a few commercial houses, by whom the great mass of the population there is held in a state of abject wretchedness and slavery; the ships made use of are, from the restricted nature of the trade, few in number, of large tonnage, and manned by a small number of seamen.

But were the Blacks set free, and the government of the islands in the hands of the inhabitants, there would be a new stimulus to the export of British manufactured goods, from the increased expenditure of a people advancing in civilization and labouring for their own comfort, as has been proved in the instance of St. Domingo; the imports from the United States and Great Britain alone into that republic, in the year 1823, having been equal nearly in value to the total amount of the imports from all countries into St. Domingo, for any year prior to the expulsion of the French planters.

An increase to our shipping would also follow, from the open competition of the merchants of small capital, who would, as in all other free trades, employ a number of small vessels, manned by a numerous body of seamen.

Nor is this merely supposition, for by the free trade of a very few years to South America, greater benefit has been already conferred on Britain, than was ever derived to Spain and Portugal from the exclusive possession of the same countries as Colonies.

There might perhaps be advantage in the possession of one or two naval stations, in the West Indies, sufficient to justify the expence necessary for their occupation. But experience has proved, that a system of extended colonization, with its attendant establishments, civil, military, and naval; that the perpetual maintenance, in an unhealthy climate, of numerous garrisons in the time of peace, to enforce submission on the part of the inhabitants, with the addition of fleets and armies in the time of war, has been the cause of loss and not of gain to every nation that has yet tried it.

The Colonies of Spain and Portugal, although furnishing silver and gold in unparalleled abundance, were the immediate cause of the ruin of those two kingdoms; both of them warlike and powerful nations, until they acquired extensive colonies; after that, weak, sunk in debt, and incapable of self-defence.

The Dutch were also a powerful and energetic people, increasing in strength for seventy years, from 1560 to 1630, amidst all the horrors of daily internal warfare; and even till 1704, in spite of all the attacks of Spain, and afterwards of France. But after they had formed Colonial establishments in the West Indies, South America, and the East Indies, those establishments, as they grew up, with their inseparable concomitant, monopoly, gradually wasted the strength and sapped the happiness of the mother country. Those monopolies constituted a privileged class, who lent their aid to the Stadtholders in all their attacks on the liberties of the people; and in return expected and received their reward, in the confiscation of the fruits of that people's industry: and what all the armies of Philip II. and of Louis XIV. attempted in vain, the silent operation of the Colonial system quietly accomplished.

Similar effects may be traced in the events of British history, although the great natural resources of the country have made these effects more slow in their developement.

In the war of the succession to the crown of Spain, which commenced in 1702, the British army, under the victorious Marlborough, controlled the destinies of Europe; when the adoption of a petty Colonial system by the Tory Ministry, and the outfit of an expedition to Canada under General Hill, the brother of Lady Masham, the favourite of the Queen, by depriving the armies in Flanders and Spain of the needful reinforcements, paralized their exertions, and finally led to a surrender of Spain to the family of Bourbon. While France by defeat gained the possession of Spain; the whole fruit to Britain of the victories of Blenheim, Ramillies, and Malplaquet, was the concession by France of the West Indian island of St. Christopher, and permission by what was called the "*Assiento Contract*," to carry annually a certain number of Negro slaves to the Spanish Main.

In 1739, that very "*Assiento Contract*" was the cause of war; and the desire to acquire new Colonial territory led to a misdirection of the strength of the country, in the fatal expedition to Carthagena, where an army perished which might have secured victory at Fontenoy. Defeat abroad was followed by rebellion at home; and the nation, which in its greed of heart had contemplated the conquest of South America, could not muster an army of native troops competent to the defence of London, against 8,000 half-armed, undisciplined men; but owed its preservation to the assistance of some Hessian regiments. Such a war was of necessity closed by a corresponding ignominious peace.

After a few years, another war came on in 1755, and Britain was found, for real warlike purposes in Europe, weaker than ever; her rank there was less than that of the Dutch in 1704. A mere detachment of the French force compelled the British army under the Duke of Cumberland to capitulate at Closterseven; and the sending of a few regiments, less in number than an Hanoverian contingent, with some subsidy money, was the total sum of the subsequent exertions of the British in Europe. Their ambition reached no higher than to claim a small portion of the honour gained at Minden by Prince Ferdinand and his honest Germans. The strength of Britain was in the meantime wasted, to acquire the burden of a perpetual establishment of garrisons over a discontented people in Canada, and the power to tyrannize over a few more of the wretched Blacks in the unhealthy West Indian islands. Fortunately, the greatest number of the conquered islands were restored to France, to make her too suffer in the same way.

In a few years after, as if to hasten the catastrophe, a quarrel was begun with the Colonies in North America; and so fond was the British government, and not less so the British people, of the garrison and tyrannising system, that they were actually mad enough to try its application on the White Colonists themselves. But here the plan failed, and the attempt ended in the acknowledgement of the Independence of the United States.

Bitter reproaches of ingratitude were cast, during the contest, by the British against the Americans; that they had accepted favours, and would make no return. But the idea never seems to have entered the dull heads of the British people, that if, while the Virginian planters were rebellious, the proprietors of West Indian estates were loyal, it was because they had the best of the bargain, in the gratuitous protection given to them against their slaves, and in the monopoly enjoyed by them of the British market. For the southern division of the United States is not so unhealthy as to prevent the increase of a White population, adequate to the coercion of the Blacks; and, in this respect, therefore, the Virginians were independent of Britain. In none of the British West Indian Islands, on the contrary, has the race of White men been able to keep up its own numbers without continued large reinforcements from the mother country; and, although a mixed breed has arisen, yet the avarice of the British men has almost universally prevailed on them to dispose of their mulatto children as slaves; so that the free part of the population has always stood in need of British garrisons to maintain its authority.

A similar Colonial system, and similar distant naval and military expeditions brought France, about the same time, to the brink of ruin. She was rescued from it by the tremendous convulsion of the Revolution, by the burning of every plantation in St. Domingo, and by the extermination from thence of all the French inhabitants.— The Republic of France started up instantaneously, with all the vigour of youth, as if Ætna had been removed from the breast of the fabled giant.

But as if the Colonial malady were at one period or another incidental to every government, Buonaparte, soon after his accession to power, became, through the intrigues and representations of the old proprietors of West Indian estates, subject to its influence. In 1801 he sent an expedition of 40,000 veteran troops under his brother-in-law, General Leclerc, to St. Domingo. In two years 30,000 of them were cut off by the yellow fever, and a few by the enemy; the rest owed their safety to the interference of the British naval commander.

Another attempt at a naval expedition was made by Buonaparte in 1805. His good fortune saved him. By the loss of the sea-fight off Trafalgar, his theatre of action was confined to Europe, which he totally overran and conquered; and if his power ultimately was destroyed, the cause was his obstinate pursuit of distant dominion.

And what was Britain doing all this while?

When, by a well-timed exertion of her strength, she might, in conjunction with her allies, during the temporary confusion of France in 1793 and 1794, have made what end she thought proper of the French and of their revolution, she was led astray, by the Colonial mania, to send expedition after expedition, naval and military, thousands of men upon thousands of men, at an enormous expence, to perish by disease in the West Indies. In twenty-eight months, from November, 1793, to March, 1796, no less than 54,212 men of the British troops, a greater number than all the White residents of the islands, were sent to the West Indies. Nearly all of them perished there.

Whilst France conquered Belgium, Holland, Italy, Prussia, Austria, Spain, and Poland, Britain conquered St. Lucia, Martinique, Tobago, Guadaloupe, and the Mauritius,—of which the entire White population might amount to 50,000 persons; and after the year 1799 it was not until the year 1808, when there were no more Colonies to be taken, that Britain could summon courage to send a single regiment on one week's European service.

Even now, when the whole nation of Spain has called on the British for assistance, when every consideration of interest and every generous sentiment urged compliance with that call, they have been obliged to confess a total defalcation of strength, brought on by the expense of former wars, which owed their origin to the Colonial system.

Such has been the train of events, from a persistance in the fatal system of West Indian colonization; a system founded in crime, and productive of merited ruin.

If Negro slavery be considered as the act of the British people, and not of their government only, then has retributive justice been made signally manifest:

> "For, in these cases,
> We still have judgement here; that we but teach
> Bloody instructions, which, being taught, return
> To plague the inventor: thus even-handed justice
> Commends the ingredients of our poison'd chalice
> To our own lips."

The original device, to unfeeling and profligate minds, had its allurements. To take advantage of their superior skill in navigation and warfare, by seizing on defenceless men and compelling them to incessant labour, year after year, generation after generation, seemed to the greedy British people a means of acquiring wealth, as easy and speedy as highway robbery and midnight murder. Accordingly it was with alacrity begun, and with relentless diligence put in practice. No means were neglected; the lash, the gibbet, the sword, and fire, were employed to enforce the labour of the weak, and the obedience of the refractory.

For the reward of these horrible atrocities, their sordid and callous hearts promised them a general diffusion of wealth, and relaxation from labour.

What has been the event?

Those West Indian Islands have been the constant object, or the never failing pretext for war, and for enormous taxation. The cunning planters have taken care to appropriate to themselves whatever could be gained. They have grown in wealth, while the people of England have sunk in poverty; till the condition of West Indian slaves has come to be thrown in the teeth of the British people, as an object of desire.

Slaveholder after slaveholder has been placed in the House of Lords; borough after borough has fallen into their hands; with its own money have they bought the stupid people, and having bought, they are ready to resell that people for fresh grants of its own money.

Every consideration, therefore, of the subject leads to one conclusion; the claims of the Negroes, the interests of the British people, justice and good policy, all demand an immediate abandonment of this long course of error and of crime.

Happily the change is of easy attainment. All that is necessary at this time, is the establishment of justice by the admission of the Black people to give evidence in civil and criminal causes; the absolute interdiction of all corporal punishment, in any other way than according to the law and usages of England; and for the proprietors of the West Indian plantations to pay the Negroes daily, weekly, monthly, or yearly wages, as may be found most convenient by mutual agreement, instead of taking upon themselves the trouble to provide that yearly supply of food and clothing which the Negroes, as slaves, receive from them.

Other requisite alterations will naturally present themselves, and can be gradually adopted.

By the measures now proposed, the chief source of the oppression exercised by the White people, and the main cause of discontent on the part of the Negroes, will at once be done away with; the necessity will cease for the presence of hired troops; and the inhabitants of the West Indian Islands will, in a short time, become fit to assume the management of their own internal and external affairs: Great Britain will be relieved from a heavy burden; and exchange the deep, the deserved hatred of the injured Negroes, and the hypocritical professions of loyalty, the insatiable rapacity, the domineering insolence, of the present race of West Indian proprietors, for the grateful and the profitable friendship of the enfranchised and happy WEST INDIAN PEOPLE.

Liverpool, March 13, 1824.

FINIS.

THE

𝕽ural ℭode

OF

HAITI;

IN

FRENCH AND ENGLISH.

WITH A

PREFATORY LETTER

TO THE

RIGHT HON. THE EARL BATHURST, K.G.

&c. &c. &c.

No.8.

LONDON:

SOLD BY JAMES RIDGWAY, 169, PICCADILLY.

PRINTED BY B. McMILLAN, BOW-STREET, COVENT-GARDEN,
Printer in Ordinary to His Majesty.

1827.

TO

THE RIGHT HONOURABLE
THE EARL BATHURST, K. G.
ONE OF HIS MAJESTY'S PRINCIPAL SECRETARIES OF STATE,

&c. &c. &c.

MY LORD,

The high station your Lordship occupies, among those who hold in their hands the fate of our West India Colonies, will, I am confident, make any apology, for addressing this Translation of The Rural Code of Haïti to your Lordship, unnecessary. Your Lordship must feel anxious to obtain every information upon a subject, so necessary to be thoroughly understood, as that of labour within the tropics; and, when those who seem to be most deeply interested in ascertaining the possibility of obtaining regular, and steady labour, in tropical climates, without compulsion, have exhibited their opinions, the results of thirty-six years' experience, it is not assuming too much, to believe, that your Lordship will favourably receive the means of facilitating your acquaintance with the result of that experience.

The following Code of Laws has been enacted,

as its Authors have told their fellow-citizens, for the regeneration of agriculture. They declare that it is *just* and *severe**. To enable your Lordship to estimate the utility of this Code of Laws, permit an humble and unknown individual respectfully to call your attention to the following observations.

The Haïtian Gentleman who furnished the copy of the Code Rural, from which this translation has been made, stated, that the Code had been received in Haïti without much dislike; because, while it fully secures the Proprietors in the possession of their lands, it only furnishes the means of exacting from the labouring population, those exertions required of them by previous laws. This Gentleman expressed himself well pleased with the salutary constraint imposed upon his labourers by the Rural Code.

The translation has been made as literally as possible, and without regard to the idioms, and modes of expression, of the English language, when an attention to such points, would have had

---

* The Chamber of Commons of Haïti, in their Farewell Address to their Constituents, at the close of their legislative existence, on the 10th of May, 1826, published in No. 20, of the "*Feuille de Commerce*," May 14th, Port-au-Prince, say,

"On n'eut pas pourvue aux soins du principe conservateur, si la *Regeneration de nos cultures* n'eut été provoquée par des lois à la fois *justes* et *severes*. Vos mandataires, en rendant le Code Rural ont pensé que le peuple reçevoit un bienfait."

the appearance of concealing the real meaning of any clause. This has been done with a view of preventing cavil.

Haïti has for some years been held up to the West Indians, as the perfect model upon which they must reform their institutions. The prosperous state of its agriculture, the industry, wealth, and happiness of its free population, have formed the never-failing theme of the speeches and writings of those persons, who can discover no merit within the tropics, under a white skin. The total ignorance of the rest of the world, as to all that has been passing in the interior of Haïti for the last thirty years, has been, unfortunately, most favourable to such declaimers. But we are at length favored with a peep behind the curtain; that glimpse, trifling as it is, suffices to dissipate all those fables with which the Public have been deceived. Instead of finding Agriculture in that palmy state represented, we find the representatives of Haïti proclaiming to their constituents, that they are compelled to endeavour to regenerate it, by enacting *" just and severe laws."* The industry of the population of Haïti, is found to require the stimulous of the bayonet. Their wealth, if measured by the remuneration reserved for the labourer, is found to be no more than sufficient to furnish subsistence, upon a scale not higher than that afforded to the Slave of the British Planter in Jamaica.

And their happiness, as far as an estimate of it can be formed from their institutions, as much inferior to that of the mass of mankind, as the happiness of the untutored savage is to that of civilised man.

The Code of Laws before us, is one, that could only have been framed by a legislature composed of proprietors of land, having at their command a considerable military power, *of which themselves were the leaders; for a population whom it was necessary to compel to labour, but whose prejudices against particular modes of expression, it was adivsable not to offend.* The Code, for this purpose, is framed with much ingenuity. Upon a casual inspection, it appears to deal lightly with the labourer, assuring him an apparently fair remuneration for his toil, and a means of subsistence adequate to his wants; and avoiding to wound his prejudices, by allowing him the choice of an employer; while to the landed proprietor, it purports to ensure that continuous exertion on the part of the labourer, which is so essentially necessary for securing adequate returns for fixed capital invested in tropical cultivation. Moreover, no obnoxious clauses for the infliction of corporal punishment, appear in this Code. It was necessary, to render a return to compulsory labour, palatable to a people accustomed to little restraint upon their exertions for more than thirty-six years; and it was judged more prudent, to leave the mode of inflicting punishment, to the discretion of those who are directed to enforce obedience—the Soldiery!

But when this Code of Laws is attentively examined, we find that the choice of a master, altho' expressly reserved to the labourer, is greatly modified by the clauses which restrain the labourer from quitting the section of country to which he belongs; and from the absence of any clause compelling proprietors to engage him; so that the cultivator must consent to bind himself to whomsoever may be willing to engage him, or remain in prison, to be employed among convicts as a public scavenger*. Again, we find that the labourer is allowed by law to bind himself for any period of time he pleases†. But this privilege is also modified by the defects above mentioned. The necessary consequence is, that these engagements will practically be for such a time as may suit the purposes of the master; and will certainly never extend beyond the period, during which the powers of the labourer may enable him to be useful to his employer; after which he may be discharged without the means of support; the wages he receives, appearing to be insufficient to enable him to make provision for old age, and the labourer having no claim upon the provision-grounds allotted to him, (which

---

* " Pour la propreté de la ville." See Article 177.
† Vide Articles 45 and 46 of the Code, and the Note at the foot of page 23.

he has been cultivating perhaps during the best years of his life), beyond the period of his engagement. Many similar instances of the art with which this Code of Laws is framed, to effect, and yet to mask its purpose, will strike every one who peruses it with attention.

It will be impossible to give your Lordship any general idea of this Code of Laws, within the limited bounds of a Letter, without giving a kind of Abstract of the whole Code. The importance of the subject induces me to entreat your Lordship's indulgence while I attempt it.

The Code begins (Article 1), by declaring Agriculture to be the foundation of national prosperity; and then decrees (Article 3), That all persons, excepting soldiers, and civil servants of the State, professional persons, artizans, and domestic servants*, shall cultivate the soil. The next clause (Article 4), forbids the inhabitants of the country quitting it to dwell in towns or villages; and every kind of wholesale or retail trade is forbidden (Article 7) to be exercised by persons dwelling in the country. Article 9, forbids building houses or huts any where but in recognized towns or villages, or upon plantations, by imposing a tax upon them; and to complete the restraint imposed upon the country people, they are forbid-

---

* By the Code Civile of Haïti, a domestic servant (domestique à gages) does not enjoy all the privileges of a citizen.

den (Article 10), to carry on the coasting trade, or to employ themselves in fishing, but for the use of the plantation to which they belong. Can any man entertain a doubt, that the object of these regulations is to confine the labour of the country population rigidly to the cultivation of the soil?

The next clauses of importance, directly relating to labourers, are Articles 36, 37, 38, and 39. They order provision-grounds to be set out for the use of the labourers. It would be singular, should it appear that these clauses have been copied in spirit, and almost literally translated in language, from the Consolidated Slave Law of Jamaica, passed in 1816 (57 Geo. III. c. 25). I have inserted the clauses of that law, which make a similar provision for the slave, at the foot of the pages in which the above Articles occur.

Articles 45 and 46, decree, That those persons, required by Article 3, to cultivate the soil, shall bind themselves as labourers, to some landed proprietor, for a term of years, varying, according to the nature of the cultivation; and Articles 73 and 74, authorize similar engagements to be made with persons having no land, but who may have contracted to procure labourers for others (labourers employed in this manner in Jamaica, are called a jobbing gang). We have then (Art. 50, et seq.) several clauses pointing out the measure of remuneration to be allowed to the labourer: we have here a distinction made between those who are hired from a job-master, and those who are bound to the proprietor himself; the former are called, " une compagnie travaillante à moitié;" and are entitled to receive half the produce, after deducting the expences of cultivation: they find themselves in every thing. The latter are called "cultivateurs travaillants au quart;" they have lands set out for them, and they are entitled to most of the advantages reserved for Negroes in Jamaica, *excepting clothing, and all foreign supplies.* They receive one-fourth of the gross produce of their labour, out of which they must find whatever they may require, beyond the produce of their provision-grounds. They are also obliged to pay taxes. It may easily be shewn, that upon a sugar estate employing 300 people, even when ably and successfully managed, the wages to be paid to either of the above classes of labourers, after deducting one-third for taxes, would never exceed 4*l.* 10*s.** per annum. Out of their miserable pittance, these Haïtian labourers are to provide themselves and their children with almost every thing, and to lay by a provision for old age.

Articles 88 and 96, limit the number of people

---

* This estimate is made for a well-managed and fertile sugar plantation in Jamaica, with a *large fixed capital* invested in works, buildings, machinery, stock, &c. If applied without reserve to Haïti, it would lead to extravagant error.

The average rate of wages in Haïti, calculated upon the *Haïtian returns* of produce and population, and calculating produce at its present price in the London market, would be about 6*s.* per annum for each person.

to be employed in keeping cattle, and require them to be bound to their employers in the same manner as other labourers.

Articles 155 to 164 inclusive, are devoted to detailing the duties of *overseers* and *drivers*. The French words used are, " *Gerans et conducteurs.*" The former of these expressions (gerant) admits of no doubt or cavil as to its proper signification. It is *overseer*, and were any evidence of its meaning wanting, the duties imposed upon such persons by this Code of Laws, would amply supply such defect. The latter word is used in the French West Indian Islands synonimously with the word *commandeur*, to signify *driver*. The word *conducteur*, is, however, frequently applied to the driver of mules. In this Code, the word "conducteur" is in one instance (Art. 116) used to signify a driver of cattle.

Article 173 says, that one of the objects of Rural Police, is the discipline of the labourer. This Article serves as an introduction to the regulations for daily labour; but before treating of them, we find several Articles recapitulating the provisions for compelling the mass of the population to cultivate the soil. These direct, that any person dwelling in the country, not being the owner or occupier of land, and not having bound himself in the manner directed by Articles 45 and 46, shall be considered a vagabond, be arrested, and taken before a Justice, who, after reading the Law to him, shall commit him to jail, until he consent to bind himself according to law. After eight days detention, should the prisoner still refuse to bind himself, he shall be put to hard labour as a scavenger.

Then follow the enactments for regulating daily labour; these, with the regulations already detailed, clearly shew what is intended to be the condition of the labouring population of Haïti. I must not call it slavery the word is objectionable; but few of the ingredients of slavery seem to be wanting. We have a whole population strictly prohibited from exercising any other mode of industry than the cultivation of the soil;—driven from the towns and villages, and compelled to remain in the section in which they are born;—forbidden to build houses or huts any where but upon plantations;—compelled to bind themselves to their employers;—overseers and drivers established by law to command them, and to direct their labours, and provision-grounds appointed to be set out for them, to be worked by themselves, *during their days and hours of rest.* They are moreover subject to the payment of all taxes.

Articles 183 et seq. decree, that labour shall commence at day-break on Monday, and never cease until sun-set on Friday; and, *in cases of necessity, it may be continued until Saturday night, under circumstances of which the master appears to be the only judge.* Daily labour must commence at day-break, and continue until sunset, with intervals of half an hour for breakfast, and two hours for dinner. Additional respite is allowed to pregnant women, and various regulations are made, even limiting the amusements of the labourers, and the power of their masters to permit their absence.

I have already drawn your Lordship's attention to the singular coincidence between some of the Articles of this Code of Laws, and a few of the Clauses of the Consolidated Slave Law of Jamaica, passed in 1816. The resemblance here becomes still more striking; the hours for labour and for rest, and the restraints upon the personal liberty of the labourer, are similar in spirit, and nearly similar in modes of expression; when any difference is perceivable, it is in favour of the Jamaica Law. The regulations respecting the treatment of pregnant women, are so extremely similar to those proved to be in general practice in Jamaica, by the evidence of persons examined before the Committee of the House of Assembly, upon the Registry Bill, that it appears to be not improbable they were framed upon that evidence.

Extracts from the Jamaica Act, (57 Geo. III. c. 25), are inserted as Notes throughout this Translation, at the foot of the pages where similar Articles of the Code occur. Their singular resemblance, both in expression and in meaning, must strike every one.

The mode appointed for carrying into effect this Code of Laws, is not less remarkable than the preceding enactments, if we look upon it as applicable to a free people. But if the Code be designed to coerce the labour of negroes under the present circumstances of the West Indies, it may be calculated to effect its object, *where fixed capital of Europeans is not at stake.* The mode is by military inspection, and military compulsion. The following is a short epitome of the principal Articles creating this military establishment.

Article 120, enumerates the Military Authorities by whom Rural Police is to be administered. They are Commandants of Districts, and Commandants of Communes; and their instruments are to be, Captains and Lieutenants of the Line, (Art. 140), and guards, armed with carbines and sabres, (Art. 154), gensd'armerie, and troops of the line. The Commandants of Districts are invested with supreme authority in agricultural affairs, and they are made responsible for the prosperity of agriculture. They are required to inspect their respective districts annually. The Commandants of Communes have similar power within their communes; they have the same responsibility, and are required to inspect each section most minutely, three times in the year. The communes are divided into sections, and a military officer placed in the command of each section; he is ordered to visit each plantation within his section, once a week, and to send one of his soldiers to visit it also, once a week; so that each plantation shall be inspected by the military, twice in the week at the least. To shew that these visits are not intended to be mere formal visits, but strict military inspections, I must refer your Lordship to Article 148. In case of illness, the duties of this officer are to be fulfilled by some other officer, from the regiment of the line quartered in the district. Some clauses then provide for the arms, accoutrements, uniforms, and pay of these police troops, who are also expressly declared to be responsible to their military superiors only, before whom they are sworn.

Every enactment in the Code of Laws before us, is directed to be carried into effect by the military, either in the first instance, or as the last resource. Their power is unbounded, and extends to the minutest detail, between the labourer and his employer; and the lower ranks of the military are directed to hold themselves in readiness, day and night, to obey the call of proprietors, farmers, or magistrates. Their authority is by no means limited to the enforcement of labour; it extends to all agricultural affairs. The Commandants of Districts and Communes, and the Officer commanding the Rural Police, are directed to view such lands as are recently granted to individuals by the State, and when, in their opinion, such a commencement of cultivation, as directed by law, has not been made within the time limited by law, *this military tribunal is directed to withdraw the grant, and confiscate the estate.*

In a few instances, it is thought necessary to make some show of a civil power. In case of any dispute arising between a proprietor and his farmers, overseers, or drivers, the dispute is to be referred, in the first instance, to the Officer commanding the Rural Police, who, if he can neither settle the difference by argument, nor by arbitration, is directed to refer it to a Justice, who must decide within 24 hours. *If the law should be silent upon the matter, the Justice must make a law to meet the case.* (See Article 84). A Council of Agriculture is also directed to be *chosen* annnally, for each section, *by the Commandant of the Commune,* assisted by the Council of Notables. The functions of this Council are principally confined to a species of espionage. They are to report to the military and civil authorities; in short, the whole establishment is a military despotism.

The Code concludes, by enacting some regulations for the repair of the roads: here again we find the military authorities directed to collect the necessary labourers from the neighbouring plantations, in rotation.

In the middle of the Code, I find a few articles,

which establish, for a limited and favoured class, a system of free, uncontrolled labour; they are Articles 75 to 80 inclusive. They enact that soldiers, not on active service, shall be permitted to make such engagements with the persons upon whose estates they dwell, written or verbal, to labour by the month, week, day, or hour, as they please; and that their wages shall be paid before those of any other class. When one of this privileged class fails to fulfil his contract, his master is not bound to pay him his wages.

I have now, my Lord, given a succinct outline of this Code of Laws. The details will be found to agree with it in every particular. My object has not been to degrade the Inhabitants of Haïti, by this exposure of their Law for controlling labour, but to make use of the testimony which this independent people have freely given, of the utter hopelessness of obtaining from the Negroes, without compulsion, that degree of regular and steady exertion, which is indispensable to secure a fair profit on fixed capital invested by European Planters in the West Indies. It matters little, under what name compulsory labour be procured, whether under the name of " slavery," or under the periphrase of " Cultivateurs, travaillants au quart." The principle is still the same—that of compelling a labouring man, having no capital, to devote his physical powers to the service of another man, possessed of capital, in such a manner, as to procure for each of them, a larger portion of the productions of the soil, than either could have obtained by his individual exertions. But, if it can be shewn, that, of the two attempts which have been made in the West Indies, to obtain this result, that which has been the most successful, by which I mean, that which has produced the greatest advantages to both parties, is the system adopted in our West Indian establishments, I have no hesitation in saying, that the attempt now making to overthrow that system, without due regard to the interests of the fixed Capitalist, is much to be deprecated. The Senate and Representatives of Haïti seem to have settled the question, that compulsion is necessary to obtain regular and steady labour in the West Indies, in their present state of population.

I have the Honour to be,

MY LORD,

Your Lordship's

Most obedient,

Humble Servant,

THE TRANSLATOR.

CODE RURAL D'HAÏTI.

RURAL CODE OF HAÏTI.

Port-au-Prince,
De l'imprimerie du Gouvernement,
Juillet, 1826.

Port-au-Prince,
Printed at the Government Press,
July, 1826.

Liberté. *Egalité.*

Liberty. *Equality.*

Republique d'Haïti.

Republic of Haïti.

CODE RURAL.

RURAL CODE.

La Chambre des Représantans des Communes, sur la proposition du Président d'Haïti, et ouï le rapport de sa Section de l'Interieur, a rendu les six Lois suivantes, formant le Code Rural d'Haiti.

The Chamber of Representatives of the Commons, upon the proposition of the President of Haïti, and having heard the Report from the Ministry of the Interior, has passed the six Laws following, which constitute the Rural Code of Haïti.

No. 1. LOI.

LAW. No. 1.

Sur les Dispositions générales relatives à l'Agriculture.

General Enactments relative to Agriculture.

Art. 1. L'Agriculture étant la source principale de la prosperité de l'Etat,

Art. 1. Agriculture being the principal source of prosperity in a State,

sera essentiellement protegée et encouragée par les Autorites Civiles et Militaires.

Art. 2. Les Citoyens de profession agricole ne pourront être detournés de leurs traveaux que dans les cas prévus par la loi.

Art. 3. Tous les Citoyens étant obligés de concourir a soutenir l'Etat, soit par leurs services, soit par leur industrie, ceux qui ne seront pas employés civils, ou requis pour le service militaire, ceux qui n'exerceront pas une profession assujettie à la patente; ceux qui ne seront pas ouvriers travaillans, ou employés comme domestiques; ceux qui ne seront pas employés à la coupe des bois propre à l'exportation; ceux enfin qui ne pourront pas justifier leurs moyen d'existence, devron cultiver la terre.

shall be specially protected and encouraged by the Civil and Military Authorities*.

Art. 2. Citizens whose employment is agriculture, shall not be taken from their labours, excepting in the cases provided for by the law.

Art. 3. It being the duty of every Citizen to aid in sustaining the State, either by his active services, or by his industry, those who are not employed in the civil service, or called upon for the military service; those who do not exercise a licensed profession; those who are not working artizans, or employed as servants; those who are not employed in felling timber for exportation; in fine, those who cannot justify their means of existence, shall cultivate the soil†.

---

* The Military Authorities appear in the very first clause of the Code. What can Military Authorities have to do with Agriculture?

† See Articles 45 and 46, and Articles 174, 175, 176, and 177.

Art. 4. Les Citoyens de profession agricole, ne pourront quitter les campagnes pour habiter les villes ou bourgs, sans une autorisation du Juge de Paix de la commune qu'ils voudront quitter, et de celui de la commune ou ils voudront se fixer. Le Juge de Paix ne donnera l'autorisation qu'apres s'etre assuré que le reclamant est de bonnes mœurs, qu'il a tenu une conduite reguliere dans le canton qu'il se dispose a quitter, et qu'il a des moyens d'existence dans la ville qu'il veut habiter. Tous ceux qui ne se conformeront pas aux regles ci-dessus etablies, seront considérés comme vagabonds, et traités comme tels.

Art. 5. Les enfans des deux sexes que leurs parens attachés à la culture, desirerons envoyer dans les villes ou bourgs pour leurs apprentissage ou pour leur education, ne pourront etre reçu, soit par les entre-

Art. 4. Citizens whose employment is agriculture, shall not be permitted to quit the country to inhabit the towns and villages, without a permission from the Justice of Peace of the commune they desire to quit, and of the commune in which they desire to establish themselves. The Justice of Peace shall give this permission *only* after having ascertained that the person asking it, is of good morals, that his conduct has been regular in the canton he is about to quit, and that he possesses the means of existence in the town he desires to inhabit. All those who do not conform to these regulations, shall be considered as vagabonds, and treated as such.

Art. 5. Children of either sex, whom their parents, being attached to agriculture, may be desirous of sending into the towns or villages, either for their apprenticeship, or their education, shall be

preneurs, soit par les instituteurs public ou particuliers, qu'avec un certificat du Juge de Paix: lequel certificat sera accordé sur la demande, soit du proprietaire, ou fermier principal du lieu, soit de l'Officier de la Police Rurale, soit du père ou de la mère de l'enfant.

Toute contravention aux presantes dispositions sera assujettie à une amende de vingt-cinq gourdes, payable par celui qui aura reçu l'enfant sans autorisation.

ART. 6. Les recrutemens militaires qui ne doivent se faire qu'en vertu des ordres du President d'Haïti, n'auront jamais lieu sur les Citoyens attachés a la culture, si l'ordre du Chef de l'Etat motivé par un danger imminent ne l'a expressement specifié.

ART. 7. Aucune boutique en-gros ou en detail ne pourra etre etablîe, aucune commerce de denrées

received by contractors, or by public or private teachers, *only* upon a certificate from a Justice of Peace. Which certificate shall be granted upon the demand of the proprietor, or principal farmer of the place; of the Officer commanding the Rural Police, or of the father or mother of the child.

Every infraction of these regulations shall be punishable by a fine of twenty-five dollars, payable by him who receives the child without a certificate.

ART. 6. Military enlistments, which can only be made by order of the President of Haïti, shall never be made of Citizens attached to agriculture, unless by express command of the Chief of the State alledging imminent danger.

ART. 7. No wholesale or retail shop shall be established, no traffic in the productions of the soil

du pays ne pourra etre fait dans les campagnes, sous quelque pretexte que ce soit; sont exceptés de cette disposition, les sucres bruts que l'on livre aux raffineries, les sirops aux guildiveries; le coton en pierre, que l'on porte aux moulins à égréner.

shall be carried on *in the country*, under any pretence whatever. Raw sugars sold to refiners, sweets sold to distilleries, and cotton in seed sold to ginning-mills, are excepted from these regulations.

Art. 8. Neanmoins, les pacotilleurs patentés ambulans resdant et sortant des villes ou bourgs, pourront vendre des provisions, marchandises etrangères, quincailleries, en parcourant la campagne.

Art. 8. Nevertheless, licensed hawkers dwelling in towns or villages, may carry about the country, and sell provisions, foreign merchandize, and iron wares.

Art. 9. Les maisons, ou cases que les particuliers ont deja fait etablir dans l'interieur des communes, là ou il n'existe pas de bourgades regulieres, mais seulement une reunion de cases, soit pour habiter eux-mêmes, soit pour louer à autrui, seront assujetties à l'imposition sur la valeur locative des maisons, comme dans les villes ou bourgs.

Art. 9. Houses or huts already built in the country parts of communes, in places where no regular villages have heretofore existed, which are only an assemblage of huts built by individuals for their own residence, or to let to others, shall be subject to a tax upon their letting value, in the same manner as houses in towns and villages.

A l'avenir, aucune case ne pourra etre batie dans les campagne où il n'y aura pas de bourgade reconnue, si elle n'est dependante d'un etablissement rural.

In future, no hut shall be erected in the country, but in some recognized village, unless it be dependant upon some rural establishment.

ART. 10. Aucun proprietaire riverain de la mer, ne pourra avoir de canots, ou embarcations, que pour le transport de ces denrées a la ville, ou bourg voisin; et pource, il aura, du Juge de Paix de la commune, une licence qui sera delivrée gratis; sous aucune prétexte, ces canots ne pourront faire le cabotage des autres ports ou ilots voisins; ni la pêche, si ce n'est pour le propre usage de l'habitation.

ART. 10. No proprietor bordering upon the sea, shall be permitted to keep boats or craft, excepting such as are necessary for carrying his produce to the nearest town or village; and for these he shall take out a license, to be delivered gratis by a Justice of Peace; these boats shall not, under any pretence, carry on the coasting trade between the neighbouring ports or islets, or be employed in fishing, excepting for the use of the plantation to which they belong.

ART. 11. Toutes les amendes confiscations prévues par le Code Rural, seront prononcées par les Juges de Paix, lorsqu'elles n'excederont pas une va-

ART. 11. All fines and confiscations imposed by the Rural Code, not exceeding one hundred dollars, shall be adjudged by a Justice of Peace;

leur de cent gourdes, et par les Tribuneaux Civils, lorsqu'elles excéderont cette somme. La moitié des dites amendes et confiscations appartiendra à la caisse publique, et l'autre moitié a celui qui aura fait connôitre le delit.

exceeding one hundred dollars, by the Civil Tribunals. Half of all fines and confiscations shall belong to the treasury, and half to the informer.

ART. 12. Le jour de la fête de l'agriculture, des groupes de cultivateurs de chaque section se présenteront au lieu où siège le Conseil des Notables, avec des échantillons de leurs travaux. Les Conseils des Notables, en présence de toutes les autorités couronneront le cultivateur qui aura mieux cultivé son champ dans chaque section, et dans chaque espèce de culture, lequel recevra un prix d'encouragement. Il sera dressé, de ces ceremonies, des procés verbaux qui seront rendu publics.

ART. 12. On the day of the festival of agriculture, groups of cultivators from each section shall present themselves at the place where the Council of Notables assembles, with samples of their labours. The Council of Notables, all the authorities being present, shall crown the cultivator (in each section for each species of cultivation) who shall be found to have cultivated his field in the best manner; he shall also receive a prize of encouragement. Accounts of these ceremonies shall be drawn up, and made public.

ART. 13. Chaque année, au premier Septembre, les

ART. 13. On the 1st of September in each year,

Conseils des Notables adresseront un rapport circonstancié au Président d'Haïti, sur l'etat des cultures de chaque commune, avec leurs observations sur ce qui pourrait tendre à l'amelioration des dites cultures.	the Council of Notables shall make to the President of Haïti, a circumstantial report on the state of cultivation in each commune, accompanied by their observations upon what may tend to the improvement of cultivation.
ART. 14. A la fin de l'année, les Commandans d'arrondissement rendront egalement compte au Président d'Haïti, de l'etat des cultures des arrondissemens et en outre de l'etat des chemins et routes publiques.	ART. 14. At the end of each year, the Commandants of districts shall report to the President of Haïti, the condition of agriculture, and the state of the public roads in their respective districts*.

---

* See Article 125, where this regulation is repeated, and the matter to be reported, set out more minutely.

No. 2. LOI.
Sur l'Administration en general des divers Etablissemens d'Agriculture.

CHAP. PREMIER.
Des Régles relatives à l'Administration fonciere des Etablissemens d'Agriculture.

Sect. Premiere.
Des Limites, Abornemens, et Etablissemens.

Art. 15. Tous les terrains situés dans la campagne, et provenant des concessions faites par l'Etat, soit à titre de propriété nationale, soit a titre de don partiel, qui n'auraient pas été arpentés jusqu'à ce jour, devront l'etre dans l'espace d'une année à compter de la date de la promulgation du présent Code, sous peine d'une amende d'une gourde par carreaux de terre, payable par les proprietaires.

Afin de parvenir à l'execution de la disposition

LAW. No. 2.
General Administration of Agricultural Establishments.

CHAP. I.
Regulations for the Administration of the Landed part of Agricultural Establishments.

Sect. 1.
Of Limits, Boundaries, and Establishments.

Art. 15. All lands situated in the country, which have been granted by the State to be holden as national, or as individual property, which have not yet been surveyed, shall be surveyed within one year from the publication of this Code, under a penalty of one dollar for every three acres of land, to be paid by the proprietor.

To ensure the due execution of the above enact-

ci-dessus presente, le Juge de Paix de la commune, sur la declaration qui lui en sera faite, apres l'expiration du delai fixé, requerra un Arpenteur dûment commissionné, pour mesurer et lever le plan des concessions non arpentées, aux frais des concessionnaires en defaut; alors l'amende sera prononcée et perçue avec les frais d'arpentage.

ment, the Justice of Peace of the commune, upon a declaration being made to him after the expiration of the delay allowed, shall call in a Surveyor duly appointed, to survey and lay down plans of the grants not surveyed, at the expence of the grantee, the Justice shall thereupon adjudge and levy the fine and expences.

Art. 16. A partir de la meme promulgation, aucune vente de propriété, sise dans les campagnes, ne pourra etre passée pardevant Notaire, si cette propriété n'a été prealablement arpentée ou si les abornemens n'en sont positivement reconnus par les titres. Dans tous les cas, toute vente partielle ne pourra avoir lieu, que le terrain ne soit prealablement arpentée. Les notaires que contreviendront a cette defense, encourront les peines de droit.

Art. 16. From, and after the date of the publication aforesaid, no sales of property situated in the country, shall be made before a Notary, unless the lands have previously been surveyed, or the boundaries be distinctly laid down in the title deeds. In no case shall any partial sale take place, unless the ground have previously been surveyed. Notaries who neglect to observe these formalities, shall be subject to the penalties imposed by law.

ART. 17. Toute concession de terre accordée jusqu'à la promulgation du présent Code, et qui, un an après, n'aura pas un commencement d'etablissement; et toute concession posterieure au present Code, qui n'aura pas un an après la date du titre de cette concession un commencement d'establissement, seront reunies aux domaines de l'Etat, le titre sera retiré et renvoyé au Gouvernement.	ART. 17. Every grant of land dated before the publication of this Code, which shall not be begun to be cultivated within one year from its publication; and every grant which may be made hereafter, and which shall not be begun to be cultivated within one year after the date of such grant, shall be re-united to the domains of the State, the title shall be withdrawn, and returned to the Government.
ART. 18. Pour parvenir a la reunion mentionnée en l'article précédent l'Officier de la Police Rurale, conjointement avec le Conseil d'Agriculture, fera le rapport au Juge de Paix, et au Commandant Militaire de la commune, de l'etat d'abandon de la concession, ceux ci apres s'etre assurées de l'exactitude du rapport, le viseront, et l'adresseront au Commandant de l'arrondissement, qui, apres avoir la preuve	ART. 18. To carry into effect the provision of the preceding article, the Officer commanding the Rural Police, in conjunction with the Council of Agriculture, shall make a report of the state of abandonment of the grant to the Justice of Peace, and to the Military Commandant of the commune, who, after having enquired into the correctness of the report, shall sign it, and address it to the Commandant of the

du fait retirera le titre, et l'enverra au Gouvernement.

Art. 19. Un établissement sera reputé commencé, lorsqu'il y aura un jardin de travaillé dans les régles établies par la loi, et dont la contenance sera proportionnelle au nombre des cultivateurs attachés à la proprieté.

Art. 20. Les proprietaires des terrains cultivés, et qui sont contigus, seront tenus, a frais communs, de faire cloturer convenablement leurs prorietés.
Celui qui s'y refusera sera contraint par de voies de droit.

Art. 21. Les proprietaires des biens ruraux sont tenus de faire placer, lors des operations d'arpentage, faites a leur re-

district, who, after having duly verified it, shall withdraw the title, and send it to the Government.

Art. 19. An establishment shall be held to be commenced, as soon as a garden shall be planted according to the rules established by law, and the extent of which shall be proportioned to the number of labourers attached to the property.

Art. 20. Proprietors of cultivated lands bordering upon each other, shall enclose their lands at their joint expence.

The proprietor who may refuse to do so, shall be compelled, by proceedings at law.

Art. 21. Proprietors are bound, when their grants are surveyed, to cause proper landmarks to be erected, either in

quisition, des bornes solides en fer, en maconnerie, ou en bois incorruptible, sous peine d'une amende de cinq gourdes pour chaque borne manquant a sa place.

Art. 22. Les proprietaires qui auront negligé l'execution de l'article precedent, seront, apres avoir payé l'amende, obligé de payer l'ouvrier qui aurait été employé, par l'ordre du Juge de Paix de la commune, à etablir la borne necessaire.

iron, in masonry, or in durable wood, under penalty of a fine of five dollars for each landmark which may be wanting.

Art. 22. Proprietors who may have neglected to obey the preceding enactment, shall, after having paid the fine, be compelled to pay the workman employed by the Justice to erect the landmark

Sect. 2.

Des Obligations imposées aux Proprietaires, ou a ceux qui sont chargés de l'Administration des Propriétés Rurale.

Art. 23. Il est specialement défendu d'abattre des bois sur la crête des montagnes jusqu'a cent pas de leur chûte, ni à la tête et à l'entour des sources, ou sur le bord des rivieres, les proprietaires des ter-

Sect. 2.

Duties imposed upon Proprietors, or Persons having the Management of Rural Properties.

Art. 23. It is particularly forbidden to cut down woods upon the summits of hills, or within one hundred paces from their summits, at the head or in the neighbourhood of springs, or upon the banks of

rains arrosés par des sources ou rivieres, devront entourer la tête de ces sources, et planter les bords des rivieres de bananiers, bambous, ou autres arbres propres a entretenir la fraicheur.

streams; proprietors of lands watered by springs, or rivers, are bound to plant bananas, bamboos, and other trees capable of preserving moisture, around the springs, and upon the banks of the rivers.

ART. 24. Le proprietaire qui voudra bruler un bois neuf, un champ de vieilles cannes, des savannes, où tout autre terrein, sera tenu d'en avertir vingt-quatre heures d'avance, tous les voisins limitrophes, sous peine de repondre de tout le dommage que le feu pourrait occasionner.

ART. 24. Proprietors intending to burn woodland, old canes, savannas, or other land, shall give twenty-four hours' notice to the neighbouring proprietors, under pain of being otherwise responsible for all damage the fire may occasion.

ART. 25. Lorsqu'un incendie se declarera sur une propriété, les proprietaires et agriculteurs voisins seront tenus de s'y transporter afin d'aider a en arrêter les progrès.

ART. 25. When a fire breaks out upon a property, the neighbouring proprietors and labourers shall attend and assist to extinguish it.

ART. 26. Il est defendu d'allumer du feu dans les savannes, les champs, ou

ART. 26. It is forbidden to light fires in the savannas, fields, or gardens of

jardins des habitations, sans la permission expresse des proprietaires, fermiers, gérans, ou conducteurs d'icelles.

ART. 27. Il ne pourra etre entretenu sur les propriétés destinées a la culture, aux manufactures, ou autre établissemens, que les bestiaux necessaires à leur exploitation, ou à l'usage des proprietaires, gerans, conducteurs, fermiers, ou agriculteurs ; mais tous ces animaux devront etre gardés le jour en troupeaux, et la nuit, dans les parcs ou savannes closes.

ART. 28. Les bêtes cavalines, les bêtes a cornes, cochons, &c. destinées a la multiplication ne pourront être gardés que sur des hattes établies en vertu, de la Loi, No. 4, relative aux Hattes.

ART. 29. Aucum proprietaire, fermier, ou gerant d'habitation, ne pourra

plantations, without express permission of the proprietors, managers, overseers, or drivers upon them.

ART. 27. No cattle but those absolutely necessary for carrying on the cultivation, or for the personal use of the proprietors, overseers, drivers, farmers, or labourers, shall be kept upon estates intended for cultivation, for manufactories, or for other establishments ; and these shall be kept by day in herds, and by night in enclosed pastures or parks.

ART. 28. Horses, mules, horned-cattle, swine, &c. intended for breeding, shall only be kept in pens established according to Law, No. 4, on Pens.

ART. 29. No proprietor, farmer, or overseer of a plantation, shall adopt a

etablir chez lui un système contraire a l'ordre etabli par la loi.

system contrary to that established by law.

Art. 30. Aucune reunion ou association de cultivateurs fixés sur une même habitation, ne pourra se rendre fermière de la totalité du bien qu'ils habitent, pour l'administrer par eux memes en société.

Art. 30. No union or association of labourers settled upon an estate, shall be permitted to farm the whole estate, to cultivate it themselves in partnership.

Art. 31. Les cases ou logemens des cultivateurs ne pourront être construits que sur un même point de l'habitation à laquelle ils seront attachés.

Art. 31. The huts of labourers shall all be built upon the same spot, upon the plantation to which they are attached.

CHAP. II.

Des Cultures in general.

Art. 32. Les cultures principales consistent dans les etablissemens des plantes et arbres qui produisent des denrées propres à être exportées à l'etranger, et en grains de toutes qualités; en toutes especes de vivres ou racines destinés à la subsistence de la population.

CHAP. II.

Of Cultivation in general.

Art. 32. The first class of cultivation consists in plantations which yield produce for exportation, every kind of grain, and the provisions necessary for the subsistence of the people.

Art. 33. Tous ceux qui s'occupent des principales cultures ne sont assujettés à l'imposition territoriale et fonciere que sur la masse des denrées qu'ils auront recueillies, et propres a l'exportation.	Art. 33. Those who carry on this class of cultivation, shall be subject to the territorial and land taxes upon the gross amount only of the produce they raise fit for exportation.
Art. 34. Les cultures secondaires sont la culture seulement des potagers, des fleurs, des arbres fruitiers, des vivres et du fourrage, lorsque ces exploitations ont lieu sur les biens, dont l'etablissement n'a pas pour but la culture des denrées principales.	Art. 34. The second class of cultivation consists of kitchen and flower gardens, fruit trees, provisions, and forage, when these are raised on estates not destined to raise produce of the first class.
Art. 35. Tous ceux qui dans un établissement, s'occupent spécialement des cultures secondaires, sont assujettés à l'imposition territoriale et foncière, sur la valeur estimative de leurs productions de chaque semestre.	Art. 35. Those who carry on this class of cultivation, shall be subject to the territorial and land tax upon the estimated value of the weekly produce they raise.
Art. 36. Sur chaque établissement rural, on sera tenu de cultiver des vivres, grains, arbres fruitiers, tels	Art. 36. The proprietor of every plantation shall be compelled to cultivate provisions, corn, fruit trees,

qu'arbres à pain etc : suffisans pour la nourriture des personnes qui y sont employées.

such as the bread-fruit, &c. sufficient to provide for the people employed*.

Art. 37. Tous les jardins, soit de denrées, soit de vivres ou grains devront etre soigneusement entretenus, sous la responsabilité du propriétaire fermier, ou gerant qui, en cas de negligence pourra être condamné a l'amende, depuis trois jusqu'à quinze gourdes.

Art. 37. Gardens, whether of produce, provisions, or corn, shall be carefully cultivated, for which the proprietor, farmer, or overseer, shall be responsible, under a penalty of from three to fifteen dollars †.

Art. 38. Sur chaque

Art. 38. The labourers

---

* Consolidated Slave Law of Jamaica, 57 Geo. III. c. 25, (1816), Section 6, after directions for the inspection of provision grounds, "And whereas it "may happen, that on some plantations or pens, settlements and towns, in "this island, there may not be lands proper for the cultivation of provisions, "or when by long continuance of dry weather, the negro grounds may be "rendered unproductive ; then, and in that case, the masters, owners, or "possessors, do, by some other ways and means, make good and ample "provision for all such slaves as they shall be possessed of, equal to the "value of 3s. 4d. currency per week for each slave, in order that they may "be properly supported and maintained, under a penalty of fifty pounds."

There is no such humane and excellent provision as this in the whole Rural Code.—*(Translator).*

† The first part of the clause of the Consolidated Slave Law of 1816, cited in the preceding note, says, "That every master, owner, or possessor of any "slave or slaves, or his or her overseer or chief manager, shall, under the "penalty of *ten pounds* for each neglect, personally inspect into the con"dition of the negro grounds once in every month at least, in order to see "that the same are cultivated and kept in a proper manner, of which oath "shall be made, as in this act is hereafter directed."

habitation les cultivateurs y attachés travaillant au quart seront tenus d'avoir, pour leur usage personnel, un jardin de vivres qu'ils cultiveront *pendant leurs heures ou jours de repos.*

attached to any plantation labouring for one quarter of the produce, shall have assigned to them for their personal use, a garden for provisions, *which they shall cultivate during their hours and days of rest.*

Art. 39. A l'effet de l'article précédent, les proprietaires, fermiers ou gerans, seront tenus de mettre à la disposition des agriculteurs, le terrain necessaire pour l'etablissement de leurs jardins particuliers.

Art. 39. To effect the preceding article, proprietors, farmers, or overseers, shall place at the disposal of the labourers sufficient ground for their gardens*.

Art. 40. Les digues, bassins de distribution et canaux qui servent a fournir l'eau necessaire aux habitans, tant pour l'arrosage que pour toute autre utilité seront entretenus par tous les interessés, lesquels seront tenus de contribuer à tous les travaux

Art. 40. The dykes, ponds, and canals which supply the water required by the inhabitants for irrigation, or for any other purpose, shall be kept in repair by the parties interested, who shall contribute to the labour necessary for their repair. No one shall

---

* "Every master, &c. shall, under a penalty of one hundred pounds for "every neglect, &c. declare on oath, that he has inspected the negro grounds "(where such negro grounds are allotted), of such plantation, pen, or "settlement, according to the directions of this act, and that every negro "on the property is sufficiently provided with grounds" (57 Geo. III. c. 25, sec. 8).

pour leur entretien. Nul ne pourra se refuser a ces travaux, ni disposer de la portion d'eau de son voisin, sans son consentiment. Tout contrevenant aux dispositions ci-dessus, paiera une amende de dix à cinquante gourdes, et sera tenu, en outre, de reparer, a ses frais et depens, le canal qu'il aura obstrué ou detruit.

be permitted to evade this work, nor to appropriate the water belonging to his neighbour, without his consent. Persons guilty of infractions, shall be liable to a fine of not less than ten dollars, nor more than fifty dollars, and shall moreover repair at their own charges the canal they may have obstructed or destroyed.

Art. 41. Lorsque les denrées seront sur le point d'être ensachées, emballées enfutaillés, on empaquetées, sur une propriété rurale, l'Officier de Police Rurale de la section, aura le droit d'examiner les dites denrées afin de s'assurer qu'elles ne sont pas fraudées; et dans le cas ou elles le seraient, il en arrêtera la livraison, et en fera immediatement son rapport au Juge de Paix de la commune; si elles sont seulement mal preparées, il en empêchera le transport, et obligera l'habitant à les renettoyer.

Art. 41. When produce is about to be put into sacks, bales, casks, or packages, upon a rural property, the Officer commanding the Rural Police of the section, shall have the right of inspecting the produce, to ascertain that it is not adulterated; and should it be so, he shall stop the delivery, and report it to the Justice of Peace of the commune. Should the produce be badly manufactured only, he shall stop its removal, and compel the proprietor to clean it.

ART. 42. Le Juge de Paix, en recevant le rapport, nommera des experts pour prendre connaissance de la denrée, et s'il y a fraude, et qu'elle soit constatée, la denrée sera confisquée au profit de l'Etat.

ART. 43. Les denrées d'exportation ne pourront sortir des habitations pour etre portées dans les villes ou bourgs, et etre livrées au commerce que sur un permis des proprietaires, lorsqu'ils resideront sur leurs biens, et pour celles des habitations ou les propriétaires ne resideront pas de l'Officier de la Police Rurale de la section. Le permis sera delivré gratis sur papier libre, par l'Officier de la Police, qui sera tenu de l'enregistrer.

ART. 44. Toute denrée transportée en contravention à l'Article precedent, sera arrêtée sur la route, et conduite chez le Juge de Paix de la commune, qui s'assurera si la denrée

ART. 42. The Justice, upon receiving the report, shall name skilful persons to examine the produce; and should the adulteration be proved, the produce shall be confiscated to the State.

ART. 43. Produce fit for exportation, shall not be removed from the plantations to towns or villages, and sent into circulation, but with a permit from the proprietor, when resident, or from the Officer commanding the Rural Police, when the proprietor is not resident. The permit shall be delivered gratis, upon unstamped paper, by the Officer commanding the Police, who shall enregister it.

ART. 44. All produce removed in contravention of the preceding Article, shall be stopped on the road, and taken before the Justice of Peace of the commune, who shall en-

n'a pas été volée, afin d'en faire remise au proprietaire, et de poursuivre le présumé coupable. Dans le cas ou ce serait le proprietaire de la denrée qui aurait manqué de donner le permis, il payera une amende de trois a cinq gourdes.

quire whether the produce have not been stolen, for the purpose of restoring it to the owner, and pursuing the supposed guilty person. Where the owner of the produce shall have neglected to furnish the permit, he shall be subject to a fine of not less than three dollars, nor more than five dollars.

No. 3. LOI.

Sur les Contrats synallagmatiques entre les Proprietaires, ou Fermiers principaux, et les Agriculteurs, Cultivateurs, ou Travailleurs, et sur les Obligations reciproques des uns envers les autres.

LAW. No. 3.

Upon the mutual Contracts to be entered into between Proprietors, or Chief Farmers, and Agriculturists, Cultivators, or Labourers, and their reciprocal Obligations.

CHAP. PREMIER.

Dispositions generales.

ART. 45. Les personnes qui ne seront pas en activité au service de l'Etat, comme militaires, ouvriers, ou employés quelconques, et dont la profession sera de cultiver la terre, ou de

CHAP. I.

General Enactments.

ART. 45. All persons not in active employment of the State, as soldiers, workmen, and others, and whose business it is to cultivate the soil, or to fell timber for exportation,

travailler aux coupes des bois d'exportation, seront tenues pour la garantie mutuelle de leurs interets, de passer un contrat synallagmatique, avec le proprietaire, ou fermier principal de la propriété rurale, ou de la coupe, sur la quelle elles devront exercer leur industrie. Le contrat pourra être passé collectivement ou individuellement au gré des contractans.

shall, for the security of their common interests, enter into a mutual engagement with the proprietor, or chief farmer, of the plantation or wood upon which they are destined to exercise their industry. The engagement with the labourers may be made either collectively or individually.

Art. 46. La durée des contrats ne pourra être pour un temps moindre que deux ans, ni plus long que neuf années pour la culture secondaire et les manufactures; pour un temps moindre que trois années, ne plus long que neuf pour les autres cultures; moindre que six mois ni plus long qu'un an, pour la coupe des bois pour l'exportation.

Art. 46. No engagement for the second class of cultivation, or for manufactures, shall be for a shorter period than two years, nor for more than nine years; for all other species of cultivation, for less than three years, nor more than nine years; and for felling timber for exportation, for less than six months, nor more than one year*.

---

* In what do these persons, thus bound to their employers, differ from slaves, but in the name? the substance of slavery is here; the name is not far off.—See 15 Geo. III. c. 28, for the name given by the British Parliament to voluntary engagers of this description. See Articles 96 et seq.; and for exceptions, see Articles 75 et seq. The principles, as to the connection

ART. 47. Le contrat sera fait sur papier timbré par-devant Notaire, lequel en gardera la minute: il devra expliquer clairement toutes les conditions arretées entre les contractans qui pourront y faire telles stipulations qu'ils jugerons convenables, pourvu qu'elles ne soit pas contraires aux dispositions du present Code.

ART. 48. Tout proprietaire, fermier, ou gerant d'habitation, qui y recevra ou y suffrira des-cultivateurs ou agricultures, sans avoir fait avec eux le contrat exigé par les Articles 47 et 49, sera condamné pour la premiere fois à un amende de dix gourdes par chaque personne reçu sans contrat; du double, en cas de recidive, et en outre, ce pro-

ART. 47. The contract shall be made upon stamped paper, before a Notary, who shall keep a minute of it: it must express distinctly all the conditions agreed upon by the contracting parties, who may insert any stipulations they please, provided such stipulations be not in opposition to the enactments of this Code.

ART. 48. Any proprietor, farmer, or overseer of a plantation, who shall receive, or employ upon the plantation, any cultivators or labourers, without having made with them the contract required by Articles 47 and 49, shall be condemned, for the first offence to a fine of ten dollars for each person so employed; and in case of a repetition of the offence,

---

between labour, and the profitable employment of fixed capital, here exhibited, are very important. The Code wisely extends the period for which contracts for labour are to be in force, in proportion as a greater portion of fixed capital is dependent on labour for its profitable employment. In felling timber, little fixed capital is employed, and, in that case, the legal period for engagement with the labourer is the *shortest*.

prietaire, fermier, ou gerant, ne pourra exercer aucune action en justice contre les agriculteurs qui auraient manqué envers lui à leurs conventions verbales, il en sera de même, à l'egard des ouvriers travaillant aux coupes des bois d'exportation.	to double the amount, and moreover, shall be deprived of any remedy against the labourers for default of their verbal engagements. This enactment extends to labourers employed in felling timber for exportation*
ART. 49. Tout contrat passé avec un agriculteur, dont le contrat antérieur n'etait point encore arrivé à son terme, sera nul de plein droit; et l'agriculteur qui aurait passé ce second contrat, sera reconduit à ses frais, sur la propriété ou il s'etait engagé et sera assujetti á l'amende fixé par l'Article 48.	ART. 49. Any contract entered into with a labourer, whose preceding contract shall not have expired, shall be absolutely void, and the labourer who shall have made such second contract, shall be reconducted, at his own expence, to the plantation where he had previously engaged himself, and shall be subject to the fine imposed by Article 48.
ART. 50. Les chefs des compagnies travaillant de moitié dans les produits,	ART. 50. Headmen of parties working for one half the produce, shall

---

* Exceptions to these regulations, are made in favour of a particular class, by Articles 75 to 80 inclusive.

devron partager par egale portion, avec le proprietaire principal de l'habitation, tout ce qu'ils recolterons sur la-terre donnée de moitié, en fait de fruits, vivres, légumes, grains et denrées quelconques.

share in equal portions with the principal proprietor of the plantation, all fruits, provisions, vegetables, grain, and produce they may raise upon the land cultivated by halves*.

ART. 51. Lorsque dans les habitations sucreries, le travail se fera de moitié, le propriétaire prelévera, avant le partage, un cinquième du revenu brut pour tenir lieu de loyer des usines ou ustensiles, bestiaux, etc. employés a l'exploitation, ou frais de réparation; dans les autres cultures, le montant des depenses occasionnées par la faisance-valoir ou frais d'exploitation, sera prélevée avant le partage.

ART. 51. When sugar plantations are worked by halves, the proprietor shall, before the division takes place, deduct one fifth of the gross produce for the use of the works, utensils, stock, &c. employed, or for the expences of repairs; and in other cases, the amount of the plantation expences shall be deducted before the division.

ART. 52. Les cultivateurs travaillans au quart

ART. 52. Labourers working for one quarter

---

* Wherever parties cultivating the land for half the produce, are mentioned, their headman is the person with whom the proprietor is made to contract; and by Article 161, he is declared to be their *driver, (conducteur)*.

des revenus par eux produits participerons pour un quart brut dans tout ce qu'ils produiront : ils jouiront en totalité des fruits recoltés dans leurs jardins particuliers travaillés eux, aux heures, ou jours de repos.

of the revenue raised by themselves, shall divide one clear quarter of the gross produce they may raise; they shall likewise enjoy the whole of the fruits raised in their individual gardens, cultivated by themselves during their hours and days of rest

ART. 53. Lorsque, dans les grandes manufactures en sucreries, caferies, cotonneries, indigotories, la saison exigera que les travaux soient poussés avec activité, les diverses sociétés de moitié que se trouveront sur la même habitation devront s'entraider dans leurs travaux, en se donnant mutuellement un même nombre de journées de travail; l'administrateur de la propriété regléra ces sortes des compensation.

ART. 53. When the seasons require that the works upon great sugar manufactories, coffee, cotton, and indigo estates, shall be pushed with activity, the different parties upon the same plantation, who work for half produce, shall assist each other in their labours, affording to each other an equal number of days' assistance; these mutual aids shall be regulated by the manager of the estate.

ART. 54. Lorsque les denrées ou recoltes quelles

ART. 54. When the produce or crop has been

* These two Articles clearly make the same distinction between the two classes of labourers, as now exists in Jamaica. Article 51 relates to jobbing gangs; Article 52, to negroes belonging to the estate.

qu'elles soient, seront fabriquées ou ramassées, soit qu'elles proviennent de travaux faits au quart, ou en societé de moitié, le déplacement ne pourra s'effectuer de la proprieté qui les aura produites, qu'apres le partage en nature aura en lieu entre le propriétaire, ou fermier principal, et les agriculteurs travaillant au quart, ou associés de moitié.

ART. 55. Sur les habitations sucreries, le partage des portions afferentes aux cultivateurs devra se faire apres la roulaison de chaque piece de cannes; sur les habitations ou l'on ne cultive que des vivres ou grains, ou se fait la coupe du bois à bruler, le charbon, ou la coupe des bois à marqueterie ou de construction, du fourage, ou d'autres exploitations irregulieres, les repartitions ne se feront aux travailleurs que tous les six mois; sur les autres habitations telles-que caferies,

manufactured or gathered in, whether it be made or gathered by parties working for half or quarter produce, it shall not be removed from the estate until after a division has been made between the proprietor, or head farmer, and the labourers working at half, or quarter produce.

ART. 55. Upon sugar estates, the division shall be made after the working of each patch of canes; upon estates cultivated in corn or provisions, woods fallen for firewood, charcoal, cabinet-making, or building, in forage, and other irregular productions, the division shall be made every six months; and upon all other estates, such as coffee, cotton, cocoa, indigo, &c. the division shall take place after crop.

cotonneries, cacaoyères, indigoteries, etc. Les partages auront lieu a la fin des recoltes de café, indigo, cacao, coton, etc.

ART. 56. Lorsque les epôques de la repartition des deniers afférens aux cultivateurs arriveront, l'Officier de la Police Rurale de la section, dans laquelle sera située l'habitation, sera appelé par le proprietaire, fermier principal, ou leur gerant, pour etre témoin du partage ; les comptes des denrées fabriquées, ou autres produits recoltés, seront exhibés, ainsi que le certificat du prix courant, et celui de l'acquéreur des denrées mentionnées en l'Article 55. La liste des compartageans sera établie, et les denrées seront comptés.

ART. 56. When the time for dividing the proceeds of the produce belonging to the labourers' arrives, the Officer commanding the Rural Police of the section, shall be called in by the proprietor, head farmer, or their overseer, to witness the division. The accounts of the produce manufactured, or crops gathered in, and a certificate of the price current, shall be produced, together with a certificate from the purchaser of the produce enumerated in Article 55. A list of all persons entitled to share shall be made out, and the produce shall be enumerated.

ART. 57. Chacun des compartageans sera porté sur la liste de partage à

ART. 57. Each individual entitled to share, shall be inscribed upon

faire par premiere, seconde, et troisieme classe, en raison de leur force et activité et du temps de leur travail.	the list in one of three classes, according to his strength and activity, and the time he has worked.
Les deniers à partager seront devises en quart de parts, demi-parts, et parts entieres. Les conducteurs des travaux au quart, ou les chefs des societés de moitié, auront trois parts entières.	The monies to be shared, shall be divided into quarter shares, half shares, and shares. The drivers, and head-men, shall be entitled to three shares each.
Les maitres-sucriers les maitres-cabrouettiers, et en un mot toute maistrance, auront deux parts.	Sugar-boilers, and chief carter, and other head-men, two shares each.
Les bons travailleurs de première classe, hommes ou femmes, auront une part et demie.	Good working men and women of the first class, a share and a half each.
Ceux de seconde classe, auront une part.	Those of the second class, a share each.
Ceux de troisieme classe, auront trois-quarts de part.	Those of the third class, three-quarters of a share each.
Les enfans de douze a seize ans revolus, qui sont utilisés selon leurs capacité, et les vieillards qui ne travaillent que mediocrement, auront demi-part.	Children from twelve to sixteen years of age, and elderly people, half a share each.
Les enfans de neuf a	Children from nine to

ouze ans revolus, qui sont occupés selon leur age ou leurs forces, les infirmes, auront un quart de part.	twelve, and weak infirm people, a quarter share each.
Les fort deniers resultans de la formation des parts serviront à augmenter la portion des travaillieurs qui auront montré le plus d'exactitude, et de persèvérance dans leurs travaux.	Any monies remaining over and above the shares paid to each person, shall be divided among those who have shewn the most steadiness and activity in their labour.
ART. 58. Il sera fourni aux travailleurs journalieres des-cartes pour constater leurs journées de presence au travail.	ART. 58. Tickets certifying the days they have been present, shall be given to day-labourers.
Chaque semaine les cartes journalières seront retirées, et remplacées par des cartes de semaine, lesquelles seront reglées, lors des partages des deniers provenant des revenus*.	These day tickets shall be withdrawn once in each week, and weekly tickets substituted for them. Account shall be taken of these weekly tickets at the time of the divisions of produce, or crop.
ART. 59. En aucun cas, l'Officier de la Police Rurale de la section, ne pourra retirer de la masse à partager aucune portion	ART. 59. In no case shall the Officer commanding the Rural Police, deduct from the amount to be divided, any thing for him-

---

* This article relates to the class of labourers recognized in Article 75. et seq.

pour se l'attribuer, il dressera procés verbal de ces partages, qui sera adressé avec les pieces à l'appui, au Conseil des Notables de la commune, pour y avoir recours au besoin.

ART. 60. Les proprietaires, fermiers principaux, ou gerans, ne pourront donner un permis à un agriculture ou sous fermier pour voyager dans la même commune, pour s'absenter de son domicile et de ses travaux, pour *plus de huit jours;* lequel permis sera delivré gratis sur papier libre, et visé par l'Officier de la Police Rurale. Lorsqu'il faudra un permis pour un plus long espace de tempts, le proprietaire, fermier principal, ou gerant, en referra au Commandant de la commune.

self. He shall draw up a written account of these divisions, and shall send it, with the necessary vouchers, to the Council of Notables, as a document of reference in case of necessity.

ART. 60. Proprietors, farmers, and overseers, are forbidden to give permission to any labourer to travel in the commune, or to absent himself from his domicile, and work for *more than eight days:* the permit shall be on unstamped paper, delivered gratis, and signed by the Officer commanding the Rural Police. When the parties require a longer leave of absence, the proprietor, farmer, or overseer, shall refer them to the Commandant of the commune*.

---

* Consolidated Slave Law, 57 Geo. III. c. 25, sec. 30, provides that no slave shall travel without a ticket from his master; and sec. 31, says, " that no ticket shall be given any slave, or slaves, for any time exceeding " *one calendar month.*"—See Articles 180 and 187.

CHAP. II.

Des Obligations des Proprietaires, Fermiers, ou Gerans, enver les Agriculteurs.

Art. 61. Les proprietaires, fermiers, ou gerans, ne pourront employer qu'a des travaux agricoles, ou a cëux qui en dependent, les cultivateurs qui auront contractés avec eux. Ils devront les traiter en bons pères de famille.

Art. 62. Les proprietaires, ou fermiers principaux, fourniront a leurs frais et depens, les outils ou instrumens aratoires aux cultivateurs travaillans au quart, ces outils ne pourront etre remplacés qu'en justifiant qu'ils sont usés, ou brisés au service des proprietaires. Cependant le cultivateur qui perdra les outils qui lui auront été fournis, sera tenu de les remplacer; s'il ne le fait pas,

CHAP. II.

Of the Duties of Proprietors, Farmers, or Overseers, towards the Labourers.

Art. 61. Proprietors, farmers, or overseers, shall employ the labourers with whom they have contracted, at agricultural labour, or at labour relating to agriculture *only*. They shall treat their labourers as parents would their children.

Art. 62. Proprietors, or head farmers, shall supply at their own expence, the labourers working at quarter produce, with tools and farming implements; these tools shall only be replaced when proved to have been worn out, or broken, in the service of the proprietor. The labourer who loses the tools supplied him, shall replace them himself; if he do not, he shall receive others, the

il lui sera fourni d'autres, dont la valeur sera retenue sur sa portion du revenu.

ART. 63. Le proprietaire, ou fermier principal, sera obligé de fournir, sans frais, aux agriculteurs travaillant au quart, les moyens de transporter leurs portions de denrées au lieu ou elle sera vendu; les associés de moitié feront les transports à leurs propres frais.

ART. 64. Lorsque le proprietaire ou fermier principal se chargera de vendre ou faire vendre la portion des denrées afferentes aux cultivateurs travaillant au quart, ou revenant aux associés de moitié, il sera tenu de faire constater, de la maniere la plus legale, le prix courant des denrées au moment ou il vendra ou fera vendra les portions de ces

price of which shall be deducted from his share of the produce.

ART. 63. The proprietor, or head farmer, shall supply the labourers working at quarter produce, the means of conveying their share of the produce to the place of sale, free of expence; the labourers working at half produce, shall convey their produce at their own expence*.

ART. 64. When the proprietor or chief farmer undertakes to dispose of the portion of the produce applicable to the labourers working at quarter produce, or belonging to those at half produce, he shall be bound to prove, in the most legal manner, the price current of the produce at the time of sale, and to produce, at the time of the division of the

---

* See Note to Articles 51 and 52.

cultivateurs et de produire, lors du partage des deniers, le certificat de l'acquereur ainsi que l'attestation du prix courant.

ART. 65. Lorsque les portions de denrées revenant aux agriculteurs, travaillant au quart ou de moitié, seront vendues par les conducteurs des ateliers, ou chefs de moitié, ceux ci ne seront pas moins obligés de faire constater le prix courant de la denrée au moment de la vente, et d'exhiber le certificat de l'acquereur, comme il est etabli en l'article ci-dessus afin de prouver que les copartageans recoivent justement la part a laquelle ils ont droit sur le produit de leurs travaux.

ART. 66. Dans aucun cas, les proprietaires ou fermiers principaux, ne pourront prélever aucune portion sur la part afferente aux cultivateurs travaillant au quart, ou aux

proceeds, a certificate from the purchaser, as well as the price current duly attested.

ART. 65. When the portion of produce belonging to the labourers, is sold by the drivers or jobbers, these shall likewise be bound to produce the price current at the time of sale, duly attested, and a certificate from the purchaser; for the purpose of proving that the sharers have received their fair and just rights.

ART. 66. The proprietor or head farmer, shall in no case deduct any thing from the share of produce due to the labourers, for the payment of the salaries of over-

associés de moitié pour payer leurs gerans. Le salaire des dits gerans sera au compte du propriétaire ou fermier principal.

seers. These salaries shall always be paid by the proprietor or head farmer.

ART. 67. Les proprietaires ou fermiers seront obligés, sous peine d'une amende de cinq a quinze gourdes, de s'abonner avec un officier de santé, pour soigner les agriculteurs; et de fournir les medicamens necessaires, lorsqu'ils y en aura dans la commune; ces medicamens seront fournis gratis aux cultivateurs, lorsqu'ils auront contracté au quart; ils serons remboursés au prix coutans lorsqu'ils seront fournis à des associés travaillant de moitié, ou comme sous-fermiers.

ART. 67. Proprietors or farmers shall be required, under penalty of not less than five dollars, nor more than fifteen dollars, to engage with a medical man for attendance upon the labourers, and to supply medicines when any are to be procured in the commune: these medicines shall be supplied gratis to labourers working at quarter produce*; they shall be paid for at the cost price by all others.

ART. 68. Les proprietaires ou fermiers principaux de biens ruraux, devront veiller à ce que les enfans en bas age qui se trouveront sur la propriété

ART. 68. Proprietors and principal farmers of rural properties, shall take care that infant children are properly taken care of: one or more nurses shall

---

* See Note to Articles 51 and 52.

soient bien soignés, a cet effet, une ou plusieurs gardiennes seront expres affectées a ce soin; le paiement de ces soins sera supporté par les agriculteurs, en raison du nombre de leurs enfans.

be appointed for this purpose; the expences attending this, shall be borne by the labourers.

CHAP. III.
Des Obligations des Agriculteurs, envers les Propriétaires, Fermiers, ou Gerans.

CHAP. III.
Of the Duties of Labourers towards Proprietors, Farmers, or Overseers.

ART. 69. Les agriculteurs seront soumis et respectueux envers les propriétaires et fermiers avec lesquelles, ils auront contractés, ainsi qu'envers les gerans.

ART. 69. Labourers shall be submissive and respectful to the proprietors and farmers with whom they have contracted, as well as to the overseers.

ART. 70. Les agriculteurs devront exécuter avec zèle et exactitude tous les travaux agricoles qui leur seront commandés par les proprietaires, fermiers, ou gerans, avec lesquels ils auront contractés.

ART. 70. Labourers shall perform with zeal and exactitude, whatever agricultural labours may be required of them by the proprietors, farmers, or overseers, with whom they have contracted.

ART. 71. Les agriculteurs, a quelque titre ou

ART. 71. Labourers, under whatever name, or

condition qu'ils aient contractés seront obligés de consacrer tout leurs temps aux dits travaux et de ne s'en detourner aucunement, ils ne pourront s'absenter de leur demeure que du Samedi matin au Lundi avant le lever du soleil, sans le consentèment des propriétaires, fermiers principaux, au gerans; pour tous les autres jours ouvrables; ils seront tenus d'avoir un permis du proprietaire, fermier principal, ou grant, s'ils ne doivent pas sortir de la commune; dans le cas contraire ce permis sera vise de l'Officier de la Police Rurale de la section, et du Commandant de la place.

upon whatever condition they may have bound themselves, shall consecrate the whole of their time to such labour, and shall not quit it upon any pretence whatever; they shall not absent themselves from their houses at any time, but from Saturday morning until Monday before sun-rise, without permission from the proprietor, farmer, or overseer; on all other days of labour, they shall be required to have a permit from the proprietor, head farmer, or overseer, if they are not to go beyond the bounds of their commune; for all other purposes, the permit must be countersigned by the Officer commanding the Rural Police of the section, and by the Commandant of the place*.

Art. 72. Les cultivateurs travaillant au quart, ou associés de moitié dans

Art. 72. Labourers working at quarter produce, or those entitled to half pro-

---

* See Article 187.

les produits, serons tenus de preparer et mettre en etat de livraison la portion de denrées du proprietaire ou fermier principal, de conduire cette denrée, au lieu de la livraison, moyennant que le proprietaire ou fermier principal fournisse les moyens de transport.

duce, shall be bound to prepare, and to put into condition for delivery, the part of the produce appertaining to the proprietor or farmer, and to convey it to the place of delivery, the means of transport being provided by the proprietor or farmer.

CHAP. IV.

Des Sous-Traités entre les Agriculteurs de Moitié et les Cultivateurs employés par eux.

CHAP. IV.

Of the Sub-Treaties between Agriculturists at Half Produce and the Labourers employed by them.

ART. 73. Les sous-fermiers, et les chefs de sociéte sur les habitations, auront la faculté de soustraiter directement avec les agriculteurs : mais ils demeureront responsables envers le proprietaire ou le fermier principal des faits des sous-contractans.

ART. 73. Sub-farmers, and head-men of bands upon plantations, shall have the power of sub-contracting with labourers; but they shall be answerable to the proprietor or head farmer, for the conduct of the persons they engage.

ART. 74. Le nombre des sous-contractans ne pourra

ART. 74. The number of sub-contractors shall ne-

exceder celui de dix par chaque sous-fermier ou chef de societé.

ver exceed ten for each sub-farmer or head-man*.

CHAP. V.

Des Regles relatives a ceux qui sont au Service de la Republique, et qui demeurent et travaillent sur les Proprietés Rurales.

CHAP. V.

Rules respecting Persons in the Service of the Republic, residing and working upon Plantations.

ART. 75. Les militaires en activité de service, ou autre personnes employées par l'Etat, pourront prendre des arrangemens avec les propriétaires ou sous-fermiers principaux, des chefs de societé de moitié ou sous-fermiers pour travailler a l'agriculture, soit au quart ou a la moitié, soit comme sous-fermiers: dans ce cas, ils seront soumis a toutes les obligations qu'ils auront contracté, et qui seront compatibles avec leurs devoirs publics.

ART. 75. Soldiers in active service, and other persons employed by the State, shall be permitted to engage themselves to proprietors, farmers, headmen of bands working at half produce, or sub-farmers, for agricultural labour, either at quarter or half produce, or as sub-farmers: they shall be liable to all the engagements they may contract, so far as the same may be compatible with their public duties.

---

* This and the preceding article savour strongly of personal slavery. Here we have persons having no land of their own, allowed to procure others to bind themselves to them, and they are authorized to sell the labours of these bondmen.

ART. 76. Lorsque les militaires, ou autres employés au service de l'Etat, qui ont fixé leur demeure sur une habitation, n'auront aucune contrat avec le proprietaire, ou fermier de cette proprieté; ils pourront prendre avec lui verbalement, ou par ècrit, des arrangemens pour travailler par semaine, par mois, ou à l'entreprise, d'apres les prix et conditions qui seront convenu entre eux; mais ces militaires seront obligés de concourir, sans paiement particulier, a tous les travaux relatifs a l'entretien des canaux d'arrosage et autres, des puits, et citernes, de la propriété, des entourages ou clotures des jardins, et savannes, et au maintien du bon ordre sur la propriété.

ART. 76. When soldiers, or other persons in the employ of the State, who have taken up their abode upon a plantation, shall have entered into no engagement with the proprietor or farmer of the plantation; they may make a verbal or written contract with him, to labour by the week, by the month, or by the piece, upon whatever terms and conditions they please; but these soldiers shall be obliged to join, without remuneration, in all labours necessary for repairing the water-courses, wells, and cisterns upon the estate, the hedges and enclosures of gardens and meadows, and in maintaining order upon the plantation.

ART. 77. Lorsque les militaires, ou autres employés au service de l'Etat, ne se conformeront pas, envers les proprietaires ou fermiers principaux des biens sur lesquels ils resideront,

ART. 77. When soldiers, or other persons in the employ of the State, shall not comport themselves towards the owners or farmers of the estate upon which they dwell, accord-

aux Articles 75 et 76 de la presente Loi, ils pourront être renvoyés de la dite propriété.

Art. 78. Les militaires, ou autres employés au service de l'Etat, qui contracteront avec des proprietaires ou fermiers, pour travailler à gages par semaine ou autrement, devront respecter les dites proprietaires, fermiers, ou gérans de la propriété sur laquelle ils travailleront, et leur obeir.

Art. 79. Lorsque les militaires, ou autres employés au service de l'Etat, auront été requis par le proprietaire, fermier principal, ou gerant, pour travailler a la journée, a la semaine, a l'entreprise ou autrement, dans un champ cultivé par les agriculteurs travaillant au quart, ou pour aider à la manufacture, ou à faire la recolte des denrées; les gages payés a ces sortes de travailleurs, seront deduits

ing to Articles 75 and 76 of this Law, they may be sent off the property.

Art. 78. Soldiers, or others in the service of the State, who engage themselves to proprietors or farmers, to labour for wages by the week or otherwise, shall respect and obey the owners, farmers, or overseers of the estate, to whom they have engaged themselves.

Art. 79. When soldiers, or others employed in the service of the State, are required by the proprietor, farmer, or overseer, to work by the day, the week, the job, or otherwise, in a field cultivated by labourers working at quarter produce, or to assist in gathering in its produce, or the manufacture of it, their wages shall be deducted from the gross amount of the proceeds of such labour, before the quarter

de la masse du revenu provenant de ce travail, avant que le quart afférent aux cultivateurs soit prelève.

Art. 80. Lorsque des travailleurs, tels que ceux mentionnés en l'Article précédent, seront requis par des chefs de societé de moitié, afin de les aider dans leurs travaux, les gages payés a ces travailleurs seront prelévés par la portion revenant aux associés de moitié avant que le partage puisse s'effecteur entr'eux.

Si ces travailleurs quittaient de leurs propre volonté, le travail pour lequel ils auraient été requis, avant la fin de la semaine, ils n'auront rien a prétendre pour le temps qu'ils auront travaillé pendant le commencement de cette même semaine.

belonging to the other labourers is separated.

Art. 80. When labourers, such as those mentioned in the preceding Article, are called upon by head-men of bands entitled to half the produce, to aid them in their labours, their wages shall be paid out of the moiety of the produce coming to such labourers, before the division of it takes place.

If these labourers quit the work they have contracted to do, of their own free will, before the end of the week, they shall be entitled to no remuneration for the time they may have laboured during the beginning of the week*.

---

* This, and the nine preceding Articles, recognize a class of labourers who are the only free labourers in Haïti.

CHAP. VI.

Du Mode pour regler et terminer les Difficultés entre les Proprietaires, Fermiers, Gerans, et les Agriculteurs, Associés de Moitié, Sous-Fermier, etc.

Art. 81. Lorsqu'il surviendra entre des proprietaires, agricoles, fermiers principaux, gerans, et les agriculteurs, associés de moitié, ou sous fermiers, des differends ; les parties porteront *d'abord* leur plaintes ou reclamations pardevant *l'Officier de la Police Rurale de la section,* lequel, assisté si besoin est, du Conseil d'Agriculture du quartier, s'occupera de suite de terminer a l'aimable les differends, en ce qui sera de sa compétence.

Art. 82. Dans le cas ou les differends seraient de nature à ne pas être terminés par l'intervention de

CHAP. VI.

Of the Mode of deciding all Disputes between Proprietors, Farmers, Overseers, and Agriculturers at Half Produce, Sub-Farmers, &c.

Art. 81. When difficulties arise between proprietors, agriculturists, farmers, overseers, and agriculturers at half produce, or sub-farmers, the parties shall *in the first instance* carry their complaints before *the Officer commanding the Rural Police of the section,* who, being assisted, if necessary, by the Council of Agriculture of the district*, shall endeavour to bring about a compromise between the parties, in all matter falling within his jurisdiction.

Art. 82. When the matter in dispute cannot be settled by the Officer commanding the Rural Police,

---

* See Article 165, for some account of this Council.

l'Officier de la Police Rurale, assisté du Conseil d'Agriculture, il invitera les parties a se choisir des arbîtres, dans la section même, pour regler et terminer leur differends.

Art. 83. Dans le cas ou les differends ne pourraient pas encore se terminer par l'arbitrage sur les lieux, ou que les parties n'auraient pas nommé leurs arbitres, l'Officier de la Police Rurale attendra un Samedi, ou un Dimanche pour renvoyer les parties devant le Juge de Paix de la commune: le tout devra se faire dans le delai de six jours au plus.

Art. 84. Le Juge de Paix sera tenu de decider du differend, *et ne pourra, sous peine de deni de justice, arguer du silence de la Loi sur le cas qui sera présenté a sa decision.*

Art. 85. Le Juge de

assisted by the Council of Agriculture, he shall require the parties to name arbitrators within the section, to regulate and terminate their differences.

Art. 83. When the matters in dispute cannot be decided by arbitration on the spot, or where the parties have neglected to name arbitrators, the Officer commanding the Rural Police shall wait until Saturday or Sunday, to refer the parties to the Justice of Peace of the commune: the delay must not exceed six days.

Art. 84. The Justice of Peace is bound to decide the matter in dispute, *and shall not alledge the silence of the Law on the matter in dispute, as a ground for refusing to give judgment, under penalty of a denial of justice.*

Art. 85. The Justice of

Paix devra prononcer *dans le delai de vingt-quatre heures,* ou plus, apres la comparation des parties,

Peace shall give judgment *within twenty-four hours* after the appearance of the parties.

No. 4. LOI.

SUR LES HATTES.

Des Etablissemens et de l'Administration des Hattes.

LAW. No. 4.

UPON CATTLE-PENS.

Establishments and Management of Cattle-Pens.

Art. 86. Les hattes ne pourront être etablies que dans les lieux suffisamment eloignés des habitations cultivées en denrées, et a une lieu de distance au moins.

Art. 86. Cattle-pens shall only be established at places, at the least one league distant from plantations.

Art. 87. A l'avenir, pour établir une hatte, il faudra être proprietaire au moin de cinquante carreaux de terre garnie des pâturages necessaires pour bêtes à cornes, et de vingt cinq carreaux pour pourceaux.

Art. 87. Hereafter no one shall establish a pen for horned cattle, who has not at the least 150 acres of pasture land; and for hogs 75 acres.

Art. 88. Le nombre des gardeurs des hattes ne pourra exceder cinq hommes y compris le maitre-

Art. 88. The number of keepers shall not in any case exceed five men, including the head-keeper,

hattier, ayant avec eux leurs femmes et leurs enfans.

with their wives and children*.

ART. 89. Tout gardeur de hatte qui trouvera dans les troupaux confiés a ses soins, ou dans les savannes de la hatte sur laquelle il est employé, des animaux etrangers a ceux qu'il garde, sera tenu d'en avertir sur le champ les hattiers voisins, et si ces animaux ne sont pas de leurs hattes, il en sera donné connaissance à l'Officier de la Police Rurale de la section.

ART. 89. When a keeper finds among the herds entrusted to him, or in the meadows belonging to the pen in which he is employed, stray-cattle, he shall forthwith give notice thereof to the neighbouring keepers, and if the cattle do not belong to their pens, he shall send notice to the Officer commanding the RuralPolice of the section.

ART. 90. Après que les animaux mentionnés en l'Article ci-dessus, seront resté trois mois dans la savanne d'une hatte, sans être reclamés par leur propriétaire, ils seront conduits par le hattier au Juge de Paix de la commune, afin de les faire mener aux èpaves.

ART. 90. When the cattle mentioned in the precedingArticle have remained three months in a pen, unclaimed, they shall be conducted by the penkeeper to the Justice of Peace of the commune, to be placed among the strays.

---

* This limitation is doubtless intended to check the natural inclination of the negro population to a life of indolence. This clause is conceived in the same spirit as Article 7.

Art. 91. Aussitôt qu'un animal d'une hatte sera reconnu être attaqué d'une maladie contagieuse, il devra, sous peine d'une amende de dix à vingt gourdes, payable par le hattier, etre separé, et mis hors de toute communication avec les autres bestiaux, pour etre traité jusqu'á sa guerison ou sa mort.

Art. 92. Tout animal mort sur une hatte d'une maladie contagieuse ou epizootique, sera brulé ou enterré.

Art. 93. Il est defendu, sous peine d'une amende de dix à vingt gourdes payable par tout contrevenant, de brûler les savannes des hattes sans la permission de l'Officier de la Police Rurale de la section.

Art. 94. Lorsqu'il arrivera que des bestiaux mourront sur les habitations de maladies ordinaires, ou

Art. 91. When any animal in a pen shall be found to be attacked by any contagious disease, it shall be instantly separated from the other cattle, and taken care of until its recovery or death, under penalty of a fine of not less than ten, nor more than twenty dollars, to be paid by the penkeeper.

Art. 92. Every animal which dies in a pen of a contagious or epizootic disease, shall be burnt or buried.

Art. 93. It is strictly forbidden, under penalty of a fine of not less than ten, nor more than twenty dollars, to burn the savannas or meadows of pens without the permission of the Officer commanding the Rural Police.

Art. 94. When cattle upon plantations die from ordinary disease, or accident, in the absence of the

par accident, si le proprietaire ou fermier, principal de la hatte n'est pas present, le mâitre-hattier sera tenu de faire constater, par l'Officier de la Police Rurale, ou des voisins, la mort de l'animal; la peau, ayant l'étempe ou la marque sera produite au proprietaire; à defaut de quoi, il sera tenu de remplacer l'animal.

ART. 95. Les animaux tant des hattes, que ceux servant a l'exploitation des habitations, ne pourront être étempés qu'avec des étempes moulées, il est defendu de faire, sur ces animaux, des marques a la main.

proprietor or farmer, the head pen-keeper shall procure a certificate of the death of the animal from the Officer commanding the Rural Police, or from the neighbours; and the skin, having the stamp or brand, shall be produced to the proprietor; in default of which, the pen-keeper shall replace the animal.

ART. 95. Animals belonging to pens, as well as those used in cultivation upon plantations, shall be stamped with brand-marks only—it is strictly forbidden to make any marks upon them by the hand.

CHAP. II.

Des Contrats entre Propriétaires ou Fermiers de Hattes, et ceux qui y sont attachés.

ART. 96. Les proprietaires ou fermiers de hattes, ne pourront recevoir

CHAP. II.

Of the Engagements to be entered into between the Proprietors or Farmers of Cattle Pens, and those attached to them.

ART. 96. Proprietors or farmers of cattle pens, shall not receive or employ

sur leurs hattes, aucuns gardiens ou autre gens, qu'au prealable ils n'aient contracté avec eux, conformement a l'Article 47 de la Loi, No. 3.

upon their pens, any keepers, or other persons, who have not previously bound themselves, as directed by Article 47, of Law 3.

Art. 97. Les obligations imposées reciproquement aux proprietaires ou fermiers ruraux, ainsi qu'a ceux qui cultivent, seront communes aux proprietaires ou fermiers de hattes et leurs employés en tout ce que concernera le bon ordre et la police generale.

Art. 97. The duties reciprocally imposed upon proprietors and farmers, and those who labour, shall also extend to proprietors or farmers of cattle pens, and those employed by them, so far as the same relate to order and general police.

Art. 98. Ne pourront les maitres hattiers, ou les autres hattiers recevoir sur les hattes ou ils seront employés, pour autrui des animaux ou bestiaux, sans le consentement du proprietaire ou fermier de la hatte.

Art. 98. Keepers of cattle pens shall not be permitted to receive upon their master's pen, any cattle or beasts, without permission of the proprietor or farmer of the pen.

Art. 99. Ne pourra le maitre hattier ni les autres hattiers, deplacer ou vendre aucun animal de la hatte, sans avoir, par

Art. 99. The pen-keeper shall not remove or sell any animal belonging to the pen, unless he produce the permission of the pro-

ecrit l'agrement de proprietaire ou fermier, et sans un permis, sur papier timbré, de l'Officer de la Police Rurale de la section, qui sera tenu d'enregistrer le permis avec l'étempe des animaux.

prietor or farmer in writing; and a permit upon stamped paper from the Officer commanding the Rural Police of the section, who shall register the permit and the brand of the animal.

No. 5. LOI.

Sur la garde et la conduite des Animaux, et sur les Degats qu'ils commettent dans les Champs.

ART. 100. Les bestiaux des cultivateurs, seront gardés en troupaux avec ceux du proprietaire, et les gardiens seront payés de leur salaire, moitié par le proprietaire, et moitié par les agriculteurs.

ART. 101. Il est defendre de mutiler, estropier, ou tuer les bêtes de charge ou les bêtes a cornes, que l'on pourrait trouver dans les champs cultivés ou jardins, pour en avoir franchi ou forcé les clotures.

LAW. No. 5.

Upon the care and keeping of Animals, and upon the Damage they may do in the Fields.

ART. 100. Cattle belonging to labourers, shall be kept in herds along with those of the proprietor, and the keepers shall be paid their salaries, half by the proprietor, and half by the labourers.

ART. 101. It is forbidden to kill or maim beasts of burden, or horned cattle, found trespassing upon cultivated land, or in gardens.

Art. 102. Il est egale-
ment defendre de blesser
ou de tuer les moutons
qui se seront introduits
dans les jardins en culture
et clôtures.

Art. 103. Il est permis
de tuer les cochous et ca-
bris trouvés dans les jardins cultivés et clôtures.

Art. 104. Les bestiaux
mentionés aux Articles 101
et 102, du present chapitre
qui seront trouvés dans
des jardins en culture seront conduit vingt-quatre
heures apres leur arrestation au Juge de Paix pour
les envoyer aux épaves de
la commune si avan ce
delai, le proprietaire des
animaux arretés, ne les fait
retirer du parc de l'habitation, dans les jardins de
laquelle ils auraient été
arretés.

Art. 105. L'Officier de
la Police Rurale de la section sera tenu de constater
par proces-verbal dans les
vingt-quatre heures de la

Art. 102. It is likewise
forbidden to kill or maim
sheep found trespassing
in fenced gardens, or en-
closures.

Art. 103. Pigs and goats
found trespassing in fenced
gardens or enclosures, may
be killed.

Art. 104. The animals
enumerated in Articles 101
and 102, which may be
found in cultivated gar-
dens, shall be conducted
24 hours afterwards, before
a Justice of Peace, to be
sent to the pound, unless
within that time the owner
of them withdraw them
from the pen belonging to
the plantation upon which
they may be found.

Art. 105. The Officer
commanding the Rural
Police shall, within twenty-
four hours after complaint
made by the parties in-

declaration des parties interessées, les degats commis par les animaux, et d'envoyer proces-verbal au Juge de Paix, si l'indemnité du degat n'est pas volontairement payée au proprietaire du jardin ravagé.

jured, draw up in writing, a statement of the damage done by the animals, and send it to the Justice of Peace, unless compensation be voluntarily made to the owner of the garden.

Art. 106. L'Officier de la Police Rurale aura soin d'adresser au Juge de Paix de la commune, le procés verbal en bonne forme mentionné en l'Article 105, pour être par le dit Juge de Paix, statué ce que de-droit.

Art. 106. The Officer of Rural Police shall take care that he send the written statement to the Justice of Peace, duly certified, that the said Justice may be able to decide according to law.

Art. 107. Le gardeurs qui auront laissé echapper les animaux mentionnés en l'Article 27, confiés a leur garde, seront tenus de payer la prise des dits animaux d'apres le tarif établi par la loi.

Art. 107. The keepers who may have suffered the animals mentioned in Article 27, to escape, shall pay the expences attending their recapture, according to the tarif established by law.

Art. 108. Il est expressèment dependu aux proprietaires, fermier, ou gerans des habitations de se servir aucunement des bestiaux arretés dans leurs

Art. 108. Proprietors, farmers, or overseers upon plantations, are expressly forbidden to work, or use in any manner, the animals found in their gardens,

jardins, pendant le temps qu'ils resteront dans leur parcs, avant d'etre envoyé aux épaves ; toute contravention a cet egard sera punie d'une amende de cinq a quinze gourdes.

during the time they may remain in their pens before they are sent to the pound ; any infringement of this article shall be punished by a fine of not less than five, nor more than fifteen dollars.

Art. 109. La prise des animaux mentionnée aux Articles 101 et 102, de la presente loi, dans les jardins, lorsque ces animaux auront été conduits jusqu'aux épaves de la commune sera payée comme suit : chaque bête cavaline, une gourde, chaque asine, soixante quinze centimes, chaque bête a cornes, une gourde cinquant centimes; chaque bêlier ou brébis vingt - cinque centimes, dont la moitié appartiendra au capteur, et l'autre moitié aux gardes champêtres.

Art. 109. The capture of the animals enumerated in Articles 101 and 102, taken in gardens, and conducted to the pound, shall be paid for as follows : for each horse or mule, one dollar; for each ass, seventy-five cents ; for each head of horned cattle, one and a half dollars ; and for each sheep, twenty-five cents : one half to belong to the person taking them, and one half to the guards.

Art. 110. Lorsque les animaux arretés dans les jardins, auront été retirés du parc de l'habitation avant d'être envoyés aux

Art. 110. When animals taken in gardens, are withdrawn from the pen before they are sent to the pound, the owner shall

epaves, alors ou payera qu'aux capteurs seul, pour leur prise, la moitié de la taxe etablie en l'Article precedent.

pay half the above fines to the person who takes them, only.

ART. 111. Si un animal arreté dans un jardin, et conduit au parc de l'habitation, vient à mourir par accident ou autrement, pendant le peu de temps qu'il doit y rester, ou si l'animal mourait dans le trajet de l'habitation a la demeure du Juge de Paix de la commune, l'Officier de la Police devra faire constater, par temoins, les causes de la mort de l'animal.

ART. 111. When an animal taken in a garden, and sent to the pen, happens to die by accident, or otherwise, during the short time he remains there, or while it is being conducted to the residence of the Justice of Peace belonging to the commune, the Officer commanding the Police shall call for witnesses, to prove the cause of the death of the animal.

ART. 112. Dans le cas ou la mort de l'animal aurait été provoquée par negligence, par defaut de nourriture, ou par violences, le proprietaire, fermier, ou gerant de l'habitation, devra rembourser la valeur de l'animal à dire d'arbitres nommés par le Juge de Paix de la commune. Le montant ainsi payé sera

ART. 112. When the death of the animal shall prove to have been occasioned by negligence, want of food, or violence, the proprietor, farmer, or overseer of the plantation, shall pay for it according to its value, to be estimated by arbitrators named by the Justice. The amount thus paid, shall be remitted to

adressé en place de l'animal, au ministère public du ressort pour etre remis au proprietaire, s'il se presente, ou versé à la caisse. Dans tous les cas, les degats commis par l'animal seront payés sur ce produit.

the administration of the district, to be paid to the owner of the animal, should he appear, or to be paid into the treasury. In all cases, the damage done by the animal shall be paid for out of this money.

ART. 113. Lorsque les animaux arrêtés dans les jardins, en vertu de l'Article 104, seront conduits chez le Juge de Paix de la commune, pour etre envoyés aux épaves, si le proprietaire consentait à payer les degats commis par l'animal, ainsi que les frais de prise, avant l'entrée aux épaves, le Juge de Paix devra y acquiescer.

ART. 113. When animals taken in gardens, by virtue of Article 104, are conducted to the Justice of Peace of the commune, to be sent to the pound, if the owner consent to pay for the damage done, and the expences of capture, before the beast be sent to the pound, the Justice of Peace shall consent.

ART. 114. Ceux qui conduisent les troupeaux de bestiaux d'une commune à une autre, soit pour le commerce, soit pour l'agriculture, seront tenus de se munir de permis, mentionnant la nature et la quantité d'animaux qu'ils me-

ART. 114. Persons conducting herds of cattle from one commune to another, whether for sale, or for agricultural purposes, shall provide themselves with a permit, setting forth the kind and number of the animals they are conduct-

nent, leurs signalemens et etempes.

ing, their description and brands.

Art. 115. Les permis seront delivrés par les Commandans des communes, ou visés par eux sur les permis des proprietaires, ou sur les certificats des Officiers de la Police Rurale des sections d'ou seront sortis les animaux. Les permis seront enregistrés par ceux qui les delivreront, et visés par les Commandans de toutes les communes ou passeront les troupeaux.

Art. 115. These permits shall be delivered by the Commandants of communes, or countersigned by them, upon permits given by the owners, or upon certificates furnished by the Officer commanding the Rural Police of the sections from whence the animals come. These permits must be registered by those who give them, and countersigned by the Commandants of the communes through which the herds may pass.

Art. 116. Les conducteurs* de troupeaux qui seront rencontrès par la police rurale ou la gendarmerie, seront tenus sur la demande qui leur sera faite, d'exhiber leur permis; et dans le cas ou le nombre des animaux et leur signalemens ne se-

Art. 116. The drivers of herds, who may be met by the police or gend'armerie, shall, upon demand, shew their permits; and where the number of beasts, or their description, shall not be found to agree with the enumeration in the permit, they may, should

---

* This expression is likewise applied to the head-man of a gang of labourers.

raient pas, d'accord avec l'énoncé, du permis ils pourront, s'il y a des causes de suspicion contr'eux, être arretés et conduits au poste le plus voisin, avec les animaux, pour-etre menés pardevant le Juge de Paix de la commune.

cause of suspicion exist, be taken up, and conducted to the nearest post, with the animals in their possession, to be taken before the Justice of Peace of the commune.

ART. 117. Si les personnes menées pardevant le Juge de Paix ne prouvent par leur droit de propriété sur les animaux pour lesquels il n'y aurait pas de permis, si elles ne donnent pas de caution valable pour rapporter dans le delai qui leur sera accordé, et qui ne pourra excéder la quinzaine, la preuve de ce droit de propriété, elles seront envoyées à la maison d'arret et les animaux arrétés seront conduits aux epaves.

ART. 117. If the parties taken before the Justice, cannot prove their right of property in those animals not included in the permit, and if they cannot give good and sufficient security for their re-appearance with such proof, within the time to be allowed them, not exceeding fifteen days, they shall be committed to prison, and the animals sent to the pound.

ART. 118. Dans le mois a dater du jour de l'arrestation, le Juge de Paix sera tenu d'ecrire au Juge de Paix de la commune d'ou serait sortie cette per-

ART. 118. Within one month from the day of the arrest, the Justice shall write to the Justice of the commune from which the party committed may

sonne, ou à l'Officier de la Police Rurale de la section (si c'est dans la même commune) afin d'avoir des renseignemens, tant sur la personne, que sur les animaux arrètés, lesquels renseignemens seront addressés, a leur reception, au Ministre Public avec le procès verbal de la Justice de Paix, et feront piéces au dossier à charge contre le prevenu, s'il y a lieu à le poursuivre.	come, or to the Officer commanding the Rural Police of the section to which he belongs, if within the same commune, to make enquiries about the person committed, and the animals stopped: upon receipt of this information, it shall be forwarded to the Public Minister, together with a written statement from the Justice, as the grounds of ulterior proceedings against the party detained, should sufficient cause appear for such proceedings.

No. 6. LOI. / LAW. No. 6.
SUR LA POLICE RURALE. / RURAL POLICE.

TITRE PREMIER. / FIRST HEAD.
Dispositions Générales. / *General Enactments.*

ART. 119. La Police Rurale embrasse tout ce qui tient à l'administration et a la prosperité des propriétés rurales.

ART. 119. Rural Police embraces every thing that concerns the administration and prosperity of rural properties.

ART. 120. La Police

ART. 120. Rural Police

Rurale se fait sous l'inspection des Commandans d'arrondissement et des Commandans des communes; par des Officiers de Police Rurale placés dans les sections de chaque commune, par les gardes champetres, par la gendarmerie, et, au besoin *par des detachemens de troupes de ligne.*

Art. 121. Les Juges de Paix exercent aussi la Police Rurale dans les cas prevus par le loi.

Art. 122. Les Conseils des Notables des communes, et les Conseils d'Agriculture assistent, au besoin toutes les autorités, pour le maintien parfait de la surveillance de la Police Agricole.

shall be carried into effect under the inspection of Commandants of districts and Commandants of communes; by Officers commanding the Rural Police, to be stationed in sections of each commune, by guards, by gendarmerie, and, in cases of necessity, *by detachments of troops of the line.*

Art. 121. Justices of Peace have also authority to exercise Rural Police in the cases provided by law.

Art. 122. The Councils of Notables, and the Councils of Agriculture, assist the authorities, in cases of necessity, to secure perfect superintendance and inspection by the Agricultural Police.

TITRE SECOND.
DE LA SURVEILLANCE.

CHAP. PREMIER.
De la Haute Inspection des Commandans d'Arrondissement.

Art. 123. Le Commandant d'arrondissement militaire ayant l'inspection generale sur les cultures de l'arrondissement qui lui est confié, il reunit toute l'autorité necessaire pour la mise en activité de la culture; il est responsable,

1. De l'etat de deperissement des cultures dans l'etendu de son commandement.
2. De l'execution du tout ou partie du Code d'Agriculture dans l'etendu de son arrondissement.
3. De la negligence des Commandans des communes sous ses ordres, relativement a la surveillance sur l'agriculture dans la commune qui leur est

SECOND HEAD.
OF THE INSPECTION.

CHAP. I.
Of the Supreme Inspection of Commanders of Districts.

Art. 123. The Commandant of each military district, having the general inspection of the cultivation of the district entrusted to him, unites in his own person, all the authority necessary for enforcing agriculture; he is responsible,

1. For the decay of agriculture in his district.

2. For the due execution of all, or part of the Code of Agriculture within his district.
3. For the neglect of Commandants of communes under his command, to inspect and superintend agriculture within their respective com-

confiée, lorsqu'il n'aura pas reprimé cette negligence.

munes, when he has not prevented such neglect.

Art. 124. Le Commandant de l'arrondissement est obligé de faire une fois chaque année dans toutes les sections rurales des differentes communes composant l'arrondissement, afin de s'assurer par lui meme de l'execution des lois, des progrès, et de la situation des travaux, et en faire le rapport détaillé au President d'Haïti*.

Art. 124. The Commandant of each district shall inspect once in each year, each rural section in the several communes composing his district, and inform himself personally, of the due execution of the laws, and of the progress and state of labour; and make a detailed report of these matters to the President of Haïti.

Art. 125. Le rapport que doit faire le Commandant d'arrondissement, chaque année au President d'Haïti, fera mention de la quantité d'habitations de chaque section, qui sont entretenues, de leur genre de culture, de leur amelioration, ou de leur deperissement, et en-

Art. 125. The yearly report which the Commandant of each district is required to make to the President of Haïti, shall state the number of plantations kept up in each section, the nature of their produce, an account of their improvement or falling off, and lastly, the

---

* Some word appears to be omitted here. I have been careful to copy the Rural Code verbatim from the printed copy, retaining even all its faults of French.

fin, de l'etat des routes et chemins publics et particuliers.

state of the public and private roads*.

CHAP. II.

De l'Inspection des Commandans de Place et Commune.

Art. 126. Le Commandant de-place ou de commune à l'inspection principale des culture de la commune qui lui est confiée; s'il a sous ses ordres des cantons ou paroises erigés en postes militaires, les Commandans de ces postes ont l'inspection particulière de la culture dans l'étendu du territoire qui forme leur commandement.

Art. 127. Le Commandant de la commune est responsable des decroissemens dans l'etendu de son commandement, lorsque le fait proviendra

CHAP. II.

Of the Inspection of Commandants of Places and Communes.

Art. 126. The Commandant of the place or commune, has the chief inspection of the cultivation of the commune; if he have within his command, cantons or parishes erected into military posts, the Commandants of such posts have the inspection of the cultivation of the territory under their command.

Art. 127. The Commandant of the commune is responsible for the deterioration of the commune within his command, when it arises from negli-

---

* See also Article 14.

de la negligence de quelque parties du service.

ART. 128. Le Commandant de place ou de commune, est obligé de faire trois fois chaque année la tournée des differentes sections dans l'etendu du son ˋcommandement.

ART. 129. Le Commandant de la commune, dans ses tournées, visitera les jardins de denrées, de vivres, les clotures, les nouvelles plantations; il entrera dans tous les details prèvus par le Code Rurale; en s'assurant si l'Officier de la Police Rurale de la section a satisfait a tous le devoirs qui lui sont imposés par la loi. Il reprimera les negligences, les irregularités qu'il reconnaîtra et de tout il sera dressé proces-verbal dans la forme prescrite pour chaque section, le double en sera addressé au Commandant d'arrondissement.

gence in any part of the service.

ART. 128. The Commandant of the place or commune, shall go the round of the different sections within his command, three times in every year.

ART. 129. The Commandant of the commune, in his rounds, shall visit the fields, provision-grounds, enclosures and new plantations. He shall examine into all the details set forth in the Rural Code; he shall enquire whether the Officer commanding the Rural Police has duly performed all the duties imposed upon him by law. He shall repress all negligences and irregularities, and shall draw up a report of the whole in the form prescribed for each section, a copy of which shall be forwarded to the Commandant of the district.

CHAP. III.

Des Sections Rurales, des Officiers de la Police Rurale, des Gardes Champêtres, des Gerans et Conducteurs d'Habitations.

Sect. Première.
Des Sections Rurales.

Art. 130. Les communes seront, par un reglement particulier du President d'Haïti, pour chaque arrondissement militaire, divisées en sections agricoles, dans la plaine de quatre lieues environ; et dans les mornes, suivant la nature du terrain.

Art. 131. Chaque section sera designée par un nom qui lui sera propre; ses limites et abornemens seront determinés.

Art. 132. Aussitot apres la formation des sections il sera dressé par le Commandant de la commune, le Conseil des Notables,

CHAP. III.

Of Rural Sections, Officers commanding the Rural Police, Guards, and of Overseers and Drivers upon Plantations.

Sect. 1.
Of Rural Sections.

Art. 130. The communes shall, by an ordinance for that purpose, to be made by the President of Haïti for each district, be divided into agricultural sections, of about four leagues extent in the plains; and according to the nature of the ground in the mountains.

Art. 131. Each section shall be named, and its limits and boundaries fixed.

Art. 132. As soon as the sections are formed, the Commandant of the commune, assisted by the Council of Notables, and

et un des arpenteurs particuliers, en triple, sur des cahiers cotés par le Juge de Paix, le role de toutes les propriétés rurales qui se trouverout situées dans chaque section, avec designation des noms des proprietaires, de la contenance de chaque propriété et du genre de culture qui s'y fait. Un des cahiers sera deposé au bureau du Commandant de la commune, un au Conseil des Notables, et l'autre es mains de l'Officier de la Police Rurale de la section.

one of the private surveyors, shall draw up, upon schedules prepared by the Justice of Peace, triple rolls of all plantations situated in each section, with the names of the proprietors, the extent of each property, and the kind of tillage carried on upon each plantation. One of these rolls shall be deposited in the office of the Commandant of the commune, one with the Council of Notables, and the third in the hands of the Officer commanding the Rural Police of the section.

ART. 133. Le Conseil des Notables fournira au Juge de Paix de la commune une copie collationnée du cahier deposé en son greffe. Le Commandant de la commune fournira au Commandant de l'arrondissement une copie du meme cahier deposé en son bureau. Le Commandant d'arrondissement, apres avoir réuni les roles des pro-

ART. 133. The Council of Notables shall furnish the Justice of Peace of the commune with an examined copy of the schedule deposited in their office. The Commandant of the commune shall furnish the Commandant of the district with a similar copy of the schedule deposited in his office. The Commandant of the district, after

priétés de toutes les sections des communes composant l'arrondissement sous ses ordres, en formera un cahier dont il addressera une copie certifié au President d'Haïti.

having collected the rolls of plantations of all the sections of each commune forming his district, shall draw up a schedule of the whole, a copy of which he shall forward to the President of Haïti.

ART. 134. A chaque mutation de propriété d'un bien rural situé dans une section, a chaque changement de culture, l'Officier de la Police Rurale en donnera avis au Commandant de la commune, que en fera mention sur le rôle deposé en son bureau et en transmettra l'avis au Commandant de l'arrondissement, qui, lui même, apres avoir fait inscrire le changement à la copie du role dont il est depositaire en informera le Gouvernement.

ART. 134. The Officer commanding the Rural Police shall give notice to the Commandant of the commune, of each transfer of a rural property situated within the section, and of each change in the mode of cultivation adopted. The Commandant of the commune shall note such transfer or change of cultivation upon the roll deposited in his office, and shall give notice of the same to the Commandant of the district, who shall likewise note the same upon the roll in his hands, and inform the Government of it.

ART. 135. Le Conseil d'Agriculture de la section, donnera au Conseil des Notable de la commune,

ART. 135. The Council of Agriculture of the section, shall give the notice mentioned in the preceding

l'avis mentionne en l'Article precedent; et le Conseil des Notables, apres en avoir pris note, en donnera connoissance au Juge de Paix, que fera inscrire la mutation sur la copie du role deposée en son greffe.

Art. 136. Chaque année, du premier au quinze Fevrier, les Officiers de la Police Rurale de chaque section, recevront, des agens de l'administration des finances de leur commune, un nombre determiné des etats de population en blanc, et timbrés, qu'ils seront tenus de fournir au proprietaire, fermier, ou gerant, de chaque habitation de la section, avant le fin du meme mois, en recevant le prix du timbre qu'ils verseront à l'agent de l'administration des finances; cette repartition se fera comme suit: aux proprietaires des biens contenant jusqu'a dix carreaux de terre, l'etat de population sera du timbre de *douze*

Article to the Council of Notables of commune; and the Council of Notables, after having noted it, shall inform the Justice of Peace, who shall cause the same to be inscribed upon the copy of the roll deposited in his office.

Art. 136. Every year, between the first and fifteenth of February, the Officers commanding the Rural Police of each section, shall receive from the agents for taxes of their commune, a certain number of stamped schedules of population in blank; which they shall furnish to the proprietor, farmer, or overseer of each plantation of the section, before the end of the same month; receiving from them the value of the stamp, which the officer shall pay over to the agent for taxes. This stamp duty shall be as follows: the stamped schedule of population for an estate containing thirty acres of land, shall be

centimes et demi; a ceux d'ouze jusqu'a vingt carreaux *vingt cinq centimes;* a ceux contenant depuis vingt et un carreaux et au-dessus, *cinquante centimes.*

twelve and a half cents; for *thirty-three* to *sixty* acres, twenty-five cents; for sixty-three acres and upwards, fifty cents.

ART. 137. Les proprietaires, fermiers, ou gerans d'habitations, seront tenus de remettre l'etat de population rempli de la manière qui leur sera indiquée, a l'Officier de la Police Rurale, au plus tard, le vingt mars suivant, sous peine d'une amende qui ne sera pas moindre de quinze ni qui n'excédéra pas cinquante gourdes par chaque délinquant.

ART. 137. The proprietors, farmers, or overseers of plantations, shall return the schedule of population, filled up in the manner pointed out, to the Officer commanding the Rural Police, at the latest on the 20th of March following, under penalty of a fine of not less than fifteen, nor more than fifty dollars.

ART. 138. L'Officier de la Police Rurale de chaque section sera tenu de faire remise au Conseil des Notables de chaque commune, des etats de population de sa section, ou de signaler les delinquans, le cinq Avril, ou plus tard, sous peine d'etre passible, lui même, de l'amende determiné en l'Article precedent.

ART. 138. The Officer commanding the Rural Police of each section shall, on the 5th of April at the latest, return all the schedules of population of his section, or the names of the defaulters, to the Council of Notables of each commune, under penalty of the fine imposed by the preceding Article.

ART. 139. Chaque année, au premier Mai, les Conseils des Notables de chaque commune addresseront au Gouvernement les originaux des etats de population qu'ils auront reçus, en vertu de l'Article précédent.

ART. 139. On the first of May in every year, the Council of Notables of each commune, shall forward to Government the original schedules of population which they may have received, in virtue of the preceding Article.

SECT. 2.

Des Officiers de la Police Rurale, et des Gardes Champêtres.

SECT. 2.

Of the Officers commanding the Rural Police, and of the Guards.

ART. 140. Dans chaque section rurale, il sera placé, par le choix du President d'Haïti un officier militaire de grade subalterne (depuis sous lieutenant jusqu'á capitaine), lequel officier sera chargé de la surveillance de la section, et la police y relative.

ART. 140. A military officer of subaltern rank (from sub-lieutenant to captain) to be named by the President of Haïti, shall be stationed in each rural section: this officer shall be charged with the superintendance of the section, and with its police.

ART. 141. Les Officiers de la Police Rurale des differentes sections, seront independans, les uns des autres et n'auront de rapport qu'avec le Commandant de la commune, et

ART. 141. The Officers commanding the Rural Police of the different sections, shall be independent of each other, and shall report only to the Commandant of the commune,

celui de l'arrondissement sous les ordres desquels ils sont placés ; il correspondront en outre avec les autorités civiles, et déféront a leurs requisitions.

Art. 142. La residence de l'Officier de la Police Rurale, sera fixée au centre de la section dont il est chargé, et sur le chemin public qui la traverse.

Art. 143. L'Officier de la Police Rurale, est specialement chargé de faire prospèrér la culture dans la section qui lui est confiée, d'y faire respecter les lois et les propriétés. Il est responsable dans l'etendu de cette section,

1. De l'execution du Code Rural, en ce qui le regarde, ainsi que tous les autres actes du gouvernement relatifs a l'agriculture, ou a la police rurale.

and the Commandant of the district under whose orders they are placed; they shall also correspond with the civil authorities, and attend to their requisitions.

Art. 142. The dwelling or station of the Officer commanding the Rural Police, shall be in the centre of his section, upon the public road which traverses it.

Art. 143. The Officer commanding the Rural Police, is particularly bound to push agriculture to the utmost extent within the section confided to him, and to cause the laws to be observed, and property to be respected. He is responsible in the whole extent of his section,

1. For the due execution of the Rural Code in what is of his competence, as well as of all other acts of the government relative to agriculture, and to rural police.

2. De toutes negligences dans la surveillance et le travail manuel des habitations de la section.	2. For every neglect of superintendance and manual labour upon the plantations of the section.
3. De tous vagabondages, desordres, contraventions de police dans l'etendu de la section, lorsqu'il ne les aura pas reprimés ou signalés à l'autorité superieure.	3. For all vagrancies, disorders, and disobedience to the police within his section, when he has not prevented them, or reported them to superior authority.
Il pretera serment, avant d'entrer en fonctions entre les mains du Commandant de l'arrondissement.	He shall make oath before the Commandant of the district, before entering upon the duties of his office.

ART. 144. L'Officier de la Police Rurale, aura a ses ordres, et a poste fixe, trois gardes champêtres; dont un sera au grade de marechal des logis, et fera fonction de secretaire; l'autre au grade de brigadier; et le troisième, simple dragon. Les susdits gardes champetres seront assermentés; le serment sera prêté, entre les mains du Commandant de l'arrondissement.

ART. 144. The Officer commanding the Rural Police, shall have under his command, at some fixed station, three guards, one of whom shall be of the rank of quarter-master, and perform the duties of secretary; one of the rank of sergeant; and the third a private dragoon. These guards shall be sworn; the oath shall be taken in the presence of the Commandant of the district.

ART. 145. L'Officier de

ART. 145. The Officer

la Police Rurale devra faire, une fois chaque semaine, la tournée et visite de chaque habitation de la section.

commanding the Rural Police, shall make the round of his section, and visit each plantation once in the week.

Art. 146. L'Officier de la Police Rurale, se rendra a toutes les requisitions des proprietaires, fermiers, ou gerans des habitations de la section, soit de jour, soit de nuit; on y enverra de gardes champêtres pour l'execution de la loi et le maintien de l'ordre.

Art. 146. The Officer commanding the Rural Police, shall hold himself in readiness to attend to the requisitions of proprietors, managers, or overseers, by day and by night, and to send guards to them to enforce obedience to the law, and to maintain order.

Art. 147. Un des gardes champêtres répétera chaque semaine sur chaque habitation de la section, la visite de l'Officier de la Police Rurale, de sorte que ces habitations seront visitées au moins deux fois chaque semaine.

Art. 147. One of the guards shall repeat every week, upon each plantation of the section, the visit of the Officer, so that each plantation shall be visited at the least twice in every week.

Art. 148. Lorsque l'Officier de la Police Rural ou les gardes champêtres dans leurs tournés ordinaires, se presenteront sur une propriété, ils s'addres-

Art. 148. When an Officer, or his guards, in their ordinary rounds, arrive upon any plantation, they shall call first for the proprietor, or, in his absence,

seront d'abord au proprietaire, s'il est present; au fermier principal, ou au gerant, en l'absence du proprietaire : pour s'informer si tout est dans l'ordre : apres cette formalité ils se mettront en devoir d'inspecter les travaux pour s'assurer si ils s'executent dans la regle convenable; ils veréfieront si tous les travailleurs sont a l'ouvrage; ils prendront connaissance des causes d'absence de ceux qui ne se seront pas trouvé au travail, et ageront suivant la loi.

for the chief farmer, or manager, and shall enquire if every thing has been orderly : after this formality, they shall inspect the labours personally, to satisfy themselves that these are properly conducted; they shall ascertain that all the labourers are present, and at work; and they shall enquire into the cause of the absence of any of them, and shall act therein according to law.

ART. 149. Dans le cas ou l'Officier de Police Rurale d'une section sera, par cause legitime, empéché de faire la tourné et visite indiquée pour les Articles 145 et 146 il sera tenu d'en donner avis au Commandant de la commune, qui le fera remplacer, pendant que durera la cause de l'impêchement, par un officier de

ART. 149. When an Officer commanding the Rural Police of a section, is prevented by any lawful excuse, making the round and visit directed by Articles 145 and 146, he shall give notice thereof to the Commandant of the commune, who shall appoint an officer of gendarmerie, or of the troops of the line quartered in the commune,

gendarmerie, ou de la troupe de ligne en garrison dans la commune.

to do the duty for him, while the impediment lasts.

ART. 150. L'Officier de la Police Rurale, qui sans empêchement legitime se dispenserait de faire les tournées, et visites exigées par les Articlet 145 et 146, sera passible d'une punition, qui lui infligera le Commandant de la commune; en cas de recidive et de negligence, il sera signalé au Commandant d'arrondissement qui sera tenu d'en rendre compte au President d'Haïti.

ART. 150. The Officer commanding the Rural Police, who, without lawful excuse, shall neglect to make the rounds and visits directed by the Articles 145 and 146, shall suffer a punishment, to be inflicted by the Commandant of the commune; and in case of repetition of the omission, he shall be reported to the Commandant of the district, who shall report him to the President of Haïti.

ART. 151. Tous les Dimanches matins l'Officier de la Police Rural sera tenu de se presenter en personne, ou d'envoyer un de ses gardes champêtres sous ses ordres avec un rapport ecrit au Commandant de la commune, pour lui faire connâitre ce que se sera passé de plus remarquable dans la section.

ART. 151. Every Sunday morning, the Officer commanding the Rural Police shall present himself in person, or send one of his guards, with a written report, to the Commandant of the commune, to inform him of whatever remarkable circumstances may have occurred in his section.

ART. 152. L'Officier de

ART. 152. The Officer

la Police Rurale, et les gardes champêtres recevront leurs appointemens et soldes, suivant leurs grades, a chaque fois que l'armée de ligne en activité de service sera soldé.

Art. 153. L'Etat fournira aux gardes champêtres l'armement, l'equipment, et l'habillement, comme aux troupes de ligne.

Art. 154. L'uniforme des Officers de la Police Rural, sera habit vert retroussé, a revers, poches en travers, collet et paremens rouges, passepoil rouge, doublure blanche, boutons blancs, bombés a moitié, avec une corne d'abondance, surmontée du Bonnet de la Liberté, ayant pour legende, "*Republique d'Haïti;*" chapeau retapé.

Ils porterons en outre, en argent, les epaulettes et franges de leur grades;

commanding the Rural Police, and the guards, shall receive their pay and allowances, according to their respective ranks, at the same time when the troops of the line in active service are paid.

Art. 153. The State shall supply the guards with arms, accoutrements, and uniforms, in the same manner as to the troops of the line.

Art. 154. The uniform of Officers commanding the Rural Police, shall be a green coat, with flaps and lappets turned back, collar and cuffs red, facings red, white lining, plated buttons, with a cornucopia surmounted by the Cap of Liberty, and the words, "*Republique d'Haïti,*" engraved upon them; a cocked hat.

They shall also bear the epaulettes and fringes of their respective ranks, wear

gilet et pantalon blanc, avec des bottes à l'ecuyère.

Celui des gardes champêtres sera habit veste, drap de même couleur et même façon que ceux des officiers de la police rurale, avec les marques de leurs grades, en galons d'argent ou de lain blanche, casques argentés; ils auront pour armure le sabre de dragon, la giberne, et le mousqueton: ils porterons de droite a gauche une bandouliere rouge, sur laquelle il sera ecrit en lettres blue, "*force de la loi.*"

white waistcoats and pantaloons, and boots.

The uniform of the guards shall be a jacket, of cloth of the same colour and make as their officers, with the distinctive marks of their rank in silver or white worsted lace, and plated helmets; their arms shall be the dragoon sabre, carbine, and cartouche-box: they shall wear a red belt from right to left, with the words, "*force de la loi,*" inscribed upon it in blue letters.

Sect. 3.

Des Gerans et Conducteurs* d'Habitations.

Art. 155. Sur chaque habitation ou le proprietaire ne residera pas, et ou il n'y aura pas un fermier principal residant, il y aura un gerant au choix du proprietaire, ou du fermier principal.

Sect. 3.

Of Overseers and Drivers upon Plantations.

Art. 155. Upon every plantation where the proprietor is not resident, and where there is no principal resident farmer, there shall be a manager, or overseer, to be appointed by the proprietor, or farmer.

---

* See Article 116, where this word is used to signify drivers of cattle.

Art. 156. Le proprietaire, ou fermier principal, apres avoir fait choix du gerant qui lui conviendra, devra passer avec ce gerant un contrat synallagmatique, devant notaire, les conditions duquel sont laissés a leur volonté, apres quoi, il fera connâitre le gerant à l'Officier de la Police Rurale de la section.

Art. 156. The proprietor, or farmer, after having selected the manager, or overseer, who suits him, shall enter into a mutual contract or agreement with him, in the presence of a notary, upon such terms and conditions as the parties may agree upon. The proprietor, or farmer, shall afterwards make known the manager, or overseer, to the Officer commanding the Rural Police of the section.

Art. 157. Tout proprietaire, ou fermier principal d'un bien rural, ne residant pas sur leur propriété, qui n'auront pas nommé et choisi un gerant pour la propriété, si le nombre de cultivateurs est au dessus de dix, seront passibles d'une amende de dix à cinquante gourdes, suivant l'étendu de la propriété : si le nombre des cultivateurs n'excéde pas dix, l'administration pourra être confiée a un conducteur.

Art. 157. Every resident proprietor, or farmer, of a rural property, upon which the number of labourers exceeds ten persons, and who shall not have appointed a manager, or overseer, shall be subject to a fine of not less than ten, nor more than fifty dollars, according to the extent of the property : when the number of labourers does not exceed ten persons, the management may be entrusted to a driver.

Art. 158. Les obligations du gerant sont, de surveiller, dans l'interet du proprietaire qui l'emploie les travaux de l'habitation dont il est chargé.

Art. 159. Les gerans d'habitation seront responsables envers les proprietaires, ou fermiers principaux, de toutes negligences, abandon de travaux, ou ils seront employés; ils seront, dans ce cas, poursuivis par qui de-droit.

Art. 160. Le gerant jouira du respect de tous les agriculteurs de la propriété sur laquelle il est employé.

Art. 161. Sur une propriété ou les terres ou jardins seront distribués par societés de moitié, ou a de sous-fermiers, chaque chef d'association de moitié ou chaque sous-fermier, devien conducteur de son

Art. 158. The duties of the manager, or overseer, are to superintend, in the interest of the proprietor who employs him, the labours carried on upon the plantation entrusted to him.

Art. 159. The managers, or overseers, upon plantations, are answerable to the proprietors, or chief farmers, for every neglect or abandonment of labour where they are employed; they shall be prosecuted by the parties injured.

Art. 160. The manager, or overseer, shall be respected by the labourers upon the estate where he is employed.

Art. 161. Upon estates where the fields or gardens are parcelled out among associations working at half-produce, or to sub-farmers, or jobbers, each head-man of association, and each sub-farmer, or

atelier, ou de sa société; il est responsable des travaux des membres de sa société.	jobber, becomes the driver of his gang, or of his association; he is answerable for their labour.
Art. 162. Les devoirs des conducteurs sont de faire executer les travaux par les ateliers qui leur sont confiés, sous la direction des proprietaires, fermiers principaux, ou gerans.	Art. 162. The duties of the drivers are, to cause the work to be done by the gangs entrusted to them, under the directions of the proprietor, farmer, manager, or overseer.
Art. 163. Le conducteurs seront responsable de toutes les negligences dans les travaux; de toute absence de travailleurs lorsque cette absence n'aura pas été legitiment autorisée; de tous desordres et vagabondages de cultivateurs, lorsqu'ils ne les auront pas fait connâitre a l'autorité compétente.	Art. 163. The drivers are answerable for every neglect of work, for every absence, without leave, of the labourers, and for every act of misconduct, excess, or idleness, committed by the labourers, when they have not reported the same to the proper authorities.
Art. 164. Les conducteurs seront payés sur les produits des revenus recueillis par les ateliers qu'ils dirigent suivant l'Article 57, de la Loi, No. 3.	Art. 164. The drivers shall be remunerated from the proceeds of the produce raised by the gangs they direct, according to Article 57, of Law, No. 3.

CHAP. IV.

Des Conseils d'Agriculture dans les Sections Rurales.

Art. 165. Dans chaque commune, le Commandant d'icelle, le Juge de Paix, et le Conseil des Notables, conjointement choisiront chaque année au premier de Mai, jour de la Fête de l'Agriculture, dans chaque section rurale, trois citoyens des plus notables, et qui seront proprietaires, fermiers principaux, ou gerans, pour former le Conseil d'Agriculture de la section.

Art. 166. Le choix des membres du Conseil d'Agriculture, sera aussitot communiqué, par le Commandant de la commune, au Commandant d'arondissement, qui en rendra compte au Gouvernement.

Art. 167. Les membres les Conseils d'Agriculure n'exercent leur fonc-

CHAP. IV.

Of the Council of Agriculture in the Rural Sections.

Art. 165. On the first of May in every year, being the day of the Festival of Agriculture, the Commandant of each commune, assisted by the Justice of Peace, and the Council of Notables, shall select from each section, three of the most respectable citizens, being proprietors, farmers, managers, or overseers, to form the Council of Agriculture of the section.

Art. 166. The appointment of the members of the Council of Agriculture, shall be immediately made known by the Commandant of the commune to the Commandant of the district, who shall communicate it to the Government.

Art. 167. The members of the Council of Agriculture are elected for one

tions qui pendant l'année; ils pourront etre chaque année, ré-élus, en raison du zele qu'ils auront apporté dans leurs fonctions pendant l'année precédante.

Art. 168. Les Conseils d'Agriculture etant composés d'habitans cultivateurs interessés au bon ordre dans le service rural, chacun des membres doit, sans se deranger essentiellement de ses propres travaux s'enquerir de tout ce qui se passe dans sa section, afin d'en faire le rapport au Conseil des Notables.

Art. 169. Les attributions des Conseils d'Agriculture sont,

1. De veiller à ce que les dispositions des lois relatives a la culture, ne soient pas tronquées dans leurs execution.

2. De chercher, par des experiences nouvelles, et

year only; but they may be re-elected each year, when the zeal they have shewn in the execution of their duties justifies it.

Art. 168. The Councils of Agriculture being composed of inhabitants cultivating the soil, and interested in the preservation of order in rural economy, each of the members is bound, when he can do so without essentially neglecting his own labour, to enquire into all that passes in the section to which he belongs, and report the same to the Council of Notables.

Art. 169. The duties of the Councils of Agriculture are,

1. To see that the dispositions of the laws relating to tillage, are not infringed or weakened in their execution.

2. To endeavour, by means of experiments, and

par le maintien de la concorde entre tous les interessés à la culture à augmenter progressivement ses résultats.

3. De signaler au Conseil des Notables, et aux autorités militaires, tous les abus ou negligences qui pourront avoir lieu dans la section qu'ils habitant.

ART. 170. Les membres du Conseil d'Agriculture correspondent individuellement, ou collectivement, avec les fonctionaries ou autorités, avec lesquels ils doivent avoir des rapports.

ART. 171. Les fonctions de membre du Conseil d'Agriculture sont honorifiques.

by maintaining concord among all those interested in tillage, to increase progressively its results.

3. To report to the Council of Notables, and to the military authorities, every abuse or neglect which may occur in the section in which they dwell.

ART. 170. The members of the Council of Agriculture may correspond, individually or collectively, with the functionaries or authorities to whom they are required to make their reports.

ART. 171. The appointment of a member of the Council of Agriculture is honorary.

TITRE III.

DE LA POLICE RURALE.

ART. 172. La Police Rurale se fait specialement par les officiers chargés des sections rurales des communes, assistés des gardes champêtres.

ART. 173. La Police Rurale a pour objet,
1. La repression du vagabondage.
2. L'ordre 'et l'assiduité dans les travaux des champs.
3. La discipline des ateliers.

4. L'entretien et les reparations des routes publique et particulieres.

CHAP. PREMIER.

De la Repression de Vagabondage.

ART. 174. Toutes personnes qui ne seront pas proprietaires, ou fermiers

THIRD HEAD.

OF RURAL POLICE.

ART. 172. Rural Police is to be specially maintained by officers appointed to command each rural section of the communes, and by guards.

ART. 173. The purposes of Rural Police are,
1. Repressing idleness.
2. Enforcing order and assiduity in field labour.

3. The discipline of the labourers, collectively, or in gangs.
4. Making and keeping in repair public and private roads.

CHAP. I.

Repressing Idleness.

ART. 174. All persons who are not proprietors, or renters of the land on

du bien rural où elles sont fixées, ou qui n'auront point fait un contrat avec un propriétaire, ou fermier principal, seront reputées vagabonds, et seront arretées par la police rurale de la section dans laquelle elles seront trouvées, et conduites devant le Juge de Paix de la commune.

which they are residing, or who shall not have made a contract to work with some proprietor or renter, shall be reputed vagabonds, and shall be arrested by the rural police of the section in which they may be found, and carried before the Justice of Peace of the commune*.

ART. 175. Le Juge de Paix, apres avoir interrogé et entendu la personne menée devant lui, lui fera connaitre les articles de la loi, qui l'obligent à contracter pour se livrer à des occupations agricoles, et apres cet avertissement, l'enverra ou detention dans le maison d'arret, jusqu'à ce qu'il ait contracté, aux termes de la loi.

ART. 175. The Justice of Peace, after interrogating and hearing the person brought before him, shall make known to him the articles of the law, which oblige him to employ himself in agricultural labour; and after that communication, he shall remand him to prison, until he shall have bound himself by a contract, according to the provisions of the law.

ART. 176. Le Juge de Paix veillera à ce que le detenu contracte avec un proprietaire, un fermier ou

ART. 176. The Justice of Peace shall allow the person arrested, to make his own choice of the in-

---

* See Articles 3, 45 et seq.

sous fermier, ou avec un chef de societé agricole, a son choix.

ART. 177. Si apres huit jours de detention le detenu n'avait pas pris un parti pour se livrer à des occupations agricoles, il sera employé aux travaux publics, pour la propreté de la ville ou bourg ou sera située la maison d'arret, et y sera employé jusqu'a ce qu'il se decide a contracter pour se livrer aux travaux de la campagne, quiconque détournera ces detenus des travaux public, pour les employer à des travaux particuliers, sera passible d'une amende de cinquante gourdes, dont la moitié sera allouée au detenu plaignant.

ART. 178. Si la personne arretée etoit un enfant en minorité, le Juge de Paix s'enquerra de ses pere et mere, et l'enverra les rejoindre pour suivre leur condition.

dividual with whom he is to contract to labour.

ART. 177. If, after eight days of detention, the prisoner shall not have agreed to bind himself to field labour, he shall be sent to the public works, for cleaning the town or district where he may be arrested, and there he shall be employed until he shall consent to bind himself to field labour. Any person who removes any labourer from the public works to employ him in private work, shall be subject to a fine of fifty dollars, of which a moiety is to be paid to the prisoner complaining.

ART. 178. If the prisoner be a child under age, the Justice of Peace shall enquire out his parents, and send him to them, to follow their condition of life.

Art. 179. Trois mois apres la publication du present Code, la rigueur sera employée contre les delinquans.

Art. 180. Toute personne fixée dans les campagnes comme agriculteur qui sera trouvée un jour ouvrable et pendant les heures de travail, dans l'inaction, ou en courses et promenades sur les chemins publics sera considerée comme oisive, sera en consequence arretée et conduite chez le Juge de Paix, qui l'enverra en prison pendant vingt-quatre heures pour la premierè fois; et en cas de recidive aux travaux publics de la ville.

Art. 181. Les Officiers de la Police Rurale, veilleront à ce que des vagabonds et des oisifs ne se cachent pas sous l'uniforme de militaires des differens corps: lorsqu'ils trouveront, dans les sections

Art. 179. After the expiration of three months from the publication of this Code, rigorous measures shall be enforced against delinquents.

Art. 180. Every person attached to the country as a cultivator, who shall, on a working day, and during the hours of labour, be found unemployed, or lounging on the public roads, shall be considered idle, and be arrested, and taken before the Justice of Peace, who shall commit him to prison for twenty-four hours, for the first offence; and shall send him to labour on the public works, upon a repetition of the offence.

Art. 181. The Officers commanding the Rural Police, shall take care that vagabonds and idlers do not conceal themselves under the uniforms of soldiers of the different corps? when they discover, in the sec-

sous leur surveillance, des hommes qu'ils ne connaitront pas personnellement pour être en activité de service dans le corps dont ils porterons l'uniforme, ils les arreterons et les enverront au Commandant Militaire de la commune pour verifier si la personne arretée avec l'uniforme d'un corps en fait partie. Dans le cas ou l'individu ne serait pas militaire, il sera déposé en prison suivant l'Article 175 jusqu'a ce qu'il ait formé un contrat pour travailler à la culture.

tions under their superintendance, men whom they do not personally know to be in active service in the corps whose uniform they wear, they shall arrest them, and send them before the Military Commandant of commune, that enquiry may be made if the individual arrested really belongs to the corps whose uniform he wears. If the party prove not to be a soldier, he shall be committed to prison, according to Article 175, until he enter into a contract to labour in agriculture.

Art. 182. Les Officiers de la Police Rurale, veilleront à ce que, dans l'etendu des sections sous leur direction, personne ne demeure dans l'oisiveté; à cet effet, ils sont autorisés à se faire rendre compte par les individus qu'ils ne trouveront pas au travail, du genre de leurs occupations, et si ces individus ne prouvent pas qu'ils cultivent la terre, ou

Art. 182. Officers commanding the Rural Police, shall take care, that in their respective sections, no person shall live in idleness; for this purpose, they have authority to oblige such persons as are not actually employed in labour, to give an account of their occupations; and such persons as cannot prove that they cultivate the soil, or are keepers of

sont employés sur des hattes, suivant la Loi, No. 4, ils seront regardés comme gens sans aveu et arretés comme vagabonds.

cattle-pens, shall be considered as without visible means of procuring their livelihood, and shall be arrested as vagabonds.

CHAP. II.
De l'Ordre et de l'Assiduité dans les Travaux des Champs.

ART. 183. Les travaux des campagnes commenceront le Lundi matin, pour ne cesser que le Vendredi au soir (les jours de fêtes légales exceptes) neanmoins dans les cas extraordinaires, tant dans les interets des proprietaires que des agriculteurs le travail se prolongera jusqu'au Samedi.

CHAP. II.
Of ensuring Order and Assiduity in Field Labour.

ART. 183. Field-labour shall commence on Monday morning, and shall never cease until Friday evening, (legal holidays excepted); and in extraordinary cases, when the interest of the cultivator, as well as of the proprietor, appears to require it, work shall be continued until Saturday evening*.

---

* And be it further enacted by the authority aforesaid, That from and after the commencement of this Act, the slaves belonging to, and employed on any plantation, shall, over and above the holidays hereinafter to be mentioned, be allowed one day in every fortnight, to cultivate their own provision-grounds, exclusive of Sundays, except during the time of crop, under the penalty of twenty pounds; to be recovered against the overseer, or person having the care of such slaves. Provided always, that the number of days so allowed to the slaves for the cultivation of their grounds, shall be at least twenty-six in the year.

And be it enacted by the authority aforesaid, That not only shall slaves,

ART. 184. Aux jours ouvrables les travaux ordinaires des champs commenceront le matin à la pointe du jour, pour durer jusqu'à midi; dans l'intervalle, il sera pris une demi heur pour le dejuner qui se fera toujours dans le lieu même ou l'ou sera occupé à travailler. L'apres midi, le travail commencera à deux heures pour durer jusqu'au coucher du soleil.

ART. 184. On working-days, the ordinary field-labour shall commence at day-dawn; to continue until mid-day, with the interval of half an hour for breakfast; which shall be taken on the spot where the work is carrying on; after mid-day the field-labour shall commence at two o'clock, and continue until sun-set*.

ART. 185. Les femmes ne seront employées qu'à des travaux legers, dès qu'elles seront enceintes, et lorsqu'elles auront at-

ART. 185. Pregnant females shall be employed on light work only; and after the fourth month of pregnancy, they shall not

---

as heretofore, be exempted during the crop, from the labour of the estate or plantation during Sundays, but that no mills shall be put about or worked, between the hours of seven o'clock on Saturday night and five o'clock on Monday morning, under the penalty of twenty pounds; to be recovered against the overseer, or other person having the charge of such slaves.—*Consolidated Slave Law of Jamaica*, 57 Geo. III. c. 25, Sections 4 and 5.

* And be it further enacted by the authority aforesaid, That every field-slave on any plantation or settlement, shall, on work-days, be allowed half an hour for breakfast, and two hours for dinner; and that no slaves shall be compelled to any manner of field-work upon a plantation, before the hour of five o'clock in the morning, or after the hour of seven at night, except during the time of crop, under a penalty of 50*l.*; to be recovered against the overseer, or other person having the charge of such slaves.

teint le quatrieme mois de leur gressesse, elles ne seront pas assujetties a travailler aux champs.

be obliged to do any work in the field.

ART. 186. Quatre mois apres leurs couches, elles seront tenues de reprendre le travail, mais elles ne se rendront aux champs, le matin qu'une heure apres le lever du soleil pour quitter à onze heures et l'apres midi qu'à deux heures, pour quitter une heure avant le coucher du soleil.

ART. 186. Four months after delivery, they shall be obliged to resume labour in the field; but they shall not turn out to work until one hour after sunrise; they shall continue to work until eleven o'clock, and from two o'clock until one hour before sun-set*.

---

* The Legislature of Jamaica, after very careful inquiry, did not think it necessary to make any regulation upon the subject of this and the preceding Article; but they have published the evidence they received, on the general practice of the Island, and the Haitian Legislature has embodied that practice in these two Articles. The following are the heads of the evidence of some of the witnesses:

The pregnant women are put to light work, and continued so till within a short time of their confinement; for experience has proved, that those women have the easiest time of labour, and bring the healthiest children, who are kept in a moderate state of exercise. They return to light work about six weeks after confinement.—*Examination of William Murray, Esq.*

Great indulgence is allowed, as to the hours of labour of pregnant women. —*Examination of R. W. Harris, Esq.*

Pregnant women are usually employed in some light work, till they have advanced about five or six months, when they seldom do any thing for their master.—*Examination of James Stewart, Esq.*

See the Minutes of Evidence taken upon oath before the Committee on the Slave Registry Bill, in Jamaica, 1815.

ART. 187. Nul agriculteur fixé sur une proprieté rurale, ne pourra s'absenter du travail qui lui sera assigné, sans la permission du gerant, en l'absence du proprietaire ou fermier principal, lequel n'accordera cette permission que lorsque le cas sera urgent.	ART. 187. No labourer attached to an estate in the country, shall absent himself from the labour assigned him, without the permission of the overseer, in the absence of the proprietor or farmer; and no person shall give that permission, unless the case be urgent*.

CHAP. III.	CHAP. III.
De la Discipline des Ateliers.	*Of the Discipline of Gangs of Labourers.*
ART. 188. Les ateliers sur les propriétes rurales, devront etre obeissans envers leurs conducteurs des travaux, chefs de societés de moitié, sous fermiers, fermiers principaux, proprietaires et gerans, chaque	ART. 188. Gangs of labourers upon estates, shall be obedient to their drivers, jobbers, sub-farmers, farmers, proprietors, and managers, or overseers, whenever they are called upon to execute the labour

---

* Section 30th, That no slave, such only excepted as are going to market and returning therefrom, shall hereafter be suffered or permitted to go out of his or her master's, or owner's plantation or settlement, or to travel from one town to another, unless such slave shall have a ticket from his master.

Section 31st, That no ticket shall be granted to any slave or slaves, for any time exceeding one calendar month.—*Consolidated Slave Law*, passed 1814, (57 Geo. III. c. 25).—See Art: 60.

fois qu'il seront requis d'executer les travaux pour lesquels ils auront contracté.	they have bound themselves to perform.
ART. 189. Toute desobeissance et toute insulte de la part d'un travailleur commandé pour faire un travail auquel il serait assujetti par un contrat, ou une convention reciproque, sera puni de la prison, selon l'exigence du cas, d'apres decision du Juge de Paix de la commune.	ART. 189. Every act of disobedience or insult, on the part of a workman, commanded to do any work to which he is subjected, shall be punished by imprisonment, according to the exigency of the case, in the discretion of the Justice of Peace of the commune.
ART. 190. Les Samedis, les Dimanches, et jours de fêtes etant à la disposition des agriculteurs, ils ne pourront, les jours ouvrables, abandonner leurs travaux pour se livrer à des dances ou festins, ni jour, ni nuit, les delinquans à cette disposition seront passibles de trois jours de prison pour la premiere fois, et du double en cas de recidive.	ART. 190. Saturdays, Sundays, and holidays, being at the entire disposal of the labourers, they shall not be permitted, on working days, to leave their work, to indulge in dancing or feasting, neither by night nor by day. Delinquents shall be subject to imprisonment for three days for the first offence, for six days for the repetition of the offence*.

---

* Section 21, That for the future, all slaves shall be allowed the usual number of holidays that were allowed at the usual seasons of Christmas,

CHAP. IV.

De l'entretien, et de la Reparation des Routes Publiques.

Art. 191. Les routes publics seront entretenues et reparées par les agriculteurs à tour de role, de toute la section qu'elles traverseront, toutes les fois que leurs étât de deterioration exigera la reparation. Les routes particulieres seront également entretenues par ceux des agriculteurs des establissemens de la section que se serviront habituellement des dites routes.

Art. 192. Aussitot qu'une route publique ou particuliere necessitera des travaux de reparation l'Officier de la Police Rural

CHAP. IV.

On making and keeping in Repair the Public Roads.

Art. 191. The public roads shall be kept up and repaired by the labourers of the whole section they pass through, in rotation, whenever their state of deterioration may require repair. The private roads shall also be repaired by the labourers of the estates in the habit of using them.

Art. 192. Whenever a public or private road requires repair, the Officer of Rural Police shall give notice of it to the

---

Easter, and Whitsunday. Section 36.—But nothing herein contained, shall be construed to prevent any master or overseer from granting liberty to the slaves, upon his plantation only, when, and as often as they please, for assembling together upon such plantation or settlement, and playing and diverting themselves at any innocent amusement: provided that such amusements are put an end to by ten of the clock at night. (57 Geo. III. c. 25).

en donnera avis au Commandant de la commune.

Art. 193. Le Commandant de la commune ordonnera le travail s'il est partiel, ou de peu d'importance; il en donnera avis au Commandant d'arrondissement, si le travail exige un grand concours de bras, afin d'etre promptement accéleré : le Conseil d'Agriculture de la section, avisera le Conseil des Notables de la commune, des travanx que se feront.

Art. 194. D'aprés le role des habitations des sections mentionné en l'Art. 132, il sera pris le nombre de travailleurs necessaires pour executer les travaux de reparation, en proportion de la population travaillante de chaque habitation qui doit toute concourir un travail.

Art. 195. Les proprietaires qui n'auront pas le

Commandant of the commune.

Art. 193. If the repairs required be local, or of trivial importance, the Commandant of the commune shall order them to be done. But if the work to be done require many hands, he shall give notice of it to the Commandant of the district, that hands may be promptly supplied. The Council of Agriculture shall inform the Council of Notables of the work to be done.

Art. 194. The number of labourers required for any particular work upon the roads, shall be taken from the plantation rolls ordered by Article 132, in numbers proportioned to the labouring population, all of whom are bound to assist in the work.

Art. 195. Those proprietors who have not four

nombre de quatre travailleurs attaché sur leur propriété, n'en fourniront, dans tous les cas, qu'un seul pour les travaux de reparation de route.

labourers attached to their estate, shall in no case be called upon to furnish more than one labourer for repairs upon the roads.

Art. 196. Tout agriculteur commandé pour un travail de reparation de route qui ne se rendra pas à ce travail payera six gourdins par semaine d'amende, ou sera detenu une semaine en prison, et ne sera pas pour cela exempt du travail, la semaine suivante.

Art. 196. Every labourer ordered to work on the roads, who shall absent himself from that work, shall pay a fine of six quarter dollars a week, or suffer imprisonment for one week, which fine or imprisonment shall not exempt him from working the week following.

Art. 197. Tout proprietaire, fermier principal, ou gérant d'habitation qui, ayant reçu la demande de travailleurs pour reparation de route, n'en fournirait pas, sera passible d'une amende de trois gourdes par sermaine pour chaque travailleur non fourni, la moitié a la caisse des amendes et l'autre moitié pour servir à remplacer les travailleurs.

Art. 197. Any proprietor, farmer, or overseer of a plantation, who, having received a requisition for labourers, shall neglect to furnish them, shall be liable to a fine of three dollars per week for each labourer short of the number; half the fine to be paid to the treasury of fines, and half to be employed in hiring other labourers.

Art. 198. Les travailleurs commandés pour les travaux de reparation de route, devron se presenter avec les outils et instrumens aratoires, dont ou se sert sur l'habitation, sans quoi, il en sera fourni à ceux qui n'en auraient pas, par l'Officier de la Police Rurale qui les recevra de l'administration, et sur le rapport qui en sera fait au Juge de Paix de la commune, il condamnera le proprietaire de l'habitation du delinquant, ou son represantant à rembourser à l'administration la valeur double des outils fournis.

Art. 199. Lorsque les travaux de reparation de routes publiques ou particulieres exigeront des transports, les propriétés ou il y aura des cabronets ou tombereaux seront obligées d'en fournir, à defaut des tombereaux ou cabrouets, ou fournira des bêtes à charge.

Art. 198. Labourers called out for repairing the roads, shall bring the agricultural instruments and tools used on the plantation, in default of which, the Officer commanding the Rural Police shall give them tools, to be supplied by the administration, and upon a report of the same being made to a Justice of Peace for the commune, he shall adjudge the proprietor of the plantation to which the defaulters may belong, or his representative, to reimburse the administration in double the value of the tools so furnished.

Art. 199. When means of transport are required for the repair of public or private roads, such estates as possess wains or carts, shall send them; in default of wains or carts, cattle for draft shall be supplied.

ART. 200. La fourniture de huit bêtes de charge equivandra à la fourniture d'un cabronet attêlé.

ART. 201. Nul ne pourra, dans un interet particulier, detourner ceux qui seront envoyés au dits travaux. Tout contrevenant à cette disposition paiera une amende de cinquante gourdes par cultivateur detourné, ne fu ce qu'un jour. Tous les matins, le directeur des travaux de la journée, fera l'appel des travailleurs commandés, afin de constater leur presence.

ART. 202. Les travailleurs commandés pour les travaux, devront s'y presenta le Lundi matin, pour ne quitter, tant que durera le travail, que le Vendredi au soir.

Donné en la Chambre des Communes, au Port-au-Prince, le 21 Avril, 1826,

ART. 200. Eight beasts of burden supplied, shall be equal to one cart and team.

ART. 201. No person shall, for his private interests, take from the repair of the roads, those who are sent to work upon them, under a penalty of fifty dollars for each labourer so withdrawn, if even for one day only. The director of the work shall call over the names of the labourers every morning, to ascertain their presence.

ART. 202. Labourers ordered to work on the public roads, shall present themselves early on Monday morning, and shall not absent themselves, unless the work be finished, until Friday evening.

Passed in the Chamber of Commons, at Port-au-Prince, the 21st of April,

<table>
<tr><td>

an 23 de l'Independance.

Le Président de la Chambre,
(Signé) MUZAINE.

Les Secretaires,
Pre. JUNCA, et ARDOUIN.

La Senat decrete l'acceptative du Code Rural d'Haïti, lequel sera, dans les vingt-quatre heures, expedié au President d'Haïti, pour avoir son exécution, suivant le mode etabli par la Constitution.

A la Maison Nationale au Port-au-Prince, le 4 Mai, 1826, an 23 de l'Independance.

Le President du Senat,
P. ROUANEZ.

Les Secretaires,
GAYOT, et F. DUBREUIL.

Au Nom de la Republique:

Le President d'Haïti ordonne, que les Lois, ci-dessus formant le Code Rural d'Haïti, soient re-

</td><td>

1826, 23d year of Independence.

MUZAINE, President.

Pre. JUNCA, and ARDOUIN,
Secretaries.

The Senate decrees the Rural Code of Haïti, and orders it to be sent, within twenty-four hours, to the President of Haïti, to be confirmed, and carried into execution, in the manner directed by the Constitution.

At the National House at Port-au-Prince, this 4th day of May, 1826, 23d year of Independence.

P. ROUANEZ,
President of the Senate.

GAYOT, and F. DUBREUIL,
Secretaries.

In the Name of the Republic:

The President of Haïti orders, that the above Laws, constituting the Rural Code of Haïti, be

</td></tr>
</table>

vetues du Scèau de la Republique, et qu'elles soient publiées et executées.

Donné au Palais National du Port-au-Prince, le 6 Mai, 1826, an 23 de l'Independance.

BOYER.

Par le President,
Le Secretaire General,
B. INGINAC.

sealed with the Seal of the Republic, and be published and executed.

From the National Palace at Port-au-Prince, this 6th day of May, 1826, 23d year of Independence.

BOYER.

By the President,
B. INGINAC,
Secretary-General.

No. I.
London, January 1, 1827.   No. 9.

THE

WEST INDIAN REPORTER.

"In setting about the conversion of more than 800,000 Black Slaves into free citizens, we must act sensibly and discreetly; especially we must begin with the beginning, for IT IS NOT A MATTER OF DECREE, EDICT, or ACT OF PARLIAMENT; there is no *hocus pocus* in the thing, there are no *presto* movements. It is a mighty work; yet mighty as it is, it must be effected, if at all, in the order, and by the rules, which reason and experience have proved to be alone effectual. If we attempt to reverse the order, or to alter the mode, we shall not only fail ourselves, but make it impossible that any should succeed."
Coleridge's Six Months in the West Indies.

"IF THE CONDITION OF THE SLAVE IS TO BE IMPROVED, THAT IMPROVEMENT MUST BE INTRODUCED THROUGH THE MEDIUM OF HIS MASTER. The Masters are instruments through whom, and by whom, you must act upon the Slave Population; and if by any proceedings of ours we shall unhappily place between the Slave and his Master the barrier of insurmountable hostility, we shall at once put an end to the best chance of emancipation, or even of amendment. Instead of diffusing gradually over those dark regions a pure and salutary light, we may at once kindle a flame only to be quenched in blood."
Mr. Canning, March 16, 1824.

"*From the general and prominent charge of cruelty, active or permissive,* towards the Slaves, I, for one, ACQUIT THE PLANTERS. I have been in twelve of the British Colonies; and have gone round and across many of them, and have resided some months in the most populous one for its size in the whole world. I have observed with diligence, I have inquired of all sorts of people, and have mixed constantly with the colored inhabitants of all hues, and of every condition. I am sure I have seen things as they are, and I am not aware of any other bias in my mind, except that which may be caused by a native hatred of injustice, and a contempt and disdain of cant and hypocrisy."
Coleridge's Six Months in the West Indies.

ADDRESS TO THE PUBLIC.

The design of the present publication is, to afford an antidote to the mischief disseminated through the country by the proceedings of a party who, professing to aim at the Abolition of Slavery, are carrying on a systematized plan of hostility against the very existence of the West Indian Colonies of Great Britain. In a variety of publications of all shapes and sizes, continually issuing from the press, adapted to the taste of all conditions of readers, and circulated with the most unwearied assiduity, the characters of the West Indian Planters are vilified, their actions traduced, their proceedings garbled and distorted, till the nation has almost been persuaded to believe that the destruction of the West Indian Colonies is essential to her own prosperity; and that the West Indians must be ruined before the extinction of Slavery can be accomplished.

"THE WEST INDIAN REPORTER" is therefore established for the double purpose, on the one hand, of investigating and exposing the incorrectness of such statements as are brought forward in support of conclusions so preposterous: and, on the other hand, of laying before the public a true and fair account of those transactions both at home and in the Colonies, which tend to that "progressive im-"provement in the character of the Slave population, which is to "*prepare* them for a participation in those civil rights and privileges "which are enjoyed by other classes of His Majesty's subjects."

The want of such a publication has long been felt; and, with a view to supply the deficiency, it is proposed to publish, *as often as circumstances may dictate*, a sheet of the size of the present, which shall contain extracts from the Colonial and British journals relative to the measures carried on for the Abolition of Slavery; and all other intelligence which may serve to show the injustice of the attacks which are from time to time made against the West Indian name and interest.

The publication will be named "THE WEST INDIAN REPORTER." Copies will be forwarded, at the request of any individual friendly to its object, at the rate of eight shillings per hundred. It is requested that all persons wishing to receive a regular supply, will make application to Mr. Wilson, Royal Exchange, and mention the conveyance by which they may be most conveniently sent. They might, in many cases, be sent at very little expense, enclosed in booksellers' parcels, or along with the Monthly Publications of the various religious or charitable Societies; permission to that effect being obtained from the country booksellers or others to whom the parcels are addressed.

It is further earnestly recommended to all the real friends of Negro improvement, to promote the circulation of the intelligence contained in "THE WEST INDIAN REPORTER," by lending their own copies, or encouraging others to purchase.

It is anticipated that much benefit will arise from the proposed publication; and, in particular, a large accession of strength to the cause of real humanity and benevolence, from numerous and influential classes of the community, not yet sufficiently informed as to the true state of society in the West Indies, and of the rapidly increasing moral and religious instruction of the Slaves. It is by no means intended in "THE WEST INDIAN REPORTER," to impugn the object of the Anti-Slavery Societies, or to cavil at *all* the measures which they may use to effect it; but merely to refute and expose those enthusiasts who would endeavour to obtain the freedom of the Slave by the ruin of the Master.

PETITION OF THE SURREY ANTI-SLAVERY ASSOCIATION.

It being the principal object of "THE WEST INDIAN REPORTER" to notice the transactions, either at home or in the Colonies, which bear upon what is commonly called, "the West India Question," in looking back upon the occurrences of the past month, our attention is called to the Petition which was presented by Mr. Dennison to the House of Commons, from the Surrey Anti-Slavery Association, praying for a repeal of the protecting duties on West India sugar. In this petition will be found stated the whole of the topics usually urged against the Planters. By examining these topics point by point, we shall be enabled to place before the eyes of the public, in one view, the principal arguments and facts on both sides of the question, to serve most opportunely as a preliminary to our future labours. A rational and dispassionate examination of the *pro* and *con*, thus contrasted, will, it is confidently anticipated, procure for the West Indians support against the inveterate persecution which they have long undergone; always premising, that in appealing to the public for protection, the West Indians are NOT, as they are daily asserted to be, *the defenders or upholders of slavery*. They are opposed only to a hasty and compulsory emancipation of the Negroes: as individuals, because it would destroy their property, obtained and sanctioned by British law; as subjects of the British *Empire*, because it would annihilate a large portion of the commercial, maritime, and manufacturing interests of their native country; as members of society at large, because it would be fatal to the interests of those Negroes whom it is designed to benefit; and if it abolished slavery in one part of the globe, would only accelerate its growth in another. They cannot, and have not, any objection to ultimate emancipation, " at the earliest period, COMPATIBLE WITH THE WELL " BEING OF THE SLAVES THEMSELVES, WITH THE SAFETY OF THE " COLONIES, AND WITH A FAIR AND EQUITABLE CONSIDERATION " OF THE INTERESTS OF PRIVATE PROPERTY."

Resolutions of Parliament.

In urging the above considerations on behalf of the West Indians, as to the general question, whenever and wherever it may be discussed, it is particularly desirable to keep them steadily in view, in judging of the object of the Petition of the Surrey Anti-Slavery Association. In the 19th Number of " The Monthly Anti-Slavery Reporter[*]," we find that this Petition is recommended to " universal attention," as a model of force and eloquence, and as " not more distinguished by " those qualities, than by its truth and justice." The " eloquence" of the Petition is certainly much upon a level with its " truth " and justice." Our business, however, is solely with the latter-mentioned qualities.—Its truth we shall consider in examining the Petition itself—its justice consists in proposing *the ruin of the*

[*] To this work we shall have frequently occasion to refer.

West India Planters, as a necessary, or, at least, a convenient and easy, mode of obtaining the extinction of slavery. Let it be remembered, then, that the remarks here made upon it, are directed not against the *object*, but against the *means* proposed, which are as inconsistent with justice, policy, and humanity, as the language in which the Petition is couched is at variance with sound sense.

House of Commons, Dec. 13, 1826.

Mr. DENNISON said, he rose to present a Petition against Negro Slavery from the Surrey Anti-Slavery Association. It was the first Petition that had been presented upon the subject in the new Parliament. The Petitioners complained of the high protecting duties upon West India produce, and calculated, that the people of England had, in the last twelve years, paid equal to a tax of £18,000,000 in the additional price of sugar, created by the duties on that article of consumption. The Petitioners trusted, that as Portugal was protected by the blood and treasure of England, our Government would insist that the Portuguese flag should no longer be allowed to protect the nefarious traffic in Negroes (hear, hear).

Mr. BROUGHAM said, he would take the present opportunity of asking whether any intimation had been received by Government since last Parliament, relative to the Colonial Legislatures acquiescing in the views of Ministers with respect to the Slaves?

Mr. HUSKISSON said, the Honorable Member connected with the Colonial Department was not then in his place, and he could not take upon himself to say, that no satisfactory returns had been received from Jamaica.

Mr. BROUGHAM said, he regretted that the communications made by his Majesty's Government had not been obeyed by those to whom they were addressed. He understood that the Colonial Assembly of Jamaica had expressed their determination to resist the views of the Home Government.

Mr. HUSKISSON said, that he believed the Assembly of Jamaica had expressed their willingness to take the subject into consideration.

Morning Chronicle.

Two Petitions of the Members of the *Surrey* Auxiliary Anti-Slavery Society, and other inhabitants of the said County of *Surrey*, whose names are thereunto subscribed, were presented, and read; setting forth,

PETITION.	REMARKS.
That the population of the *West Indian* Colonies belonging to the Crown of *England*, consists chiefly of Negroes, who are either unoffending foreigners, carried thither by force, or *British* subjects, born within the King's allegiance;	This description of the Slave Population may pass as correct; but it is necessary to warn the reader of the insidiousness of the design with which it is introduced. That "unoffending foreigners" were carried into the West Indies by the *Slave Trade*, was an act, whose injustice no one disputes; but it was the act, not of the Colonists, but of the nation, the Legislature of which, pronounced the trade which carried those foreigners thither, to be a trade "very advantageous" to Great Britain.

PETITION.	REMARKS.
	The descendants of these "fo-"reigners," who comprise the other portion of the Slave population, are certainly " *British subjects, born within the King's allegiance;*" but they are placed by the accident of their birth (an accident which in all ages and countries has occasioned some to be destined to labor for others), and by British laws, under the condition of servitude, in return for protection, food, and raiment.
That these unoffending foreigners possess rights under the Law of Nations which *England* is bound to recognize and uphold, as a civilized State; and for the violation of which, in the persons of other foreigners, a *British* fleet was sent only a few years since to lay the Port of *Algiers* in ruins; That *England*, on that occasion, justly resented the barbarous practice adopted by the *Algerines*, of converting their enemies taken in war into slaves, as an uncivilized modification of the right assumed by savages of putting the prisoners to death;	This paragraph contains a particular instance brought forward in support of the truth of a general proposition; but the proof altogether fails. England attacked Algiers for a direct aggression upon the persons of her own subjects, and of those of Christian Potentates with whom she was in alliance; and not for any violation of the " Law of Nations," in the persons of unoffending foreigners, who had no other claim to her protection. She justly resented the " barbarous practice," because it was carried on against herself, or her allies. But even were the case as here represented, it would not affect the present state of the West India Question; since if England, for the sake of consistency, is bound to recognize and uphold the " right" of the Negroes to liberty, she is equally bound to provide a compensation for the Planters whose property her actions made dependant upon their Slavery.
That *British* subjects, born within the King's allegiance, and innocent of all crime, cannot be deprived of their civil existence, and reduced to a state of slavery, by any power known to the Constitution of this Country;	It can scarcely be said that the descendants of the Negroes are " *deprived*" of liberty, or " *reduced*" to Slavery, since they cannot be deprived of that which they never possessed, or " reduced" into a state to which they are destined

PETITION.	REMARKS.
	by laws, sanctioned by English Sovereigns and English Ministers. This assertion, theoretically true, is practically false. A system of Slavery, however much opposed to the *spirit* of the British Constitution, has been not only allowed, but *encouraged*, by the British Legislature, to take root in British possessions, from a notion that it was highly advantageous to national prosperity. But it would be a most gross violation both of the theory and practice of her constitution, were England to attempt to repair the injustice committed on one portion of her subjects, by an act of equal injustice committed upon another.
That such a power necessarily supposes the annihilation of every principle on which the reciprocal claims of allegiance and protection are founded, and at once destroys the basis of the social compact; that such a power, if it could exist, might reduce to slavery all the born subjects of the King, as justly as any particular portion of them;	This paragraph is mere declamation. Even the little portion of argument which it contains, consists in the assertion of abstract principles; a mode of reasoning upon this subject which exposes the Petitioners to the reproof conveyed in the following words of Mr. Canning.

If there be those again who think that this important question, involving, as it confessedly does, THE LIVES, THE INTERESTS, AND THE PROPERTY OF OUR FELLOW-SUBJECTS, is to be determined on the abstract proposition---" That man cannot be made the property of man,"---I take the liberty of relegating them to the schools; and of telling them that they do not deal with this grave and complicated matter as members of the British Parliament, or as members of a society constituted, like that in which we live, of long-established interests, of conflicting claims to protection, of modifications and involutions of property, not to be changed and simplified by a sudden effort, and of usages which, however undesirable, if the question were as to their new institution, are too inveterately rooted to be destroyed at a single blow. I must tell them, Sir, that the practical adoption of their speculative notions would expose our West India possessions to ravage and desolation, which, I think, those Honorable Gentlemen themselves would be as little satisfied to behold, as I hope they are prepared wilfully to produce them.

| That while in *Russia* civil death has been awarded as an appropriate punishment for high treason, and in *Algiers* slavery is substituted for the savage right of taking the life of a captured enemy, in the *West Indian* dominions of | The essence of this declamatory sentence is, that the negroes are deprived of their liberty " for " the emolument" of the West India Planters. It does unfortunately happen, that " THE LIVES, " THE INTERESTS, AND THE PRO- |

PETITION.

the *British* Crown unoffending aliens and unoffending *British* subjects are deprived of their civil existence by thousands, and hundreds of thousands, solely for the emolument of private individuals, who, for that purpose alone, by a monstrous and illegal usurpation, condemn their fellow subjects to a state of irremediable slavery, and extend the dreadful curse to their children, and their children's children;

REMARKS.

" PERTY" of " thousands and hundreds of thousands of unoffending" British subjects, fellow countrymen of the Petitioners, are, as Mr. Canning states, " *confessedly involved*" in the *gradual* decay of Slavery; but before any individual can with prudence or justice come to the conclusion, that " *those lives, interests, and property*" ought to be sacrificed, as the Petitioners desire, to the natural right of the Negroes to their liberty; he must take into consideration two questions; first, Is it true that the Negroes are deprived of their liberty SOLELY for the emolument of the PLANTERS? next; whether the Planters were the SOLE agents in the guilt of producing the slave system? To both of these the answer will be in the negative; as the following quotation will most distinctly prove.

" Great Britain established the Slave Trade in the reign of Queen Elizabeth, who personally took a share in it.

" The Colonies did not then exist.

" Great Britain encouraged it in the successive reigns of Charles I., Charles II., and James II., by every means that could be devised. But it was William III. who outdid them all. With Lord Somers for his Minister, he declared the Slave Trade to be " *highly beneficial to the* NATION;" and that this was not meant merely as beneficial to the nation, through the medium of the colonial prosperity, is demonstrated by the Assiento treaty in 1713, with which the Colonies had nothing to do, and in which Great Britain binds herself to supply 144,000 Slaves, at the rate of 4,800 per annum, to the Spanish colonies. From that time till within a few years of the present time, our history is full of the various measures and grants which passed for the *encouragement* and protection of the trade.

" The Colonies all this time took no share in it themselves, merely purchasing what the British Merchants brought them, and doing therein what the British Government invited them to do by every means in their power.

" So much as to those who created and fostered the trade; and now let us see who it was that first marked it with disapprobation, and sought to confine it within narrower bounds.

"The Colonies began in 1760. South Carolina (then a British Colony) passed an Act to prohibit further importation.

"Great Britain rejected this Act with indignation, and declared that the Slave Trade WAS BENEFICIAL AND NECESSARY TO THE MOTHER COUNTRY. The governor who passed it was reprimanded, and a circular was sent to all other governors, warning them against a similar offence.

"The Colonies, however, in 1765, repeated the offence; and a Bill was twice read in the Assembly of Jamaica, for the same purpose of limiting the importation of Slaves.

"Great Britain stopped it, through the governor of that island, who sent for the Assembly, and told them, that, consistently with his instructions, he could not give his assent: *upon which the bill was dropped.*

"The Colonies in 1774 tried once more; and the Assembly of Jamaica actually passed two Bills to restrict the trade;

"Great Britain again resisted the restriction; Bristol and Liverpool petitioned against it. The matter was referred to the Board of Trade, and that Board reported against it.

"The Colonies, by the Agent of Jamaica, remonstrated against that report, and pleaded against it on all the grounds of justice and humanity; . . . . . but

"Great Britain, by the mouth of the Earl of Dartmouth, then President of the Board, answered by the following declaration: ' We cannot allow the Colonies to check or discourage, *in any degree,* a traffic so beneficial to the nation,' and this was in 1774!"

PETITION.

That the claim set up by the *West Indian* Slave-masters to their fellow subjects, and to helpless strangers, as their property, rests on no better basis than the claim of robbers and receivers to goods which they have stolen, or purchased knowing them to be stolen;

REMARKS.

If the West Indians are to be considered as robbers, and receivers of stolen goods, for having imported or purchased Negroes the Petitioners themselves are liable to the charge of being also robbers, and vendors of stolen goods, for having exported and sold them. Of the Slave Trade, the British Legislature distinctly stated that the *nation* received the benefit. The nation, of whom the Petitioners are part, now feel some scruples of conscience, and wish to make restitution to those who have been robbed. Nothing can be more laudable than such a feeling, but it is most iniquitous that the robber should retain his portion of the plunder, while he compels the receiver to refund his.

This hardy assertion was brought forward by the Duke of Devonshire at a County Meeting, and was thus replied to by Viscount St. Vincent in the House of Lords, on the 7th of March, 1826.

It was reported, and he believed truly reported, that a noble duke, whom every one regarded who did know him, and every one respected who did not know him, that this noble duke (Devonshire) should have said at a recent county meeting, that he considered the claims of the West Indian to compensation, *if his property were destroyed, as the claim of a receiver of stolen goods.* Had he (lord St. Vincent) been present at that meeting, he would have asked that noble duke, who stole those goods, who sold them, who pocketed the money for them? who but the people of England! The ancestor of that noble duke had taken a conspicuous part at the memorable era of the revolution, at the passing of the Bill of Rights, but the Bill of Rights was the Bill of Wrongs to the sons of Africa. It was in consequence of a doubt whether the Bill of Rights opened the African trade, that the act of 9 and 10 of William and Mary (cap. 26) was passed. Before that period, the African slave trade was exclusively limited to a few chartered companies. But, after the Bill of Rights, this was deemed too precious for a chosen few, and was extended to all the good people of England. So precious, indeed, was it deemed, that whereas all other articles of that trade were subject to a duty of five or ten per cent., gold, silver, and silver ore, and slaves, were alone exempted from any. In fact, slaves were put on the same footing as gold and silver. He (lord St. Vincent) was descended from one of the receivers of that period. The noble duke was descended from one of the *licencers of the thieves.* Had the noble duke been in his place, he (lord St. Vincent) would have called upon him to support him in his title to that estate *which the ancestor of the one had bought* under a system *not only sanctioned but encouraged by the ancestor of the other.*

PETITION.	REMARKS.
That the crime of depriving an innocent man, whether a foreigner or a *British* subject, of his civil existence, immeasurably exceeds any one of those descriptions of theft for which the punishment of death is usually awarded in this country, as it includes them all;	In this paragraph there is a vagueness of expression similar to that previously noticed, adopted apparently for the purpose of insinuating assertions too preposterous to be directly made. In its literal meaning, it goes merely to the proposition of an abstract principle, into the discussion of which it is unnecessary to enter; those who bring it forward, as a foundation for attacks upon the West Indians, being liable to the censure conveyed in the words of Mr. Canning, already cited. If, however, the holding of the Negroes in Slavery (hyperbolically described as depriving innocent men, or British subjects, of their civil existence) be a crime, it is, as has been repeatedly shown, a crime chargeable upon the whole British nation.
	The declamatory nature of the following sentence renders it scarcely capable of reply. As a metaphorical description of the evils attendant upon all slave sys-

PETITION.	REMARKS.
	tems, it might pass; but we are gravely told that these are " no " fancied horrors, but positive and " admitted facts." It is not clear what are intended for statements of facts, but by analyzing the whole we shall see how many it contains, and how far they are " positive" or " admitted."
That it is one continued system of daily and hourly robbery,	Declamation.
wresting from the miserable victim	This expression is not applicable to the Slaves in the British West Indies, who are any thing but " miserable," if contrasted with the laboring population of any other country *.
his rights as a man,	Declamation.
as a husband, as a father,	As far as this includes a statement of fact, it is certainly not " positive," or " admitted."
his rights as a *British* subject by the Constitution of his Country, or as an innocent foreigner by the Law of Nations;	These assertions, as applied to the present question, have already been investigated, and the fallacy of them as the foundation of argument shown.
That the crime is nothing less than that of robbing a human being of all his mental and moral energies,	It would be difficult to prove that the Negroes in the West India Colonies are inferior in mental or moral energies to those resident in Africa. At all events, this is a

---

* Mr. M'Donnell, in his " Considerations on Negro Slavery," has shewn that " the " Negroes are not that degraded, miserable set of beings they are so generally supposed to " be."---" The first sensation," he observes, " which a stranger experiences on visiting an " estate, is that of an unqualified surprise. In place of beholding that scene of chains and " cruelty which had been associated with his idea of slavery, he finds every thing indicative " of cheerfulness and content; an active, animated picture of industry lies before him; every " now and then is heard a loud and general laugh, evidently that of persons free from " care: in his walks about the grounds, he is saluted with courtesy; and he sees the pro- " prietor received really with affection. After the work of the day is over, if he proceed " to the Negro-Houses, he will be still more gratified; he there beholds apartments well " fitted up, and comfortable; the little children before the doors gamboling about in " sportive innocence: and the whole presenting such an appearance of satisfaction and " happiness, that he is at once prompted to exclaim, ' What is it Mr. Wilberforce would " ' have?' "---*Considerations*, p. 213.

PETITION.	REMARKS.
	mere hyperbolical description of the crime, and is by no means admitted as a correct delineation of the state of Slavery in the West Indies.
of keeping his mind in darkness,	The reader is referred in contradiction to this assertion to the measures now in active operation for diffusing among the Negroes religious and moral instruction, brought forward by the Bishops of Jamaica and Barbadoes, and enthusiastically adopted by the Planters.
lest he should become acquainted with his rights,	As the fact is not admitted, it is needless to observe upon the motive here alleged.
and of reducing him for all civil purposes to the condition of a murdered man;	This is unintelligible. The *real* "condition" of the Negroes may be learned from Mr. Coleridge, who tells us that the

"Slaves receive no wages, because no money is paid to them upon that score; but they possess advantages, which the ordinary wages of labor in England *doubled* could not purchase. The Slaves are so well aware of their comforts which they enjoy under a master's purveyance, that they not unfrequently forego freedom rather than be deprived of them. A Slave beyond the prime of life will hesitate to accept manumission. Many Negroes in Barbadoes, Granada, and Antigua, have refused freedom when offered to them."

| That the *West India* Negro, though born to all the privileges of a *British* subject, is allowed no inheritance but Slavery; | This assertion, as far as it can be understood, is untrue. |
| That if he attempts to assert his just claims, he is consigned to the gallows or the stake as a traitor, on the principle by which pirates put to death those who do not quietly submit to their injustice, and thus natural death is added to civil death, and judicial murder to robbery in its most complicated form; | If the Negro attempts to regain his liberty *by the destruction of his Master's property, or by an attempt upon his life,* he is condemned to death by laws sanctioned and approved by British Ministers and British Kings, whom these Petitioners, by implication, charge with the guilt of "piracy," and the commission of "judicial murders." The first steps of a Negro to "assert his just claims," are those of the incendiary and murderer. Do the Petitioners wish the laws denouncing the punishment of |

PETITION.	REMARKS.
	death on such criminals to be repealed? If they do, what becomes of their humanity to their white brethren?—the history of St. Domingo will show what would be the result.
To robbery momentarily repeated through a life of terror, of scourgings, and of mental and bodily degradation;	To say the life of a Negro is like what is here described, is to utter a calumny which admits of no answer but a direct and positive denial.
The Petitioners beg leave to observe that these are no fancied horrors, but positive and admitted facts, and that they are here speaking of the sufferings of innocent aliens, whose privileges are consecrated by that Law of Nations which *England* has shed her bravest blood to maintain, and of *British* subjects born in the King's allegiance, whose rights have the same foundation and are as inalienable as those of every Member of the House;	This is a mere summary of the previous statements, and needs therefore no detailed examination; but in talking of rights which are inalienable, it is well to bear in mind, that the West Indians have also rights equally inalienable. Preparatory, therefore, to the examination of the prayer of the Petition, the object of which is, to annihilate the property of the West Indians, it may be as well to refer to the nervous reasoning comprised in the following extract from the Petition of the West Indians to the King, presented in 1823.

We humbly conceive that in a case in which the parties are—the State on the one hand, and any class of your Majesty's subjects on the other---it cannot be necessary to prove any other title to property than that it has been recognized by the State itself; and we humbly conceive that, as against the right of the State to annihilate or to injure in any degree that property, such proof is conclusive.

It has been urged, with a view of shaking the title to such property, that in its origin it will be found to have been vitiated by acts of injustice or violence. We might ask, how much of the property of your Majesty's subjects---property held the most sacred---could shew a title in its origin free from injustice or violence?---Whether your Majesty's title to those very Colonies, though sanctioned by treaties, and recognized by the law of nations, could stand that test?---Whether it could be shewn that the original occupation of those countries by the nations of Europe was unstained by acts of cruelty or violence towards the native inhabitants?---or, how much of the landed property of Great Britain or Ireland could be retained by the present possessors if such a title were required to be shewn? The general admission of this principle would shake property of all descriptions throughout your Majesty's dominions; and against a partial application of it to the property of your Majesty's subjects in the Colonies, we appeal in confidence to your Majesty as the dispenser of equal justice to all your subjects.

If the State considers that the property of the West India Planters in their Slaves interferes with a great national object, it has a clear course, as in all cases where the property of individuals interferes with a public object, by offering them a fair compensation for the surrender of their property.

If that object is one which is required by a high moral duty, the same sense of duty commands that it should be accomplished by the fair purchase of that property, rather than by a forcible violation of it. If the right to compensation be admitted in case of injury, but if it be maintained that the object can be accomplished without injury to the Planters, the State has also a clear course by offering a distinct pledge, and making provision for a contingent compensation. If no loss should be incurred, this will cost the State nothing---if the injury should be inflicted, it will be only the satisfaction of a claim previously admitted to be just.

PETITION.

That the Petitioners, regarding the slavery of their fellow subjects in the *West Indies* as an outrage upon all justice, and sensible of the duty of putting an end, with as little delay as possible, to a system which is pregnant with such complicated evils, confide in the wisdom of the House for the adoption of such measures as may be necessary for the speedy attainment of that desirable object; but, at the same time, they beg leave respectfully to submit, that there is one measure which, while it is unquestionably safe, would also prove a most efficacious corrective of many of the immediate evils of Colonial Slavery, and might be carried into effect without loss of time; the Petitioners allude to the abrogation of the Bounties and Protecting Duties on Sugar;

REMARKS.

From the introductory part of this paragraph, it really might be inferred, that the Petitioners are not aware that the British Parliament is already pledged to the adoption of measures calculated to put an end to the system of Slavery;—it is, however, by no means an uncommon practice of the Abolitionists to argue in this question, as if the English Slave Trade had not been abolished ; as if no measures were in operation tending to the gradual emancipation of the Negro ;—and as if no improvement whatever had taken place in the condition of the Slave. Were this indeed the case, there might be some shadow of an excuse for the inveterate persecution which they carry on against those unfortunate individuals, whose property is embarked in the West India Colonies; but the flagrant injustice of schemes like that which they here propose as *safe* and efficacious for the extinction of Slavery, becomes still more apparent when it is remembered how perfectly *unnecessary* they are. Parliament has declared that Slavery must be gradually extinguished ;— the Ministers of the Crown are employed in arranging and perfecting the schemes already in force for the accomplishment of their wishes ; the condition of the Slaves themselves is gradually but perceptibly advancing in comfort, by the result of natural causes, as well as the *voluntary enactments of their Masters* ; every thing is

PETITION.

REMARKS.

proceeding slowly but safely towards the wished-for result; yet the Petitioners come forward now with the proposition of a plan, which involves the *ruin* of the Masters, and the Colonies, as a means for accomplishing the freedom of the Slave.

That these Bounties and Protecting Duties prevent Sugar, now become one of the necessaries of life, from being imported from various parts of the world, at a price so much below the Sugar from the *West Indies*, as to make a difference to the *British* public of one penny per pound, or about one million and a half sterling on the aggregate annual consumption of the people of *Great Britain and Ireland;*

This sweeping assertion can for the present be met only by as sweeping a denial of its correctness.

That sugar is a " necessary of " life," is readily admitted ; but that it is the " *protecting duties*" that prevent its more general consumption, is absolutely denied. The true cause of the high price of sugar is the enormous taxation imposed upon it, amounting to nearly 100 per cent. upon the value :---a taxation at once oppressive to the producer, and injurious to the consumer.

That these Protecting Duties have now been in force twelve years, many of them years of great distress to the agriculturists and manufacturers of this country, during which the *West Indian* Sugar Farmers have received eighteen millions sterling for their Sugars over and above the price at which Sugars might have been purchased in the markets of *England,* if the *West Indian* Planter had not been protected from the effects of fair competition;

A more insidious statement was never inserted in any public document. It is the evident intention of the framer of the Petition to insinuate that twelve years of great distress to the public, were twelve years of great prosperity to the Colonies; while it is a fact, notorious as the sun at noon, that during those twelve years, the distresses of the West Indian Planters have far exceeded those of any other part of the community: they commenced earlier, and still continue very little diminished. The price of sugar has been long under the average which is necessary to give the Planter even a bare subsistence, much less any adequate return for his labour or capital.

Allowing then, for the sake of argument, that the English public have paid eighteen millions more

PETITION.	REMARKS.

REMARKS (cont.): than they ought to have done for sugar, it is a fact, of which none are better aware than the Abolitionists, that the West India Sugar Planter has not received the benefit, but that if there has been any gainer, it has been the *Revenue of England.*

PETITION: That it is from the forced and unremitted cultivation of Sugar in the comparatively inferior and exhausted soils of the *British West Indian* Islands, excited by the hope of high profits, that the sufferings of the Negroes chiefly arise, and that, upon the showing of the Planters themselves, this forced cultivation is solely kept up by the artificial stimulus of Bounties and Protecting Duties, which impede the commerce of *Great Britain,* and operate as an oppressive tax on the public ;

REMARKS: We find here some expressions, which, without being absolutely false, are calculated to produce very erroneous impressions of what is the truth. The Slaves in the West Indies, are the labouring population of the country: all over the globe this class of persons are compelled to " unremitted culti- " vation" of the soil. The English labourer is " forced" to work by the fear of starvation ; the Negro by the fear of punishment. Any " sufferings" arising from labour are the result, therefore, of the general laws of society, and are shared by the larger portion of the inhabitants of every country in the world. But to say that the labour of the Negro produces " sufferings" beyond those of the *labouring population* of any country, is an assertion directly untrue, as the following extract from " Coleridge's Six Months in the West Indies," will show :—

" IT IS A CERTAIN TRUTH, THAT
" THE SLAVES IN GENERAL DO
" LABOUR MUCH LESS, DO EAT AND
" DRINK MUCH MORE, HAVE MUCH
" MORE READY MONEY, DRESS
" MUCH MORE GAILY, AND ARE
" TREATED WITH MORE KINDNESS
" AND ATTENTION, WHEN SICK,
" THAN NINE-TENTHS OF ALL THE
" PEOPLE OF GREAT BRITAIN,
" UNDER THE CONDITION OF

PETITION.	REMARKS,
	"TRADESMEN, FARMERS, AND DOMESTIC SERVANTS."*

The assertion here implied, that the soils of the British West Indian Islands are " inferior and " exhausted" is only partially true, and is quite erroneous as applicable to Jamaica and most of the Colonies.

The statement is worth notice only to show the general inaccuracy of this " model of truth."

If it is meant by the latter part of the paragraph to assert, that, without the aid of "Protecting Duties," the British West India Planters would be unable to compete with the foreign Planter in the British market; that he would be obliged to abandon the cultivation of his property; that the production of sugar would totally cease in the British Colonies, these are conclusions which the West Indians are by no means called upon to deny; but when it is considered that such cultivation of sugar here referred to, occasions the employment of 25,000 British seamen, and 230,000 tons of shipping, produces an annual revenue of nearly £6,000,000 sterling, occasions the annual consumption of British manufactures, to the value of nearly £5,000,000 sterling, it is difficult to imagine how the cessation of this cultivation can be recommended as a measure useful to Great Britain.

---

* It is curious to observe the measures which the " free community" of Hayti have been obliged to resort to, in order to procure the very small portion of labour which is there exerted. In that island, when a Proprietor wants to have his canes cut, he applies to a Contractor, who engages to supply labourers. For this purpose, the Contractor goes, not to the advertising-office, or to the market-place, but to the military police, who sweep together all the idle Negroes they can collect, and keep them to labour till the work is done. The Contractor then pays the Negroes whatever wages he pleases, which, in some cases, is none at all. This is the general custom at *Aux Cayes*, where the gentleman who furnished this statement resided nine years. And this is in Hayti; for the encouragement of whose FREE labour, the Petitioners gravely request the destruction of the British West India Colonies.

17

PETITION.	REMARKS.
	As to the general question, considered merely as one of political economy, it need only be remarked, that sugar and coffee are to the Colonial agricultural interest, what grain is to the British agricultural interest, the staple of the country, and the British Colonial landholder is equally entitled to, and has enjoyed protection against, foreign competition*.
That when the exhaustion of the soils, and the ruinous and expensive system of slave cultivation and of non-residence, prevent the importation of Sugars from the *West Indian* Islands at the price for which they could be obtained from various parts of the world, the Petitioners humbly conceive that the *West Indian* Planters have no just claim to Bounties and Protecting Duties to enable them to continue an improvident speculation;	The high price of Sugar is occasioned by the high rate of duty imposed upon it, and not by Protecting Duties. This sentence altogether affords an amusing specimen of logic and "justice." The "Slave cultivation of Sugar" is certainly not "ruinous" to the nation, who derive from it an annual revenue of 6,000,000*l*. The Petitioners here call upon the nation not to support the Planters in "an improvident speculation," from which the nation has reaped the benefit.
That the Petitioners humbly submit that the Bounties and Protecting Duties on Sugar, for the benefit of a comparatively few individuals, who hold their fellow-subjects in Slavery, ought not, in justice to the agricultural and manufacturing interests of this country, to be continued;	The Protecting Duties enable the West Indians, amid all their distresses, to pay 6,000,000*l*. annually to the English Government, and to consume British manufactures to the annual value of 5,000,000*l*.; yet the Petitioners call these Protecting Duties beneficial to a comparatively few individuals.
That, next to *British* farming produce, Sugar is the chief article	This is admitted; and when the West Indians apply for a reduc-

* The claim of the British West India Planter to a Protecting Duty on Sugar, cannot be discussed in the short limits that can be allowed to the "Remarks." A most able and satisfactory answer to the statements and arguments of the Petitioners, with regard to that Protection, and the benefits alleged to be derived from the Bounties, will be found in a letter in "The British Press," of the 10th of May, 1825†. It is to be noticed that the Petitioners have omitted all reference to the fact, that the Bounties, from which the Colonies did derive any benefit, HAVE CEASED TO EXIST.

† It shall be reprinted in another portion of this work.

PETITION.

of domestic consumption, and ranks among the necessaries of life;

That the effect of abrogating the Bounties and Protecting Duties on Sugar would be, to transfer the cultivation of that article to the *East Indies*, and other places, where it can be produced by the free labor of native farmers, and at little expense;

REMARKS.

tion of the Duties on Sugar, the support of the Petitioners may be confidently relied on, as that reduction will necessarily increase the consumption of this " necessary of life" among the lower classes of society.

It is somewhat surprising that the judgment of those who drew up this Petition should have suffered these words, "transfer of cultivation," to slip in, as they clearly indicate that they contemplate nothing short of the DESTRUCTION of an important branch of industry in one British possession, to foster it in another, or in other words, to ruin the West India, for the sake of the East India Colonies. Without inquiring at present whether the " transfer of cultivation," here spoken of, *would* ensue; what the " other places" referred to are; whether East India sugar would indeed be the produce of *free* labour : (all opinions liable to objections :) it is now asked, Are not the Petitioners, from their own words, convicted of the grossest injustice in praying for a measure which they *avow* must involve the destruction of the property of their fellow-subjects ? The absolute " TRANSFER OF CULTIVATION" of the STAPLE PRODUCTION of the West India Colonies, is the object which they coolly and deliberately propound, without even a word of pity or regret, by way of propitiation to their unfortunate fellow-countrymen, whom such consequences would necessarily plunge in utter and irremediable distress. Those who are now petitioning for a repeal of the Corn Laws, do so upon the allegation, and endeavour to prove, that the introduction of

PETITION.	REMARKS.
	foreign corn would *not* occasion a " *transfer* of cultivation of grain" to other countries, but the Petitioners boldly assert this to be their aim. It is difficult to avoid the strongest expressions of disgust at such barefaced injustice, (to say nothing of the folly,) when it is remembered that the Petitioners profess to plead in the cause of humanity, and in the name of that Religion which commands us to " do unto others as we wish they " should do unto us."
That this transfer would tend to increase the growth of the proper food of the Negro *British* subject in the *West Indies*, diminish his fatigues, his privations, and his sufferings, and by rapidly increasing the black population, would so reduce the price of Slaves, and facilitate manumissions, that the Slave system would gradually become extinct, without violence or commotion;	There is not a word here stated as to the effect of the " TRANSFER " upon the proprietors of land, nor any account of the *means* by which it would produce so much benefit to the Negro. One general observation will be sufficient in answer; that it would occasion the greatest distress to the Master, and, as a natural consequence, a corresponding degree of distress to the Slave; for while they continue in their relative situations, the prosperity of the Master is the prosperity of the Slave in the British West India Colonies. From the " transfer of " cultivation" two consequences would most probably ensue, both leading to the same result---first, that many proprietors would throw up their estates, and leave their Negroes in the uncontrolled possession of the *rights of man*; secondly, others would be obliged so to diminish the food and enjoyment of their Slaves, that the latter would be driven by distress to *insurrection* and *rebellion*. Whether this mode of extinguishing the Slave system, would be without " violence or commotion," or is preferable to the measures adopted by Government, (which, if inaccurate in details, have the PROTEC-

PETITION.	REMARKS.
	TION OF THE MASTER as one of their bases,) are questions left to the decision of the reader.
That the Petitioners, therefore, on behalf of the thousands of innocent foreigners, and of hundreds of thousands of their fellow subjects ! forcibly held in slavery ; on behalf of the people of *England*, whose rights and liberties are invaded in the persons of innocent *Englishmen*, denied that justice which ought to be extended with rigid impartiality to the powerful and to the helpless, to the black Colonist as to the white; on behalf of the King, nearly seven hundred thousand of whose natural-born subjects are wrested from the guardianship of his protecting hand within his own dominions, by those who strip their sovereign of the attributes of his Crown, and annihilate the civil existence of a portion of his people equal in number to the population of a Principality ; on behalf of the consistency and the credit of the nation, whose cannon so recently swept the ramparts of *Algiers*, and dealt death to thousands on the *African* shore, that a barbarous people might be compelled to abstain in future from reducing into Slaves, not the subjects of this country merely, but those of all other *European* Powers, and to act on principles of which *Britain* is the public champion, and of which her *West Indian* Slave-owners are as publicly the unpunished and daily violators ; on behalf of the suffering manufacturers of *England*, whose trade with nearly the whole of *South America*, with *Mexico*, with *Hayti*, with *China*, with *New Holland*, and above all	To this extravagant mixture of falsehood and rodomontade it is scarcely possible to reply, from the difficulty of meeting with a tangible proposition. Much of it, bearing the shape of assertion, has been already replied to, and that which is not, is only a continuation of that system of laying down propositions, true in themselves, but falsely applied to the case at issue, of insinuating charges, which cannot openly be made, and of immoderate abuse of their West Indian fellow-subjects, which prevails through the writings of the Abolitionists, from Mr. Stephen, down to the Editor of the " Monthly Anti-Slavery Reporter." The West Indians are here upheld to public detestation, as " wresting from the King the " guardianship of his natural-born " subjects ;" those very West Indians who were *invited, encouraged,* and almost *compelled* by English Kings and English Parliaments, to engage in the Slave-trade, and to cultivate their estates by Slave-labour. " Stripping the " Sovereign of the attributes of " his crown, and annihilating," &c. are phrases absurd in expression, and untrue in spirit. If the West Indians are " un- " punished," it is certainly not the fault of the Petitioners, whose language, in this portion of their *tirade,* is somewhat of the strongest kind. " Violator" is a hard word to be applied even to " Slave-owners," who are so by descent, purchase, and inheritance, and no more chargeable with the guilt of

PETITION.	REMARKS.
with *India* and her one hundred millions of inhabitants, is checked and stunted in its growth, because Protecting Duties and Bounties prevent those countries from sending to *England* their sugars in exchange for the products of *British* industry ; and this in order that the Slave cultivation of the *West Indies* may be exclusively encouraged ;	the system than the Petitioners themselves. " The suffering manufacturers of England !" It would be an admirable mode of relief to them, who now find in the West Indies a vent for their production, to the value of £5,000,000, annually, to stop that vent, as the Petitioners propose, by the destruction of the Colonies. The folly of the last part of the paragraph, relative to the trade which is stunted in its growth, will be evident from one or two remarks :--- South America, Mexico, Hayti, and *China!* are not British Possessions, and therefore, no reasonable man would wish to destroy the trade of British Proprietors, to " transfer" it to them. As to South America, is it the Brazils to which the Petitioners refer ? In the last year 25,000 Slaves were imported thither from Africa, and Slavery is there in full force and vigor. Do the Petitioners wish to transfer the trade from a British Slave-owner to a foreign *Slave-owner* in the Brazils, other parts of South America, and in Mexico ? As to Hayti, it is wonderful the Petitioners can venture to refer at all to this island. Some remarks will be found upon this part in other pages of the West Indian Reporter. *New Holland.* How trade can be checked with that Colony, by the protecting duties on West India Sugar, must first be stated, before it can be answered. It is a most flourishing Colony, *without* the trade, and it would be, at all events, questionable policy to destroy the cultivation of sugar, which is a staple article of commerce in

PETITION.	REMARKS.
	one British Colony, to force its cultivation in New Holland, where it is not a staple article.
As to India, and her 100,000,000 of inhabitants, the same remark will apply that has just been made with regard to New Holland. The East India Proprietors can exist without the production of Sugar; the West Indian Proprietor *cannot:* the East Indies were *not* colonized for the purpose of producing sugar; the West Indies *were.*
As to the last clause, it is a complete misrepresentation. The protecting duties were not imposed to foster West India trade, *because Slave labor was employed in these Colonies,* but because they were British Colonies, and cultivated by the aid of British capital; and because, also, the West Indians were not allowed to have their wants supplied from any other source but the mother country. They were obliged by law, to come to Britain for every single article of consumption, in the way of trade or manufactures. In the words of Lord Chatham---" They had not " the right to manufacture a nail."
On behalf of every virtue, and of every interest, that is dear to *Englishmen,* the Petitioners implore the House to take into their earliest consideration the repeal of the Protecting Duties and Bounties granted to the cultivators of sugar by Slave labor; that whatever difficulties the Slavery Question may present under other aspects, the people of *England* may at least be delivered from the bitter consciousness of maintaining by oppression, and unnecessary premiums, a system of iniquity degrading to the national character, criminal beyond all other modes	This winding up being a mere summary of the declamations and assertions already examined and exposed, needs no detailed reply. It is an appeal to the people to *rob* one portion of the empire, to atone for " *robbery and violence*" committed by the whole: an act than which nothing could be more " subversive of every legal and " constitutional principle, or more " at variance with the dictates of " sound policy, humanity, and " justice;" and we cannot conclude better than with the following words of Mr. Barham.
" If the Legislature, with a view

PETITION.	REMARKS.
of robbery and violence, subversive of every legal and every constitutional principle, and equally at variance with the dictates of sound policy, humanity, and justice.	" to NATIONAL ADVANTAGE, has " committed injustice, and now, " with a view to NATIONAL JUS-" TICE, would repair the wrong, " it is for the NATION to pay the " price of its wrong, and NOT " for the INDIVIDUAL who acted " in conformity to the law. To fix " on the present Proprietor the " cost of redeeming the acts of " the Nation at large, would be " concluding a series of INJUSTICE " TO AFRICA by an act of INJUS-" TICE TO A PORTION OF THE SUB-" JECTS OF THIS COUNTRY, with " regard to whom, the first laws " would have been a FRAUD, and " the last would be a ROBBERY."

THE EDINBURGH REVIEW ON WEST INDIAN SLAVERY.

In No. 89 of this Review, recently published, the writer endeavours to prove, that the " West Indians themselves will never reform " the system confided to their Administration." The documents quoted in support of this proposition, are some which were laid before Parliament in the spring of 1826, and which of course cannot embrace any transactions in the Colonies *since last February*. Admitting, therefore, for the sake of argument, what is far from true in fact, that those documents *do* warrant the inference of the Reviewer; still it is dishonest in the extreme to attempt to delude the public mind by arguing from events which are superseded, as the foundation of inferences of this nature by transactions which have since taken place.

That the cause of Negro improvement has made rapid strides in the Colonies since that time to which the Reviewer refers, is a fact upon record; and there are documents daily arriving from the West Indies, all tending to disprove his hardy assertion, and to show how sincerely the Colonial Legislatures are disposed to meet the wishes of this Nation to the utmost limits of what is safe and practicable.

JAMAICA.

It has been stated (among other matter), unaccompanied by any explanation, that the " Bill permitting Slave Evidence to be received in certain cases, has been rejected." This is in part true; but it should be added, that the Bill had been ordered to be read a second time on that day three months, on the ground, that it formed a part of those measures which had been referred to a Committee, and would be included in the enactments of the then intended Bill for the amendment of the Slave Code.

It is not pretended to assert that the Assembly will adopt all or any of the amendments and additions recommended by their Committee; but the facts, that such a Committee has been appointed, and that it has recommended the important and extensive alterations in the Slave Code, which it is known to have done, are sufficient to prove that the Assembly of Jamaica is well inclined to adopt such measures for the improvement of our peasantry, as their long experience and local knowledge may point out as likely to be productive of benefit to the Slave, without injury to the Master, or detriment to the right of Property.

BARBADOES.

In this Colony, by letters received very recently, it appears that the Legislature has gone far beyond any other West Indian Colony in the measures which they have adopted for the amelioration of the Slave system. The particulars at present are not publicly communicated.

ST. KITT'S.

Heads of the St. Kitt's Melioration Bill, which passed the Assembly.

1. Limiting Sunday markets to the hour of eleven in the morning.
2. Directing a constable to ring a bell to disperse them at a quarter before eleven.
3. That all female slaves that have five children, on any estate, shall have 52 days in the year to themselves; also prohibiting the employment of slaves on Sunday, with a few unavoidable exceptions.
4. Abolishing the use of the cart-whip and cat as emblems of authority.
5, and 6. Allowing slaves to give evidence in the Courts, provided they produce certificate of sufficient religious instruction, signed by a Minister of the Church of England, or Scotland.
7. Allowing the slaves to contract marriage, and appointing the course to be pursued in case of owner's refusal.
8. Empowering slaves to hold, enjoy, and alienate real and personal property, and to maintain suits at law in respect thereof.
9. Directing freedom to be presumed until slavery be proved.
10. Restraining punishment to 25 stripes; slave not to be whipped when marks of recent flogging are visible on his body, nor until the day after the offence committed, nor unless one person of free condition other than the person inflicting the punishment be present, under certain penalty.
11. Prohibiting the exposure of females.
12. Book of punishment to be kept on each estate; all floggings exceeding 12 stripes to be recorded with all particulars and names of witnesses.
13. Fixing penalties for infringement of last clause, and in case of injury, or obliterating the said book.
14. Directing the production of the said book, and how the Court and Jury to determine in case of prosecution for flogging.
15. Husbands, wives, and children, not to be separated by seizure or sale of any of them under execution, and how the Marshal shall act therein.
16. Clause establishing Savings Banks for the slaves, and placing the same under the superintendence of the Colonial Treasurer.
17, 18, 19, and 20. Slaves allowed to purchase their freedom, and consequent regulations, and how the Magistrates shall act therein.
21. Penalties provided for.
22. Repealing clauses of former Act.

Published and Sold by Effingham Wilson, No. 88, Royal Exchange, where communications are requested to be addressed to the Editor.

Price, 3d.

No. II. will be published immediately.

London: Printed by D. Cartwright, 91, Bartholomew Close.

No. II.

London, 1st February, 1827.

THE

WEST INDIAN REPORTER.

"IN setting about the conversion of more than 800,000 Black Slaves into free citizens, we must act sensibly and discreetly; especially we must begin with the beginning, for IT IS NOT A MATTER OF DECREE, EDICT, or ACT OF PARLIAMENT; there is no *hocus pocus* in the thing, there are no *presto* movements. It is a mighty work; yet mighty as it is, it must be effected, if at all, in the order, and by the rules, which reason and experience have proved to be alone effectual. If we attempt to reverse the order, or to alter the mode, we shall not only fail ourselves, but make it impossible that any should succeed."
Coleridge's Six Months in the West Indies.

"IF THE CONDITION OF THE SLAVE IS TO BE IMPROVED, THAT IMPROVEMENT MUST BE INTRODUCED THROUGH THE MEDIUM OF HIS MASTER. The Masters are instruments through whom, and by whom, you must act upon the Slave Population; and if by any proceedings of ours we shall unhappily place between the Slave and his Master the barrier of insurmountable hostility, we shall at once put an end to the best chance of emancipation, or even of amendment. Instead of diffusing gradually over those dark regions a pure and salutary light, we may at once kindle a flame only to be quenched in blood."
Mr. Canning, March 16, 1824.

"*From the general and prominent charge of cruelty, active or permissive, towards the Slaves, I, for one,* ACQUIT THE PLANTERS. I have been in twelve of the British Colonies; and have gone round and across many of them, and have resided some months in the most populous one for its size in the whole world. I have observed with diligence, I have inquired of all sorts of people, and have mixed constantly with the colored inhabitants of all hues, and of every condition. I am sure I have seen things as they are, and I am not aware of any other bias in my mind, except that which may be caused by a native hatred of injustice, and a contempt and disdain of cant and hypocrisy."
Coleridge's Six Months in the West Indies.

PROTECTING DUTIES AND BOUNTIES ON WEST INDIA SUGAR.

"Our trade to the West Indies is saddled with almost all the expense of their civil and military establishments, and with a bounty of 1,200,000*l*."---*Edinburgh Review,* No. 82.

"And when this quantity, upon which drawback is allowed on excess re-exported, is taken into consideration, and added to the 1,600,000*l*. arising from the 10s. duty, the annual tax on the public will be found to exceed 2,000,000*l*."---*Speech of Mr. W. W. Whitmore, 22d May,* 1823.

"The best way to attack the system of slavery, was undoubtedly through the sugar duties; for if they would but call to their recollection the amount of those duties, 1,200,000*l*., or as the noble Chairman (the Duke of Gloucester) had observed to him, 1,500,000*l*., they must be sensible that if these duties were taken off, the whole machinery must drop to pieces."---*Speech of Mr. Sykes, at the anniversary of the Anti-Slavery Society.*

"There was a bounty allowed on the exportation of sugars, but it could be easily shown that that bounty, without effecting any benefit to this country, generally, by increasing the supply and diminishing the price, served only to put a million into the pockets of the West Indians."---*Speech of Mr. F. Buxton, 24th February, 1825.*

"We have hitherto paid a tax to the West Indians of at least a million and a half in the price of their sugars, owing to bounties and protecting duties."---*Observations on West India Company Bill.* Hatchard, 1825.

The above quotations afford some specimen of the arguments reiterated with unwearied assiduity by the anti-colonial party. By asserting that the West Indies enjoy a monopoly greatly detrimental to the public, they excite a strong prejudice against those possessions; and perhaps there are few, even among the intelligent, who are not more or less influenced by this feeling, whenever the Colonial question is agitated. It is true, our opponents, in their statements, carefully abstain from any attempt at analysis or calculation. Bold assumptions and sweeping conclusions compensate, in their opinion, for the absence of reasoning. The continual cry is simply that a million and a half or two millions are annually paid by the people of this country to the West Indians; but in regard to the manner in which this amount is distributed, they supply us with very scanty information. *The more cautious of the party generally connect the protecting duty and bounty together, with the wary design that if they are driven from the one position, they have still another resource to cover that retreat.* The impartial inquirer cannot fail to be surprised in perceiving the great discrepancy which exists in their statements, whenever they attempt to particularise what portion of benefit belongs to each of, the regulations respectively. *Some make* the protecting duty amount to upwards of a million, and merely add, that besides there is a large bounty given on the exportation of West India sugar. Others state, that the latter alone is more than this sum, and that of the extent of the protecting duty the public may judge, when it is considered that the duty on West India sugar is 27s., while that on East India sugar is 37s. Mr. W. Whitmore, whom we might be disposed to deem the most intelligent of the party, is also the most explanatory on the subject. He expressly states, that the bonus conferred is 2,000,000l., of which 1,600,000l. arises from the protecting duty, and that the remainder has to be classed under the denomination of bounty.

It is my intention to investigate these points a little in detail; correct information must be particularly useful to many Members of the House of Commons, as debates on the subject are continually occurring; and to the mercantile community at large any illustration relative to so extensive an article in commerce as sugar, cannot fail to be interesting. For the sake of greater clearness, I shall consider the matter under two heads ---the protecting duty and the bounty.

PROTECTING DUTY.

To any person at all acquainted with political economy, it will doubtless appear superfluous to waste time in showing, that *so long* as a surplus is obliged to be exported, *the West India planter can derive no advantage from the nominal protection given to him by the legislature.* The quantity of sugar annually imported into Great Britain from her colonies, it is well known, very greatly exceeds her consumption; a large export has consequently to take place to the Continent, no matter what price is likely to be obtained. In other commodities, shipments in general are made to a foreign port in consideration of the prices there being higher than at home; if such be not the case, the article is held over, if it cannot, in the mean time, be sold favourably, in expectation of a shorter supply coming forward, and the market taking a more favourable turn; but as to sugar, where heavy capitals are invested in its cultivation, which cannot be withdrawn, and where, from time immemorial, the supply has greatly exceeded the home consumption, it would be quite useless to hold over in expectation of a more favourable state of things. Shipments must unavoidably take place to the only vent for the article, the Continent, where it necessarily sells at the same rate as sugar from other quarters, be that rate high or low. The quantity exported consists, it may be said, entirely of refined sugar, and in this case the price of all of similar quality in London must be adjusted to the same scale as what is existing abroad. Were it either higher or lower, the thing would soon rectify itself, by the merchants either forbearing to ship, or increasing the competition to send their goods forward. This operation is well known by every intelligent merchant. Whenever a fall, say of 5s. per cwt., takes place in any of the leading continental markets, this enables the refined sugar to be sold in the interior of Germany so much cheaper. British sugar abroad must consequently also fall; prices in England again follow this reduction; and the refiner being able to give so much less to the merchant, the price of raw must be equally reduced.

There are, however, many persons who, while they admit the general correctness of this principle, at the same time maintain that so large a quantity as is exported from England must certainly have some effect on the continental markets. Should it be withdrawn, it must obviously cause some deficiency, the natural effect of which would be to raise prices; and if we allow this to be the case, we must grant that it unites with other markets in determining the rate at which sugar can be sold. This opinion, which seems to have been maintained by Mr. Huskisson in the debate in May, 1823, can certainly be demonstrated erroneous.

It appears by the continuation of the slave trade in full activity by foreign powers, that the supply of sugar is so abundant as to beat competition from other quarters entirely out of the field, and to render any effect produced by the exports from England comparatively insignificant. Without going into a tedious analysis on the point, the fact can be fully established by merely contrasting the exports a few years back, with what they are at present.

	cwts.
In the year ending the 5th January, 1818, the quantity exported was..	1,443,309
In 1819	1,476,616
1824	959,408
1825	998,947

There is here a diminution in the exports of at least 40,000 hogsheads, and, if there were any truth in the position, that a large or a small quantity going from England exercised any influence on prices abroad, the natural inference would be, that some advance should have taken place in consequence of the deficiency. But directly the reverse has been the case. Prices on the Continent have materially fallen since 1818. The increased supply from foreign colonies, owing to the continuation of the slave trade, has still kept adjusted to the demand required, totally independent of the exports from England.

The following table will afford some information as to the imports of sugar into the two principal continental ports at the different periods I have alluded to:—

1819.

AMSTERDAM.		HAMBURGH.	
Havannah and Brazils, chests....	5,006	Brazil, chests	20,155
Surinam, &c., casks............	14,666	Havannah, chests............	19,424
East India, canisters	10,673	Great Britain, chests	3,900
——— bales and matting	20,849	——— casks *	25,360
		East India, bags	39,133

1824.

AMSTERDAM.		HAMBURGH.	
Havannah and Brazils, chests....	11,358	Brazil, chests	44,841
Surinam, &c., casks............	16,484	Havannah, chests	23,957
East India, canisters	2,287	Great Britain, chests	1,723
——— bales and matting....	27,833	——— casks............	10,953
		East India, bags	12,252

From what is here exhibited, two important facts will be strikingly evident. First, that, in markets open to all the world, free-labor sugar, as it is termed, cannot compete with that produced by slave labor; and, secondly, as the price of sugar in England is entirely dependant on that of the cheapest market on the Continent, the West India interests have not, hitherto, derived the slightest advantage from their nominal 10s. protecting duty. If East India sugar regulated prices abroad, there might be some grounds for the assertion; but when such event arrives, it will be time enough to speak of the monopoly of our Western Colonies.

BOUNTY.

We have now to investigate the nature of the Bounty. By the Consolidation Act of Customs, 59 Geo III. cap. 52, the duty on sugar was fixed at 30s., and the drawback on single refined at 46s. per cwt. But permission was given to the Lords of the

---

* These casks are almost entirely refined sugar.

Treasury, to remit 1s. of the duty, if the average price in the Gazette should be below 49s. per cwt.; 2s. if below 48s.; and 3s. if below 47s.; while the drawback of 46s. continued as before. It is well known the price of sugar has long been far below 47s.; the 3s. duty has consequently been remitted, making the duty now paid 27s. It is apparent, therefore, at once, that the exporter of refined sugar possesses an advantage of 3s. per cwt. on Muscovado, or 4s. 7¼d. on refined; and the first object is to ascertain what this costs the nation. Very considerable delusion exists in this particular. By the returns ordered to be printed by the House of Commons on the 30th of March last, the bounty is stated at 844,441*l*. 8s. 11¾d.; a person would thus, on first consideration, be prompted to exclaim, what a large boon do the West Indians enjoy! He would, however, in so doing, run into a very great error. Much the larger portion of this amount, classed under the head of bounty, should be denominated *drawback*, being merely the repayment of the duties when exportation takes place. It is certainly not in conformity with the usual accuracy of Mr. Irving (the Inspector-General of Imports and Exports), to have given rise to this ambiguity, from the manner in which he has made out the returns. It is unnecessary to observe, that before the refiner commences his manufacture, the duty has been paid; and, as we have no right to tax the people abroad, on shipments being made to the Continent, the duty originally paid must be drawn back by the exporter. In place, then, of so large a sum going into the pockets of the West Indians, as is insinuated, the account will stand as follows:—

The total amount of payments made on British refined sugar amounts, as has been stated, to 844,441*l*.; and it is to be observed, that this appertains to the year ending 5th January, 1824, and not the 5th January, 1825.

The quantity then of refined sugar which has received the drawback, will be 367,147 cwt. equal to 624,153 cwt. Muscovado, according to the Government proportion of 34 cwt. of the latter to 20 of the former.

Three shillings per cwt. has been remitted; and, it is obvious, that this taken on the above quantity, will give the net amount of what should be properly termed bounty. This sum, amounting to only 93,623*l*. falls far short of what is stated by the Anti-Colonial writers. To prevent misunderstanding in this respect, the returns should have been made out differently.

The drawback would then appear to be............. £750,821
Bounty 93,623

Total repayment out of the Customs £844,444

Having shown that the clamour against the amounts of this boon are perfectly unwarranted, a few observations are necessary to explain its further operation as concerns the West India interests. For this purpose I cannot do better than quote the words of the Chancellor of the Exchequer on opening his Budget the 28th of February last. He stated, " that it appeared the drawback was calculated upon the high duty, and in point " of fact the revenue received a duty of 27s. and paid a drawback of 30s. This could " be founded on no true principle, and could be favorable to none of the interests of this " country. It could not be expected that foreign powers, who were always quicksighted " enough to see opportunities of heaping all sorts of restrictions upon our commerce, should " not perceive that this difference of three shillings between the duty and the drawback " would come to their treasury. And the fact was, that it did so; for they imposed " higher duties upon sugars imported from this country than from any other, or than it " was reasonable they should pay."

The accuracy of this may be judged of from the conduct of the Continental States. On the 1st of January, 1824, the Russian Government published an ukase, imposing a duty of 2 sil. R. and 50 cop. on every pood of sugar. The effect of this duty has amounted nearly to a prohibition. We find by official documents, that the quantity of refined sugar exported to Russia, year ending 5th January, was, 1820, 153,585 cwt. 16lb.; while that ending the 5th January, 1825, the quantity was only 2,822 cwt. 8lb.

This measure of Russia has been imitated by the Austrian Government. In the port of Trieste, to which we were in the habit of exporting largely, the duties have been materially advanced.

According to the new tariff of October last,   fl.   fl.
  Refined Sugar, in loaves, is raised from .... 15 to 16¼
  Crushed Sugar ...·.. 11 7-10 16½

		fl.	fl.
All other Powder Sugar for Grocers		9	12
White Sugar for Refiners are		6	8
Grey brown ditto		3	4

The effect of this regulation must be very apparent. By levying a higher duty relatively on Refined Goods, it must operate seriously to the detriment of our trade, and mercantile men in Mincing Lane know well that comparatively few shipments have latterly been made to this former outlet for the staple of our colonies.

Even in Holland the same system prevails. The duty on Muscovado is only about 6d. per cwt. if imported in Dutch ships; 14d. if in foreign ships. But refined sugar is visited with a duty of 30s. per cwt. which, when contrasted with that paid on the raw article, may justly be termed an entire prohibition.

These circumstances fully corroborate the views of the Chancellor of the Exchequer, and they imperiously demand the consideration of every Member of Parliament, both for the purpose of showing the true manner in which the West India interests are affected, and of exhibiting the mode in which foreign Governments meet the commercial liberality of our own Legislature.

There is yet one word more to advance relative to the bounty, and that is as to the principle of its continuance.

On this head the regulation can be satisfactorily defended. To the supporters of free trade, the very name of bounty is peculiarly repugnant. But it must not be for a moment supposed that the principles on which this bounty rests are in the least degree at variance with a free trade, or with that policy which the administration is now so judiciously adopting. Its advocates never contended that it should continue perpetually, but only so long as to prevent its cessation from being injurious either to particular interests or to the general welfare of the country. Supposing it to be a benefit, it was urged that its removal would necessarily reduce prices, which would have the effect of putting some of the exhausted lands of the old Colonies out of cultivation, and that thus diminishing our exports, would naturally hold out a direct stimulus for Foreign Powers to prosecute the Slave Trade with increased ardour. It was even admitted, that if this disposition on the part of the Continental Nations should be presumed always to continue, it would be difficult to justify it, as a lapse of some years would still give rise to similar arguments. But it was on account of ministers continually declaring that they would eventually succeed in stopping the traffic in slaves, that remonstrances were used for them, not to impede their own efforts until the trade was generally determined piracy. On their own grounds did the appeal rest; for as they maintained that in a few years they would have succeeded in their negociations, so for those few years only was the bounty demanded. It ought, moreover, to be observed, that if it be an advantage, East India sugar equally participated. Now, as the anti-slavery party uniformly advances the interests of the East India traders, in opposition to those of the West Indies, it will afford an admirable specimen of its fairness and impartiality, denouncing to the public that undue preference is granted to the one, while in reality that of the other is similarly benefited.

The President of the Board of Trade has just introduced some measures affecting very considerable changes in our Colonial policy. The bounty also it is intended shall expire on the 1st of July, 1826. It cannot for a moment be doubted but that the same strict regard to justice and vested rights will here be observed, as has marked other innovations. The relations between mortgagee and planter, and indeed the general nature of the Colonial trade, oblige the greater portion of the produce of the West Indies to be shipped to this country. No new arrangements, therefore, as to facilities of trade, given to the Colonies in their intercourse with Foreign Nations, can come into operation for a considerable period; and it would be most unjust not to delay the removal of the bounty until such arrangements are completed. This has no relevance to its being or not being an advantage; it is simply, that the change may not inflict an injury on the refiners, or on other interests.

I have now, I hope, satisfactorily shown that the assertions of the individuals whose names are prefixed to this communication, are utterly destitute of foundation. If they again come forward in public with such idle declamation, let them at all events, at the same time, attempt some reply to this exposition. If not, the voice of public opinion cannot applaud either their knowledge of political economy or their candour.

May 15, 1825.   INVESTIGATOR.

THE EDINBURGH REVIEW, AND WEST INDIAN SLAVERY.

It is confidently rumoured, that it is the intention of "The Abo-"litionists" to introduce into Parliament, during the present session, a Bill, containing all the regulations of the Order in Council for Trinidad; and to propose that those regulations shall thus be adopted as law in every portion of the British Empire. It might be doubted, whether any attempt of this kind would be made, when it is considered how surely the loss of the Colonies would follow such an attempt to exercise a paramount right of legislation over the Independent Assemblies; and how inevitably, also, the very menance of assuming it would exasperate the minds of the Colonists into more determined opposition. That there is some foundation for the rumour, we are, however, inclined to believe, from the style and tone of the article which we alluded to in our last, on the subject of " West Indian Slavery" in the Edinburgh Review. In that article the immediate assumption of that right is recommended as "the only effectual " remedy" to be applied to what they state to be the "determination" of the Colonists *never* to " reform the system confided to their administration."

In unqualified terms, we state that the Colonists have come to a determination precisely the reverse, and that we have official proofs of their endeavours " to reform that system to the utmost limits of what is " safe and practicable." We wait only till we can collect the requisite information from *all the islands*, and we pledge ourselves to our readers, to lay before them very shortly, such details as shall at one view expose a mass of long accumulated assertions and accusations.

In the meantime, we subjoin some remarks upon this part of the subject, which strongly corroborate the sentiments to which we would lead our readers. They are taken, it is to be observed, not from the work of any partizan of the West Indians, but from a volume * in which the authors profess themselves to be guided by no motives but the common interests of mankind, and who examine with consummate ability and closeness of argument the various measures which were brought forward in 1826, by men of all parties, and who judge of those measures solely by their tendency to promote or retard the improvement and happiness of this Empire. Such testimony is, therefore, not a little important; as it shows how very small is the support given to the Ultra-Abolitionists, even by those who are the most strenuously attached to liberty, and *disproves* their vaunting assertions that the country at large support them in their designs. We refer our readers to the whole of the article entitled " Negro Slavery" in this work, as it contains a very able examination of the real points of dispute in this very important question.

Although there is a broad distinction between the plans of the Government and those of the Abolitionists, the West Indians either will not or cannot observe it: they persist in confounding them; and, perhaps the causes of this confusion may be traced (in some degree) in the proceedings of parliament. The Abolitionists began the discussion, and have ever since kept the advanced ground in complaining, and proposing measures, and the Government, in the steps it has adopted, and even in the language which individual ministers have held, has as uniformly appeared to *yield* to their suggestions, and to follow their driving. When the question was introduced in the House of Commons, in 1823, *on the strength of petitions remarkable for their intemperance both in language and project*, the ministers, without taking breath, proposed only an alteration in the proposition, which, to this day, sounds in most ears like an insignificant verbal change. *If they had rejected the proposition altogether, and condemned the violence with which it was brought forward, they might* have

---

* Parliamentary Review, for the Session of 1826. Longman and Co.

found an after opportunity for producing their own plan independently; by which they would at least have conciliated the more reasonable of the Planters. In addition to this, the Planters are well aware that the management of the Colonies on the African coast (the establishment of which they regard as a standing censure on themselves), is committed by the Government to the most intemperate of the Abolitionists. This, then, is the actual situation and state of mind of the West India Planter. Confounding the two parties together,—believing the ministerial plans a mere cloak for ulterior measures intended to deprive him of his property—surrounded by a hostile population, in the proportion of nearly twenty to one—placed within a few days sail of a Colony where a formidable rebellion was lately quelled with much loss, and nearly within sight of an island, on which, thirty years ago, half the whites were killed by the Negroes, who have succeeded in preventing the restoration of their property, with the exception of a trifling indemnity of a tenth, or a twelfth promised thirty years afterwards—placed in this situation, entertaining, groundlessly or not, apprehensions like these, *he talks of resisting the authority from which the source of his apprehension emanates.* But to what does this resistance amount? Mr. Brougham said last session, that the promises of the Colonists "had ended in nothing." *The assertion is not exactly true,* although much of Mr. Brougham's statement is undeniable. That statement itself, however, proves that the resistance of the Colonists *is rather the effect of (be it hoped) a momentary passion, than of deliberate intention.* Four of the islands, (Tobago, Grenada, St. Vincent's and Dominica) according to the Parliamentary papers, have given a species of protection to the property of slaves. Two (Tobago and Grenada) have diminished the quantity of punishment to be inflicted by the master. One (the Bahamas) has totally prevented the separation of families by private or judicial sale; and one (Grenada) by judicial sale only; in which the former goes further, and the latter as far as the Trinidad Order. Tobago, Grenada, and St Vincent's have gone further than the latter regulation on the subject of slave evidence, by the express reception of slave evidence against whites in capital cases. This is one of the topics which has excited the warmest opposition in Jamaica, and many of the other islands: the discrepancy proves that there is no combination or concert between the Colonies. Some weight will also be attributed to the effect of the imperfect success, (if we may trust the Jamaica Assembly,) which has attended the Government experiments. For these experiments, Trinidad and Demerara were selected; *of which, the former, has at present been only eighteen months in trial, the latter hardly one year.* Mr. W. Horton (in February last) describes the success of the experiments. But at a later period, the Jamaica House of Assembly deny the facts; for in an address to the Duke of Manchester, in October last, they state that they had received accounts of the operation of the experiment in Trinidad, from the date of the order in council, which disagreed with Mr. Horton's representation[*].

But suppose the resistance of the Colonies to have arrived at the point which Mr. Canning styles "confirmed contumacy," and that the time is come for the application of the means recommended by Mr. W. Smith—"fear or force." According to Mr. Canning, there are two methods of applying "fear or force"---the one by fiscal, the other, by military operations. Fiscal vexations are of various kinds. The ports or harbours might be removed from such towns as should exhibit marked opposition, as in the case of the Boston Port Bill, before the American war; but as such a measure would be plainly inapplicable to the small islands, and to such of the large ones as have not a second port, we conceive that it could not be executed with any general effect. The Government at home might lower the duties on East India sugar, or impose a high duty on West India exports or imports. If the reader will refer to our last year's volume on the subject of East India sugar, he will find that the mischief apprehended by the West Indians from diminishing the duty on that article, is altogether unfounded; West India sugar being able to compete in the foreign market with that of the East Indies, with the trifling aid of a bounty of 3s. per cwt. on its transit through this country. But even on the supposition that the lowering of the duties would be mischievous to the West Indians, it would be undeserved by such of the Colonies as would submit, (as all the smaller ones must do immediately,) in the event of an ultimate resort to force. The imposition of a high duty on the export of West India produce, would only be mischievous to the Planters in proportion as it would lessen the quantity sold; but exactly as that effect should ensue,

---

[*] Kingston Chronicle, October 19.

the consumers at home would be mulcted by a rise in price on West India commodities; to which must be added the decrease in the production of those commodities, cottons, provisions, and the like, for which the West India produce is exchanged. *The infliction would fall as heavily upon the mother country as upon the Colonies.* The effect of a duty on articles imported into the West Indies, would depend on its amount. If it were not heavy, the consumption might go on as at present; but if too heavy, it would be lessened exactly in proportion to the heaviness; if it amounted to a prohibition, it would, of course, cease altogether. The moment a decrease of consumption should begin, a diminution in West India produce would commence. The infliction on the West Indians would be much the same as in the case of imposing a duty on West India exports. The Planters would go without our commodities, and give us less sugar and coffee; and this country would produce less cottons and provisions, and pay dearer for sugar and coffee, or go without them. The Planters might follow the foolish example of other countries, and revenge themselves by an independent duty of their own; in that case, both parties would be worse off than before. *Before the home Government ventures to vex the Planters with duties, it must ascertain with what portion of good-will the mother-country will lay the rod on its own back.* The Abolitionists have had for a little while anti-saccharine and anti-sugar societies; but as they did not succeed any more than the anti-beef and mutton associations, projected by the late Mr. Ritson against graziers and butchers, we should infer that the main body of sugar consumers would be altogether recusant. Neither would the decrease in the revenue be a consideration entirely to be rejected.

Lastly comes the resort to military force. If the Government withdrew its troops, the slaves would put an end to the subject, after the example of the Haytians. The military force, therefore, must remain at all events. But as the troops already in the Colonies are now barely sufficient to intimidate the slaves, an additional force must be sent over to intimidate their masters. The success of such a step in the smaller islands, in every respect, may be looked upon as certain. But it would be a hazardous assertion to say that the effect on the tranquillity of the slaves in the larger Colonies, would not be serious in the highest degree. If it ended in actual conflict, their rising must be looked upon as inevitable. And such are the extraordinary facilities for negro operations, presented in the interior both of Jamaica and Demerara*---such, too, is the fatal effect of the climate upon European soldiers, especially whilst in campaign, that no man can say when, or at what cost of life and money, such a rising would be quelled, or whether it could be quelled at all. By some, this part of the subject has been treated lightly, nor do we question that the terrors of the Planters are greatly exaggerated; but we cannot help calling to mind, *that within ten years we have witnessed two formidable insurrections, connected in some sort with the plans of the Ultra-Abolitionists, and quelled only at the expence of many lives, and that the late slave trials in Jamaica exhibit, beyond question, considerable indications, that something serious was in preparation amongst the negroes in that island.*

But let not the reader infer from the difficulties in the way of *coercing* the Colonists, that no improvement can or will take place in the condition of the Slaves. *Something,* we have seen, though little, *has been done*; and when the Planters shall grow cool enough to note the distinction between the Government plans and those of the violent Abolitionists,—when, moreover, they shall witness the successful issue of the former, we may hope for more extensive amendments. The good opinion of the mother country is of importance with all Colonies; with such as are so dependent, and so small in point of white society as the West Indies, it is of the very first importance. The Planters and other parties, connected with the Colonies, who reside in this country, and commonly called the West India interest, have accorded their approbation to the Government plans. *Before resorting to measures of coercion, it is the part of wise men at least to await the effect of these circumstances upon the resident West India Planters.*

---

* See the accounts of the two Maroon wars in Jamaica, contained in Bryon Edwards' work, and Captain Stedman's Expedition to Surinam.